*Social Responsibility
and the Business
Predicament*

Studies in the Regulation of Economic Activity
TITLES PUBLISHED

Studies in the Regulation of Economic Activity

JAMES W. McKIE, Editor

Social Responsibility and the Business Predicament

Essays by James W. McKie
Marvin A. Chirelstein
Thomas C. Schelling
Roland N. McKean
James Q. Wilson
Martin Bronfenbrenner
Jerome Rothenberg
John F. Kain
Benjamin Chinitz
Raymond Vernon
Charles A. Myers

The Brookings Institution / *Washington, D.C.*

Library of Congress Cataloging in Publication Data:
McKie, James W
  Social responsibility and the business predicament.
  (Studies in the regulation of economic activity)
  Includes bibliographical references and index.
  1. Industry—Social aspects—United States—
Addresses, essays, lectures.   I. Title.   II. Series.
HD60.5.U5M3   658.4'08   74-23967
ISBN 0-8157-5608-9
ISBN 0-8157-5607-0 pbk.

9 8 7 6 5 4 3 2 1

THE BROOKINGS INSTITUTION is an independent organization devoted to nonpartisan research, education, and publication in economics, government, foreign policy, and the social sciences generally. Its principal purposes are to aid in the development of sound public policies and to promote public understanding of issues of national importance.

The Institution was founded on December 8, 1927, to merge the activities of the Institute for Government Research, founded in 1916, the Institute of Economics, founded in 1922, and the Robert Brookings Graduate School of Economics and Government, founded in 1924.

The Board of Trustees is responsible for the general administration of the Institution, while the immediate direction of the policies, program, and staff is vested in the President, assisted by an advisory committee of the officers and staff. The by-laws of the Institution state, "It is the function of the Trustees to make possible the conduct of scientific research, and publication, under the most favorable conditions, and to safeguard the independence of the research staff in the pursuit of their studies and in the publication of the results of such studies. It is not a part of their function to determine, control, or influence the conduct of particular investigations or the conclusions reached."

The President bears final responsibility for the decision to publish a manuscript as a Brookings book or staff paper. In reaching his judgment on the competence, accuracy, and objectivity of each study, the President is advised by the director of the appropriate research program and weighs the views of a panel of expert outside readers who report to him in confidence on the quality of the work. Publication of a work signifies that it is deemed to be a competent treatment worthy of public consideration; such publication does not imply endorsement of conclusions or recommendations contained in the study.

The Institution maintains its position of neutrality on issues of public policy in order to safeguard the intellectual freedom of the staff. Hence interpretations or conclusions in Brookings publications should be understood to be solely those of the author or authors and should not be attributed to the Institution, to its trustees, officers, or other staff members, or to the organizations that support its research.

Foreword

PUBLIC DEMANDS on private business have expanded greatly during the twentieth century. Business enterprise was once expected to devote its efforts to producing and distributing goods and services as efficiently as possible and to making innovations and improvements in products and processes. Now, business is increasingly called upon to promote a variety of social purposes in addition to these long-standing economic ones. The demands for "social responsibility" have provoked extensive discussion and debate on what new roles, if any, business firms should play in the social system. The novelty and variety of these demands have raised profound questions about the extent to which it is possible or desirable to vest in the business firm the duty to cure social ills.

The Brookings Institution invited a panel of nine economists, a political scientist, and a legal scholar to examine the question of the social responsibility of business from a variety of viewpoints. Though normative judgments are necessarily a part of any conclusions and recommendations on this issue, these scholars were asked to apply their own special knowledge to it in order to discern what is sensible and workable in the demands for social responsibility, and to make specific recommendations on how much and what kinds of responsibility business enterprise can usefully be expected to assume. James W. McKie served as editor of the panel's report and provides a summary of its approach and findings that appears as the first chapter of this book.

Some of the essays presented here analyze the question of social responsibility in general; others consider the responsibility of business toward particular social problems. Among the general surveys, Thomas C. Schelling finds that "responsibility" has to be defined as the responsibility of business firms (not the business *system*) toward concrete problems which can effectively be assigned to them for solution; yet some troublesome problems arise in fixing responsibility on particular persons or groups within the firm. James Q. Wilson concludes that government is usually unsuccessful when it tries to introduce social objectives into business management through administrative regulation. Roland N. McKean offers a parallel analysis of the limitations of behavioral codes and voluntary "responsible" action by businessmen. Marvin A. Chirelstein concludes that reform of the law of corporations can do little to further the objectives of social responsibility.

The skepticism of these scholars is strongly reinforced by the conclusions of those investigating the special problems. Business firms perhaps cannot be expected to move voluntarily very far from their traditional economic role to assume new responsibilities for social problems, external costs, and social benefits unless they see some long-run gain to themselves in doing so. Social responsibilities can be assigned to them by government to some degree, through mixtures of compulsion and inducement, but still others must probably remain in the province of governmental action if they are to be assumed by anyone.

Writing from the perspective of specialists in sectoral problems, Jerome Rothenberg, John F. Kain, and Benjamin Chinitz investigate, respectively, the extent to which responsibilities for protection of the physical environment, for reducing urban ills, and for developing backward regions and distressed areas can be expected of business, and which of these responsibilities are likely to be assumed voluntarily by business firms. Raymond Vernon examines the social responsibilities that multinational corporations may be inclined to assume voluntarily and the conflicts in demands that various interests and governments may impose upon such corporations. The results do not encourage the belief that there is much scope for the exercise of voluntary responsibility by business other than its observance of basic codes of conduct and its obedience to unenforceable aspects of regulation and public policy. Even in employee relations, the area of business policy on which new concepts of responsibility have perhaps had their strongest influence, Charles A. Myers concludes that change has resulted largely from external pressures, including governmental coercion, rather than from voluntary action. Martin Bronfenbrenner suggests that the best way to make business more responsible to consumers is through effective competition. Of course, to the extent that social responsibility coincides with the interests of the firm (even in the long run) its successful exercise by private business is to be expected.

The authors and the editor owe a considerable debt to Joseph A. Pechman, director of the Economic Studies program at Brookings, who helped to organize and encourage the project and offered many valuable comments and suggestions on the various chapters. Many anonymous readers in the academies, in business, and in the Brookings Institution contributed comments and criticisms that improved the volume. Robert Erwin edited the manuscript and Evelyn P. Fisher checked the accuracy of sources and data cited. The index was prepared by Florence Robinson.

This book is the eleventh in the Brookings series of Studies in the Regulation of Economic Activity. The series presents the findings of a program of research focused on public policies toward business. The work on this volume was supported by a grant from the Rockefeller Brothers Fund.

The views expressed in this book are solely those of the authors, and should not be attributed to the trustees, officers, or staff members of the Brookings Institution or to the Rockefeller Brothers Fund.

KERMIT GORDON
President

October 1974
Washington, D.C.

Contents

Tables

CHAPTER ONE

The Issues

JAMES W. McKIE

THE ESSAYS in this volume present the views of specialists in economics, political science, and law on an issue that has recently become prominent. The "social responsibility" of business was not widely considered to be a significant problem from Adam Smith's time to the Great Depression. But since the 1930s, and especially during the last decade, social responsibility has become an important issue not only for business but in the theory and practice of law, politics, and economics.

The scholars represented here have each considered an aspect of the issue of social responsibility (indicated by the chapter titles) to see what their own disciplines had to say about what the responsibility of the business firm should be and what it appears to have become. We all recognize that such an inquiry is not purely "scientific," leading to hypotheses that one can confirm or disprove empirically or to a set of theorems linked together in an impeccable system of logic that all rational persons must accept. Judgments about social responsibility are in part value judgments, like many other judgments in social sciences and law. But analysis of the problems construed in the way that these investigators see them should help business, government, and other interested parties in the community to understand the consequences of assuming certain kinds of responsibility and to avoid some mistakes in the assignment of responsibility to private business organizations.

The issue of social responsibility has grown to very large proportions in recent years. Public concern with it stems largely from the growing interdependence and complexity of society, which has greatly increased the mutual involvement and vulnerability of individual persons and organizations. No individual can rely wholly on himself, free of the tyranny of his neighbors' presence; no business firm can assume that it is surrounded entirely by an impersonal and automatic market; no organization can operate

1

without considering the ties and external effects linking it to the rest of society. These interrelationships have become so pervasive and so intricate that the traditional mechanisms of interaction among independent organizations and individuals, each following its own interests in a private enterprise market economy, no longer seem to work effectively. Moreover, dissatisfaction with the performance of the social system, which surfaces from time to time in the course of history, has again become widespread and has focused as it usually does on the leading institutions of American society. Business, though one of the most prominent of those institutions, is not the only one, and the issue of "responsibility" is not confined to business alone. But it is certainly one of the institutions whose responsibility has been widely debated of late.

Demands that business enterprise improve its performance by assuming more responsibility and new kinds of responsibility have emerged in part from political influences, including the development of public regulation. Business firms (especially big ones) are now expected to contribute to purposes of society such as community service, equitable employment opportunities, and improvement of the quality of life. Furthermore, regulations and inducements are often aimed at business firms simply because they may be the best *available* institutions to accomplish some public purpose. Demands have also come from philosophical critics of the business system; from new constituencies representing disadvantaged minorities and previously powerless or inarticulate groups in society; and from those concerned with new issues of the environment and other hitherto neglected physical and cultural dimensions of social organization. Business enterprise itself has been attempting to redefine its role—partly in response to the criticisms and demands laid on it by others, but partly following from its own institutional development and its changing conceptions of the world.[1]

The contemporary impact of these new conceptions of responsibility on various problem areas such as the environment and the urban predicament are described in Chapters 7–12. Some of these conceptions, such as business responsibility for alleviating racial discrimination, seem to have grown from changes in fundamental social attitudes as influenced by reformers and by spokesmen for previously hidden constituencies. Other new concerns, such as area redevelopment, have emerged chiefly from public

---

1. See in Chapter 2 my discussion of the classical view of business responsibility and the views that developed later.

policy initiatives, while still others such as employment security seem to result in the main from evolution of traditional roles of business and labor unions. But few if any redefinitions and extensions of business responsibility have had simple causes. The influences are intermingled.

Whatever the origins of demands for greater responsibility, we must also consider the business entities that are (or should be) the recipients of these demands.

The System, the Firm, and the Individual

"Business" has at least two connotations.[2] One suggests the process of production in industrial society: a material, technological, physical process. The other is the system of private ownership and profit motivation: a legal and social process. They need not correspond. In some countries without a private enterprise system, the productive process nevertheless generates problems like those discussed in this book. Potato chip factories, oil tankers, and electric power generators appear to constitute much the same kind of pollution problem in countries where they are not "business" as in countries where they are. Sonic boom does not depend on whether the airline is nationalized. In a mixed economy, municipal power plants may be no different from private power companies with regard to the environmental problems they pose. So one can talk about the responsibilities that ought to be associated with electric power production, irrespective of ownership; alternatively one can talk about the responsibilities that ought to be assumed by, or placed on, private corporations, which are legally and bureaucratically not expected to share the particular responsibilities that go with government enterprises and charities. Even in America the correspondence between these two elements of economic organization—the productive technology and the business institutions—is only partial. The contributors to this book focus on "business" in the second sense, the private, profit-oriented part of the economy, the part that hires and purchases and sells for private gain.

One way to think about the social responsibility of private business is to inquire what we can legitimately expect of the sector as a whole, how we should react when our legitimate expectations are disappointed, and

2. This section is excerpted and condensed from a contribution by T. C. Schelling. See Chapter 4 for a further development of the distinctions formulated by Professor Schelling.

what to do about it. But there is a great difference between what we can expect of the "business system" in America—the private enterprise economy, business in the aggregate—and what we can expect of particular business firms. The system may fail to provide full employment, fail to innovate vigorously, fail to weed out the inefficient, fail to invite entrepreneurship, fail to respond to the needs of consumers, and may obviously fail to provide "public goods" and things that fall somewhat beyond its domain. Yet some of these "failings" represent expectations we should not have had in the first place, and others are aggregate failings rather than the shortcomings of individual firms.

Innovation and invention, vigorous competition, and quick response to needs that can be felt in the marketplace may legitimately be expected of the system. These expectations, too, may lead to disappointment; but again it is hard to focus the disappointment on particular firms. To some extent this distinction corresponds to that between sins of omission and sins of commission. The "system" may be poor at developing innovations for fighting fires rather than fighting nuclear wars. The "system" may be poor at producing a harmless substitute for the cigarette. The "system" may be poor at producing and selling containers that don't litter the countryside. But it is not easy—indeed, it is almost meaningless—to affix responsibility.

What are the responsibilities of private enterprise in America? This is very different from the question of what are, or ought to be, or could be made to be, the responsibilities of particular business. This book mainly concerns itself with what can be expected from existing firms. Both the system and its concrete units are important, possibly too important to permit us simply to make a choice between them. But the distinction is significant; and the policy implications for the two are quite different.

If the system disappoints us, one possible response is to revise our expectations downward. Another is to supplement or augment it from outside the business system. A third is to take generalized measures for the health of the economy. But the word "responsibility" has moral and legal connotations. It suggests something that a person or a social entity can recognize and act upon. And the emphasis in this volume is on what people or organizations might do or abstain from and what might be expected from them.

The distinction cannot be drawn with complete clarity. The "system" may be a social aggregate that reflects the individual businesses, and a disappointing performance of the system as a whole may prove to be analyzable into the disappointing behavior of the entities that comprise it. Just as the weakness of an army or of a medical system may in the end be resolvable into the individual weaknesses of the individuals who comprise it, the failure of the "system" may prove upon analysis to be a composite of the failures of a multitude of individuals. But it may not. A traffic jam is not best analyzed in terms of the individual pathologies of the drivers, and the failure of anyone to compose music comparable to what Bach composed cannot be analyzed as the sum of the failures of a population of identifiable musicians who collectively fell short of the mark.

Similarly we have to distinguish between a "business" and the *people* —call them "businessmen"—who manage or control or bureaucratically conduct the enterprise. Individual businessmen may lie, cheat, steal, or subvert the organizations they work for. They may do it for personal gain, for political motives, or for the public good. They may be bold or timid, sensitive or callous on public issues, personally innovative or lacking in imagination. They can be "responsible" or "irresponsible," without the businesses they work in being the image of the people who manage them and without the "business" being analyzable as the equivalent of a businessman.[3] The firm is a "black box" whose conduct and purposes do not relate in any simple way to those of the people who constitute it. For this reason the task of assigning responsibility is greatly simplified whenever it can be directed to the firm as an organization, instead of to the several motives and behavior of the individual employees.

Immanent Responsibility and Assigned Responsibility

Is responsibility solely a question of ethics? The ethical approach holds that responsibility consists of observing moral imperatives: these are axiomatic; they reflect natural justice or obligation or legitimate moral expectation; all responsible agents should act accordingly in

3. See Chapter 3, by Marvin A. Chirelstein, on the conflicts that arise among internal constituents of the firm and the attitude of the law on responsibility of management to other constituents. It can be said, for example, that charitable contributions by corporations begin mainly as a result of management's conscience, or at least management policy, and not mainly from actions or initiatives of stockholders. But the views of managers (as persons) are checked by other constituencies and by impersonal constraints.

matters of morality and conscience. The other concept of responsibility is assigned responsibility: allocation of function to the organization or entity best fitted to discharge it.

The analysis of different problem areas in Chapters 7–12 reaches tentative conclusions concerning how much and what kinds of responsibility can legitimately be assigned to business firms primarily on the basis of their suitability for handling those responsibilities, not primarily on the basis of ethical imperatives. But business ethics which reflect the views of ethical behavior held by the general community do have a strong effect on business behavior.[4] Ethical codes induce businesses (and businessmen) to accept constraints and follow rules of behavior that are frequently essential to the operation of society.[5] Any explanation of how business views its responsibilities must take them into account.

Externalities

Demands for "responsible" social action are largely directed at problems that are in whole or in part external to the business firm. Assignment of responsibility for them implies that the firm can help to alleviate them and may wittingly or unwittingly have helped to produce them. *Some* of these external problems originate out of the firm's operations, which generate costs (such as atmospheric pollution) or benefits (such as the social benefits of education/training on the job) that are transmitted to other parties or to society at large but which escape accounting by the firm itself. These externalities should in theory be counted in with the other costs and benefits generated by the firm. The costs to other parties, or the social costs to the community, may exceed the private costs as seen by the firm, or the social benefits may exceed the benefits (such as profit) counted by the firm. If no offset or correction results from the countervailing action of affected parties, an uneconomical imbalance between costs and benefits can result unless the firm itself takes account of these external effects of its operations. Other problems actually arise outside the operation of business enterprises, as

4. See Roland N. McKean's remarks in Chapter 5.
5. But not always; appeals to "business ethics" have sometimes been used to justify cartels and agreements limiting competition and to fix moral opprobrium on "chiselers." See Chapter 2, p. 24, n. 9.

a result of imperfections in social organization. Though the firm did not originate them (and hence was not "responsible" for them if that word is used to denote "guilt"), it may create some external benefits by assuming responsibility for them. But which ones, and to what extent, and by what means?

Criteria for Business Responsibility

It is clear that most business managers are quite responsive to the traditional criteria of business performance: economic efficiency, progressiveness and innovation, contribution to growth and development. They are less so to demands for "responsibility" that go into other kinds of social action which one group or another deems to be desirable or which press the claims of constituencies other than the managers and owners to have a formal, recognized voice in management.

In Chapter 7, Martin Bronfenbrenner proposes a rigorous economic test for responsibility. He invites agreement to the proposition that a firm is behaving responsibly toward consumers to the extent that it sets prices and specifications for its products *as if* it were a pure competitor with long-term goals uppermost, *as if* all its external costs and benefits were captured (internalized), *as if* information to consumers were perfect and costless, and *as if* the firm were fully liable for all acts of its employees and agents.[6] Assuming that the firm is free to exercise discretion, responsibility to the consumer interest consists in moving toward such norms.

Most economists would probably agree that these conditions do encompass the applicable economic tests of optimum performance by business firms. Generally speaking, a closer approach to pure competition in the business system might alleviate much of the criticism that has been directed against it and deflect many of the demands for greater social responsibility that have been leveled against large business firms. The

6. Compare with Bronfenbrenner's "test" the definition formulated by Raymond Vernon to use in drafting Chapter 11, on business operations abroad: "I shall think of social responsibility as including: (1) a concern to minimize external diseconomies wherever business operations create such diseconomies; and (2) a readiness to apply the resources of the enterprise for social ends whenever there is a reasonable possibility that the application would eventually generate some net benefit to the enterprise."

norms of economic performance may be all that is necessary for some aspects of business responsibility, such as responsibility for the interests of consumers. But in some other fields of concern, problems of equity, aesthetics, life styles, social development, and even of politics may arise. Are these "externalities" in the sense of the above definition? Are they among the external costs and benefits to be internalized? Though some of the problems that firms are now being invited to solve or alleviate result from production externalities that should be completely internalized within the firms' business operations if we can find a way to do it, others involve functions that have little relation to traditional economic missions (despite the fact that they might generate external benefits).

The presence of so many unconventional or noneconomic problems in the offing creates some potential conflicts among criteria of performance, notably conflicts between the traditional criterion of economic efficiency and profits and a number of other social values. Inevitably, these conflicts generate differences in value judgments concerning the kinds and extent of responsibilities that should be assigned to business firms. These judgments reflect different views of social priorities. It is obvious that no matter how they approach these problems, business firms are not going to be able to satisfy everyone.

The problem of conflicting norms is vividly illustrated by Raymond Vernon's description in Chapter 11 of the difficulties faced by multinational enterprises, especially in emerging nations:

In most situations, there is no such thing as a social standard that is universally acceptable. . . .

For example, if U.S. drug companies should decide to adhere to U.S. labeling standards in the sale of their products abroad, they would be unwise to assume that they could count on escaping criticism. Rather, they might be charged in the importing country with administering an implied rebuke to the local government for failing to protect its consumers adequately; or they might be charged with imperiling all sellers in the local market in ways that powerful foreign firms can afford but fledgling local firms cannot. Any U.S. company that decides to avoid apartheid practices within the limits of South Africa's tolerance must count on being charged from some quarters with holding back; and if such a company manages to get itself ousted, it must anticipate that it will be charged from other quarters with abandoning the Bantu. If foreign enterprises raise local wages, they must be prepared to be accused of trying to hold local labor in thrall; if they increase local exports, of increasing the dependence of the local economy upon them; if they train local workers or give jobs to those that are trained, of monopolizing local talent.

Processes and Instruments for Assigning Responsibility

If society is to assign responsibility for any problems outside the usual or traditional concerns of the firm, whether they entail economic costs and benefits or not, it must have some means to induce, persuade, or require business organizations to accept it. At one extreme is pure coercion, or the application of collective decisions by force. Public power may "assign" tasks in that manner, but organizations or persons subjected to that kind of requirement are not assuming "responsibility" in the relevant sense of accountability for something that is to some degree within their power, control, or management. But pure coercion is usually an inaccessible option anyway. "Responsibility," referring to that part of the spectrum short of pure coercion and extending to purely voluntary action, implies some freedom of decision by business (or by other organizations). It is not confined to *purely* voluntary action in the sense of acts initiated and performed by the business firm at its sole and unfettered discretion. Such acts are hardly likely to result from distilled rationality or pure altruism, in any event; they are influenced by codes of conduct and all manner of social controls, general and specific, subtle and unsubtle. Most questions of business responsibility involve a mixture of voluntary action and compulsion of one kind or another.

Yet the spectrum between pure coercion and purely voluntary acts is not a transition in one dimension. Society may choose to use the political machinery to provide public goods and services to remedy failures of the private sector. It may regulate, leaving some decisions about the problems to the private decisions of business firms. The government may use inducements, threats, exhortations, specific or unspecific promises of benefit. It may provide information to awaken a voluntary response. It can influence codes of behavior.[7] It may apply pressure or inducements to third parties in the expectation that these will be transmitted to business firms. Other constituencies than the government may also use most of these methods to mobilize opinion, publicize issues, focus pressure on business, and induce extensions of responsibility or changes in policy. Nongovernment groups can also use a third-party approach, via government organizations. Business firms can influence or pressure each other. Constituencies *within* the firm (such as dissident groups of stock-

7. For fuller discussion of ways in which government may influence the social outlook of business, including noncoercive ways, see McKean, Chapter 5; Schelling, Chapter 4; and Charles A. Myers, Chapter 12.

holders) exert pressures on management.[8] Finally the underlying force of public opinion can change the viewpoint of any organization, "voluntarily" or not. The machinery for assigning responsibility is a multifocus system. Certainly there is no mutual exclusion between "coercion" and "voluntary" exercise of responsibility; nor do these correspond to "private" and "public" mechanisms.

Business firms are more willing to accept responsibilities thrust on them by other constituencies if they can see a reasonable probability that these actions will pay off in the long run. By reducing and internalizing the external costs, they hope also to internalize some corresponding benefits. They expect to preserve the enterprise and increase its long-run profitability by enhancing the stability, productivity, and reliability of the labor force, by improving the business environment, by forestalling burdensome regulation, etc.[9]

The long-run benefits for the firm and for society are often shrouded in uncertainty.[10] Naturally, there is always *some* social benefit associated with elimination of a social cost. Firms considering whether to assume or internalize a social cost or to undertake a beneficial social service may not be able to capture enough of the social benefit even in the long run to repay their own private costs of doing so. Or too many may hope to be "free riders" on the altruism of other firms, benefiting from the improvement in the condition of society without bearing any of the costs themselves. When confronted with free riding by noncomplying firms, their competitors often find themselves unable to accept responsibilities they would otherwise be willing to assume. A trade or industry can only capture benefits or bear external costs collectively.[11] Hence business

---

8. Chirelstein (Chapter 3) evaluates some proposals for legal certification of the "rights" of various groups in the firm to influence managerial decisions.

9. Jerome Rothenberg in Chapter 8 gives some concrete examples of long-run profit maximization. "Managers of nuclear power plants," he writes, "generally plan to install—on their own initiative—cooling towers to lessen thermal pollution of waterways from their emissions. The main London airport has set up self-operating rules for takeoffs and landings to mitigate noise disturbance to neighboring households. Through such acts, firms seek to allay or prevent public hostility and fend off governmental intervention."

10. Note Vernon's description in Chapter 11 of the policies of the International Petroleum Company in Peru. He believes the company followed generally enlightened policies in that country and unquestionably (from the point of view of an outside observer) generated social benefits for Peru. "But there is no evidence that this had any bearing on the eventual nationalization of the enterprise in Peru."

11. Schelling in Chapter 4 and McKean in Chapter 5 touch on this subject.

groups develop codes or rules and instigate governmental imposition of them on all members of the industry. Society also assigns some responsibilities to business firms that are not expected to bring them *net* benefits, though the assignment may benefit other constituencies. It must usually use some form of compulsion to do that; firms, like other organizations, will voluntarily assume responsibility only when they see (or can be made to see) a net benefit in doing so. But it is worth emphasizing again that what appears to be a voluntary act usually results from some complex forms of social pressure.

Quasi-Voluntary Response

Several instances are given in this book of internalization of costs and benefits by a process that illustrates the mixture of voluntary action and pressures from outside the firm. Business is familiar with such a process through experience with charitable contributions, community improvement, and other contributions toward alleviation of local problems of the social environment of the firm.[12]

There is also an extended record in redefining responsibilities toward employees (summarized by Charles A. Myers in Chapter 12). Historians would doubtless have some difficulty in determining how much change has come from purely voluntary or paternalistic or philanthropic acts by management; how much from managerial recognition of inexorable market forces; how much has been extracted by effective union pressure; what management would have granted anyway but held back to grant during collective bargaining; and what has resulted from moral suasion, government threats, legislation, or changes in management philosophy. Many business firms have improved safety conditions on the job; they have set up pensions and company-paid insurance coverage; they have provided severance and relocation support for displaced employees; they have endeavored to enrich employment experiences in recent years and to make certain kinds of work less monotonous (though perhaps with less success than they hoped for); they have helped to set up child-care centers, clinics, and even counseling services for various needs of their employees. They have thus substituted the action of the employer for the unlimited responsibility and even the free-

12. See Chirelstein in Chapter 3 on the feasible limits to such actions and the difficulties in establishing the corporation's right to do this.

dom of the employee, while endeavoring to avoid the excesses of nineteenth-century paternalism. They have done these things as a result of
the pressures mentioned above. Not many actions have been taken because of pure coercion originating with the government and forced on
business, though not many were entirely voluntary either. *Some* firms
had to be coerced, as is true for any other kind of social responsibility
or even of simple obedience of the law.

Sometimes "voluntary" responsibility is a question mainly of perceiving opportunities and obligations and not allowing strict conventions of
profit accounting to obscure the real choices. Benjamin Chinitz, who in
Chapter 10 analyzes the problem of industrial location and business responsibility for depressed areas, makes this point several times: decisions
to locate plants are not entirely determined by the distribution of resources and markets as "given" elements; the firm itself often has an
impact on these. Innovative efforts, developmental energy, and personal
views of the parties to such decisions have powerful effects in some
cases. A range of choices is usually open to the firm, without decisive
differences in probable expected costs. Development decisions, in other
words, can be substantially self-validating.

The Firm as Collective Instrument:
Compulsion and Its Limits

Once it departs from altruism and from voluntary acceptance by the
firm of responsibilities assigned to it by such mechanisms as the pressure
of public opinion, the assignment of business responsibility must usually
be mixed with some elements of compulsion. The chapters in this volume identify a range of activities which mingle some elements of coercive or collective assignment with some elements of voluntary acceptance, or occasionally initiative, by the business firm.

For example, Rothenberg's analysis (Chapter 8) leads him to doubt
strongly that private altruism can be very successful in dealing with the
problems of pollution: "The prospects rest on the willingness of equity
holders to sacrifice income and other goals; on the ability of managers
to formulate consistent rules of behavior; on the amassing of very sizable amounts of difficult and intrinsically ambiguous information beyond
what is required for each firm's own operations; and on the ability and
desire of numbers of altruistic firms to coordinate their efforts."

Each of these forms of support has its limits. Rothenberg does think (p. 204) that firms can take the initiative in cleanup campaigns as a call to direct action and a means of involving the public sector in enforcement of policies on all. But a centralized approach with private cooperation (such as public subsidy for private waste treatment) is the only one that is likely to be effective for most environmental problems.

John F. Kain in Chapter 9 identifies four factors that are central to the urban predicament of the mid-twentieth century: racial discrimination and poverty (and their spatial distribution); outmoded institutional arrangements for financing public services in metropolitan areas; and obsolescent private and public capital in old cities.

Kain doubts whether business will voluntarily undertake actions that are not in the interests of its owners, managers, or workers. It will not undertake clearly unprofitable ventures. Business firms can do very little directly to correct current fiscal and governmental deficiencies, but indirectly they can do much by "placing their prestige and political power behind the development of more suitable fiscal and governmental arrangements for metropolitan areas" (p. 244). They can make a more direct contribution to elimination of urban poverty by setting up programs to train and employ disadvantaged workers; but the success of these programs will be enormously enhanced if the government maintains full employment and enacts national wage subsidy and income maintenance programs. Their best opportunity for making a large contribution toward resolving the urban crisis lies in vigorous efforts to combat racial discrimination in all aspects of life—an approach that has virtually become part of the ethical imperatives or "immanent responsibilities" of all organizations but whose concrete effect on the urban predicament will be realized only slowly. It appears that much of the contribution of business to "solution" of the urban crises must be indirect and dependent upon parallel efforts by government.

Chinitz (Chapter 10) concludes that business firms may voluntarily act to develop depressed areas and to ease the problems that result when they exit from a dependent community. But these individual decisions will not add up to an optimum pattern of distribution of population or of help for underdeveloped areas. Nationally, those things will depend on a "consensus"—i.e., a national policy to stem "urban crowding and rural decline or otherwise redirect the geographic pattern of population growth" (p. 273). The government is the agency for such decisions; business firms cannot cooperate with national policy until one is formulated. When a policy is formulated, success will certainly depend on business cooperation and response to incentives.

Perhaps the widest range for successful assignment of responsibility to business enterprises has been demonstrated in the category of relations with employees—in part (though not entirely) because the constituencies affected have some power that they can use to bring pressure on management. But even in this field of action, progress toward social goals, in which participation by employing firms is a necessary action, cannot be achieved without government policy in a central role. Full employment, for example, along with other macroeconomic norms, has long since been assigned to the government to bring about; the individual firm cannot produce this result by the exercise of responsibility or even assume an important part in the effort without government controls and specific incentives.

In short, the chapters presented here come down to prescriptions for business firms to discharge their traditional economic responsibilities of producing efficiently and contributing to growth and progress. Society may assign responsibilities beyond what the firm owes to its owners only to a quite limited degree. It may also expect adherence to the law, to standards of conduct that are universally accepted, and to the minimum rules that eschew violence and renounce fraud. Society may have to threaten to enforce these on some firms by coercive methods, to reinforce voluntary adherence to them. Public policy, of course, has the converse responsibility of providing inducements for responsible rather than for irresponsible business behavior.[13]

Beyond these basic expectations, responsibility legitimately includes community service, participation in philanthropic and charitable enterprises, and a number of other activities that could produce long-run benefit for the firms and its stockholders by improving its social environment, including its employee relations. Society may realistically expect business firms to experiment with some relatively cost-free ways of meeting social norms and to participate in formation of public policy on matters that pertain to business operations.

Business responsibility also implies compliance with that public policy, once it is determined. Even when the government decides to assign a task to business by fiat, "coercion" is limited in effect. It is a common-

13. See Rothenberg, pp. 211ff.

place observation that the government in a country like the United States cannot regulate effectively without at least some cooperation from the regulated. The self-assessed income tax is the archetypal example, but there are many others in the annals of regulation to achieve the purposes discussed in this volume. Without voluntary compliance from at least part of the business community, controls become unenforceable. Hence we observe many instances of "responsibility" within a regulatory mode which is apparently coercive but actually mixed. We can define "business responsibility" in that context, as in many others cited in this volume, as obedience to the unenforceable.[14]

Merely stating these conclusions does not necessarily imply that American business firms have all tried conscientiously to live up to legitimate expectations of responsibility. No judgment is rendered here on actual average performance. The authors of this volume offer their conclusions as a guide to expectations. As long as the business firm remains an essentially private organization, distinct from the state and with private ownership substantially intact, it cannot accept general responsibility for problems that lie any appreciable distance outside its traditional economic concerns. Collective responsibilities other than those validated in these essays are more efficiently assigned elsewhere.[15]

Some responsibilities have long been neglected by everyone. If society does pick them up out of limbo and assign them to various organizations and agencies, large corporations are not the only ones eligible. Government has often neglected its own social responsibilities. Aside from the remediable shortcomings of regulation (and avowedly anticonsumer actions such as encouragement of price-fixing cartels), government frequently fails in its responsibility to control crime, to stabilize prices, to build safe highways, and to protect the rest of us from drunken

14. See Chapter 6 by James Q. Wilson (as well as McKean, Chapter 5).

15. A large multinational corporation in a backward country which has no institutions (not even a government) capable of bearing the kind of responsibilities that come with economic growth and the transition to a market economy more or less tests the outer boundary of what is possible for corporate responsibility. The problems arising out of such situations are painfully well known. Vernon, pp. 289ff., notes that some multinationals in such circumstances have developed "illusions of absolute sovereignty." But a test of adequate political development in those circumstances is the establishment of government control of the activities of private firms, its ability to use them for its own purposes instead of vice versa, and the rapidity of its creation of genuine collective agencies to supersede the corporation outside the legitimate economic domain of the private firm.

drivers. It has even engaged in misleading advertising, as for U.S. savings bonds.[16] And what of consumers themselves? Bronfenbrenner (Chapter 7) leads us to wonder whether assignment of additional responsibility might produce less shoplifting, fewer abuses of consumer credit, less destruction of rental housing by its tenants, and so on. And what shall we say of the responsibilities of other institutions of society such as universities? This book does not address that question; but our inquiry into the social responsibilities of business may reveal issues that have to be faced in judging the obligations of any agency or organization.

16. See Roland N. McKean, "Government and the Consumer," *Southern Economic Journal*, Vol. 39 (April 1973), pp. 481–89.

CHAPTER TWO

Changing Views

JAMES W. McKIE

THE CONCEPTION of business responsibility that held a dominant position up to about fifty years ago gave primary emphasis to the obligations of the profit-seeking private enterprise toward its owners. Historians of the distant past might classify this outlook as "early modern," but from the viewpoint of recent generations it can be called classical or traditional, since it reached its full development in the late eighteenth century. In recent years the traditional view has been rather extensively modified; the approach of most large corporations nowadays to questions of responsibility is no longer austerely classical. There are also pre-classical traditions of responsibility which have never died out completely. Those older views of responsibility, applicable to both individuals and organizations, are now taking on renewed significance for the business firm. They derive largely from nonbusiness institutions and from moral and religious precepts which predated the appearance of the business firm as we know it.

Even after "business" emerged as a set of organizations, habits, functions, purposes, ideas, and methods of action and control separate from other social institutions, it took some time to define a creed of its own. During the seventeenth century in Western Europe, for instance, well after the establishment of capitalism and of a full-fledged business community, the business creed still carried a strong tincture of religious principles which did not really distinguish between the moral duties of a business organization and those of individuals who owned it and directed its affairs. The medieval view of society as a mystical body unifying members of different purpose and degree still survived; but even the more "individualistic" Protestant creeds did not look on business pur-

17

suits as autonomous and ethically self-contained. Each man was morally responsible for his acts, in economic transactions as in everything else.[1]

The doctrine of the stewardship of wealth was another manifestation of this moral view of business obligations. The moral doctrine never entirely disappeared; but as time went on, ethical concern tended to focus on the individual's disposition of his wealth and his conduct in nonbusiness pursuits rather than on the behavior of the businessman or the business enterprise in the generation of wealth. By Adam Smith's time the distinction between business behavior (controlled by the external, automatic, impersonal mechanism of the market) and other kinds of social relations had become well established. Its implications were well expressed in the following famous passage:

Every individual necessarily labours to render the annual revenue of the society as great as he can. He generally, indeed, neither intends to promote the public interest, nor knows how much he is promoting it. . . . By directing that industry in such a manner as its produce may be of the greatest value, he intends only his own gain, and he is in this, as in many other cases, led by an invisible hand to promote an end which was no part of his intention. Nor is it always the worse for the society that it was no part of it. By pursuing his own interest he frequently promotes that of the society more effectually than when he really intends to promote it. I have never known much good done by those who affected to trade for the public good. It is an affectation, indeed, not very common among merchants, and very few words need be employed in dissuading them from it.[2]

The Classical View

The basic idea can support a rather simple philosophy of business responsibility, which was the prevailing view in the nineteenth century. The simplified classical view embodied these cardinal points:

1. Economic behavior is separate and distinct from other types of behavior, and business organizations are distinct from other organizations, even though the same individuals may be involved in business and nonbusiness affairs. Business organizations do not serve the same goals as other organizations in a pluralistic society.

2. The primary criteria of business performance are economic effi-

1. Richard H. Tawney, *Religion and the Rise of Capitalism: A Historical Study* (Harcourt Brace, 1926), p. 184.

2. Adam Smith, *The Wealth of Nations*, bk. iv, chap. 2 (Modern Library, 1937), p. 423. First published 1776.

ciency and growth in production of goods and services, including improvements in technology and innovations in goods and services.

3. The primary goal and motivating force for business organizations is profit. The firm attempts to make as large a profit as it can, thereby maintaining its efficiency and taking advantage of available opportunities to innovate and contribute to growth. Profits are kept to reasonable or appropriate levels by market competition, which leads the firm pursuing its own self-interest to an end that is no part of its conscious intention: enhancement of the public welfare. It need not recognize any responsibility to the public to accomplish this result.

A contemporary version of this view has been eloquently expressed by Milton Friedman:

> The view has been gaining widespread acceptance that corporate officials and labor leaders have a "social responsibility" that goes beyond serving the interest of their stockholders or their members. This view shows a fundamental misconception of the character and nature of a free economy. In such an economy, there is one and only one social responsibility of business —to use its resources and engage in activities designed to increase its profits so long as it stays within the rules of the game, which is to say, engages in open and free competition, without deception or fraud. . . . Few trends could so thoroughly undermine the very foundations of our free society as the acceptance by corporate officials of a social responsibility other than to make as much money for their stockholders as possible. This is a fundamentally subversive doctrine. If businessmen do have a social responsibility other than making maximum profits for stockholders, how are they to know what it is?[3]

The classical approach dominated the economic theory of the firm, as well as middle-class ideology, for a long time. Economists tended to conclude that the profit-seeking business firm, under the pressures of the market, would produce good economic performance in terms of the relevant criteria of performance: efficiency and progress. They did recognize that certain "externalities" (costs or benefits arising from a firm's operations but having an impact on someone or something else) escaped proper accounting and could lead to inefficient use of resources. Much of the debate about social responsibility really concerns externalities of one kind and another, and specifically how much of the responsibility for external costs and benefits a firm should be obliged to assume. The viewpoint of orthodox economics on external costs and benefits was not entirely clear. It implied that "social" costs and benefits—the kinds

3. *Capitalism and Freedom* (University of Chicago Press, 1962), p. 133.

of externalities that had a diffused effect on society and that could not be defrayed or compensated by contractual agreement and payment between specific parties generating them and specific parties feeling their impact—were the responsibility of government, i.e., a collective responsibility. If necessary, the government could take steps to assess the costs and benefits against the right parties and limit or enlarge them to the right proportions, but business firms could not be expected to do this voluntarily.[4]

Equity and Security as Criteria of Business Responsibility

Society demands more of its economic *system* than efficiency, growth, and technological progress. The additional demands are economic norms in their own right to some extent. But in the classical view, which still survives in considerable measure, the individual business *firm* is in no way responsible for attaining them, even assuming that they can be given unequivocal expression as standards of performance.

Equity in income distribution—a political issue—is not necessarily what results from market competition or from attainment of a fully efficient allocation of resources. Business firms must pay people what their services are worth on the open market; they must pay competitive prices for land and capital resources; the income distribution that results is largely determined by the distribution of marketable skills, abilities, credentials, and property ownership in the community. If this distribution does not meet with social approval, said the orthodox approach, it is not up to the firm to change it. A business cannot pay less than competitive prices for particular factors of production, and should not pay more; that would distort efficient allocation of resources. Nor can it redistribute its owners' property to satisfy its own conception of equity.

---

4. Economists have often found it convenient to follow a dualistic approach to the "firm" and the "government" as theoretical models. The theoretical "government" model seems to be a monolithic mechanism guided by an unambiguous set of "policy" choices and collective ends which it attains with perfect efficacy. It is the abstract embodiment of the collective will. No one would mistake this theoretical government for a real one. The difference corresponds to that between the theoretical model of the firm and the real business organization. Neither theoretical model is "wrong," or inappropriate, for the purpose for which such models are employed by economic theory.

It is up to the government to change the distribution of income. Further-more, any government seeking to change the distribution should take care not to interfere with the efficiency of markets. Direct taxation and direct payments, preferably in the form of lump sum transfers, are advisable. Clearly, this is not the business of the firm. Efforts to redis-tribute property and to remedy educational inequality are likewise re-served to the government.

As for stability in employment, income, and prices, the firm (even a relatively large one) is too small in relation to the total economy to have much impact on these things. Besides, according to classical eco-nomic theory, the pressures of the competitive market will keep a com-pany's prices in line with those of other firms; and it cannot employ unnecessary workers in slack times without incurring a cost disadvan-tage which could threaten its survival. Even if the firm has no com-petitors, it cannot do much about fluctuations in aggregate income and unemployment, and it is still obliged to concern itself with minimizing costs. Prices, employment, and aggregate income are a collective respon-sibility—only the government can control them, through monetary policy, compensatory fiscal policy, and other weapons of economic stabilization.

Thus postulates orthodox theory. The successors to the classical view tend to agree with it on these points, though there are some critics of the private enterprise *system* who assign blame (and hence responsi-bility) to individual business *firms* for inequities in income distribution and for inflation and unemployment.

The Legal Model of Business Responsibility

The contemporary legal view of business responsibility is developed in the next chapter. We shall note here only that the traditional legal approach meshed very nicely with the traditional economic formulation to produce a distinctive view of business responsibility. The orthodox juridical conception of the firm was that of private ownership of prop-erty. The firm, from this viewpoint, was an extension of the personal property rights of its owners, exemplified in the simplest form by single proprietorship. The owner had the right to use or dispose of his property as he wished (provided he did not infringe the legal rights of others) and to enter into contracts. The legitimate goal of the business firm was to make profits for the owners.[5]

Modifications of the Classical Formulation in Practice

The business community never has adhered with perfect fidelity to an ideologically pure version of its responsibilities, drawn from the classical conception of the enterprise in economic society, though many business-men have firmly believed in the main tenets of that creed. Nor did government ever take the extreme position that business firms had no responsibilities other than to make profits for their owners, even in the heyday of laissez-faire in the late nineteenth century. The following modifications in the practice of business responsibility could be observed even when the doctrine prevailed in its most classic form.

Philanthropy, Community Obligations, Paternalism

At the level of the local community, business enterprises of all forms and sizes have generally shown some willingness to recognize social as well as economic responsibilities. This propensity has not been universal, but because it was largely unrecorded in the early days, we cannot pre-cisely measure its extent. Yet there were many indications of widespread voluntary efforts by business firms to alleviate community problems, contribute to charity, and join in enterprises of civic improvement, even though those efforts did not enlarge the firm's profits in the short run or contribute to its economic self-interest narrowly defined. (Of course, many businessmen as individuals have always participated in philan-thropic enterprise and contributed to charity; we are here considering what business *firms* do, or proprietors in their role as owner-managers, using business resources.) One recorded instance is the cooperation be-tween industry and the YMCA after the Civil War, especially by rail-road corporations, to provide community services in localities served by the railroads.[6]

5. "Where orientation to profit is not socially acceptable, an organization is not considered a business enterprise in the true sense of the term." Francis X. Sutton and others, *The American Business Creed* (Harvard University Press, 1956), p. 54.
6. Most, though not all, of the services were provided to the railroads' own employees with the aid of contributions by the companies. The companies' motives were doubtless mixed but went beyond simple market calculations in dealing with

There were others. Business firms were more inclined to participate in ventures of community improvement, beautification, and uplift if those ventures promised some material benefit to the firm, even if not fully compensatory, and especially if they benefited the firm's own em- ployees. These motives, though philanthropic to a degree, sometimes went beyond that to invade areas of responsibility traditionally reserved for individual decision by employees and other dependents of the firm and to meddle with their personal lives. In their quest for responsibility, employers sometimes became paternalistic.

Many manifestations of business paternalism appeared during the late nineteenth century. Probably the most extreme was the company-town experiment of Pullman, Illinois. Again, the motives of the firm were mixed: to improve the conditions of life among the employees while insulating them from trade unionism; to maintain an agreeable and well-planned community while earning a target return on its real estate; etc. As is well known, the experiment backfired. The social conditions in the town were by no means as agreeable as the physical surroundings, and the employees resented their position of total dependence on the company. A violent and bitter strike put an end to this enterprise in paternalistic philanthropy.[7] Labor unions and other interested groups have since made their opposition to such policies unmistakably clear.

Whether company towns were run philanthropically or not, the business organization had to do much of the work of government in them; social responsibility in some form was thrust upon it. The company town, happily, has all but vanished from the American economy, but there are still plenty of instances of large-scale influence by individual firms on particular communities. In those cases, the public welfare is bound to be materially affected by what the firm does. The distinction between private and public responsibility becomes blurred. Even now they face the problem of being "responsible" without being paternalistic.

The "Ethics" of Market Behavior

From the point of view of the orthodox creed, a code of ethics (a voluntary code, resting on the moral force of business opinion) might

---

employees; the railroads themselves regarded these contributions as philanthropic. Morrell Heald, *The Social Responsibilities of Business: Company and Community, 1900–1960* (Press of Case Western Reserve University, 1970), pp. 12–14.

7. Ibid., pp. 7–9.

appear anomalous. After all, it is said that the only responsibility of management is to make profits for the stockholders; the market itself rewards good performances and punishes bad, without reference to principles of conduct. Businessmen have to observe certain rules of behavior, such as avoiding actual theft of property and violence against competitors or employees, most of the time.[8] But these rules are matters of general law, codified and enforced by the government on businessmen and other persons alike. The classical view includes no code of ethics specifically adapted to business organizations.

The dualism in theory between voluntary responsibility and compulsory rules breaks down a bit in practice here as elsewhere. Regulation of the ethics of market behavior has not resulted entirely from a reaction of the general public against the consequences of unrestrained pursuit of self-interest by business firms. The business community itself participated in that process and generated a large part of the specific codes of conduct that were legislated into compulsory rules. Many, if not most, business firms have always attempted to adhere to a code of business ethics and would observe them even without compulsion, just as most persons would not kill even if there were no law against murder. Laws fixing the minimum rules of the game are required to restrain a small minority. Moreover, there is always a voluntary ethical code over and above the letter of the law. Perhaps the most significant manifestation of responsibility is obedience to the unenforceable.

Yet there is no denying that the voluntary ethics of market behavior were not very rigorous or restrictive in the nineteenth century. Most firms would not engage in certain questionable though legal kinds of business (selling narcotics, peddling worthless medical cures, packing adulterated foods, dealing in slaves), but there were always some that would, and they probably appeared in sufficient numbers to fill the available economic space for them. Legislation and regulation, rather than voluntary responsibility, put an end to these kinds of business pursuits. The "rules" themselves were sufficiently elastic in that era to permit myriad instances of fraud, theft, and violence that would clearly be illegal under present interpretations.[9]

8. Even Milton Friedman's uncompromising position on social responsibility calls for certain "rules of the game," such as prohibition of deception or fraud, presumably to be enforced by the government, if profit-seeking enterprises are to produce good economic performance. (See p. 19 above.)

9. One difficulty with a code of market ethics is that the business community

The traditional view of business "morality" did generate some psychological strains from the beginning and led increasingly to attempts to rationalize the ethics of business and to define its aims in terms other than the pursuit of self-interest. As the authors of a study of this aspect of business put it:

On the one hand, self-interested actions by businessmen are tolerated in law and approved in social mores. On the other hand, self-interest is considered to be an unworthy goal of action which conflicts with ethical norms to which society attaches great importance. This inconsistency creates ambivalence in social attitudes toward business; and since businessmen share the values which support both sides of the dilemma, it also produces strains within businessmen themselves.[10]

In view of these inner conflicts, it was to be expected that business firms, especially large corporations with dispersed ownership, would begin to develop overt norms of service to society to supplement their goals of profit.

The Emergence of Big Business

It was the development of big corporations during the last quarter of the nineteenth century more than anything else that hastened modifications in the classical view of business responsibility. Big business had

---

often fails to distinguish adequately between the ordinary ethical limitations on conduct that ought to constitute the "rules of the game" and particular competitive practices that help to maintain the vigor of competitive markets but which may be inconvenient or bothersome to the competing firms. In some cases the desire to eliminate these practices in the name of business ethics is self-serving; the real intent is to weaken competition. Practices have to be evaluated in a market context. Price cutting by a competitor in an imperfectly competitive market may be a manifestation of healthy competition, or it may be a predatory tactic aimed at weaker competitors. The competitors themselves are likely to regard it as "vicious price cutting" in either case. Attempts to write business ethics into enforceable legal codes frequently encounter this difficulty. For example, the codes of fair competition that were drawn up in 1933–34 under the National Industrial Recovery Act proscribed misrepresentation, defamation of competitors, bribery, coercion, piracy of designs, industrial espionage, and predatory litigation. These aims would probably command universal approval. Some of these practices, indeed, were already restrained by law. But the codes also restrained price cutting, regulated methods of price quotation and bidding, provided for maintenance of resale prices, limited quality and guarantees, restricted output and capacity, and in some cases permitted allocation of customers. One may doubt whether the participating businesses felt that these were really ethical issues. See Clair Wilcox, *Public Policies toward Business* (3d ed., Irwin, 1966), pp. 680–85.

10. Sutton and others, *The American Business Creed*, pp. 354–55.

two kinds of effects. One was to increase concentration and create a high degree of monopoly in certain important markets in the U.S. economy. The evident decline of competition led to regulation—external control, rather than voluntary responsibility—exemplified by the antitrust laws and the beginning of direct regulation. The change in the climate of opinion that led to these kinds of government intervention was itself a significant alteration in the business environment, which posed (and, as time went on, intensified) the question of voluntary responsibility to forestall or supplement public regulation.

The other effect of the growth of big business was on the legal concept of the firm. The large corporation with its complex structure of ownership, its large constituencies of nonowners dependent on it in various ways, and its professional managers not identical with the owners forced some adaptations on legal theory and practice. Far from assuming responsibility for the behavior and performance of the firm and with it the sole legitimate right to its property and earnings, the typical stockholder in the large corporation is little more than an absentee investor. He has no actual control over it and no power to influence it, other than the right to vote occasionally in a stockholder revolt against an incompetent management. Nor are the stockholders any longer the principal source of equity capital for large corporations, though that situation took some time to develop. But by the turn of the century it was evident that something new had emerged in the big, publicly held corporation: an entity which did not remotely correspond either to the old legal model of proprietorship or to the economic model of the atomistic firm in the competitive market. Lawyers, social scientists, and businessmen all began to develop some fresh views of the nature of the business firm and of the responsibilities of its management.

By the beginning of the twentieth century, it was quite evident that economic activity was no longer organized entirely into small, powerless, "atomistic" firms governed entirely by the market, if indeed it ever had been. Instead, business organizations presented a spectrum of size and power. A few large firms—virtual monopolies—were well insulated from the immediate compulsions of the market and did have considerable discretion in choosing among various possible business policies. Others —oligopoly firms—were large enough to have some discretionary power but were constrained by rivalry with other large and powerful enterprises. At the lower end of the spectrum was a considerable fringe of small firms that had no power and that confronted market pressures of more or less classical type. Economic activity showed a tendency over time to concentrate in larger business units. Questions of business responsibility centered increasingly on the large corporations that had some discretionary power of decision.

The Managerial Version of Business Responsibility

What we call the managerial version is far less rationalist than its classical alternative.[11] It is concerned with the actual organization and behavior of firms in society. It takes the large corporation as the archetype of business organization and models its view of business responsibility on the role of large enterprise in society realistically conceived. It is also inclined to view the processes of government more realistically than the classical model.

The managerial view has itself undergone considerable development since its beginnings. In the 1920s, for example, managers of large firms had accepted a much more positive outlook on their responsibilities to society than their counterparts of the 1890s were wont to have, and they no longer sought refuge in the theory that the market would take care of most problems and the "government" the rest. But their definition of the sphere of responsibility was still quite limited. The issues of consumerism, minority rights, and the environment as aspects of business responsibility were as yet unknown, though management was more inclined to assert positive virtues in its services to other constituencies in the economy than to hide aloofly behind the principle of the Invisible Hand. But the principal field of action for business responsibility at this stage was community service. The most important manifestation of this new urge toward community service was the Community Chest movement, which received much of its leadership and motive force from businessmen. It was the first large-scale involvement of business leaders with other (nongovernmental) groups in the community for a common, nonbusiness purpose, requiring contribution of their time and of business funds for community welfare.[12] It signaled a change in the conception that management held of business responsibilities toward the community.

11. The phrase "managerial version" (or "view") is borrowed from ibid., pp. 57ff.

12. Heald, *The Social Responsibilities of Business*, p. 119. For an excellent history and analysis of the Community Chest movement and the atmosphere of the 1920s, see Chapters 4 and 5 of Heald's book.

The 1930s

The 1930s are often considered to be the Great Divide between an economy organized on the principle of laissez-faire with a benevolently Jeffersonian government keeping its hands off the business interests of the country and a mixed economy in which business operates as one of the constituencies monitored by an activist government with a decided flavor of syndicalism and the welfare state. Yet the threads of the events of the 1930s run back in time. The evolution of managerial concepts and practice of responsibility continued through that period, perhaps reaching full development only after World War II. For example, there was a steady growth in certain aspects of business responsibility for employee welfare, such as disability pensions and insurance, safety measures, medical care, and retirement benefits. Pension plans, which at the turn of the century would have been regarded as manifestations of paternalism or an intrusion of the employer on the employee's freedom and responsibility to dispose of his income, had become acceptable before the New Deal and commonplace among large corporations by the 1950s. These developments were spurred both by governmental compulsion and by an enlarged concept of business responsibility.

But there is no doubt that business management was severely shaken up by the Great Depression, the New Deal, and the leftward shift of political opinion. The business community itself enlarged its concepts of responsibility in many new directions but at the same time saw many problems, in whose solution it might have participated voluntarily, pass under government control. To a considerable extent responsibility was preempted by regulation, not always with the enthusiastic acquiescence of business management.

Among many developments of the 1930s that had an impact on the managerial view and practice of responsibility, we may note these:

1. The economic collapse evoked both sporadic attempts by big business to ameliorate unemployment and to contribute to recovery, and its involvement with the government in various kinds of "partnership" efforts to achieve macroeconomic stability. That these attempts were usually ill-advised and ineffectual is beside the point. They marked a further breakdown of the classical ideology and a major entanglement of "government" with the affairs of business under the label of cooperative responsibility.

2. The public loss of confidence in the competence of "private enter-

prise" to manage and sustain the economy without government control also expressed itself in a major extension of government regulation of and presence in business. The results are familiar: the Securities and Exchange Commission, the Federal Deposit Insurance Corporation, the Tennessee Valley Authority, the Federal Communications Commission, the Federal National Mortgage Association, unemployment compensation and other forms of social security, as well as major extensions of the jurisdiction and powers of established agencies. The new approach was clear enough: whenever the private business system failed in a major responsibility to the public as the government defined it, whenever its performance in some important respect became unacceptable to a major segment of the public, the government would intervene, to enforce better performance by coercive rules or to do the job itself. Private enterprise could no longer suppose that it had full powers to maintain vested rights within a defined field of activity. The managers of large and powerful corporations could draw the appropriate conclusions with respect to the responsibilities accepted by their firms.

3. In the previously developed domain of community responsibility, contributions to charity, and social uplift, corporations were now (1935) given the legal right to make donations of the "stockholders' property" and to charge them as a business expense, up to 5 percent of pretax income. Though corporate "giving" has never actually approached the maximum deductible rate, the "five percent amendment" of 1935 gave official sanction to the use of corporate income for nonbusiness contributions and thus established business as an independent source of support. Charitable and community-service agencies could look routinely to business firms as well as to individuals for financing.

4. With the encouragement of the federal government, other groups besides business interests began to form power blocs in economic society. After the enormous growth in size and power of labor unions in the 1930s, the further development of the farm bloc, and the appearance of numerous other groups that had economic power and government support, it was no longer possible for the management of a large corporation to look out on its surroundings and see nothing there but the undifferentiated purely competitive markets of classical theory. Nor could management assume that it had full control of the internal affairs of the firm. Now it was likely to collide with some countervailing power of the unions or face the intervention of a government agency in behalf of some affected group. Management perforce began to think of con-

stituencies and power interests that had claims and influence on the firm in addition to the owners, who in classical theory had the sole right to control it and enjoy its fruits. In fact, management thenceforth had to mediate as well as to control.[13]

The Essence of the Managerial View

As noted earlier, the managerial conception of business responsibility reaches its fullest development in the large corporation, though small business reflects the same viewpoint to some degree. If one word can describe the conception that corporate management has of its own role, it is "trusteeship." The large corporation is thought of as a *permanent* institution, not merely an extension of its proprietors, and is assumed to have a life and purpose of its own, involving both its internal constituencies and the groups with which it must deal. The manager/trustees believe that they should not (and in fact cannot) run these large organizations in the interests of only one of those constituencies—the (largely absentee) owners. Employees, customers, suppliers, and other parties have rights in the organization that are not merely contractual claims.[14] According to a recent publication by the Committee for Economic Development:

> The modern professional manager also regards himself, not as an owner disposing of personal property as he sees fit, but as a trustee balancing the interests of many diverse participants and constituents in the enterprise, whose interests sometimes conflict with those of others. The chief executive of a large corporation has the problem of reconciling the demands of employees for more wages and improved benefit plans, customers for lower prices and greater values, vendors for higher prices, government for more taxes, stockholders for higher dividends and greater capital appreciation—all within a framework that will be constructive and acceptable to society.[15]

13. Some advance indications of this reorientation of viewpoint were already evident in the 1920s. Gerard Swope of General Electric "held that management, in effect, was in a position to 'define its own responsibilities'; and when he did so in a 1926 speech, he astonished his audience by putting the public and the employees ahead of the stockholders in the list of those to whom managerial obligations were due. Swope acknowledged that investors were entitled to a fair return on their money and a full reporting of company undertakings; but his emphasis almost suggested that he saw these as residual, rather than primary obligations." Ibid., p. 97.

14. Sutton and others, *The American Business Creed*, pp. 57–58.

15. Committee for Economic Development, *Social Responsibilities of Business Corporations* (New York: CED, 1971), p. 22. This document is almost an official manifesto of the managerial view in its current phase of development.

This approach does not yield an easy answer to the question of how much weight the trustees are to give to each claimant and constituency.[16] It also raises the issue of whether nonowner constituents should themselves have formal representation in the control structure of the corporation and among its trustees.

The realistic view of large corporations leads managers to understand that they must assume some responsibilities just because the corporations are there, because large enterprises are such prominent features of the social landscape and have control over such a large aggregation of resources and managerial talent.

The modern breed of corporate managers seems to welcome a partnership between business and government to attack social problems, making use of the particular strengths of each and recognizing the limitations of both. Some problems that classical economics would allocate to the "government" require the effort of corporations because they have a presence and an expertise that the actual government lacks—and the two institutions working in tandem can be more effective than either alone. Of course, the limits of that partnership still remain to be determined.

Profits and Business Responsibility

Amid all this recognition of diverse responsibilities to various constituencies, management must still remember that profits are the most important variable in the control system of a firm and one of the significant indicators of its performance. Profits are important as a guide to the allocation of resources and as an inducement for good performance, not just as income to stockholders. Certainly the managerial viewpoint is not indifferent to profits. Some theorists of the managerial school have advocated including profit maximizing within a concept of "satisficing." This concept means that the firm chooses its preferred set of actions from a complex view of its own welfare, of which profit as conventionally defined is only one variable, though some firms would regard it as the only really important one. Yet even these theorists dis-

16. Sutton and his collaborators pointed out the logical problem with the concept of trusteeship: "The moral responsibilities toward others which the managerial view would have him assume are numerous, conflicting, and incommensurable. . . . If he must balance the merits of claims to higher wages, lower prices, and higher dividends, he is a judge rather than a businessman." *The American Business Creed*, p. 358.

tinguish between optimum and nonoptimum paths of decisions.[17] To introduce elements of social responsibility into the firm's long-run profit strategy is not to say that *every* action that meets someone's notion of "responsibility" would add to the firm's profits or welfare or even its satisfaction as seen by managers, owners, or anyone else. All the managerial formulation says is that a policy of recognizing responsibility for other things besides maximum short-run profits (as conventionally defined) might help the firm to follow its own best interests over the long run, at least as far ahead as it is possible for management to see—even if other groups besides owners will share in the "profits."

In the words of the Committee for Economic Development:

There is broad recognition today that corporate self-interest is inexorably involved in the well-being of the society of which business is an integral part, and from which it draws the basic requirements needed for it to function at all—capital, labor, customers. There is increasing understanding that the corporation is dependent on the goodwill of society, which can sustain or impair its existence through public pressures on government. And it has become clear that the essential resources and goodwill of society are not naturally forthcoming to corporations whenever needed, but must be worked for and developed. . . .

Enlightened self-interest thus has both "carrot and stick" aspects. There is the positive appeal to the corporation's greater opportunities to grow and profit in a healthy, prosperous, and well-functioning society. And there is the negative threat of increasingly onerous compulsion and harassment if it does not do its part in helping create such a society.[18]

Critical Viewpoints on Responsibility

The managerial view of business responsibility has not achieved total victory. Some businessmen have always held out for the austere classical position. Economists (and some lawyers) are even more inclined to adhere to the classical view and to dismiss the managerial model as inconsistent and unworkable. But dissent has also appeared on the other end of the spectrum, from those who believe that the private business firm, and specifically the large corporation, has not been responsible enough, or that its total performance has been unacceptable, or that it

17. See Herbert A. Simon, *Administrative Behavior* (2d ed., Macmillan, 1957); Richard M. Cyert and James G. March, *A Behavioral Theory of the Firm* (Prentice-Hall, 1963).
18. CED, *Social Responsibilities of Business Corporations*, pp. 27, 29.

is the wrong sort of organization to manage the economy because it is ill adapted to supply pressing social needs. These criticisms show up in a variety of forms. They have grown in vehemence since the middle 1960s. Critics have besieged business organizations, especially big business, with a succession of demands for reform and attacks on their present performance and responsibility. We shall sample only a few of these to illustrate the tone and variety of the present criticism.

The "New Industrial State"

Among the critics who have expressed skepticism about managerial responsibility and about the suitability of private business corporations as agencies for realizing social goals is J. K. Galbraith.[19] Though the managerial school may be correct in saying that profit is no longer the sole objective of the corporation, its aims, Galbraith argues, are nevertheless shaped by its private interests. The corporation may strive for social goals when these are consistent with or adaptable to its primary aims. But, in Galbraith's opinion, large corporations (which may well be necessary for management and control of large-scale technological activities) must come under much more comprehensive social control before they can meet social needs. He believes that ultimately it will happen: that the apparatus of the state will merge with that of the corporate economy to serve the ends of society. It is this coming development, and not the growth of voluntary responsibility in the large private corporation, that will finally produce acceptable social performance:

Given the deep dependence of the industrial system on the state and the nature of its motivational relationship to the state, i.e., its identification with public goals and the adaptation of these to its needs, the industrial system will not long be regarded as something apart from government. Rather it will increasingly be seen as part of a much larger complex which embraces both the industrial system and the state. . . .

If the mature corporation is recognized to be part of the penumbra of the state, it will be more strongly in the service of social goals.[20]

The same process, he says, is to be observed in technologically advanced socialist countries: the technostructure and the state converge, the goals become intermingled, and the strictly private economic goals

19. John Kenneth Galbraith, *The New Industrial State* (Houghton Mifflin, 1967).
20. Ibid., pp. 392–94.

of the organization find their place in a multiplicity of social values and responsibilities. But, obviously, this final convergence is a long way from the present formulation of the corporate role and responsibilities envisioned by the managerial view.[21]

Efficiency and Externalities

The point of view of *The New Industrial State* is that large corporations possess unchecked power which they use in ways directed by the power structure (the private managers and, eventually, the state managers), not that they are inefficient or technologically obstructive. But other critics would vehemently make those charges. They assert that large corporations are *not* efficient for the most part, that they do not perform well in terms of the economic criteria of efficiency, growth, and progress, but that they are able to conceal poor performance for long stretches of time behind a screen of monopoly power and deception of the public—even though some (e.g., Penn Central) are eventually found out.

For example, Ralph Nader and his followers frequently publicize what they find to be shortcomings of large business corporations and express doubt not only about the social responsibilities of business but about its economic performance as well. To select one instance from many possible ones, the Nader group asserts that a general agreement or "conspiracy" exists among automobile manufacturers to limit technological progress in the auto industry in order to increase short-run profits—the opposite of what one would expect in an industry dominated by the managerial philosophy. The result, as the group sees it, is shoddy engineering, poor design, lack of durability, and a concentration on showy gadgets bringing high sales potential but no real improvement. The consortium is also said to suppress innovations which might be beneficial to the general public but which do not enhance profits or sales.[22] Externalities are an obstacle to attainment of real economic efficiency, in automobiles as in other fields of industry.

21. It is not altogether clear in *The New Industrial State* whether Galbraith intends merely to observe this "technostructure" with cynical disbelief in its professions of virtue and detached distaste for the quality of the political economy that results from it, or whether he intends to urge action to convert the technostructure to serve social ends at an early date. No plans for a planned economy are included.

22. See Mark J. Green and others, *The Closed Enterprise System* (Grossman, 1972), pp. 240–65.

The muckraking tradition of exposing what the critic believes to be peculation, perfidy, predatory behavior, greed, and incompetence in big business is older than the tradition of business responsibility—as old as big business itself. It still persists, as a kind of counterpoint to the homiletics of social responsibility. A recent book labeled by the publisher "Profiles in Corporate Irresponsibility," for example, details a record of shameful behavior by corporations: falsifying the test records of aircraft brakes to get them accepted by the Air Force; deliberately lowering the quality of construction of school buses; selling pharmaceutical drugs that were inadequately tested and suppressing clinical reports of adverse side effects; bribing municipal officials; using mergers to defraud stockholders.[23] (Rebuttals to these charges were not included.)

Perhaps it is needless to assert that even if big businesses generally accepted a much larger role of voluntary responsibility, some firms would inevitably fail to measure up to it; a few would not observe even the minimum rules of the game.[24] Such episodes at least warn of the possibility of mandatory controls if voluntary responsibility should fail too often. They also serve as a reminder that larger corporations must look first to their primary economic mission of efficient production, growth, progress, and effective management of their particular segments of the national economy, within the rules of the game. If they do not do that job well, no practice of other kinds of social responsibility is likely to save them from attacks on their performance.[25]

The Radical Attack on Business

The critics named thus far have spoken in familiar terms. They have expressed reservations about the performance of the private enterprise

23. Robert L. Heilbroner and others, *In the Name of Profit* (Doubleday, 1972).

24. Robert Heilbroner, the principal author of the book cited in the preceding note, admits: "Atrocities are not, of course, the only, or perhaps even the central, issue with regard to the problem of corporate responsibility" (p. 225). But he thinks that poor economic and social performance is not an aberration but is a necessary consequence of unrestrained and concentrated corporate power. He calls for much stricter legal controls of corporate behavior (pp. 223ff.).

25. Philip Sporn, himself a member of the Committee for Economic Development, criticizes the CED report in these terms: "If business is not meeting society's requirements, it is not because they have changed but simply because business has not done a good enough job in its main area of responsibility. . . . There are many negative features to the performance of business in carrying out its basic economic responsibility, not a word of which is even hinted at in the report." CED, *Social Responsibilities of Business Corporations*, pp. 62, 65.

system: externalities, monopoly, and the instability of consumer wants, mentioned earlier as flaws in the classical system. Some have also attacked its justice as a distributor of income and provider of equal opportunity. But these critics differ with the proponents of the traditional view mainly in their understanding of what they think to be the facts and in their skepticism about the possibility that private, voluntary exercise of responsibility by business firms can or will do anything to alleviate these problems.

Farther out one finds radical critics who do not believe that satisfactory performance can be expected from private business under any circumstances. Big business organizations, representing "monopoly capitalism," in their view are inherently exploiters—both of "workers" and of the consumer. Corporations are said to survive and thrive by creating artificial wants and producing unnecessary goods to satisfy those wants, taking their profit off the top. In the opinion of the radicals, nothing less than the complete replacement of this system by another set of social institutions will solve the problem. No pursuit of responsibility by individual firms is likely to have any effect.

Radical critics differ among themselves on the causes of what they see as the failure of the present order and on the configuration of the society that should replace it, though most agree on the need for a revolutionary solution. Some see the inherent cause as private ownership of the means of production, which inevitably leads to class exploitation; their view goes back to the Old Left of orthodox Marxism. Others reject contemporary economic organization in order to follow paths that would lead to Early Christian communalism, Rousseauist pastoral simplicity, the communion of the tribe, and other conjectural states of innocence. Many other possible alternatives to the business system as a way of organizing economic activity have been advocated. Since none involve "business" responsibility, we shall not here pursue those solutions to the problem.

The following extended quotation gives several wide-ranging examples of recent criticisms:

Business is more than willing to celebrate the free-enterprise system and to take credit for the strength, growth, and affluence of the nation. But when business catalogs the social ills of the nation, the sources are found in the malfunctioning of a large variety of nonbusiness institutions and in the practices of nonbusiness groups. The president of the Chase Manhattan Bank, David Rockefeller, has been quoted as saying that the urban crisis is really a witch's brew of crises blended "from all the major ills of our country: inadequate educational systems, hard-core unemployment, hazardous pollution of natural resources, antiquated transportation, shameful housing, insufficient and ineffective public facilities, lack of equal opportunity for all, and a highly dangerous failure of communication between young and old, black and white." (*Business Week,* November 1, 1969, p. 63.) That clearly leaves the solution up to a variety of institutions and agencies, and above all, to "the people itself." The New Left, on the other hand, would link each of these major ills directly to business itself, as follows:

1. Educational systems are inadequate primarily in the poor districts. People in those districts cannot afford to vote adequate school taxes because they are poor, and they are poor because wealth is so inequitably distributed because business has vested interests in keeping wages as low as possible and in maintaining a nonprogressive taxation system with large loopholes for business and wealthy families. Furthermore, businessmen worry about the educational system only when the labor market is tight (such as when "only" about three million people are looking for work) and they cannot get well-disciplined workers cheaply, and when disorders in the schools threaten social stability.

2. Hard-core unemployment would disappear with better health measures, with housing and education for the hard-core poor (which could not materialize unless they were endorsed by business), and with better job opportunities, which business (and government) can provide.

3. Pollution of natural resources is, of course, primarily a business responsibility.

4. Antiquated transportation is a result of the investments in the profitability of the automobile, oil, and highway-construction industries, as is the cost of the air and water pollution they cause. As *Business Week* notes: "The companies involved in the building and use of highways are led by the automotive and oil industries. And it has been estimated that the so-called highway lobby accounts for more than half of all political contributions." (*Business Week,* May 15, 1971, p. 74.) The public bears the costs of building highways (which may easily come to more than $10 million a mile in cities), maintaining them, and policing them. While the poor pay for highways and their associated costs and pollution, they must also pay increasing fares for the antiquated transit systems that they must rely on.

5. Shameful housing can be laid at the door of the private-enterprise system. The United States has little low-cost public housing (far less than most other industrialized countries), but it does have highly profitable insurance and real-estate ventures, slumlords, and banks holding mortgages that pay handsome returns.

6. Public facilities are insufficient and ineffective. One needs little imagination to realize that when business fights the extension of various kinds of public facilities; when it proposes private, commercial alternatives instead; and when it resists attempts to increase the taxes of managers and stockholders, public facilities will be insufficient and ineffective. Actually, public facilities are inadequate only for the poor; they are probably adequate for the middle class.

7. The lack of equal opportunity for all exists preeminently in private

employment, and it has taken strong federal action to make a dent in this inequity.

8. Finally, the failure of communication between black and white, young and old, may be attributed at least in part to the failure of the mass media. They have the greatest communicative power to respond to these divisions. The media are corporations, of course, which operate for profit and make very handsome profits. In addition, the profit system requires that advertisers—business again—pay for communication time on television, and they have been more reluctant to use that time to promote communication between groups.

Thus the sources of urban ills, which are generously spread by business, are highly concentrated by the New Left. "Some people," mourns David Rockefeller, "are blaming business and the enterprise system" (he left off the adjective "free") "for all the troubles in our society." They surely are. Why shouldn't the rich give up some or most of their riches to help the poor in order to eliminate most of our urban problems? Because this is not the way the system is designed to operate. In the logic of the businessman, the rich must be motivated to do a good job by paying them richly; those with no future, the unmotivated, are a social problem, but they are not a problem of the business system.[26]

The State of Opinion

The general public does not consist of professional critics on the left or the right, but people still hold opinions, often strong opinions, about business performance. There are numerous warning signals. Public mistrust is growing. It seems to extend both to business performance of economic responsibilities and to social responsibilities outside that area. Opinion Research Corporation in a well-known national sampling of opinion found that the percentage of people expressing "low approval" of business had been rising rapidly, from 47 percent in 1965 to 60 percent in 1972. The ranks of "strong supporters" of business had been cut in half. The majority expressed the belief that business was doing very little (not enough) to protect the environment; that competition cannot be relied upon to keep prices at fair levels; that the consumer gets poor value from such industries as automobiles, prescription drugs, toiletries, etc. Over 75 percent want new laws and regulations for industrial products to protect health and safety.[27] Other surveys have

26. Charles Perrow, *The Radical Attack on Business: A Critical Analysis* (Harcourt Brace Jovanovich, © 1972), pp. 220–22. Perrow has attempted in this passage to summarize the views of diverse critics.

27. Reported in "America's Growing Antibusiness Mood," *Business Week*, No. 2233 (June 17, 1972), pp. 100–03.

brought the same message. (To put the matter in perspective, we should observe that these same surveys show that the American public currently holds *all* established institutions in low esteem; it has not switched its affections from business to other organizations.)

Out of these critical attitudes, both pointed and diffuse, comes a rather disorderly picture of the new demands being placed on business, along with intensification of some older ones that were already a matter for managerial concern twenty years ago. Without attempting at this point to sort them out to distinguish between practicable and impractical ones, or to suggest how corporations should respond to them, we may recognize the following principal areas of stress in the new calls for more business responsibility:

1. Demands that business do its assigned traditional job more effectively: be more efficient and more progressive, produce better services and better and more durable products, guarantee the quality of what it sells to the consumer, avoid "unnecessary" style and quality changes that increase cost, and do less injury to the public welfare of the kind mentioned earlier, resulting from failure to observe ethical rules.

2. Demands that large corporations be more responsive to interested groups other than their owners and that they give representation both to employees and to outside groups (the "public" or others) on their governing boards in a conscious effort to create "corporate democracy."

3. Demands that business assume a larger share of responsibility for the welfare and economic security of its employees.

4. Demands that corporations act as agents of national "morality" as viewed by one group or another, in actions toward foreign countries and in attitudes toward war and armaments, usually along paths differing from the official policy of the United States government (or attempting to remedy a lack of official policy). The demands associated with acts in foreign countries almost inevitably concentrate on the large multinational corporations, chiefly on those with headquarters in the United States.

5. Demands that business firms take a more positive role in the control of external costs, especially in protection of the environment.

6. Demands that business develop backward regions and contribute to the lessening of differences in prosperity and income among different parts of the country.

7. Demands that large firms participate actively in the search for solutions to the urban predicament, eradication of the ghetto, employment of disadvantaged minorities, and amelioration of urban poverty.

Along with these new thrusts, business is expected to intensify its previous involvement with the community and to enlarge its already recognized responsibilities there.

These demands, some of which would have been unthinkable a decade ago, have struck business enterprise in a short space of time with hurricane force. Management has been subjected to unprecedented pressures from organized groups; while fiduciary officers in charge of investable funds (university endowments, pension funds, investment trusts) have likewise been pressured to direct resources in consonance with the new morality and thus to transmit the pressure to management itself.[28] Corporate management has responded both with actions and with assurances of its concern. Yet the sheer volume and variety of the new demands have created some confusion. If business enterprise met them all, it would transform itself beyond recognition. But which ones can business now be expected to meet, and to what extent? The following chapters consider both general and specific aspects of this question.

28. See, for example, Burton G. Malkiel and Richard E. Quandt, "The Moral Dimension to Investment Policy," Financial Research Center Research Memorandum No. 8 (Princeton University, 1970; processed); *Report of the Committee on University Relations with Corporate Enterprise* (Harvard University, 1971)—commonly called the Austin Report.

CHAPTER THREE

Corporate Law Reform

MARVIN A. CHIRELSTEIN

WHAT CHANGES in internal governance would be likely to render the modern corporation more sensitive to public goals and more generous in committing resources to the solution of social problems? Those who assert that large business organizations have responded inadequately to contemporary social needs often also appear to believe that the blame lies wholly or partly with the way in which the law pertaining to corporations defines and allocates authority within the firm.[1] As it stands, corporate law focuses almost exclusively on the relationship between managers and security-holders; it assumes that the primary interest of the latter is in maximum financial returns for a given level of risk and that the responsibility of the former is to pursue that interest with tireless and single-minded diligence. Taken literally, the arrangement just described is one which leaves little room for the introduction of public goals or at best accommodates the public interest only as an incident of profit seeking. What is needed, therefore, in the view of many critics, is a broader framework of authority, an expanded set of reference points, whose aim would be to admit social, political, and ethical criteria to the ordinary process of corporate decision making.

As it happens, a fairly full complement of corporate remodeling plans is already on the table and available for inspection and comparison. Some of these are new in important ways; others date back to much earlier periods of corporate law reform. Surprisingly perhaps, the proposals that seem most novel today involve various measures for reviving the stockholders' role in corporate policy making. Corporate democracy,

1. See, for example, Daniel Bell, "The Corporation and Society in the 1970's," *Public Interest*, No. 24 (Summer 1971), pp. 5, 29–30; Robert Dahl, "A Prelude to Corporate Reform," *Business and Society Review*, No. 1 (Spring 1972), pp. 17–23.

an idea whose time, in the judgment of many, would never come again, is now seen by some as having a renewed potential for good, the realization of which necessitates a new interpretation of legal relations between managers and owners. Among other proposals for structural change, support can also be found for the well-worn idea of adding labor, consumer, community, and/or government representatives to the board of directors, for establishing new and higher levels of supervisory authority within the firm itself, for federal preemption of the chartering function, or for all of these in combination. Whatever its vintage, each such plan is at present conceived of as a vehicle by which public interest standards would be imposed on corporate management, in some degree supplanting the conventional profits objective. How well these devices would work—whether the behavior of corporate managers really would be moved in the direction desired—is of course the question to be asked.

The discussion that follows attempts to canvass the current literature of structural reform and, having done so, to produce a tentative appraisal of those reform proposals which are now under more or less active consideration by legal scholars and others. The existing legal structure of publicly held companies, together with some familiar perspectives on the relationship of law to a traditional concept of corporate responsibility, is first summarized briefly. Next the discussion considers how social goals are, or could be, accommodated within a structure which continues to emphasize management's obligation to shareholders (and in particular whether a larger role for shareholder initiatives is likely to be feasible and productive). The third section contemplates the admission of other interest groups—consumers, labor, etc.—to a position of influence and considers what effect their inclusion might have on the goals of the firm. Nothing is said directly about closely held concerns, both because small owner-managed firms present no significant opportunity for internal restructuring and because public companies with large resources are, for the moment at least, the major target of the responsibility movement. The conclusions to be drawn appear in a final section.

Corporate Law and Conventional Responsibility

Within the existing framework of intracorporate relationships, the law has tried to enforce responsibility in conventional terms by emphasizing the legal claims of ownership. This is done by stressing the importance of share voting rights, by requiring disclosure of accounting and other corporate data at frequent intervals, and by imposing obligations of fiduciary conduct on corporate managers. Against a background of atomized stockholdings, however, these devices are no longer seen as providing an important measure of control by stockholders over company policy or even giving stockholders an effective voice in the selection of management. Rather, the significance of traditional legal requirements in promoting responsibility is assumed to reside in the opportunities they create for surveillance and discipline via the capital market and for prosecutorial activity both by legal professionals and by government.

The threat of management displacement, for example, has long been cited as a major force for loyal and efficient performance. Proxy contests, mergers, and tender offers—which, if successful, produce the ouster or subordination of incumbent managers—pose a threat to managerial tenure and hence inhibit the systematic diversion of corporate assets by management even when competitive conditions are attenuated or relaxed. Of course, aggressive action of this sort is not without substantial costs and risks to the aggressor—including both the cost of identifying poorly managed firms and the risk that the takeover effort will fail—but as a practical as well as a theoretical matter, the danger of displacement undoubtedly sets limits on management's freedom to subordinate stockholder objectives to management goals. It confirms also that, despite the much-emphasized passivity and powerlessness of individual investors, the ability of outsiders to commandeer the stockholder vote still occupies an important place in the thoughts of the alert executive.[2] Efforts by the Securities and Exchange Commission (SEC) and stock exchanges to preserve share voting rights—by refusing to list nonvoting stock, for instance—are thus perhaps not wholly quixotic even if originally undertaken for reasons that now seem somewhat dated.

Legal regulation is active, possibly overactive, with regard to business takeovers, apparently because of what is thought to be the unprotected status of public investors caught between contending forces. To shore up the investor's strategic position, the law employs various devices—ratification, appraisal and disclosure rights, as well as an overriding

2. For a useful summary of takeover mechanisms, see Henry G. Manne, "Some Theoretical Aspects of Share Voting," *Columbia Law Review*, Vol. 64 (December 1964), pp. 1427–45; and by the same author, "Mergers and the Market for Corporate Control," *Journal of Political Economy*, Vol. 73 (April 1965), pp. 110–20.

"fairness" requirement—which are designed to compensate for presumed disparities in bargaining strength and information. The latter aim conflicts at various points with the idea of takeover as a market discipline, but the law is still in the process of evolving a theory of takeover, and developments in this area are not at an end.[3]

Federal disclosure statutes—chiefly the Securities Act of 1933 and the Securities Exchange Act of 1934—along with state blue-sky laws are likewise designed to promote responsibility in decision making by ensuring, or at least advancing the probability, that management's performance record will be made available and become known to investors who propose to buy or sell the company's shares. The objectives of the disclosure laws are several. Most important, of course, is the intention to protect individual investors or their advisers from being deceived about the value of securities issued and traded in public markets. By requiring the filing and distribution of financial and other data, the federal and state enactments are expected to ensure that outsiders will be defended from inflated claims emanating from inside sources and perhaps that bargaining inequalities attributable to disparities in access to corporate information will be reduced. In addition, the disclosure requirements are expressly designed to expose the behavior of corporate insiders to public view and in that way to have the disinfecting properties of sunlight. The assumption, quite simply, is that people will refrain from engaging in, or will find it impossible to consummate, many kinds of socially undesirable behavior if they are required to disclose what they are doing. Conceding that the evidence is impressionistic, one senses that the securities laws have been quite successful, on the whole, in inhibiting what might be called the grosser forms of discretionary conduct.

To the extent that statutory disclosure requirements are further relied on to provide a linkage between the value of the firm's real assets and the value of its outstanding securities, the accuracy of the data required is obviously critical. Largely because the federal securities laws originated in an era of promoter frauds, however, the SEC has been slow to depart from conventional accounting principles and has largely prohibited management from officially communicating the projections and estimates of income on which investment policy is likely to be based.

---

3. See Victor Brudney, "A Note on Chilling Tender Solicitations," *Rutgers Law Review*, Vol. 21 (Summer 1967), pp. 609–44.

As a result, financial analysts and other market professionals regularly take steps to obtain such data unofficially, and though the significance of the data may be no less swiftly reflected in stock prices, the securities laws themselves now hardly rank as a primary source of investment information other than for initial offerings.[4] Nevertheless, it remains true that stock ownership creates a legal right to information in the first instance and thus furnishes a basis for restricting the ability of managers to conceal performance data from the market.

The federal securities statutes—in particular the Securities Exchange Act of 1934—have also erected safeguards against management fraud through rules on insider trading. Although a willingness to translate substantial portions of management compensation into stock ownership—largely through the medium of option plans—is heavily relied on to induce behavior oriented toward higher share values, trading in the firm's securities on the strength of undisclosed information is treated as fraud under the securities laws and as the basis of a private action for damages. In recognition that stockholders relate to the corporation chiefly as investors, the purpose of the insider trading rules is to promote sanitary conditions in the securities markets: in effect, insiders are required to disclose material information or else refrain from trading. It has been argued that a relaxation of insider trading prohibitions would produce important management incentive effects, but that is hard to believe and even if true would be offset by the negative impact on investors' expectations.[5] As has been pointed out, the lack of direct stockholder control over management conduct, together with the cumbersome nature of remedies under state law for violations of fiduciary obligation, make it especially important for the market to appear to operate fairly from the standpoint of public investors and for the law to protect against overreaching by those enjoying privileged access to corporate news.[6]

4. See George J. Benston, "The Effectiveness and Effects of the SEC's Accounting Disclosure Requirements," in Henry G. Manne (ed.), *Economic Policy and the Regulation of Corporate Securities* (Washington: American Enterprise Institute for Public Policy Research, 1969). The SEC has recently reconsidered its policy on forecast data and now permits certain companies to issue income projections. See SEC, Securities Act of 1933, Release 5362 (February 2, 1973).

5. See Oliver E. Williamson, *Corporate Control and Business Behavior* (Prentice-Hall, 1970), pp. 93–96.

6. See J. A. C. Hetherington, "Fact and Legal Theory: Shareholders, Managers, and Corporate Social Responsibility," *Stanford Law Review*, Vol. 21 (January 1969), pp. 248–92.

In any event, the refusal to accord managers a property right in corporate information is plainly the major preoccupation of corporate law today. As the courts see it, the principal opportunity for management misconduct lies in the misappropriation of news values; and although the ability to police the rules against the use of inside information, whether through government or private action, may well be limited to obvious cases, the formal possibilities now cover virtually the entire field of management fraud.

The foregoing pretty much exhausts the efforts of law to promote responsibility in corporate policy making; and even when one concedes the omission of significant details, it is evident that the list is brief and that the legal weaponry is blunt and clumsy. If the scope of managerial discretion were larger than existing data indicate, however, it is still far from clear what additional steps the corporate law could usefully take. One possibility would be to reduce in some appreciable way the insulation afforded by the so-called business judgment rule, which, uniformly under state law, vests management with exclusive authority over the conduct of the company's affairs. The approach, presumably, would be to require shareholder ratification of, or expose to judicial or administrative review, certain investment and financing decisions now left entirely to management's best judgment. No doubt officers' compensation would be a prime candidate for this treatment; another might be the annual dividend decision—especially so if one accepts the argument that because compensation levels correlate more closely with growth in size than in profitability, there exists on management's part a systematic preference for retentions over payouts.

But experience with both procedures—ratification and review—particularly in connection with corporate mergers and recapitalizations, justifies considerable pessimism about their value in promoting discipline. Merger plans submitted by management are almost invariably approved by the requisite majority of shareholders on both sides of the transaction, negative views being reflected, as usual, by a decline in stock prices rather than a substantial dissenting vote. Even more striking has been the tendency of preferred stockholders to approve recapitalization plans which effect the elimination of their own dividend arrearages, and to do so without receiving anything that approaches adequate compensation for the rights surrendered. The usual explanations—stockholder apathy, management's control of the proxy machinery—are undoubtedly relevant, but it is hard to suppose that they would not apply as well to other management decisions, including compensation arrangements or the dividend rate.

Mergers and recapitalizations are also sometimes subject to review by courts or administrative agencies on grounds of "fairness," usually at the instance of lawyers and investment analysts who specialize in challenging such transactions. Assuming the merits are reached in a given case, the issue often turns upon a valuation of the enterprises being combined or of the securities being reshuffled, since fixing the entitlements of various claimants necessarily entails an estimate of the size of their competing claims. It would be agreed by many, perhaps most, observers that such valuation efforts are clumsily and erratically executed by courts and agencies. The work of the SEC and the Interstate Commerce Commission (ICC) in the field of industrial and railroad reorganizations is a frequently cited example of the failure of specialized agencies to achieve consistently respectable or even defensible valuations despite ample staff assistance and lengthy periods of consideration in individual cases. If past performance is indicative, the idea of bringing particular management decisions before the courts or agencies for periodic review is not a promising one.

At another extreme, the familiar perception that stock ownership consists of little more than a passive market claim to dividends and capital gains has led some to suggest that the shareholder's status as casual investor be formally recognized either by abolishing his voting rights entirely or by subjecting those rights to a holding-period requirement. The advantage, the advocates say, is that once the law gives up its romantic yearning for corporate democracy, concern will more properly be directed toward the expansion of investor protection and perhaps toward improvement of the stock market as an exchange mechanism. The so-called empty forms of shareholder democracy allegedly "divert attention from the real problems of holding business managements to a desirable standard of responsibility,"[7] and distract officials and the informed public from other pressing reform needs as well.

Yet it is difficult to see what could be gained in conventional terms by substituting a voteless model of the corporate structure for what we have. The development of fraud concepts under Rule 10b-5 of the Securities Exchange Act could hardly have been achieved more swiftly

7. Bayless Manning, review of J. A. Livingston's *The American Stockholder*, in *Yale Law Journal*, Vol. 67 (July 1958), p. 1489; and see Hetherington, "Fact and Legal Theory."

than it has.[8] Nor is it clear that sluggishness in other areas, such as information quality, can be explained by reference to the law's absorption in antiquated ideals of shareholder participation. Votelessness, moreover, would put an end to open competition for corporate control, since takeovers could then be accomplished only with the consent of incumbent management. This result is clearly undesirable unless measurable gains can be anticipated elsewhere.

In any event, as shown below, the voteless model is more often seen as relevant to the abandonment than the enforcement of conventional enterprise objectives, especially by those critics who incline to the view that the primacy of shareholder welfare in the present scheme of corporate law is outworn and anachronistic and deserves to be replaced by an equal or greater concern for the economic well-being of other interest groups. But as long as it *is* the shareholders' economic interest that remains the focal point of corporate law, neither the voteless model nor any other structure which displaces the imputed rights of ownership as a basis for legal regulation seems likely to attract a consensus on the part of those who consider the present situation anomalous. None has emerged so far, at any rate, although the separation of ownership and control in large corporate entities has been debated more or less continuously for over four decades.

Social Action Opportunities under Present Law

Within the present structure of management-stockholder relations, what legal basis exists for corporate social commitment? It is evident from a reading of annual company reports that managers consider socially responsive conduct of various kinds to be an appropriate exercise of powers granted by the corporate charter and to be well within the bounds of their fiduciary obligation to stockholders. How can this be justified in legal terms? And assuming justification can be found, what processes of law might be exploited to induce an even larger commitment to social goals?

The particular form in which these questions arise depends, in turn, on whether the impulse to responsive conduct is assumed to originate with management or at the stockholder level. If one presupposes some dedication on the part of management itself—a willingness to pursue

---

8. *Code of Federal Regulations*, Title 17 (1973), sec. 240, p. 329.

social interests regardless of the wishes of the firm's owners—the relevant legal inquiry concerns the limits of the business judgment rule and the extent to which that insulating doctrine frees managers from any specific obligation to account. But if one assumes that management is devoted solely to profits, and that it is the stockholders, or some of them, who assert a preference for social goals, then the question shifts to whether the latter have legal standing within the established delegation system and can find practical means to prompt adoption of an altered version of the firm's objectives.

Before taking these issues up, it will be helpful to attempt some classification of corporate social behavior, if only on the basis of what business organizations do at the present time, or say they do. Three categories of conduct suggest themselves: (1) the affirmative commitment of resources to civic betterment, whether through conventional gifts to charity or through direct investment in self-administered programs such as job training, minority business loans, and assistance to community institutions; (2) the avoidance of business activities causing social injury such as damage to the environment, consumers, or employees; (3) efforts to enhance relations with government at all levels, including law compliance, responsiveness to government policies, appearances before legislative committees and rule-making bodies, and even informal contacts with government officials. These categories obviously overlap and may not exhaust the full range of activities that can be described as social. However, they have the merit of relating somewhat differently to particular legal rights and obligations and may, for that reason, be of use in distinguishing between those types of publicly responsive conduct which the corporate law affects in some way and those which it does not.

Management Initiatives: Donations, Self-Regulation, and Willing Compliance

Management initiative in the form of charitable giving has become a widespread and accepted business practice (though carried on at a relatively low level of expenditures) and is now amply sanctioned by state corporation statutes.[9] At early common law, under a strict interpretation of charter powers, donations of corporate assets were viewed by

9. See Phillip I. Blumberg, "Corporate Responsibility and the Social Crisis," *Boston University Law Review*, Vol. 50 (Spring 1970), pp. 157–210.

the courts as *ultra vires,* and as violating the rights of stockholders, un-less justified by a showing of direct benefit to the donor, presumably in the shape of anticipated increases in net revenues. Gifts for the benefit of employees, such as the construction of a local hospital, were usually sustained under this approach, whereas donations to nonlocal institu-tions were sometimes held to be too remote. As applied from case to case, the direct benefit rule undoubtedly made corporate managers cautious in authorizing charitable contributions.

Within the past three decades, however, the courts have responded to public pressures for increased corporate philanthropy by gently abandoning the older rule of *ultra vires* and substituting a broader and much less demanding standard of corporate benefit. In the well-known *A. P. Smith Mfg. Co.* v. *Barlow* case, for example, a corporate gift to Princeton University was held to satisfy the common law requirement on the ground that the strengthening of community institutions was ulti-mately beneficial to private business, even though no direct or measur-able benefit to the particular giver could be shown.[10] Later decisions, although occasionally utilizing analogies to advertising or goodwill as a way of paying formal respect to the benefit rule, have reached similar results, and it seems safe to conclude that moderate gifts to conventional charities are no longer open to serious challenge.

Even so, the development of a legally benign attitude toward char-itable gifts cannot be taken to mean that contributions or direct invest-ments in public goods are wholly free of legal limitations. Although state statutes now expressly confirm that corporations possess the power to make donations for the public welfare or for charitable, scientific, or educational purposes, it must be assumed that such authority, like other management powers, is subject to a requirement of reasonableness in respect to both the character of the donee and the size of the amounts committed. In addition, even though the direct benefit rule has been displaced by a broader standard, the very general concept of shareholder welfare no doubt continues to be the ultimate legal test for management decisions. Though this limitation is likely to be invoked if management exercises its discretion in favor of charities having highly restricted ob-jectives or if the choice seems heavily flavored with personal ideology, its principal impact may well be on the *size* of corporate donations.[11] To be sure, references to viable social arrangements or to public expec-

10. *A. P. Smith Mfg. Co.* v. *Barlow,* 13 N.J. 145, 98 A. 2d 581 (1953).
11. On the matter of ideology, see *Medical Committee for Human Rights* v. *Securities and Exchange Commission,* 432 F. 2d 659 (D.C. Cir. 1970), vacated as

tations ordinarily suffice to meet the benefit standard as applied at current levels of commitment. However, one has a sense that a more substantial reconstruction of fiduciary premises would be needed to insulate materially higher outlays from attack. In the *Bell* case, for example, shareholders of U.S. Steel brought an action against the company's directors on the ground that voluntary annual payments of approximately $5 million to Allegheny County (Pennsylvania) constituted a "waste" of corporate assets. The company, together with other large corporations having manufacturing facilities in the area, had agreed to make such payments in lieu of an increase in real estate taxes which the county would otherwise apparently have sought to impose. The court found the payments permissible under a statute authorizing "donations for the public welfare"; but in view of their size it felt obliged to consider the question of reasonableness as well and was able to hold for the defendants only after establishing that the avoidance of higher local taxes rather than community welfare had been the directors' chief concern.[12]

Even in its emancipated form, therefore, the benefit requirement may limit management's initiative in making donations to charity and at least be partly responsible for what some regard as the disappointing level of corporate giving at present. On the other hand, for those who mistrust corporate philanthropy—whether because they feel that the funds in question properly belong to the stockholders or because they doubt the wisdom or fear the power of a "socially minded" management—the benefit rule offers some assurance both that the amounts involved will remain modest and that the chosen objects will fit within recognizable and generally accepted categories. Although "benefit" as a category could undoubtedly accommodate larger and more diverse appropriations than are now being made, it is hardly to be expected that managers and their legal advisers will wish to test the outer limits of the rule either by moving rapidly to higher levels of commitment or by developing novel programs whose public acceptance is not yet well established.

The second category of responsive behavior suggested above—avoidance of social injury—seems on the whole to be free of the implied restrictions just described and to be even less likely than the first to encounter limitations of character and size, at least insofar as those

---

moot, 404 U.S. 403, 92 S. Ct. 577 (1972), informally referred to as the *Dow* case. See also *Dodge* v. *Ford Motor Co.,* 204 Mich. 459, 170 N.W. 668 (1919).

12. *Kelly* v. *Bell,* Del. Ch. 254 A 2d 62 (1969), aff'd 266 A. 2d 878 (1970).

limitations derive from management's legal obligation to stockholders. The reason relates once more to the limited nature of judicial review when management's business judgment is placed at issue. Quite simply, business decisions which involve production techniques, research, marketing, or product characteristics—even assuming that they are ever sufficiently visible to invite attack—are almost always regarded as within the scope of management's authority to manage. As compared with gifts to charity or their equivalent, choices affecting ordinary business operations require no justification in terms of their apparent *relationship* to the company's acknowledged purposes. Hence, apart from allegations of fraud or gross negligence, any serious stockholder objection would have to be expressed in terms of profitability comparisons. In effect, the issue would be, not whether a gift to Princeton can somehow be related to the manufacture of carpets and rugs, but whether comparative profit calculations can be used to condemn management's particular choice among apparently plausible business alternatives.

But it is at precisely this level of decision that fiduciary obligation normally ceases or, more accurately, that it passes beyond the enforcement capacity of the courts. Without an admission by management itself that it has acted against the stockholders' interests, the courts would rarely if ever undertake to examine the wisdom of the choices made and, indeed, would be unlikely to intervene even if the superiority of another course of conduct were somehow conclusively demonstrated.[13] The weight of the existing delegation system, together with an extreme judicial reluctance to engage in complex present-value calculations, virtually insulates purely business decisions from review and in effect allows a management possessing some discretion in economic terms to balance the stockholders' interests against those of other affected groups without serious concern for the imposition of fiduciary liability. What this suggests, not surprisingly, is that much the larger opportunity for management social initiatives—again, as compared with donations and the like —lies in the area of self-regulation and self-restraint based upon a heightened sensitivity to the social consequences of the company's own business activities.

Within the third category of responsive behavior—willing compliance with laws and government programs—fiduciary restraints on affirmatively responsible management conduct are presumably wholly lacking,

13. See *Shlensky* v. *Wrigley*, 95 Ill. App. 2d 173, 237 N.E. 2d 776 (1968).

although, as the *Dow* case (cited in footnote 11 and discussed below) suggests, there may be rare situations in which doubt exists as to whether management is acting in support of "government policy" or in pursuit of individual political predilections. In general, however, an acceptable concept of fiduciary obligation could hardly be announced, at least in public, whose aim was to discourage management from maintaining a high level of law compliance, from keeping contacts with government officials above board, or from lobbying on the basis of public interest standards for laws of uniform application. In addition, and apart from strictly legal considerations, it appears that an exercise of responsibility on this front avoids or minimizes many of the usual objections to corporate voluntarism—i.e., that it represents an improper arrogation of power by managers, that it lacks legitimacy and authorization, or that it leads to inefficiency and competitive disadvantage. In particular, high levels of law compliance in major areas of governmental regulation, such as environmental protection, obviously import their own authorization and are likely, once adopted by major firms, to become industry enforcement norms in many instances.

It is not the case, moreover, that willing compliance with public policy represents a trivial or self-evident instance of social responsibility: regulatory codes are not self-executing, and the government's enforcement powers are obviously inadequate to assure complete obedience to rules even when supplemented by private enforcement activities. More generally, there is a pervasive tendency throughout the field of legal regulation—one which lawyers are trained to implement in their counseling role—to endeavor to meet legal standards at a minimum level of compliance and to press for interpretive rulings which constrict the application of the regulatory scheme. Though this approach may be unavoidable or at least ingrained with respect to laws which are seen (however mistakenly) as having private consequences only—the federal tax law being the most familiar illustration—statutes specifically designed to protect a public which consumes the corporation's products or shares its environment might justifiably attract a very different kind of response. In these areas, compliance at generous levels, without contest or coercion, would represent an important contribution to the achievement of *established* public interest goals (as well as a major change in private attitudes toward regulation), and in many respects would offer a greater opportunity for voluntary social initiatives than anything so far discussed.

Shareholder Social Action Proposals

In the case of the other assumption mentioned above—namely, that the impulse to social responsibility originates at the shareholder level—the legal questions that result are distinctly less familiar than those associated with management initiatives, and corporate practice is far less settled. Various current or recent developments, including the circuit court's decision in the *Dow* case, the advent of organized shareholder social movements such as Campaign GM, and the proposals and undertakings in behalf of ethical investment practices by churches, universities, and even mutual funds all suggest, as indicated earlier, that "corporate democracy" may be in the process of generating a new form of expression to which legal institutions will be compelled to adapt in one way or another. Chiefly affected are the SEC's proxy regulations, but there are also implications for other areas of corporate law and practice.

After decades of active concern with the question of corporate democracy, it is ironic that the law should now experience uncertainty in arriving at an appropriate response to public shareholders who desire to play a part in corporate affairs. Two reasons can be suggested. In the first place, despite much official utterance to the contrary, legal authorities have long been resigned to the idea that the holders of securities offered for sale to the public and traded on the market can have no active voice in management policy and that the function of stock voting rights is mainly to provide a jurisdictional base on which to build a superstructure of fiduciary duty and related ownership claims. The linking of voting rights with the expression of individual shareholder preferences has simply not been regarded as functionally significant by commentators or administrators, and the familiar maxim about selling your shares if you don't like management is accepted not only as a standard of practical investment conduct but as an expectation of legal policy as well. Second, with particular reference to ethical preferences, the confident supposition has always been that individual shareholders are inclined to embrace the traditional objectives of the firm even more doggedly and with less ambivalence than management itself. Recurring stockholder objections to company philanthropy are cited as proof (if any is needed) that managers on the whole are more socially minded than shareholders. As a result, the idea that equity owners would be concerned to promote other than traditional goals, and the further notion that atypical shareholders dedicated to nonbusiness goals might attempt to exploit the company as a means of communicating those goals to potential allies was seen until recently as no more than an occasional annoyance, requiring little attention and even less tolerance from legal rule makers.

But the developments mentioned above, and especially the *Dow* case, make it plain that a serious legal response is now appropriate. That response, moreover, pretty clearly has to begin by assuming what was previously doubted or denied—namely, that there are conventionally motivated investors who have an interest in the social characteristics of their portfolios *as well as* dividends and capital gains. To be sure, persons or groups acquiring small shareholdings solely for the purpose of bringing ideological suits are still quite visibly at work in this area. Nevertheless, the "movement" for shareholder participation in social issues now evidently also draws support from various institutional stockholders, themselves subject to fiduciary obligations to their beneficiaries. As a result, the entire question gains an element of legitimacy which it appeared to lack at an earlier date.

The main legal battleground in the current push for shareholder participation is Rule 14a-8 (the so-called shareholder proposal rule) issued by the SEC under the Securities Exchange Act of 1934.[14] The rule, which is a relatively minor element in the proxy machinery created by the SEC pursuant to its authority under the 1934 act, establishes a procedure through which corporate management can be compelled to include shareholder proposals, together with brief supporting statements, in its proxy materials (i.e., to circulate such proposals at company expense). In its present form, the rule allows management to *omit* shareholder proposals which (1) are not proper subjects for action by security holders under state law, (2) are submitted primarily for the purpose of promoting general social, economic, or political causes not related to the company's business or within its control, or (3) relate to the company's ordinary business operations. The burden of justification is placed on the company: if management decides to exclude a shareholder proposal, it must file with the SEC an explanation of its

14. The history and scope of Rule 14a-8 are extensively discussed in Donald E. Schwartz, "The Public-Interest Proxy Contest: Reflections on Campaign GM," *Michigan Law Review*, Vol. 69 (January 1971), pp. 421–538; and see "Proxy Rule 14a-8: Omission of Shareholder Proposals," *Harvard Law Review*, Vol. 84 (January 1971), pp. 700–28. Recent amendments to the rule, which are of generally minor import, appear in SEC, Securities Exchange Act of 1934, Release 9432 (December 22, 1971) and Release 9784 (September 22, 1972).

decision, along with supporting opinion of counsel. The SEC may then accept or reject management's position; in the latter event it may seek enforcement in the courts if the company remains adamant. Individual stockholders whose proposals are excluded may resort to private legal action against the company, and, as it now appears, may also obtain judicial review of an SEC determination that is adverse to inclusion.

Section 14a of the 1934 act, which gives the SEC broad power to make rules governing the solicitation of proxies, was adopted as a result of concern about the unlimited control and possible misuse of corporate proxy machinery by managers of publicly held companies. The legislative debates that preceded enactment of the section emphasize problems of proper disclosure to security owners—it being recognized that the opportunity to question management in person at annual meetings was as a practical matter unavailable to the great majority of shareholders. These same debates give evidence of concern for "fair suffrage" in the corporate election process. In effect, the proxy system was seen as the only reasonably practical substitute for physical attendance at meetings, and the absence of clear and consistent state proxy rules was deemed to establish a need for uniformity through regulation at the federal level.

Though nothing in the legislative history of the section suggests that Congress then envisioned the proxy machinery as being employed for the presentation of individual shareholder proposals, the shareholder proposal rule developed logically as an extension of the general requirement that shareholders whose proxies are solicited by management be informed through the proxy solicitation materials of all matters expected to be taken up and voted on at the annual meeting. If management has notice in advance of the meeting that a shareholder plans to introduce a resolution requiring a vote, full disclosure plainly requires that proxy solicitation materials make mention of that resolution, as well as of the usual management-sponsored proposals, so that solicitees will be in a position to exercise their voting rights intelligently. Accordingly, the SEC in 1942 imposed on management a duty to include in its proxy materials any shareholder proposal that represents "a proper subject for action by security holders."[15]

The SEC's original intention was to be guided in respect to "proper subject" by a consideration of what, under *state law*, could validly be

15. Rule 14a-8(c)(1), *Code of Federal Regulations*, Title 17 (1973), sec. 240, p. 375.

presented by shareholders for adoption at annual meetings. Nevertheless, there was and is a general awareness that state statutes and court decisions contain very little, if anything, of a specific nature on the subject of shareholder proposals. As a result, the reference in Rule 14a-8 to state law must be understood as adverting to the generally accepted allocation of powers between management and stockholders, which everywhere follows an accustomed pattern. Thus, the rule's exclusion of proposals aimed at promoting social causes and of proposals relating to the company's ordinary business operations can be taken to reflect a reasonable approximation of how the state laws would probably be read at present if state courts had occasion to pronounce on them.

Against this background, the *Dow* case is especially important because it represents the first decision by a federal court of appeals on the application of Rule 14a-8 to a shareholder social-issue proposal.[16] In *Dow,* the Medical Committee for Human Rights, having obtained by gift a few shares of Dow Chemical Company common stock, offered for inclusion in management's proxy statement a proposal asking the board of directors to consider the advisability of an amendment to the corporation's charter which would prohibit the sale of napalm unless assurance was provided that it would not be used against human beings. Dow declined to include the proposal, citing both the "ordinary business" and the "political cause" provisions of the rule (in effect arguing that the proposal was either too specific or too general), and was upheld in its refusal by the SEC. On appeal from the SEC's ruling, the court dealt chiefly with procedural issues relating to the reviewability of commission determinations. However, in remanding the case to the SEC for further administrative action, the court plainly indicated that it disagreed with the commission on the merits. Exclusion of the Medical Committee's proposal, it said, was inconsistent with the purpose of the statute to promote corporate democracy and "to assure to corporate shareholders the ability to exercise their right—some would say their duty—to control the important decisions which affect them in their capacity as stockholders and owners of the corporation."[17]

More particularly, the court found Dow's alternative reliance on the standard exclusionary provisions to be misplaced. On the "ordinary business" exclusion, Dow had argued that Delaware law gave manage-

16. *Medical Committee for Human Rights* v. *SEC* (the *Dow* case).
17. Ibid., 432 F. 2d, 680–81.

ment exclusive authority to determine what product lines a company should manufacture and that such determinations were entirely a matter of business judgment. The court, however, stressed that the Medical Committee for Human Rights proposed to *amend* the corporation's charter to remove the sale of napalm from the list of activities which the company was authorized to undertake; since state law provided for charter amendments designed to " 'change, substitute, enlarge or diminish the nature of [the company's] business,' "[18] a proposal aimed at amendment must be viewed as relevant to the company's overall purpose rather than an intrusion on management's authority to manage within the area so defined. Moreover, although Delaware law reserved to management sole power to initiate charter amendments, the committee's proposal was in the form of an *advisory*, which merely recommended that the directors adopt the resolution and submit it to shareholders for approval, and hence could not be excluded as an invasion of management's domain.

On the "political cause" question, the court noted that what the shareholder had proposed was not merely a general political posture but a restriction on the use of company property itself. "No reason," the court said, "has been advanced . . . which leads to the conclusion that management may properly place obstacles in the path of shareholders who wish to present to their co-owners . . . the question of whether they wish to have their assets used in a manner which they believe to be more socially responsible but possibly less profitable than that which is dictated by present company policy."[19] In addition, because management itself had publicly asserted that the manufacture of napalm was being continued for moral and political rather than business reasons, the court found that the company could not reasonably refuse to entertain a shareholder proposal on the same social issue.

Taken literally, the *Dow* decision thus appears to require inclusion in management's proxy materials of many, and perhaps most, kinds of social action proposals. The proponent need only show that the proposal bears a reasonably close relationship to the company's business activities and is not entirely beyond management's control. Moreover, even if decisions otherwise plainly within management's business judgment would be affected, the proponent can apparently avoid that restriction

18. Ibid., p. 680.
19. Ibid., p. 681.

by utilizing the form of a charter amendment or, if shareholders lack power to initiate charter amendments under state law, by offering the proposal in advisory terms. On the other hand, the court did not disapprove the exclusionary provisions of Rule 14a-8, so that some limitations on shareholder proposals may still be supposed to have survived. The question of what is a suitable subject for charter amendment, for example, was not carefully examined, and there remains the possibility that the courts, or the SEC, will regard some matters—those affecting the company's technology and marketing procedures, for example—as too detailed and particularized to be reflected in the company's articles of incorporation. Another or further limitation might derive from a distinction between positive action and negative restraints. Thus a proposal calling for the training and employment of minority-group workers might be viewed as less appropriate for charter amendment than one which required the termination of a product line—although in many other instances it would be simple enough to frame action proposals in negative terms. There is, of course, no certainty that other appellate courts will accept the approach taken in *Dow;* the Supreme Court, to which the SEC appealed the procedural questions, declared the issue moot in view of Dow's inclusion of the resolution in a subsequent year and failure of the proponents to obtain the minimum vote necessary under SEC rules to offer it again in less than three years.

In assessing the *Dow* case, one can begin by noting how difficult it is to integrate much of what the court said into conventional corporate legal theory. Taken broadly, the court's opinion seems to imply that the company's shareholders may decide—presumably by majority vote—to accept lower returns on their shares in exchange for more "social responsibility" in the management of company assets. In effect, if a stockholder majority prefers that management divert funds to social goals at the cost of profits, management must follow that direction whatever may be its own preference, since the shareholders, not the managers, have final control over corporate policy. But the error in this—or at any rate the departure from conventional theory—resides in the apparent assumption that mere majorities do actually possess the authority in question. In concentrating entirely on the distribution of power between managers and stockholders, the court apparently disregarded or failed to consider the rights of *dissenting* stockholders as against a would-be majority. The question of law that is really presented in *Dow* (at least at one level) is whether dissenters—who acquired their shares in the expectation that the company would pursue a policy of maximum returns for a given level of risk and who evidently continue to prefer that it should—can be bound by majority vote to accept an investment policy which expressly contemplates a reduction in the value of the company's shares. If they cannot, inclusion of a proposal calling for adoption of such a policy would appear improper.

Ordinarily, at least, the answer to the question just posed is negative: management's fiduciary obligation is independent of the wishes or preferences of controlling stockholders, whether such control is exercised by an individual, an organized group, or by public investors who concert their proxies. As a consequence, stockholder majorities have no power under state law—against the objection of even a single dissenter—to require management to execute a program whose acknowledged aim is to abandon profitable opportunities or to replace existing corporate assets with tangible property of lesser worth. It is well established in the corporate law that acts of "waste" (assuming that is what has just been described) cannot be ratified except by unanimous shareholder vote; directors and others in a fiduciary capacity who commit such acts cannot validate their behavior by obtaining approval from fewer than all of the company's shareholders.[20] No more reason exists to suppose that the waste of corporate property can be compelled by a mere majority, and if the point is carried out still further, it may well be that even a majority-approved charter amendment can be enjoined by dissenters if it calls for social initiatives at the cost of measurable profits. Again, the argument from the standpoint of conventional corporate law is that majorities can never act to impose economic sacrifices on unwilling minorities, no matter what procedure is used and however small the minority. It is of course true that majority vote controls in the election of directors and in the approval of certain other corporate transactions such as mergers and major asset sales. Here, however, the felt need is for some source of authorization for the continuation or termination of the company's existence. In brief, the law's willingness to bind

20. "It is an old saying that one should be just before being generous, and this common sense truth is especially applicable to stockholders who, for one reason or another, are willing to condone a wrong done to their corporation and themselves. They cannot be generous with the corporation's money. They, of course, may be as generous as they please when the money has become their own." *Keenan* v. *Eshleman*, 23 Del. Ch. 234, 2 A. 2d 904, 912 (1938). And see *Kerbs* v. *California Eastern Airways*, 33 Del. Ch. 69, 90 A. 2d 652 (1952); *Rogers* v. *Hill*, 289 U.S. 582, 53 S. Ct. 731 (1933).

dissenters and to allow majorities to control in these areas of decision undoubtedly presupposes that all investors have a common economic goal and that any disagreements will be limited to the choice of means and instrumentalities.

The majority-rule problem is not a great deal easier to handle merely because the resolution of the Medical Committee for Human Rights was framed as advice to management rather than as a binding direction. Advice is presumably meant to be followed, not ignored, particularly when, as in *Dow,* the advisory form was employed solely as a means of avoiding the point that state law required charter amendments to originate with management. Despite some argument to the contrary, there is really no wholly persuasive reason for treating advisory—or "precatory"—proposals differently from mandatory resolutions or for exempting such proposals from the restrictions that are otherwise applicable to shareholder initiatives. In effect, if the subject matter of the proposal is an illegal and enjoinable act, it makes little sense to allow the proponents to activate the proxy machinery in its behalf. That the proposal is designed to encourage but not compel such action plainly does not answer the objection; nor does it suffice to say that "because an advisory proposal does not commit the corporation to a course of action—only if management subsequently acts does the corporation become committed"—such a proposal cannot itself entail a violation of the legal norm.[21] On this view, a court would be "justified" in requiring inclusion of a shareholder advisory resolution only if it were confident (as of course it was in *Dow*) that the proposal would be defeated or if it felt assured that management would disregard the resolution even if the resolution somehow succeeded in attracting a majority of the proxies.

Although there was always a theoretical possibility of unanimous shareholder approval in *Dow,* that possibility could hardly serve as a reasonable basis for administering the proxy rules in respect to Dow or any other public company unless all social action proposals are to be included indiscriminately; and in any case, management opposition obviously assures a negative vote.

It may be, however, that the foregoing analysis exaggerates the degree of monetary sacrifice implied in the Medical Committee's proposal (or at least overstates the court's intention in setting up a tradeoff between

---

21. "Liberalizing SEC Rule 14a-8 through the Use of Advisory Proposals," *Yale Law Journal,* Vol. 80 (March 1971), p. 858.

profits and social responsibility). The court could have viewed the napalm resolution simply as an attempt to raise a question about short-run versus long-run business advantage or as a way of drawing attention to the company's then rather acute public image problem. However, even if the resolution is taken in this limited sense, there appears to be little conventional justification for requiring management to include it. Questions relating to the financial desirability of particular business decisions are plainly reserved to management under state law and are within the "ordinary business" exclusion of Rule 14a-8 even when thought to have a major impact on the company's business outlook. Stockholders are of course free to communicate their business ideas to management and even to do so publicly if they choose. But such action would have to be viewed as very different from making use of the proxy machinery, since the latter entails a vote that is designed to produce binding consequences if it carries.

But this approach to the *Dow* decision is evidently too coldblooded. As has been noted, Dow's directors did assert at various points that the continued sale of napalm was viewed by them as a moral and political obligation rather than as a business judgment, and in these somewhat unusual circumstances, where management avowedly subordinated stockholder interests to social goals, the reasons usually offered for giving directors exclusive power over investment choices would not apply. Indeed, if such avowal were taken seriously, not merely a proxy fight but a stockholders' action for waste might have been the appropriate response.

Suppose, however, that Dow's managers had been more circumspect in their public utterances and had mustered the usual association between the questioned activity and long-term economic goals. Even then, arguably, although management's ability to cite one or another version of enlightened self-interest would generally suffice to ward off stockholders' suits, the same familiar recitation need not necessarily foreclose shareholders from pressing their own ideas of what constitutes social responsibility and of what are the conditions for long-run economic survival. Once management acknowledges, if only tacitly, that social actions by the company are under way and that these are determined by ethical rather than business values in the narrow sense, the question of whose ethical preferences should predominate—directors' or stockholders'—becomes one for which the established delegation system provides no clear answer. Given that question in a public company setting, it may well appear that there is no other alternative to management rule than majority rule, with dissenters being bound in either case. This, presumably, was what the *Dow* court had in mind when it accused Dow's management, in effect, of treating the corporation as a "personal satrapy"; and this, rather than some novel view of the allocation of authority over conventional business decisions, may explain why the court was willing to expose the napalm resolution to a shareholder vote. As a matter of fact, much the same concept appears to be at work when shareholders propose resolutions (as they have for years) *condemning* the use of corporate assets for philanthropic purposes; such resolutions are always included without objection in the company's proxy statement (and always defeated), even though management invariably makes reference to long-term business interests in justifying its charitable activities.

Institutional Investors and Improved Disclosure

However viewed in strictly legal terms, the overall result of the *Dow* decision is to invite an annual round of competition—altogether one-sided as far as the mere matter of votes is concerned—between managers and stockholders in setting the company's course on public interest questions. Since in the present social setting shareholder resolutions almost always fail of passage, their impact and effect depend largely on management's perception of what constitutes the best strategy from the standpoint of its own public acceptance, and of course the exercise is understood in those terms by everyone involved. For this reason, the attitudes of institutional investors—perhaps especially universities—which not only command respectable voting strength but can be seen as in some sense representing a public constituency, are of considerable importance.[22] A major goal of Campaign GM, according to its counsel, was to *force* the issue of corporate social responsibility on the institutions.[23] Although it failed to attract the requisite minimum of votes for its proposals, the campaign did in fact stimulate a number of institutions to become openly and sharply critical of General Motors' activities in

22. See John G. Simon, Charles W. Powers, and Jon P. Gunnemann, *The Ethical Investor: Universities and Corporate Responsibility* (Yale University Press, 1972).
23. Donald E. Schwartz, "Towards New Corporate Goals: Co-Existence With Society," *Georgetown Law Journal*, Vol. 60 (October 1971), p. 68.

the antipollution field and, more generally, encouraged some portfolio managers to try to create internal guidelines aimed at integrating investment goals with social objectives.

The development of such guidelines presents its own difficulties, both of policy and of strategy. However, even if various practical issues could be resolved satisfactorily, there would remain two general and quite familiar objections to institutional and other responsible support for shareholder social action proposals, and these objections ultimately reach to the larger question of corporate voluntarism. In the words of Malkiel and Quandt:

> First, most of the reprehensible activities of companies that one may wish to eliminate and most of the constructive actions that one may wish to encourage have far-reaching external effects. It seems quite unlikely that the actions of decentralized pressure groups toward vaguely similar objectives will ever produce widespread and coherent corporate policies at an acceptable social cost.
>
> Second, corporations may well resist pressures brought to bear on them but not on their competitors, because yielding to such pressures could put them at a serious competitive disadvantage.[24]

The answer usually given, in the words of the same authors, is that "only strict legislation seems to promise . . . to solve these two problems by bringing about coherent plans for social improvement while ensuring that all corporations in the same line of business will be treated equally." As a result, it is said, the best use of institutional pressure is to persuade corporate managers to put their political strength and technical expertise to work in helping to develop legislative solutions to problems within their reach. Presumably also, as mentioned, the same effort would be directed toward the development of sound administrative and enforcement standards once suitable legislation had been enacted. In all this, the role of shareholders would evidently be to stress public concern for the social problem at hand—pollution, product safety, etc.—and to demand a full disclosure of the company's response.

These considerations also suggest that shareholder proposals might better be directed at obtaining more and better data on the social consequences of the company's overall business activities than at particular issues of corporate policy. Once it is accepted that investors have an interest in the development and enforcement of legal regulation, it be-

---

24. Burton G. Malkiel and Richard E. Quandt, "Moral Issues in Investment Policy," *Harvard Business Review,* Vol. 49 (March–April 1971), p. 47.

comes legitimate as well for them to call for periodic disclosures of related information. Drawing on experience under the securities laws, moreover, the hope would be that unflattering disclosures or the prospect thereof, by increasing the threat of stricter law enforcement or additional controls or even consumer retaliation, would prompt a higher order of ethical conduct on the part of company managers.[25] In legal or conceptual terms, finally, the tensions created by the *Dow* decision over respective spheres of authority would not arise or would be less acute if more performance data were accepted as the appropriate stockholder objective, because the stockholders' claim to information—within limits roughly defined by the concept of trade secret—entails no intrusion on management's powers beyond the desired intrusion of publicity.

Although data in the nature of social indicators would be technical and hence meaningless to many investors, as with technical financial information, outside experts could be called upon for explanation and evaluation both by those shareholders who were concerned with the company's social conduct and by nonshareholders who felt the same concern. To some degree, data of the sort referred to can be integrated with and made an essential feature of financial disclosures already mandatory under the federal securities laws. The SEC currently requires registered companies to disclose the capital outlay necessary to comply with antipollution laws, the expected effect on earnings, and any changes in the company's business practices, as well as information on any legal proceedings known to be contemplated by governmental authorities under environmental laws, civil rights laws, and the like. Of course, anyone with experience in the preparation of registration statements and other formal documents required by the securities laws will at once suspect that routine disclosures of pending litigation and the like will often be no more than minimally informative, and the SEC has already indicated some disappointment with the response that it is getting.[26]

Broader data categories could readily be developed, however, and, indeed, resolutions and recommendations in this direction have been

25. See Eli Goldston, *The Quantification of Concern: Some Aspects of Social Accounting* (Columbia University Press for Carnegie-Mellon University, 1972), pp. 72–75; Raymond A. Bauer and Dan H. Fenn, Jr., *The Corporate Social Audit* (Russell Sage Foundation, 1972).

26. See William J. Casey, "Corporate Responsibility," *Business Lawyer*, Vol. 27 (February 1972), pp. 51, 56–57; SEC, Securities Act of 1933, Release 5386 (April 20, 1973).

pressed for some time by leading social action organizations, universities, and even some businessmen. Management in many cases has responded voluntarily by issuing data on such subjects as pollution control, product safety, assistance to minorities, and so on. Unfortunately, the information supplied is often trivial and self-serving, and certainly it varies widely in quality from company to company, a state of affairs suggesting that outside supervision or at least an independent audit might well be useful. The SEC has been urged to assume that obligation, but to date it has declined (not unreasonably) to view its mandate as extending to the oversight and evaluation of such data. Other proposals for government supervision of social auditing—through a federal incorporation process, for example—have attracted only limited interest to date.[27]

It seems likely, nevertheless, at least for the immediate future, that disclosure will provide the chief basis for compromise and cooperation between shareholder activists and management. "Objective" verification of social responsibility, if there is to be any, is likely to remain a voluntary function of the company board, although increasingly the point is made that here at last may be a vital role for outside directors to play. The idea, expressed in one form or another by many writers, would be to constitute an independent committee of the board (a committee composed exclusively of nonexecutive members) whose job would be to require of management and then to evaluate information on the company's performance in areas of public concern specifically affected by the company's business operations. Of course, such a body would require funding, staff, and access in order to function effectively, and it should have authority to write its own report to shareholders if the company's data were judged incomplete. Technical competence rather than interest-group representation would be the criterion for membership, and its goal in general terms would be to encourage a realistic perception of the company's opportunities for responsive conduct. Especially from the standpoint of investment institutions determined to express positive social attitudes in their role as shareholders—whether through proxies, communications to management, or even divestment—a continuous flow of objective reports would be of considerable value as a substitute for costly investigation and research. Other shareholders would treat such information with indifference, to be sure, but the over-

27. See Willard F. Mueller, "Corporate Disclosure: The Public's Right to Know," in Alfred Rappaport and Lawrence Revsine (eds.), *Corporate Financial Reporting: The Issues, the Objectives and Some New Proposals* (Commerce Clearing House, 1972), pp. 67–93.

all costs for large companies would be relatively small, and in any event the securities laws even now require financial and related data which hold little interest for the great majority of shareholders.

Reform and Expansion of Company Boards

Suggestions for expanding the corporation's board of directors and/or dividing the board into two "chambers" to take care of different kinds of responsibility are on the increase. Obviously such proposals for major internal corporate reform reflect a conviction that the existing structure of management-stockholder relations can never by itself be adequately responsive to the public interest. As nearly as can be seen in the extremely general literature in this area, the existing structure is faulted not so much because shareholders lack or have lost control over corporate affairs as because shareholders are no longer thought to have a claim to corporate government which deserves to be ranked above the claims of other interest groups. In Robert Dahl's words, shareholder control, even if it can be revived in some form, is objectionable for the following reasons:

> The first . . . stems from the underlying and usually unexamined assumption that investors, whether individuals or firms, have some special right to govern the firms in which they invest. I can discover absolutely no moral or philosophical basis for such a right. Why investors and not consumers, workers, or, for that matter, the general public? It would be utterly absurd to argue that investors will suffer more from bad decisions [than others]. . . .
> Second, it cannot be argued that investors are particularly *interested* in running the firm or especially gifted with *competence* to do so. . . .
> Finally, as the Supreme Court has recently reminded us, democracy means something like one man, one vote. Certainly it does not mean one share, one vote. Yet either solution is unsatisfactory. If it is difficult to establish the general claim for stockholder control as opposed to control by consumers or workers, it is even harder to argue that by acquiring a single share of stock one should acquire a theoretically equal share in decision-making while denying any such right to an employee who may have worked the better part of his life for the corporation. If, on the other hand, stockholder control is merely intended to insure that the firm's decisions accord with the preferences of investors who own a majority of the stock, the reform seems barely worth the effort.[28]

Others have expressed similar doubts about the right of investors to

28. Dahl, "A Prelude to Corporate Reform," pp. 19–20.

control the processes of decision and have argued for the idea of broad interest-group representation in corporate government. Professor Chayes, for example, has suggested that corporate "membership" be expanded to "include all those having a relation of sufficient intimacy with the corporation or subject to its power in a sufficiently specialized way. Their rightful share in decisions on the exercise of corporate power would be exercised through an institutional arrangement appropriately designed to represent the interests of a constituency of members having a significant common relation to the corporation and its power." Chayes concedes, however (and might have stressed), that "it is not always easy to identify such constituencies, nor is it always clear what institutional forms are appropriate for recognizing their interests."[29]

Interest-Group Participation

Apart from shareholders, the constituencies usually identified as having "a relation of sufficient intimacy" are, in no particular order, labor, consumers, suppliers and other creditors, and possibly the public generally (or government). In addition to being affected in important ways by various corporate processes, these groups are thought to be sufficiently diverse and inclusive to ensure that the main concept of the group-representation idea—that corporate decisions should reflect a "balance of interests" and not merely goals that are unique to managers and shareholders—has some chance of being carried out. Regarding the question of appropriate institutional forms, one proposal would have labor and other interest-group representatives acquire permanent, but minority, representation on boards of directors of larger companies. Although lacking control, such group representatives would have access to information which is currently denied them and would supposedly be far more influential in their positions as informed board members than they are now as outsiders. Another proposal which goes much further would create a second and higher supervisory body—again, composed of interest-group as well as shareholder representatives—with power to make and enforce major corporate policy decisions, presumably through the selection and instruction of company executives. The existing board of directors would continue as a committee of active

29. Abram Chayes, "The Modern Corporation and the Rule of Law," in Edward S. Mason (ed.), *The Corporation in Modern Society* (Harvard University Press, 1960), p. 41.

management, but with an inferior status and with jurisdiction confined to day-to-day operations. Since the individual members of the supervisory body would be largely free of personal concern about job tenure and would therefore be objective in appraising the performance of operating personnel, no need would remain to include other impartial persons at either level of authority, and the much-criticized institution of the outside director could be dropped. In effect, the long-standing problem of management control would have been solved through a process of straightforward innovation—i.e., by abandoning the notion that managers derive their powers from the company's shareholders, rather than through doubtful measures aimed at invigorating the function of ownership.

Despite a certain attractiveness, it has not been difficult for commentators to raise objections to the idea of interest-group participation —objections which spring up rather naturally once some effort is made to give the idea specific content. As Melvin Eisenberg has noted in his discussion of the subject, there is, first, the quite puzzling question of how votes are to be allocated among group members for the purpose of choosing their respective representatives.[30] Where labor is concerned, the principle of one worker one vote is at least mechanically feasible. But supplier and consumer representation, if it is also to be democratic, is obviously much harder to arrange. If suppliers (including lenders) and consumers voted on the basis of average dollar volume of transactions with the company over some period, the result, as Eisenberg points out, would very often be to place a director of one giant corporation (or bank) on the board of another and thus to legitimate an element of cartelization which would otherwise be regarded as unthinkable. The notion that all big companies are supplied by small companies and that all consumer activity takes place at retail somehow seems to have woven itself into the fabric of the interest-group idea, although the facts are plainly contrary in many instances.

To this problem—especially if group membership *were* somehow confined to smaller supplier and consumer units as well as labor—might be added the question of how to relate the skills which group members possess to the powers which they would be expected to exercise as corporate directors. Assuming these powers were no narrower than the

30. Melvin A. Eisenberg, "The Legal Roles of Shareholders and Management in Modern Corporate Decisionmaking," *California Law Review*, Vol. 57 (January 1969), pp. 16–21.

powers held by boards of directors at present, interest-group representatives would need somehow to acquire conventional management
skills and to become expert in the businesses they direct, even though
the status of "representative" would be based on an entirely separate set
of qualifications and a different range of experience. "The skills needed
to be a leather merchant [or a union official] are not necessarily those
needed to decide the business or structural problems faced by shoe manufacturers, nor are such skills acquired with the purchase of one or more
pairs of shoes."[31] If shareholders are not especially competent to run a
firm, it seems equally unlikely that skilled directors can be drawn from
the ranks of consumers, labor, or the civil service. An inexperienced,
nonbusiness supervisory board, whatever its stated legal responsibilities,
would probably restrict itself to exercising authority over a very limited
range of company activities, and the role of board members, like that
of outside directors in the present system, would become merely con-
firmatory of decisions already reached at lower levels. European experience with two-tier directorates apparently supports no greater expectation.

In larger terms, however, legal criticism of direct interest-group participation derives from a feeling that the existing institutional processes
by which workers, consumers, and suppliers press their interests on the
firm—processes of negotiation, contract, and litigation—are superior on
the whole, or could be made so, to the idea of internalizing those interests within corporate government itself. In part, perhaps, this criticism
springs from an understandable reluctance to confront the massive problems that would ensue if, for example, the present system of collective
bargaining had to be revised to reflect a new and unified relationship
between labor and employers or if the same need should arise in respect
to the elaborately constructed law of creditors' rights or in the field of
consumer protection. In part, also, there is a very reasonable doubt
about whether interest groups, particularly labor, would desire to be
brought inside the firm and to assume management obligations rather
than deal with the company at arm's length as at present. More generally, the point is urged that interest-group representatives—if they remained that—would persist in emphasizing short-run goals of immediate
concern to their membership and that this might often entail a sacrifice
not merely of profits and efficiency but also of the social objectives

31. Ibid., p. 18.

whose attainment is the very goal of the restructuring plan. Again, the proponents of interest-group control seem to assume that group representatives would consistently work with fellow board members toward publicly desirable ends or else that the processes of conflict and compromise would generally produce socially beneficial decisions. Whether they would or not is unknown, but it is easy to imagine situations in which the balancing process might scant important social interests because these were unrepresented or less well informed or because they lacked the bargaining strength to obtain concessions from the others.

Public Directors

Doubts about the ability and willingness of special-interest representatives to promote broader social values have led some writers to suggest that it is not private interest groups but the public, or at least the public interest, which ought to dominate or be more prominently reflected in corporate management. Since the public is otherwise unorganized, this necessarily leads to government, and presumably the federal government, as a source both of personnel to man the directorships and guidance about what constitutes the public interest. In one version government representatives would serve as "neutrals" with a duty to arbitrate among the other interests represented on the board; in another, one or more public officials would play the role of ombudsman or compliance officer with the task of making sure that the company meets its obligations to the law and that management takes account of public policy in making corporate decisions.

Once more, however, critics have expressed doubt about whether it is really desirable to shift from a system of external regulation, which is conducted on an adversary basis and surrounded by administrative safeguards, to one in which the regulatory authority is brought inside the firm in the shape of a corporate director who also carries a government commission. Professor Vagts, in appraising the German experience with public representatives on corporate supervisory councils, has summarized the point as follows:

> The effect on a firm of having a partially public management may be compared with that of being subject to regulation. In both cases the tendency of management to maximize profits is subject to restraints designed to further other interests. The restraints imposed by public representatives are not, however, exerted in as plainly visible a fashion and there is less

need for the government to take as clear and reasoned a stand. Thus on the one hand there is considerable danger that the government may seek to achieve in the quiet of the conference room what it cannot achieve in the normal administrative process. On the other hand, the asserted tendency of administrative agencies to fall under the influence of the industry they regulate is apt to reveal itself even more with government board members who work together with the regular management and develop a common set of attitudes and a common *esprit de corps*. On the whole, one is inclined to believe that a more rational and orderly development of economic law is apt to be achieved by pursuing the American pattern of open regulation than the German form of operating through undisclosed negotiations between private and public representatives. We are too committed to disclosure and due process in the making of economic decisions to be able to accomplish easily a shift to the less public German way of doing things.[32]

Whatever may be the merits of legislating the inclusion on company boards of officially designated representatives, it appears that a number of larger corporations have created "public" directorships on a voluntary basis over the past few years. The notion, apparently, is that management's perception of public values will be enhanced through the presence on the board of one or more public-spirited individuals, especially if the latter possess some relationship to interest groups which lack adequate formal means of negotiating their objectives with the firm. Apparently no studies have yet been done on the impact of privately appointed public directors, but it is difficult to suppose that a single individual meeting with the board of a mammoth firm at quarterly intervals can do much to affect day-to-day technical decisions reached by a sizable corporate bureaucracy with which he or she has no direct contact. One can perhaps envision some opportunity for private persons to perform an ombudsman function with real effect, but plainly this would entail the usual requirements of funding, staff, and access—in effect, a fully acknowledged management status—more or less as proposed by former Justice Arthur Goldberg, among others.[33] There are only occasional indications at present, however, that public directorships are being professionalized in this way or that company boards have acquired a new significance in corporate life by reason of the voluntary addition of public members.

32. Detlev Vagts, "Reforming the 'Modern' Corporation: Perspectives from the German," *Harvard Law Review*, Vol. 80 (November 1966), pp. 86–87.
33. "Arthur Goldberg on Public Directors," *Business and Society Review/Innovation*, No. 5 (Spring 1973), pp. 35–39.

Conclusion

What has been said so far can be taken to suggest that there are, broadly speaking, two ways in which corporate law affects or might affect the question of corporate social conduct. The first and most familiar concerns the corporation in the role of volunteer—acting not so much in obedience to market forces or legal regulation as out of a sense that socially responsible behavior on the part of major firms is justified by public expectations. Here, as has been seen, the chief function of corporate law is to "enable," that is, to furnish a suitable formula within the existing system of fiduciary obligation by which corporate generosity can be approved as properly self-serving. This has not been a difficult task when the firm's social commitment comes from management itself. Within wide limits, the courts have been willing to take management's word that expenditures for improved relations with groups whose welfare may be implicated by the company's activities are in the interests of its shareholders. References to long-term planning goals routinely suffice to meet the legal standard. Rather curiously, it would appear that the most common of all corporate social gestures—small cash contributions to conventional charities—is also the least closely related to discernible business objectives; however, the enactment of enabling legislation in almost every state, together with the absence of serious objection from most stockholders, has placed the legality and, by and large, the propriety of corporate giving beyond question.

By contrast, the role of corporate law as an element in the overall strategy for bringing public pressure to bear on management is not yet well defined. As has been suggested, there may be some difficulty in squaring conventional legal theory with the right of shareholders to initiate and vote on social action proposals, particularly if such proposals expressly or by implication advocate significant departures from a profits standard. Ideals of "corporate democracy" and "fair suffrage" do not support the right of stockholder majorities to adopt a policy of economic sacrifice over the objection of dissenters; indeed, a major goal of corporate law, through many decades, has been the development of equitable restrictions and rules of restraint aimed specifically at defending the financial interests of minority shareholders. In essence, the law contemplates that corporate investment decisions shall be wholly independent of the personal tastes of the company's shareholders—whether majority or minority—and shall be based solely on a presumed universal preference for higher market values per share.

It is evident, however, that managers in practice may exercise considerable discretion in dedicating corporate resources to those social goals which they themselves find appealing. The "neutrality" of the arrangement thus appears somewhat one-sided—occasionally, as in the *Dow* case, rather glaringly so. It is not surprising, therefore, especially in the present climate of opinion, that attempts should be made to redress the balance and that the law should prove hospitable thereto. Lawyers, at least, will appreciate that a body of legal principles which has been flexible enough to accommodate corporate (i.e., management) gifts to charity can also be made to find room for shareholder social initiatives once a respectable section of investor opinion comes to regard management's efforts as inadequate or misdirected.

What is less clear, perhaps, is whether enthusiasm among shareholders themselves for this form of protest activity will remain as high as it has been in the time just past. Although the proponents of social action resolutions generally declare that as little as 3 percent shareholder support must be viewed as a victory, it seems likely that a failure to increase the vote above minimum levels over a period of years would be found dispiriting by many. Unless support levels grow, there is danger (from one standpoint) that the movement will become routine and repetitive and lose its ability to generate public attention, much as has the older struggle for shareholder influence which is identified with Lewis Gilbert. Widening support for shareholder resolutions appears to depend on institutional support (see, for example, *New York Times,* April 25, 1965) and on whether the development of ethical investment guidelines which can be defended as sensible and moderate will blunt the movement or spur it on. The very cautious investment guidelines recently adopted by Yale University, for example, which stress compliance with "rules of domestic or international law," might actually be read to preclude support for the napalm resolution considered in *Dow,* or at any rate seem to leave the university's probable reaction as shareholder much in doubt.[34] In effect, there may be considerable difficulty in developing a principled basis for responding affirmatively to individual resolutions which are offered ad hoc.

This suggests, again, that the long-run interests of shareholders who

34. Simon, Powers, and Gunnemann, *The Ethical Investor,* p. 171.

wish to encourage a larger sensitivity to moral questions might be better served by periodic disclosure of management's performance in areas of major concern than by occasional efforts to intervene in particular matters of corporate policy. The practical advantages of a public reporting system, especially from the standpoint of institutions and others holding widely diversified portfolios of securities, are surely evident. In addition, the purely strategic problems which even large institutional shareholders face in attempting to make their views on social issues felt by management might in some measure be eased by substituting disclosure, i.e., public embarrassment, for other forms of intervention. Although the resemblance between conventional fiduciary obligations, which are well defined and fairly easy to apply, and a rather vaguely stated obligation to the public interest is anything but perfect, experience under the federal securities laws does support the expectation that personal exposure will sometimes prompt higher standards of conduct on the part of company managers.

The second way in which corporate law could move in the direction of social responsibility would be through the enactment of a "balancing of interest" concept. One might suppose that this would qualify as a "reform" only if its object and effect were to overthrow existing rules of fiduciary obligation, since those rules are largely aimed at establishing shareholder wealth-maximization as the sole decision criterion for the firm. However, as Barbara Shenfield has pointed out, the commonest explanation given by company boards *themselves* of their own decision process "is to describe it as a balancing of interests in which the board takes into account the interests of various groups."[35] Accordingly, if one takes seriously the statements made by corporate managers about what they think they are doing when they exercise business judgment, the notion of "balancing" should not only be a comfortable way for management to view its own tasks but is a fair description of what has actually been going on within the firm for years.

This, of course, is not to say that managers would wish to see the balancing idea articulated in a statute—that, no doubt, would be regarded as too confining and as showing a somewhat graceless lack of trust. The resistance, fierce if clumsy, which some companies have put up against shareholder social action proposals makes it apparent that

35. Shenfield, *Company Boards* (London: George Allen and Unwin, 1971), p. 12.

managers prefer to deal with social issues on a discretionary basis, deciding for themselves what kinds of sacrifices public sentiment requires. One suspects, indeed, that it is not so much "sacrifice" or "compromise" that corporate managers have in mind when they speak of balancing group interests as it is a deftly executed decision in which all affected interests are maximized yet somehow made to coincide. In principle, as management sees it, profit making serves everyone's interest: workers, creditors, and shareholders all have a long-term interest in the firm's being profitable; profitability also shows that consumers' needs are being met; hence business may proceed as usual by "balancing" the interests of everyone concerned. No revision of corporate law is called for.

On the other hand, if the balancing concept is truly understood to refer to "sacrifice," important changes in the corporate law are certainly required. The question then, however, would be just how to reflect a complex social purpose in a set of standards precise enough to be includable in a business corporation statute, intelligible to lawyers and enforceable by the courts. To be sure, judges are well accustomed to arbitrating among competing claims, but with rare and unsatisfactory exceptions the law provides fixed points of reference by which those claims can be measured. How would this be done in the present setting? Not a hint of answer can be found in all the legal writing that has been devoted to the subject. One has the sense, however, that any effort to embody the balancing principle in a corporation statute in merely general terms and without detailed elaboration would do no more than confirm the existence of a discretionary power which management already thinks it possesses.

The difficulty of reconstructing the framework of business law so as (1) to encourage corporate social responsibility while at the same time (2) limiting management's freedom to pursue its own version of the public interest thus seems very great. Interest-group representation on company boards is perhaps the only proposal which purports to aim in both directions at once; but the problems of definition and practicability that are instantly foreseeable—identification of constituencies, selection of representatives, competence and experience of the individuals selected —as well as skepticism about whether group members would be likely, on the whole, to see the public interest as a concept separable from their own narrower objectives, have discouraged support even among those who otherwise seem most eager for change.

In the end it may be necessary, if mildly disappointing, to conclude that corporate law as such has relatively little to contribute to the realization of social goals (other than those that pertain to investors). "The prospect of a breakthrough on this front," as Wilber Katz has said, "is not encouraging, for what is demanded is a contrivance which would operate neither through individual responsibility and competitive markets nor through political controls."[36] Assuming that no such "contrivance" is waiting in the wings—and again, the question has been before the house in one form or another for nearly half a century—it may now be appropriate to suggest that the subject of corporate law reform and social responsibility be seen in reduced perspective. Corporations will undoubtedly become more responsive as a consequence of pressure from consumer organizations, labor, government, and public opinion generally. The development of an active sense of public accountability on the part of major firms is plainly welcome and might be aided or encouraged through stronger disclosure requirements, as indicated above. But apart from enlisting legal processes in a move toward wider dissemination of company performance data, it is perhaps useless to expect or insist that the corporate law itself should have more than a limited role to play in determining the social content of business behavior.

36. Katz, "The Philosophy of Midcentury Corporation Statutes," *Law and Contemporary Problems,* Vol. 23 (Spring 1958), p. 192.

CHAPTER FOUR

Command and Control

THOMAS C. SCHELLING

TRADITIONAL THEORY envisions the firm as a finely tuned machine controlled by an absolute master who not only knows what he wants, from a faultless calculation of what will maximize his profits, but who can enforce his decision on the enterprise he commands. In practice, however, it is well to recall what President Truman said in the summer of 1952, contemplating the problems that General Eisenhower would have if he won the forthcoming election. "He'll sit here, and he'll say, 'Do this! Do that!' *And nothing will happen.* Poor Ike— it won't be a bit like the Army. He'll find it very frustrating."[1] Is the President of the United States more impotent by an order of magnitude than the president of a telephone company, hotel chain, or airline? Had "Poor Ike" even found the Army as obedient as Truman thought he did?[2]

It is too bad that some of our Presidents did not become presidents of business firms after leaving public office, with analysts like Neustadt to chronicle their frustrations. Some of them might have expected that at last they could say, "Institute equal opportunity here! Eliminate noxious preservatives there! Don't spoil the quiet in that community!"— and have it done.

Part of the problem of "the social responsibility of business" is that captains of industry are hell-bent for profits or too beset by competition to indulge their social consciences. But another part is that, say, the

1. Quoted in Richard E. Neustadt, *Presidential Power: The Politics of Leadership* (Wiley, 1960), p. 9.
2. In late September 1972, the Environmental Protection Agency reported that "high" officials of a major auto company, without the cognizance of "top" officials, had falsified the results of engine emission tests, while across town the Senate Armed Services Committee sought to determine whether or not the Commander of the Seventh Air Force had had the cognizance of his theater commander or of the Joint Chiefs of Staff in willfully violating the orders of his Commander-in-Chief.

president of a telephone company may be no more able to institute equal rights for women than the president of a university or the director of a nonprofit hospital. He usually can't even fire people for disobeying his directives. And if he could, he might still be unable to devise a system that would monitor the way minority applicants were treated in a personnel office.

The problem arises in the small and in the large. The small taxi company with a fleet of twenty or thirty drivers, all known by their first names to the owner-dispatcher, may be no better able to make passengers fasten their seat belts than a large conglomerate that owns cab companies in a dozen cities. The conglomerate, in turn, is like a "government" attempting to devise policies for the decentralized firms that it owns but that it controls only in a legal sense.

One should not too much disparage the effect of adding a consumer or minority-group representative to the board of directors of some huge corporation; the symbolism as well as the authority can make a difference. But the cartoonist's image of the captain of industry should not mislead us into supposing that even the whole board of directors can make "policy" and then sit back and see its will be done. Neither conscience nor the profit motive, at the level of business management, is likely to make a captain of industry like the captain of a ship. And even the captain of a ship may suffer some of the frustrations of President Truman once in a while.

For setting public policy with respect to business, two important implications emerge from these initial insights. First, business, as a "black box" to be dealt with through government action, will not be instantly and effectively responsive either to the consciences of managers or to the market incentives—taxes and subsidies, property rights and liabilities—that may be designed as "proxies" for conscience. Second, in thinking about social responsibility, it may often be a mistake to think of "the company" as the unit of action. Business is not a population of unitary entities—"firms" in the private sector. On the contrary, it is a number of small societies comprising many people with different interests, opportunities, information, motivations, and group interests.

Taking the Lid off the Black Box

For some purposes it will be necessary to "disaggregate" the firm and to deal with the social responsibility of subdivisions and individuals, applying the incentives and sanctions directly on the people or on the transactions that constitute the business and its activity, rather than to conceptualize the firm or the industry as the target of attention.

A clear-cut example would be to impose criminal liability on individuals for, say, activity contrary to the antitrust laws. One can apply sanctions on the firm; or one can make people individually liable for their actions as managers, supervisors, even salesmen. A city can attempt to hold taxi companies liable for the safe driving, courtesy, and traffic behavior of taxi drivers; or the city can make it a personal offense of the cabby to double park or to refuse service to a member of some minority group. The government might even, though this is rarely done, attempt to influence the reward structure within the firm. Especially in matters of equal opportunity and nondiscrimination, there is developing some tendency toward disaggregating large organizations into the individuals who compose them (or at least directly scrutinizing and monitoring the policy directives and procedures). The concept of an "affirmative action program" for hiring members of minority groups is illustrative of not dealing with the industry as a population or with the firm as a black box but of getting inside the firm and monitoring the processes that govern it.

The Nuremberg trials developed the notion of "war criminals," people who could not find adequate legal defense for their actions merely in having been instructed or commanded to carry out the policies of higher authority. In some countries the acts of a functionary are immune to personal legal action, and a formal complaint has to be lodged with the government he represents; in others, individuals are personally liable for their actions, and their uniform does not make them immune even though they are merely cogs in a large machine. It is interesting that the Anglo-American legal tradition makes the policeman criminally responsible for what he does with a firearm, even when on duty and in uniform. There is apparently a corresponding distinction between the social responsibility *of* a business and the exercise of responsibility *in* a business.

It is useful to imagine how we would approach the problem of responsibility if we avoided altogether considering the "business" as an entity—as a corporate individual that could have cognizance of responsibility or that could be acted on through a centralized profit motive.

Take a few potential areas of "social responsibility," like equal opportunity or consumer protection, and imagine that we conceptually disaggregate the firm into nonexistence or deny it legal recognition. Now we cannot act on profits and the profit motive. We cannot use taxes and subsidies on the *firm* as instruments of social control. We cannot direct our persuasion at boards of directors. We cannot work with a concept of "administrative law" that identifies an individual with the firm that employs him. Instead we have to motivate people who are earning individual livelihoods. For equal-opportunity purposes we have to appeal to, or work through, the personnel officers and clerks, the people who devise questionnaires, who deal politely or impolitely with applicants, and who make actual hiring decisions. We work directly on the chemist who recommends an additive to preserve the color in a jar of jelly and on the person who designs a cheap bumper that will not withstand impact. We work on the pilot of the plane who steers his craft at particular altitudes over noise-conscious population centers. We go after the navigator who brought that tanker too close to shore in bad weather and risked an oil spill.

That is, we should recall, the way we would deal with a policeman who fired his gun in a crowd.[3]

I am drawing a distinction, not a conclusion. The question of *where* it is most efficacious to locate responsibility within the business is a complicated one. It is an enormous convenience to government if "policy" can be directed toward the firm and not toward the people who work for it. But sometimes it won't work. Sometimes the firm is impotent. Sometimes the firm is a clumsy instrument to work with. Sometimes the firm has little control over the activities that the authorities wish to regulate. (Sometimes the firm can take refuge in its own impotence!) And even when the firm is the appropriate target for policy, it is difficult to identify the level of corporate decentralization or the mixture of stock holdings that determine just which entity is "the business."

The Problem of Identification

Even legally it is sometimes difficult to identify just what a business is, or where it is. Especially for corporate business, one has to inquire whether it is the stockholder group, the board of directors, the management, or the entire social entity that engages in the business. For several decades it has been common to distinguish between ownership and con-

3. Procedurally, that is. In practice few policemen appear to be severely penalized unless they have earned the resentment and lost the support of their fellows.

trol, especially in the modern corporation; and this distinction blurs the idea of responsibility. Add a union, and it becomes even harder to decide where the firm is governed. The "production" of rock-and-roll music and the "production" of telephone service include many parties to the transaction. Baseball and prizefighting are businesses; so are newspapers and taxis, insurance and automobile sales. From the point of view of "social responsibility," it may be important to know who's in charge; and it may be as difficult as it is important.

Anyone who has shipped goods across country by moving van or across the ocean by freighter, or who has bought an automobile from a dealer or stopped at a chain restaurant on a turnpike, knows how difficult it is to find out just where responsibility is focused, who's in charge, what the "industry" is. If you like your Chevrolet or the meal at Howard Johnson's, where do you send your letter of appreciation? Many businesses are not only complex in the legality of their ownership but in the arrangements they have worked out with their laborers, distributors, even their customers. If you see a bad movie and would like to complain, to whom do you complain?

The typical commodity or transaction involves a diffusion of responsibility and, when one wants to focus liability or obligation, blame or credit, it is typically not easy to locate the target. Furthermore, it cannot be expected that the business firm, as an entity, will be the institutional equivalent of the people who work for it or a simple reflection of them. The key people in an organization may be bold or timid, sensitive or callous, innovative or lacking in imagination, "responsible" or "irresponsible," without the business they work in having corresponding qualities or being the image of the managers and without the "business" being analyzable as the equivalent of a businessman. A bunch of timid people directing an enterprise do not necessarily make for a "timid" enterprise; everybody may lack the personal boldness to oppose a rash action. "Responsible" individuals may be so loyal to the organization that they acquiesce in policies that appear "irresponsible." Responsibility may be so diluted within an enterprise that there is no one to blame when the organization seems blameworthy, no individual to reward when the organization behaves uncommonly well. An organization, business or other, is a system of information, rules for decision, and incentives; its performance is different from the individual performances of the people in it. An organization can be negligent without any individual's being negligent. To expect an organization to reflect the qualities of the individuals who work for it or to impute to the individuals the qualities one sees in the organization is to commit what logicians call the "fallacy of composition." Fallacy isn't error, of course, but it can be treacherous.

A Universal Dilemma: Internalize or Decentralize

Many problems relating to the social responsibility of business that we are conscious of in America are problems also in other countries that do not share our business system. Marshall I. Goldman has persuasively illustrated the thesis that pollution in the Soviet Union is not only a serious problem but much the same kind of problem as it is in America.[4] Part of our subject can evidently best be thought of as "the social responsibility of large organizations" (or social responsibility *in* large organizations).

Comparing the Russian economy with the American gives some appreciation of what is meant by "internalizing" externalities. The ministry that controls pulp and paper in the Soviet Union apparently no more internalizes its impact on fish and wildlife in Russian lakes and streams than does a large corporation in the United States. Just as it is useful to compare the telephone company with Columbia University, for analyzing policy and its effectiveness with respect to the employment of women, it can be useful to compare an American firm with its counterpart in a socialist country.

What emerges from the comparison is some downgrading of the profit motive as a key to the behavior of the business system. Profits, as a motivating force, become rapidly attenuated as one moves down the chain of command or through the social network of decisions in the firm, away from those individuals who have a strong and direct interest in company profits or a lively sensation that their own behavior would make a noticeable difference. (Profits are substantially "external" even to many individuals in top management.)[5]

A firm as large as General Motors apparently finds it worthwhile to decentralize management. So does a Soviet ministry. There are evidently

4. Goldman, "The Convergence of Environmental Disruption," *Science*, Vol. 170 (October 2, 1970), pp. 37–42.

5. It is helpful to recall that close-order drill in the army originated in the need to keep every infantryman within easy pistol range of his squad leader, to help that infantryman "internalize" the objective of victory, and squad leaders within similar range of platoon leaders for similar reasons.

limits to the effectiveness of hierarchical control. But there is no such thing, then, as internalizing all of the externalities if there are organizational limitations on the radius of responsibility. To decentralize in the interest of managerial incentives and effectiveness is to externalize the more diffuse responsibilities.[6] There is a sense in which the leaders of the Soviet Union are enormous monopolists; but complete hierarchical control is beyond their means. And, whether decentralization is deliberate or ineluctable, it leads to many of the same problems we impute to the profit motive in the private sector in this country.

Discipline and the Supportive Role of Government

Later I suggest that firms might, and sometimes do, submit voluntarily to "coercion" as a substitute or supplement for contract or compact, as a way of solving some of the problems of freeloaders, chiselers, and others who could not or would not join in internalizing the costs and benefits of more responsible policies. Firms have surely learned to place their activities under "outside" rules when their own security or profits, not the public interest, is at stake. The barbershops, for example, appreciate mandatory closing on Wednesday in Massachusetts, since it precludes competitors from staying open. No agency short of the federal government, to take another example, could possibly institute cotton acreage controls on a workable scale.

But there is another role that government might play in helping firms to do what they might wish they could do but cannot—or cannot as well as government, or cannot without the help of government. I earlier mentioned obstructions to command and control. It is interesting to note to what extent government may substitute for the firm's own management, or augment the firm's capability, or supplement the firm's efforts to enforce policy directives within the firm, and particularly policy directives that represent a social responsibility.

To indicate what I have in mind, let me begin with a few clear cases. Certain forms of personal violence and material sabotage are criminal

6. Decentralization of incentives to the individual motels of a large chain will make the goodwill of the cross-country traveler more proximate but external to the motel manager who affects the goodwill. Centralization to the home office makes it internal but remote. The problem may be much the same for Intourist as for Holiday Inn.

offenses, and a company is also presumably helped by the police in enforcing the rules against prostitution, drug peddling, and gambling on company time. Similarly with theft and embezzlement. Certain regulations that reduce the hazards of fire and disease are more easily enforced within the firm if there are local ordinances that can be adverted to or if certain careless actions are violations of law as well as of company policy.

For a case that is a small step closer to the government's monitoring the activities of a firm's employees, consider a taxi company. The company may want a reputation for courtesy and safety—it may even want actual courtesy and safety. But it may be unable to enforce its own regulations about seat belts, double parking, illegal U-turns, or drinking on the job. The police, the Registry of Motor Vehicles, or other public authorities may have to do the monitoring. A taxi driver who refuses to take a black passenger from the airport to a black residential district at night may be more susceptible to the command of the state trooper at the airport than to any complaints phoned in to his dispatcher. And one of the functions of metered fares, established by an agency of government, is to keep drivers from engaging in pricing practices, or subterfuge about their earnings, or intimidation of passengers, in a way that a taxi company on its own might not be able to do.

The idea extends to a number of operations that occur outside the physical reach of a company, beyond the company's power of observation, and where the company's ability to spy and detect is inadequate. This could include, of course, fishing fleets, airlines, truck drivers, repairmen, and anyone who might cheat or steal or blackmail customers. The principle extends to customers as well as employees: the airlines, left to themselves, showed no eagerness to examine passengers' handbags; if they had to do it, they preferred to be required to do it, and probably they wanted the actual job to be done by customs officials.

It is worth noticing that the licensing both of airline pilots and of cab drivers is done by government. Though one may expect the airlines to demand higher standards of pilot competence than are prescribed by the regulations, there is no thought that the profit motive alone should be counted on to guarantee the competence of those airline employees to whom are entrusted the airborne mixed cargoes of people and kerosene.

Now, how does this bear on our subject? Business firms may indeed want government to help them police their employees or their customers, to help protect the firm itself—its profits, its reputation, its legal security.

May it also need some direct intervention of government in the command-and-control process to meet some social responsibilities? What are the specific areas of social responsibility in which a business firm might lack the discipline, the information, the incentives, or the moral authority to command performance or restraint on the part of everyone whose cooperation is required?

One possibility is that employees are personally irresponsible and out of laziness or for personal gain fail in their performance. Trash collectors leave debris in the gutters; fishing boats dump garbage in the harbor; sanitary regulations are neglected in a fruit-processing plant; nurses sleep and airline ground crews drink on duty; truck drivers make up for an extra-long lunch hour by driving through an off-limits tunnel with a dangerous cargo.

Another possibility is that employees oppose some "socially responsible" policy on moral or ideological grounds; or they suspect that top management is making a pretense at demanding performance but doesn't really want its orders heeded. Discrimination in hiring, promoting, firing, and job assignment comes quickly to mind. Someone may even out of kindness turn down a job applicant who, being male or being female, being old or young, being black or white, would be uncomfortable in a particular job but may not know it. Someone can subtly discourage job applicants through procrastination, can mislay documents, misrepresent the job, or pretend it has already been filled. The question is whether government efforts to demand nondiscriminatory performance, or even "affirmative action" to compensate groups that have been discriminated against, might not be better directed in some instances toward the performance of individuals rather than toward a statistical monitoring of the firm itself. Statistically based penalties and rewards may provide adequate motivation for top management. The question is whether this motivation on the part of those whose profits are at stake, whose reputations are in the limelight, or whose moral responsibilities are being tested and challenged can be transmitted throughout the organization to show up as personal motivation in a myriad of individuals whose compliance or cooperation is required.

Whether we have in mind criminal charges or damage suits, it will turn out in many cases that the government does best to make it an obligation of *people* in a firm, not of the firm as a profit-making entity, to behave properly. Just as the police can keep a delivery truck from double parking even though the home office of the delivery truck may not be able to, the holding of individuals personally responsible for hazardous behavior in the plant, for violation of civil rights, misrepresentation of a product, or the destruction of beauty or quiet can sometimes be more effectively managed by government directly than by government attempting to manipulate rewards and penalties on stockholder dividends.

The issue is one of comparative advantage. Technology may make it easier for the trucking firm than for the Registry of Motor Vehicles to monitor the emission of gaseous pollutants. Or it may not. Or it may be that large firms owning their own tractors can be centrally penalized and can enforce exhaust-pipe standards on their own fleet; while the driver-entrepreneur who owns a single tractor and will haul anybody's trailer is too small and too itinerant to be caught by the Environmental Protection Agency, and he enjoys such a competitive advantage that eventually the task of monitoring the regulations and inflicting the fines has to be a matter between the driver and the authorities. (The company's obligation then is not to reimburse its employees for the fines levied on them in line of duty.)

In some cases the firm's inability to control the behavior of individuals within the firm is not the result of a physical incapacity to monitor performance and to identify delinquents by name but stems from some lack of moral authority to command behavior in other respects than those that go with a strict construction of job and job performance. Personal hygiene may be an example. An ordinance against spitting on the floor may work better than a company directive, either because the local authorities can enforce it or because it legitimizes a parallel injunction by the company itself. A company's efforts to test employees for communicable infections and to suspend those who are a hazard to the health of co-workers might meet resistance and malingering, whereas public health authorities could quarantine the plant until everybody had submitted and insist on treatment for the individuals who had contagious venereal and other diseases. Fire drills are carried out more seriously when attended by firemen in uniform.

Moral Choice or Policy Choice

In discussing "social responsibility" there is a tendency to take for granted that more of it is a good thing. (Those who don't think so probably don't spend much time discussing it.) There may be limits to how much one would demand, but, if one thinks of a unidimensional scale—"responsibility" at one end and "irresponsibility" at the other—responsibility seems to be something we can always wish for more of.

At least, it does until somebody feels morally compelled to persuade us to his faith in some god or some food, or to protect us from books or card games, to make us salute the flag or refuse to salute the flag, to prohibit smoking in the cafeteria or to make us stop using the masculine pronoun in referring to everybody.

There are of course situations in which responsibility means considerateness, less selfishness, helping or supporting someone and offending no one. Flammable children's pajamas without warning labels, the clandestine dumping of garbage, and reset odometers on second-hand cars are not likely to cause any moral dilemmas.[7] But at a time when, urged by the brother of two assassination victims, the Senate can barely muster a majority in moral support of suppression of the cheap and easily obtainable handguns known as "Saturday night specials"; when the town dog-catcher is still among the least-loved public servants; when abortions are construed by some as an inalienable freedom and by others as a sin to be publicly suppressed; when Academy Awards are won by pictures that couldn't have been shown ten years ago; when many black people are genuinely apprehensive about the dilution of their culture and the co-opting of their leaders by "integrationist" campaigns reflecting the best of intentions—at such a time responsibility is often not a quantity (something a person can have more or less of) but a *policy choice,* a choice among the alternative values that one can be responsible to.

There are dangers in urging business to let its responsibilities be defined by some subset of its customers, by the special interests of its employees, by whatever ethnic group in the community is most articulate or most threatening, by people who love dogs or by people who are allergic to dog hair. There is no need to be alarmist, but it is worthwhile to recall that, even in matters of business responsibility, especially social responsibility, there are always conflicts of interest to be found; and they often correspond to conflicts of responsibility. Protective tariffs, safety inspection of marginal coal mines, pets in apartment buildings,

7. Not so fast. The dealer who sold me my Mustang argued earnestly that, as a car buyer, I should oppose the unfair law against tampering with odometers, because it would lower the resale value of my automobile!

and of course the gun laws are reminders of this principle. Some of the issues may be strictly distributional: higher-cost low-sulphur fuels clean the air for the people who live downwind from the smokestacks; and use of these same fuels may add to the cost of electric power and other commodities, with an incidence that falls disproportionately on the poor. Pity the "responsible" refuse company that has to decide in which community to locate its dumping ground.

My purpose at this point is not to be destructive of the idea of responsibility or to suggest that all efforts at responsibility are doomed to violate somebody's principles. It is rather to point out that being responsible for a business firm is a little like being responsible as a senator or as a university president. Often the question is not, "Do I want to do the right thing?" It arises in the form, "What is the right thing to want to do?" The choice is not always between some selfish temptation and some obvious responsible course. The choice is often a policy decision.

What should a business do about drug addiction among its employees? What should it do about admitting men to jobs that have been traditionally women's—secretaries, receptionists, or file clerks? Or smoking on the job? Or eliminating some hazard in the product by producing it more expensively and selling it at a higher price? Or letting a black organization dictate policy toward blacks, letting a woman's organization negotiate on behalf of women? Consider the business that is under pressure to discontinue operations in South Africa, throwing people out of work there. What is the right thing to do? To whom should the company defer in deciding the right thing to do? Is there a "right thing" in this case or just a choice between equally unsatisfactory options?

Many of today's issues in business responsibility are new. There is no easy answer to the question of whether the Sierra Club or a farm group speaks for the responsible position, and they may take opposite sides. One thing seems sure: on the issues that exercise people today, especially the issues of the social responsibility of business, there is often no source of reliable guidance, no acknowledged source of policy, no easy choice between the responsible and the selfish.

Not all problems of responsibility involve dilemmas of conscience. Ambiguity about what is right is no excuse for doing wrong. But we should usually be careful not to adopt the idea that it is easy to know what is right and responsible and that the choice is only between responsibility and irresponsibility. People in business who have the decisiveness to do the responsible thing will often be the people who, because they did something decisive, are accused of irresponsibility. Even the prejudiced employer may have trouble deciding whether or not his responsibility is to his community and its traditional values; it is the unprejudiced employer who may have the hardest time deciding how much of a handicap it is appropriate to give some disadvantaged minority.

Irresponsible or Unresponsive

The vexed and ambiguous character of many modern problems of business responsibility has been exemplified, if in an exaggerated way, by the tantalizing problem of aircraft hijacking. In addition to the dramatic crisis of responsibility that is bound to occur when an actual hijacking is attempted or in process and perilous decisions of an unforeseen and often unique kind have to be reached in a hurry, a multitude of nearly routine decisions with a bearing on hijacking remained on the agenda for a good many years without being settled.

There is, for example, the straightforward matter of baggage handling, about which nothing has been done. Maybe nothing should be done. Baggage in the cabin is evidently important, as evidenced by the search procedures that were initiated in early 1973. Until a dozen years ago we checked our bags; then, with the large-diameter fuselage that goes with jet airplanes, it became feasible to elevate the seats off the floor to accommodate overnight bags. Most baggage is apparently carried aboard for quick retrieval, not because anyone wants to shave or wear his bathrobe in flight. Maybe passengers could be induced to surrender their baggage or eventually to invest in specially designed aircraft luggage that yielded more readily to search.

Instead we have search procedures. Whatever their efficacy, one thing is certain: if it made sense to institute them in 1973, it would have made sense to institute them several years earlier. There were halfhearted efforts by some airlines. Eventually federal regulation made the procedures mandatory.

There were some procedures for screening passengers, by reference to "behavior profiles" of real and potential hijackers. It was apparently left to busy passenger agents, on their own responsibility and with no very clear system of penalties for either kind of mistake—overzealous and heavy-handed screening or laxity or laziness—to enforce or even to legitimize the procedure. Little or nothing was done about airport security or the design of aircraft or of loading facilities. Nothing noticeable was done about aircraft operating procedures, personnel selection, or restrictions on passenger seating and behavior in relation to hijacking.

The point in rehearsing this unimpressive history of efforts to cope with the danger of hijacking is not to disparage what the airlines did, to give them low marks for responsibility, or to complain that solvable problems went unsolved. The point is rather to observe how difficult it may be to identify social responsibility.

In the first place, it was not clear just where primary responsibility rested. The matter involved criminal behavior and airline safety. While the federal government fumbled its own policies and failed to specify clearly where responsibility lay, an airline executive could only have been bewildered about even what responsibility would be allowed him if he were to assume it. It was by no means evident how jurisdiction was divided among agencies of the federal government or between levels of government.

Second, many of the measures that airlines might have considered depended largely on collective action, perhaps uniform arrangements common to all airlines. It may not have been clear how far the CAB (Civil Aeronautics Board) or the Antitrust Division of the Department of Justice would have let them go. And many changes in operating procedures would have required the active cooperation of air-terminal facilities, which for the most part the airlines neither own nor control.

In the third place, it is not altogether clear toward whom the airlines ought to feel responsible or whose interest the airlines should responsibly try to serve. Airline managers can feel responsible for the safety of their firm's own passengers, or for all passengers on all airlines, or more generally for helping to prevent an epidemic of violence. They could have a sense of obligation not to use ethnic data in the screening and selective search or interrogation of passengers. They could feel responsible for protecting passengers from illegal or improper search and seizure. Responsibility for the safety of employees is still another consideration, as well as a responsibility not to waste the stockholders' resources.

If a senior executive of an airline had resolved, as many of them may have done for all I know, to be guided by his sense of social responsibility on all matters relating to hijacking, it is not clear what he would have done. A responsible objective could have been to avoid unduly alarming passengers, to avoid making a dramatic and enticing game out of efforts to thwart hijackers, to avoid burdening passengers or crew with any sense of obligation to risk their lives in heroics, and of course to avoid any behavior that would so exaggerate the hazards of flying as to impair airline travel seriously, at high cost to passengers and stockholders alike.

Just as banks may be wise, individually and collectively, and responsible as well, not to do anything drastic to counter the threat of bank robbery, maybe the airlines were wise to keep their response to the hijacking threat within bounds. But there is no dearth of alternative hypotheses to explain the haphazard, desultory, and indecisive small efforts that punctuated the basic trend of nonresponse, nor any sign that the airlines responded as they did out of wisdom and self-discipline, forgoing the competitive public relations of individual action in the interest of a calm, collectively "low profile" treatment of the problem.

And if a case can be made that the social responsibilities of the airlines with respect to the hijacking problem are enormously complex and fraught with potential conflict, it should also be kept in mind that these are not naive little suburban taxi companies but large corporations engaged in high-technology interstate commerce, a line of business that from the outset was beset by dramatic hazards to life and property. If any business in America should be able to cope with the prospect of armed, possibly crazed men and women taking customers hostage in a risky and unstable environment, it ought to be the airlines. A small soup company may not know how to cope with botulism, but one might expect the major airlines to rise to the occasion when a new hazard confronts them.

But even more, one might expect the federal government to rise to the occasion. In a matter involving airline safety, criminal activity under federal jurisdiction, and possibly airline costs and rate schedules, there is a presumption that the social responsibilities of the airline companies would be defined for them by some cognizant federal agency. At least, the auspices existed under which the airlines might have come together to arrive at collective policies and uniform practices.

One cannot easily make a case of *irresponsibility* against the airlines. What we have instead is simply a *lack* of any commanding sense of *responsibility,* of any initiative toward assumption of responsibility, of any leadership or collective action inspired by social responsibility. The lack seemed even more conspicuous on the part of federal agencies than on the part of private airlines. One of the differences between irresponsibility and lack of responsibility may be that conscience or legal liability can help to safeguard against the former, but some real initiative is required to overcome the latter. The diagnosis involves the organizational basis for behavior, not merely the private consciences of people. The discouragement of wrongdoing is different from the stimulation of something right.

Immanence or Assignment

There are two quite different notions of responsibility. One is like the doctrine of immanence: the responsibility is there. Duty exists. It ought to be perceived and acted on by the responsible agent. It reflects some natural notion of justice, obligation, or legitimate expectation.

The other is that responsibility is something to be assigned or created or invented.

In matters of morality and conscience one typically assumes that responsibility is not manipulable. It exists and is to be recognized. But there is also the notion that responsibility is an assignable or allocable obligation, that the responsible persons or entities are the ones to whom responsibility has been delegated or imputed or otherwise affixed. Within an organization the assignment of responsibility—deciding who is supposed to look out for something, to be blamed or credited, to have the power of decision or to be morally cognizant of a decision—is part of skillful management. Judicial decisions often reflect the conflict between identifying, for retrospective justice, where responsibility naturally inheres and calculating, as a matter of policy, where responsibility can best be placed to be effective.[8] *Legislative* cognizance of a problem usually has to do with where responsibility can most efficaciously be assigned.

The question arises with, say, accidents resulting from defective auto parts. If the problem is simply to do justice, once an accident has occurred, there is a retrospective interest in who really failed to meet traditional expectations. Somebody was at fault, and the problem is to decide who. But prospectively the situation is different. Prospectively, we usually want to assign responsibility in an effective way. We want to decide

8. This seems to be the heart of the matter discussed by Richard A. Wasserstrom in *The Judicial Decision: Toward a Theory of Legal Justification* (Stanford University Press, 1961), especially Chap. 7, pp. 138–71.

who is in a position to know what is defective and what to do about it. If we are concerned only about somebody who has already died because of a defective tie rod connecting the steering mechanism to the wheels, we have a very different problem from deciding where, in the future, we want to affix responsibility so that somebody knows that, if there is a fatal accident, he is going to be liable for damages.

There is usually some leeway. We can put somebody on notice that he is responsible and induce a legally enforceable sense of responsibility. We can tell the restaurateur that, if somebody dies of food poisoning, he's liable. Or we can tell the meat wholesaler that, if anybody dies of food poisoning after dining at a restaurant, the immediate source of the meat is responsible. Or we can tell the customer that he's supposed to learn how to tell healthy from unhealthy meat. Sometimes it is more important just to identify the responsibility than to identify it in the technically most accurate way; what matters is that the responsible person know that he is responsible. Other times it is important to see that legal responsibility be sensitively placed where it can be responded to. We could decide that whoever last lubricated the automobile is responsible for failing to notice a defect; whether or not this is a smart way to assign responsibility is an empirical question. Is the person who lubricates the car in the best position to respond to incentives, to process information, to spot the defect and warn the motorist? Or is it the firm that assembled the car? Or the producer of the defective part?[9]

To sum up, the question of the social responsibility of business is sometimes the question of who is or was responsible, legally or morally, as though responsibility was immanent in the situation. For policy making, however, the question becomes that of assigning or identifying responsibility at the socially expedient point, so that cognizant parties are able and motivated to act responsibly.

Business as an Agent of Government

Most discussion of the social responsibility of business is really about *irresponsibility*—how to redress it, penalize it, inoculate against it, com-

9. The work of Guido Calabresi is among the most lucid on this subject. See, for example, "Does the Fault System Optimally Control Primary Accident Costs?" *Law and Contemporary Problems,* Vol. 33 (Summer 1968), pp. 429–63. E. J. Mishan and Roland McKean have emphasized the same issues.

pensate for it, or otherwise overcome it. We discuss pollution, equal opportunity employment, safety on the job and nonhazardous consumption goods, the need to internalize costs and benefits that are already "there" but external to the firm's accounting, and occasionally, going a little further, landscaping the buildings or helping to support a museum. When we look for more positive contributions, like developing a better contraceptive or a better washing machine or a substitute for having to make beds every morning, we have in mind business as a system, it not being the responsibility of any particular firm to accomplish what we would like at least one of them to achieve. But there are some matters of social policy that go beyond the normal business of the firm, beyond the ordinary responsibility that goes with being in business. They involve the business firm as an *agent* of social policy or social reform.

To make clear what I have in mind, let me use the analogy of the school system. Public schools are nominally supposed to teach children certain intellectual and manual arts and skills and sciences, to make them better able to earn a living, to get along in the world, to meet the obligations of citizenship. Schooling is also expected to civilize them by teaching them to sit still, to be punctual, and to get along in a group. Schools often go further and try to teach children how to dress and to cut their hair, to teach them personal hygiene or the evils of tobacco and other stimulants, and sometimes how to pay their respects to God and country.

Most schools go further still and provide sports and contests. They often provide skin tests for tuberculosis, eye tests and hearing tests, and some inoculations. Some schools aim to improve the diet with hot lunches and fresh milk. Some try to teach children how to save money, through arrangements with local savings banks. Schools organize social activities and a variety of clubs and hobbies, to keep children off the streets, to separate the boys from the girls or to mix the boys with the girls, sometimes to make up deficiencies in the local community.

Which among these activities are the central purposes and which have been added on because school is where a child is conveniently captive for several hours five days a week and therefore a convenient place to give him his shots or to teach him how to clean his teeth? If the age groupings were just a little different, schools might become the locus of registration for voting, the draft, and social security cards.

Just as it's hard to draw the line between activities central to schooling and those added for social convenience, it is difficult to draw the line in business. But the effort can sensitize us to this kind of activity, making us alert both to opportunities and to possible dangers.

Let me cite a few activities in which business appears to be used as a *social instrument*—as a convenient organizational setting for getting things done that might otherwise be done elsewhere. An example is the withholding of income tax. Unlike an excise or sales tax, which is a tax on business activity, the withholding of income represents a drafting of the firm into the service of the Treasury. True, the income originates within the business; and one might construe the whole thing as the firm's rendering to Caesar what is Caesar's before turning the residue over to the employee as take-home pay. But a more practical interpretation is that the business firm can cheaply, conveniently, and reliably take care of the employees' periodic tax installments and is in a good position to police them on behalf of the Internal Revenue Service. (The employer could instead send periodic wage statements to the IRS, which could monitor the taxpayer directly: it would take more postage stamps.)

As a second example, there is a policy consensus that working people ought to put something aside for retirement. The organizations that employ people have been identified as the "chosen instruments" to make this easy, or even mandatory. (It is slightly reminiscent of savings bank day when I was in sixth grade.) Just as we could pay our income tax installments by ourselves, we could save money on our own for our retirement years; if we didn't trust ourselves, we could do as the Christmas savings people do and buy annuities as we went along. But for most people it makes sense to relate the amount saved for retirement to the amount currently earned; a simple withholding formula at the source of the income takes care of it, and there are administrative savings in letting the employer do the paper work. It is furthermore easier to have statutory safeguards if retirement plans are managed through large organizations, like the firms that hire many of us.

"Affirmative action programs" in the hiring and promotion of women and minorities are another example of business used as a social instrument. The responsibility of the firm might plausibly be construed as the absence of adverse discrimination and a little bending backward to avoid inadvertent discrimination. Going beyond that, to deliberately giving advantage to groups that are universally disadvantaged, to help solve a universal problem, is a social program using the firm as a social instrument. The conscious activity in making arrangements to give special attention to the disadvantaged, to avoid practices that *could* discriminate whether or not in fact they do, to avoid language that might offend, and so forth has and is probably intended to have an educational effect on people within the business, an effect that will carry over outside working hours and that may affect, and is intended to affect, customs, speech, and self-consciousness, in a manner not altogether different from what is attempted in the schools.

Health is another field in which business firms for adults, like schools for younger people, are uniquely convenient agents. I have in mind not programs oriented toward occupational hazards (such as are found in coal mines or factories that use radioactive materials) but the promotion of general health care, physical exams, tuberculosis tests, screening for heart disease, tests of eyesight and hearing, and programs to encourage the drinking of milk or the avoidance of alcohol. The Nixon administration proposed, in the Comprehensive Health Insurance Act of 1974, that employers be required to offer employees a private health insurance plan with comprehensive benefits (including eye examinations for children under thirteen).[10] The plan would make the employing firm the chosen instrument for medical and hospital coverage, as it already is for retirement but without quite the same rationale.

A related development that could arise through governmental pressure or through the demands of employees or customers is the discouragement of smoking. Airlines reintroduced the no smoking sections, and I think I detect a slight increase in the frequency of signs requesting that for the comfort of others and the health of everybody tobacco not be smoked. It is not out of the question that an emergency program for flu inoculation or the treatment of venereal disease would take advantage of the fact that most people have a regular place of work where they can be located and identified, that many work in places large enough to enjoy economies of scale in examination or administration of vaccine, and that business firms might be prevailed on to encourage or slightly to coerce their employees and to make time and space available.

Other possibilities are more controversial. Encouragement of patriotism and worship can go beyond good taste or the civil liberties of

10. U.S. Social Security Administration, "National Health Insurance Proposals: Provisions of Bills Introduced in the 93rd Congress as of February 1974" (1974; processed), pp. 3–4.

employees and customers (though I have not come across any objection to the chapels located in air terminals). Testing urinals for narcotics, educating people in the recognition of drug addicts or enemy agents, and coercing dress and hair styles would surely meet with objection.[11] (The banning by some states of bare feet in retail establishments probably has more than a public health motivation.) Unions and customer boycotts, not merely state, municipal, and federal programs, can sometimes be the motivating force.

Business is already expected to participate to some small extent in encouraging people to vote and in making it convenient for them to do so. More could be done, if it were thought appropriate, in connection with voter registration. Income tax advice is available in many business organizations; time off for daily prayer is a little more controversial.

In the United States it is probably nonbusiness organizations that engage most conspicuously, most self-consciously, and most paternalistically in social programs. The armed forces, the Job Corps, and some prisons are examples. In other countries, especially underdeveloped countries, literacy, public health, and family planning have been encouraged or organized through the place of employment.

In America the history of business' own efforts to encourage or coerce conformity to "accepted" social standards does not command universal admiration. *The Organization Man* was an exposé of "business responsibility" as defined by business itself.[12] Indeed, a good deal of political power has been exercised by business firms, especially in local communities, under the heading—innocent or contrived and probably some of both—of "business responsibility." Some of the most criticized practices of real estate boards come readily to mind. Indeed a history of political reform and civil liberties in America is likely to devote a chapter to the repudiation of many responsibilities that business arrogated to itself.

It is one thing to exercise an acknowledged responsibility. It is quite another to define that responsibility. And business itself is only one of the contenders for defining it.

---

11. For an attempt to advise business on a controversial social responsibility that cannot always be rationalized away as merely the employee's own private affair, see Carl D. Chambers and Richard D. Heckman, *Employee Drug Abuse: A Manager's Guide for Action* (Cahners Books, 1972).

12. William H. Whyte, Jr., *The Organization Man* (Simon and Schuster, 1956).

The Two Faces of Regulation

It is hard to escape the impression that the attitude of the airlines toward hijacking was about as zealous as the attitude of the automobile companies toward safety in the middle 1950s. There was, until the mandatory procedures of 1973, something so desultory about the inspection of briefcases and handbags, even the magnetic inspection that turned up keyrings and pocketknives, that the airlines almost appeared to be spoofing. (Pilots were concerned; but pilots have to fly.) The occasional intensive examination of passengers, with attendant congested queues and delayed departures, seemed almost intended to sabotage the campaign and to provoke passenger discontent.

Auto safety was for years apparently not "commercial" enough to feature in the advertisements. "Danger" being implied in concern over "safety," it was considered poor merchandising to call attention to the risks of motoring. Besides, focusing upon auto safety might have led to a more critical attitude on the part of car buyers toward the entire subject of auto engineering; and critical customers scrutinizing auto design were a less attractive prospect than happy motorists buying their machines uncritically.

A preoccupation with air safety must appear even more threatening, both to the airlines and to the aircraft manufacturers, because so many millions of people traditionally considered air an unstable substance on which to travel. Cocktails aloft helped, but airplane travel had an uphill struggle to eliminate the image of daring and danger.

Evidently to the airlines the greatest fear is fear itself—fear on the part of passengers. And newspaper accounts of hijacking, especially of hijacking not accompanied by violence, may inhibit flying less than the sight of pistoled, uniformed guards in the terminals and cabins.

So it may not be hard to understand why the airline companies were among the more silent of those involved. Indeed, when the question arose about who should foot the bill for protective measures, it was not immediately apparent who had the greatest interest in reducing the hazards of airline piracy. It is by no means clear that the interest is even confined to people who have any connection with flying.

Consider some alarming byproducts of ordinary commercial activity. There is the dumping of noxious substances into rivers and lakes; there is strip mining; there is the production of electric power by combustion of cheap fuels that fill the air with sulphuric acid. It appears to be typical of producers that they resist being identified with the harms that they promulgate and being saddled with compulsory efforts to clean up or to change their technology. In some cases there is a transparent motive behind their resistance: fear that they will be put out of business by an aroused populace. In some cases there may be fear that the image of their product will be contaminated by association with noxious by-products. People may come to associate potato chips with dead fish or associate the harmful effects of insecticides with the foods protected by them, even though there is no physical connection between the harms and the foods.

But suppose all the barbers in Massachusetts were threatened with a law requiring everyone to get a shampoo with his haircut. Suppose all the building contractors in California were required by law to put external fire escapes on new three-story houses. How would we expect the barbers and the contractors to react?

The answer is not easy. It is not easy to guess; and it may not be easy for them to decide. The consequences depend on the elasticity of demand for the product, on the vertical integration of the industry, and on traditional pricing. Mandatory shampoos may so raise the price of haircuts that barbershop business declines, or it may double the activity of shops that install sinks and get $5 per customer.[13] Surely a law requiring everybody to get his hair regularly trimmed would not be viewed as an onerous interference in the barbering trade. Regulations on the sulphur content of fuels used in electric power production might be welcome or not to the power industry, according to whether the industry were so integrated that expensive production of fuels was internal to the industry.

Why did the automobile manufacturers not lobby for expensive anti-pollution devices on automobiles? Why—to go further—were the auto companies not demanding, in the early 1970s, abolition of the internal combustion engine by the year 1980?

I am not now raising a question of responsibility. I am trying only, in an area related to "responsibility," to get at the question of what business motivation ought to be expected to be. One of the phrases that has been popularized in the last decade is "built-in obsolescence." It is alleged that automobile companies and companies that produce television

13. This number is projected from prices in May 1974.

sets or electric freezers like to see this year's product become unacceptable to consumers next year or the year after. What could more reliably promise "built-in obsolescence" than a federal law prohibiting internal combustion engines in automobiles after the year 1980?

Several hypotheses come to mind. One relates to the *elasticity of demand*. Just as painters may not benefit from a law restricting the width of brushes, nor barbers from a law requiring shampoos, people may not only buy fewer automobiles but spend less money altogether on automobiles if the cost of cars increases. The auto companies may worry that demand is price elastic and that mandatory cost increases will lead to a reduced dollar volume.

A second hypothesis relates to the *vertical integration* of the industry. If the law requires that all cars be equipped with something not produced by the firms that produce cars, the industry that produces the item will be delighted but the auto producers will not. A law that required everybody who got a haircut to buy a bottle of shampoo at the nearest drugstore would raise the total cost of haircuts and do the barbershops no good; a law that required the internal fumigation of all houses painted on the outside would not help the painters unless they were simultaneously fumigators. Mandatory safety glass is most interesting to auto manufacturers if they produce glass.

A third possibility is that traditional firms fear the *entry* of new firms. If it were assured that external combustion engines could be produced only by Ford, General Motors, Chrysler, and American Motors and that cars would forever be produced by the firms that produce them now, mandatory obsolescence of the internal combustion engine might appear a splendid way of getting fifty million cars off the road in the near future. But suppose the ultimate technology of an external combustion engine (or of other alternatives to the internal combustion engine) is so different that it isn't clear whether producers of sewing machines or submarines are likely to get into the business. Then it will not be obvious to the auto manufacturers that they benefit from a technology that opens up the industry to new entrants.

I haven't the answer. There is even a fourth interesting possibility. It is that the auto manufacturers haven't learned to think like painters and barbers and building contractors. They may be unaware that cost-increasing regulations are often good for the business.

Of course there is a strong sentiment against antibusiness regulation. There may be great apprehension, not always unjustified, that, when government intrudes into a field of production, it bodes ill for the companies intruded on. This attitude may not have much to do with profits: people don't like, or pretend not to like, being told what to do. One is provoked to wonder, nevertheless, whether government regulation is quite as menacing as it is seen to be.

There is growing recognition that firms may acquiesce in standards that penalize them no more than their competitors. A "responsible" firm can wish to comply with some social standards but refuse to adopt them unilaterally while its competitors ignore them. My suggestion here is that the standards, once adopted by all, may not even turn out to be onerous. Often measures that perforce increase business costs (or internalize costs) turn out to be neutral or even beneficial in relation to business profits.

The False Dichotomy of Voluntarism and Coercion

The question is sometimes posed where the line should be drawn between reliance on the voluntary assumption of responsibility by business and the coercion of "responsible" performance by government sanctions. So many techniques, instruments, and philosophies exist beyond or in addition to these two rather pure forms that that may be a poor way of posing a choice.

Posing the question in terms of drawing a line suggests gratuitously that what is needed is something business firms "ought" to have done voluntarily but did not, so that coercion is both corrective and punitive. It may also suggest, inadvertently and often wrongly, that business firms prefer (or naturally should prefer) public reliance on their voluntary assumption of responsibility and that coercion is what they always and naturally wish to avoid.

Taking off from that last point, an interesting alternative approach is that of permitting businesses *to coerce themselves*. "Mutual coercion, mutually agreed on," a term recently publicized by Garrett Hardin in connection with population policy, could appeal to firms that are prepared to incur costs but only on condition that competitors do also. The coercion could take the form of the government's responding to a plea to enforce a mandatory regulation. Alternatively, the government might allow, in the public interest, a voluntary contractual arrangement that would otherwise run afoul of the antitrust laws. As still another arrangement for the same purpose, there could be legislation that would make mandatory the application to all firms in an industry of an agreement that had been ratified by some substantial number; retail price maintenance in some states may be a near example.[14]

Sometimes what business may need is an ability to *concert on a uniform practice* or simply the information by which they could coordinate their activities. Heterogeneous phonograph speeds may not have been a sufficient nuisance to consumers to arouse a demand for regulatory action, but bumper heights are a different matter. The sheer power of suggestion could become almost "coercive" on domestic automobile manufacturers if a simple, identifiable, easily remembered standard could be impressed on consumers and insurance companies. The primary enforcement of daylight saving is merely the publicized announcement of the date for setting clocks forward or backward and everybody's expectation that, if they don't participate, they'll only confuse themselves and their friends.

Another alternative to the voluntarism-coercion dichotomy (one much discussed recently in the professional economics literature) is the *relocation of legal obligations.* Property rights and liabilities for damage are important ways of dealing with externalities. No-fault insurance is a current, dramatic example.

Still another approach is *leadership in the public sector.* In addition to setting an example, government purchasing power can often overcome the overhead costs of, say, redesign of a product; and government contracting has long been used as a way of enforcing, with at least some success, certain hiring practices. The government may reach an industry indirectly through its powers of regulation over suppliers to that industry. Both these techniques have affected automobile design: seat belts, direction signals, and bumper standards can be influenced by requiring police cars and other government vehicles, and taxis, to meet the new

14. Henry C. Wallich and John J. McGowan make an interesting point in their section on "Stockholder Interest and the Corporation's Role in Social Policy," in *A New Rationale for Corporate Social Policy,* CED Supplementary Paper No. 31 (New York: Committee for Economic Development, 1970), pp. 39–59. It is that many costs and benefits external to a firm are substantially internalized by stockholders, who are simultaneously stockholders in other corporations that suffer the costs or enjoy the benefits. An example is training on the job, the benefits of which may be lost to the firm when an employee switches to another firm; but if the firms are similarly represented in a stockholder's portfolio, the benefits remain internal to the portfolio. The principle applies equally to collusion on prices or lobbying against the public interest and does not mean that stockholder interests in general coincide with everybody else's. But for good or ill, for responsibility or for irresponsibility, the point can be important. In particular it may be a powerful argument

standards. (Now that legislation protecting pension plans has been enacted, the federal government can help reform retirement practices in private business by remodeling its own practices to set the example.)

Changing the rules of the game has been another important way that government has redefined and restructured the responsibility of business. The National Labor Relations Act is an example. Both legislatively and through the courts a similar shift of bargaining advantage may occur, or may now be occurring, with respect to multiple-tenant landlords.

Schemes that operate in the market can have an element both of the voluntary and of the coercive. A tax that is discretionary rather than prohibitive is a flexible kind of coercion. Subsidies are much the same, though harsh words like "coercion" are typically not used when the firm is, on balance, a beneficiary and not a victim. Tax relief and cost-sharing arrangements are somewhat less "coercive" than straightforward regulation.

Similarly, government-financed research and development and government provision of goods and services (not necessarily "public goods" in the economist's jargon) offer a way of bypassing the coercion-voluntarism issue.

Thus the coercive and the voluntary are not exhaustive alternatives. They are not even opposite ends of a scale, since many techniques have little to do with either category.

The Marketplace Is No Excuse

It is sometimes argued, by economists as well as by businessmen accused of neglecting the public interest, that the business of business is just business. A firm is expected to compete for the consumer's dollar by ruthlessly cutting costs and single-mindedly attending to what the consumer will buy. When the firm tries to do some conscionable thing like planting trees or suppressing noise or designing automobiles that meet aesthetic standards that the car buyer is not interested in, the result is higher prices or lower wages or the squandering of potential dividends on things that, though usually harmless and often quite good, merely

---

rationalizing, if not quite justifying, "enlightened" voting by institutional investors. This is merely the brighter side of the story about "interlocking directorates" and other modes of concentration. It is one that may have been too little recognized and exploited.

represent some executive's notion of what he'd appreciate if he were the public, or what he'd like to be remembered for. Even the beneficiaries would usually be better off with a lesser amount of cash instead of "public goods" paternalistically provided.

The individual proprietor, of course, is free to spend his money as he pleases. If he wants to provide for his customers a higher-quality product than they'd be willing to spend their own money on, or play music for his employees, or subsidize some group by hiring them at wages they cannot earn, at least it's his own money he's spending, and only the Internal Revenue Service need wring its hands at the potential waste. But when the semiautonomous managers of a large, publicly owned corporation choose to invest in good works, so the argument goes, they are not only spending somebody else's money but indulging their personal whims in the process.

This argument, which begins by making fun, perhaps properly, of what businesses may actually accomplish when they try to do good, can easily be pushed to the point of proposing that all is fair in business and that a sufficient excuse for ruthlessness in competitive business is that the marketplace demands it. According to the hard line, if the firm that cuts corners didn't cut corners, it would lose ground to its competition and possibly become extinct. Business is business, and the fittest survive. Just as governments are often alleged to have a higher obligation to national survival than to any virtuous aspirations of the electorate, and just as the Constitution appears to many not to countenance philanthropy at the expense of some national interest, the corporation is expected to follow what people sometimes call the law of the jungle.

This view unduly depreciates the law of the jungle. Konrad Lorenz, in his widely read book *On Aggression* (Harcourt, Brace and World, 1966), gave numerous illustrations of how biological evolution reflects the survival needs of the species as well as of the individual. Time and again, modes of behavior are suppressed that, though advantageous for the individual, would be inefficacious for the larger community. The nervous system of the adult wolf makes it incapable of attacking the cub. If this restraint were not built into the wolf's nervous system, the adult wolf itself would never have survived as an infant, nor would its parents have survived to give it birth. The law of the jungle contains its own commandments. Without them, without nature's restraints, the species does not flourish. Lawlessness is not the way of the jungle.

A second difficulty with the notion that business should merely maximize profits no matter what is that it conflicts with what we expect of ordinary people. We would condemn doctors who promoted disease in the interest of selling their services more dearly. We don't expect the motorist with a disabled car to have to pay $10 to get a passing motorist to phone for help. We disparage the repairman who installs an expensive replacement part that the ignorant consumer doesn't need, and we disparage him because, if we were repairmen, we wouldn't want our children to know we did that. Some personal morality is an enormous social asset. It helps to keep us all from getting small personal advantage at large expense to each other, with a net loss all around. Trust and honesty are of great social worth. Konrad Lorenz may have had it backward when he characterized animal restraint as "behavioral analogies to morality" (p. 109): maybe our human morality is a necessary substitute for those instinctual commandments that beasts of the jungle are neurologically incapable of violating.

The question is whether the modern business corporation has to be thought of as a solvent within which personal morality becomes unstuck. Should human decency be considered incapable of surviving the sterile atmosphere of the business firm? Can we not demand of a large corporation—or, if not demand, wish for—the same decency that we think we have a right to expect from our paper boy?

It is asking too much to expect the profit-motivated pharmaceutical firm to share the ethics of our family physician. But we are not surprised when an ordinary person sacrifices earnings to do the decent thing. Individual people are allowed to be as sentimental as they please toward fellow human beings. If they combine to form a corporation, must they be denied the same sentimentality? May they not be encouraged, at least, to forgo profits, consciously and openly, in the interest of behaving, as a firm, the way they would all wish to behave as individuals? Shouldn't it be considered merely the decent thing for a firm to go to the wall competitively, perhaps to succumb and go out of business, rather than violate the spirit of the law or take deceitful advantage of somebody's ignorance?

The difficulty is one of diffusion of responsibility. Decisions are made by a multiplicity of individuals in a large organization. Ultimate liability is to a multiplicity of owners, stockholders who are unknown and unknowable. The sheer organizational process seems to be inhospitable to the softer sentiments that we appreciate so much in individuals or small organizations.

There is no sense in expecting a large organization—the organization itself, as distinct from the people within it—to have the corporate self-respect that we hope for in a person. An organization is not a person, and it will have neither the same strengths nor the same weaknesses. But maybe we could expect people in organizations to continue to be people, even though they are executives of large firms. Maybe the guideline for executives who want advice on what their social responsibilities are or ought to be might as a rough approximation be just to be themselves. The standard to which they should hold the organization is the standard they would set for themselves if they were in it alone.

CHAPTER FIVE

Collective Choice

ROLAND N. McKEAN

IT IS MADE abundantly clear in other chapters of this volume that the phrase "social responsibilities" has several possible meanings.[1] Here I will use the term to mean taking actions that affect *others* in ways generally regarded as desirable. In some instances, decisions by just a few businessmen have direct repercussions on other persons. In other instances, little decisions by millions of individuals have powerful indirect or "Rube Goldberg" repercussions on everyone (including themselves). Often the impacts are undesirable, and changing the decisions might have beneficial impacts on others.[2] For example, as firms and households expand their use of internal combustion engines and electricity, they inflict noise, air pollution, ocean pollution, and health hazards on all of us without anyone deliberately choosing those consequences. Many persons may feel that it would be desirable for firms as well as households to behave differently—to take into account such impacts on other persons and be more responsible toward others.

In connection with the behavior of business firms, collective choices affect, and are sometimes influenced by, managerial decisions. By collective choices I mean those that are made for the group, that cannot usually be made by any one person acting alone, and that affect many members of the society. First of all, there is the official mechanism for collective choice: government. Actions by government help shape businessmen's decisions, affecting their ability to take various steps. To in-

1. See especially Chapter 4 by Thomas C. Schelling and Chapter 2 by James W. McKie. I will henceforth refrain from putting quotation marks around this phrase, but the reader should keep in mind that others may attach different meanings to it.
2. For some of the thoughts expressed here, I have drawn on related work done by me under a grant made by the National Science Foundation to the Thomas Jefferson Center Foundation—work on the implications of different configurations of resource rights.

109

quire into the social responsibilities of business while ignoring the public sector would be like asking how much cotton Minnesota can produce—while ignoring the climate. It becomes relevant to ask what kind of social-responsibility climate one can realistically expect government to provide. Furthermore, firms themselves influence the public choice process and hence this climate (which in turn affects business decisions). For example, as vividly illustrated in 1972, corporations try to buy political protection or influence when the latter are offered for sale.

Second, there is a crucial *unofficial* process of collective choice—the formation and maintenance of ethical codes—that affects both government and business decisions and is in turn affected by those decisions. Moral and behavioral codes are not "passed" by any formal legislative body and are not directly enforced by policemen and courts. Yet they are much like laws and affect us all through group choices that cannot be determined by any individual or business firm acting alone.

What are some of the factors shaping ethical and behavioral codes? In his particular milieu, what should the businessman do?

In an effort to shed light on these matters, I shall in this chapter explore (a) the "free rider" problem as vitally important background for collective choice, (b) the theory of government choice, as well as realistic expectations about governmental behavior, (c) the economics of ethical codes, as well as realistic expectations about conformity to such codes. Then, in view of the outlook for these collective choices, I shall examine what businessmen should do about social responsibilities. In investigating such issues, no one can come up with a fully satisfying analysis; the "realistic expectations" will inevitably be imprecise generalities, and the actions suggested will sound like the Cub Scout motto: Do your best. Nonetheless, just trying to examine these topics systematically may yield a better appreciation of the difficulties besetting group choice and a sounder basis for individual judgments and decisions.

Background for Collective Choice: The Free Rider Problem

Before examining either governmental behavior or ethical codes we should look at a basic reason for having institutions affecting the whole group. In looking at that question, we will learn why to expect failures there as well as market failures. The basic reason for having both government and behavioral codes is the "free rider" problem. Many other variables obviously affect the specific choices made, but the phenomenon of the free rider is a fundamental condition shaping the process of collective choice.[3] People value numerous things, such as lighthouses or air pollution abatement, which, if produced at all, cannot economically be denied to nonpayers. In economics such outputs are called "public goods that cannot be privately produced." With respect to these goods, people can if they wish have a free ride, since they face the same outcome whether or not they make any payment or sacrifice.[4] It would be difficult, for example, to single out nonpayers and prevent them from enjoying whatever air pollution abatement or lighthouse beams were produced.

Goods which cannot be withheld from people who do not pay are unlikely to be produced by business. To be sure, some quantities of such items—listener-supported radio programs, for instance—can be financed by voluntary contributions. Also, certain public goods, discussed below, can be financed through ethical rules inducing people to contribute out of a sense of duty. Moreover, in some instances, limited quantities can be financed by tie-ins between the public good and marketable products; pharmaceutical houses undertake some basic research, because the benefits that no one can be excluded from consuming are sometimes tied in with capturable gains. For the most part, however, private cost-covering enterprises cannot be expected to turn out such goods.

It is vital that we recognize how pervasive this public goods problem is. It arises in connection with a host of important "products"—not merely in connection with defense, the beams of a lighthouse, and listener-supported radio. Consider an atmosphere of law and order. Private entrepreneurs would find it profitable to sell some guard and police services, and individuals would voluntarily finance a certain amount of policing, but it is too difficult to exclude the nonpayer from, and charge prices for, many benefits of a general atmosphere of security. An air of justice, greater cohesiveness or consensus, a degree of monetary stability, the expectation of contract enforcement, the promotion of free entry and

3. Though he never uses the term "free rider," Mancur Olson, Jr., has written an entire book—an excellent, highly significant volume—about this motivation. Olson, *The Logic of Collective Action: Public Goods and the Theory of Groups* (rev. ed., Harvard University Press, 1971).

4. The hallmark of the "pure public good" is the fact that its services can be provided to an extra consumer at zero extra cost. But the "public good that cannot be privately produced" is one whose benefits cannot economically be denied to particular individuals who do not pay.

competition—at least some benefits of these "products" would accrue to most persons whether or not they "bought their tickets." As a consequence, firms cannot sell tickets to these extra benefits so as to finance large-scale production of such items. As for each individual trying to create law and order or a general atmosphere of justice, each correctly views his input as a drop in the bucket and therefore anticipates the same benefits whether or not he exerts effort or otherwise contributes. In other words, each person is a free rider with respect to the production of all but small quantities of these "products."

For our purposes here, however, the significant thing is that many less obvious items have this public characteristic. Consider abatement of congestion, noise, distrust, racial discrimination, fossil-fuel consumption, or social unrest. Or even things like reducing rapid technological and cultural change, as might be desired by many citizens. If one values these abatements, trying to produce them individually is like *not* standing on tiptoe at a parade. Why should one sacrifice his effort, money, convenience, or view of the parade, when the benefits to himself (and indeed to others) are not noticeably increased?

There is one slight difference between this kind of abatement of an undesirable "product" or condition and the pure public good. My contribution to finance a public good like a lighthouse that someone else produces makes no difference in the benefits, whereas my contribution to air-pollution abatement (e.g., by reducing *my* automobile travel) makes an infinitesimal difference in the benefits. But the hallmark of public goods that cannot be privately produced remains: the noncontributor faces essentially the same situation as the contributor. As Olson stresses, the crux of the matter is that an individual can have no perceptible effect on the production of such goods.[5]

Most outputs that we label social responsibilities are public goods like those discussed. That is why I have placed so much emphasis on the free rider problem. This phenomenon makes us turn, for these forms of social benefits, to collective choice—to government action that will produce public goods, to formal regulations that will modify the social-responsibility climate, and to informal behavioral codes that may alter that climate. Unfortunately, we will find that the free rider difficulty may plague collective choice, through either government or ethical rules, as much as it handicaps market production.

5. Olson, *The Logic of Collective Action*, p. 64.

Theory of Government Choice and Realistic Expectations about Government Behavior

When people turn to government, or when businessmen make decisions in the light of the government's functioning, they need to have some feeling about what to expect. One should not naively assume that government will automatically behave in accordance with one's own concept of the "public interest." Even though systematic thought about public-choice processes may not carry us far, let us see what a few theorists have said about government behavior.

Governments, like business firms, consist of individuals who make choices and take actions. What forces shape these choices, and what predictions, if any, can be made about them? With respect to firms, economists' abstract representations of the real world seem to yield useful predictions. For example, most models predict that firms will shift resources into an industry if the demand for its product rises (other things remaining the same); they predict that firms will employ an input, such as a river (for waste disposal), as long as the gain exceeds the extra cost to the firm. With respect to government, what can economic theory say? By making assumptions about what government officials try to maximize and about the constraints on officials, some theorists have developed models that yield implications regarding government behavior. Naturally, the models are oversimplified representations of the public-choice process, and the predictions pertain to only a few kinds of behavior, but they offer some aid in understanding the public sector.

Voting Models

Even before we take the free rider into account, voting models imply serious shortcomings in government as a route toward socially responsible behavior. First of all, individual preferences may not be translatable into a set of preferences (a "social welfare function") that fulfills certain sensible conditions for group rationality.[6] For example, if voters try to choose between pairs of policies, it may turn out that A is preferred to B, B is preferred to C, yet C is preferred to A. Second, voting outcomes inevitably neglect the preferences of, or impacts on, many groups. For

6. Kenneth J. Arrow, *Social Choice and Individual Values* (Wiley, 1951; 2d ed., Cowles Foundation for Research in Economics at Yale University, 1963).

example, simple majority voting would result, for certain kinds of decision, in approving the demands of the "median voter."[7] If voters were ranked according to how much they wanted to spend on a program and if this middle voter wished to spend a million dollars, half the others would vote against spending less and half would vote against spending more. Hence the amount with the most support would be one million dollars. If such a public good is provided in one lump, voters other than this middle voter cannot buy the size or design they prefer (as they might buy the size or design of shoes they prefer). Also, many actions approved by the majority will have sharply adverse consequences for minorities, "spillover" impacts that the majority may not have worried about.

Government actions based on votes may yield the best attainable outcome. Many public imperfections, like many attributed to the private sector, are shortcomings in comparison with a hypothetical ideal. Nonetheless, these shortcomings help explain why government will at best be a frustrating affair, yield numerous "irresponsible" impacts on subsets of citizens, and provide a less-than-ideal climate for promoting social responsibility by business.

When we add to these voting models the complications caused by the free rider phenomenon, the prospects become still less encouraging. Consider the voter. As Anthony Downs has stressed, any *individual* voter's efforts to inform himself, vote, or write his congressman will have little or no impact on an election, on other voters' decisions, or on the governmental process.[8] Like other public goods, the same government is available to the average individual regardless of the sacrifices (e.g., monitoring efforts) that he might make. Why then should he incur information, decision-making, and monitoring costs in a futile effort to influence outcomes?[9] What citizens *will* find it economical to do is to (a) act when the stakes for them individually are relatively high—e.g., when they are members of producer groups such as land owners in an irrigable area or

7. James M. Buchanan, *Public Finance in Democratic Process: Fiscal Institutions and Individual Choice* (University of North Carolina Press, 1967), pp. 144–59. For several basic contributions to the theory of public choice, see James M. Buchanan and Gordon Tullock, *The Calculus of Consent: Logical Foundations of Constitutional Democracy* (University of Michigan Press, 1962).

8. Downs, "An Economic Theory of Political Action in a Democracy," *Journal of Political Economy*, Vol. 65 (April 1957), pp. 135–50.

9. It might be noted that ethical codes are employed to cope with this free rider situation—"It is your duty to inform yourself and vote."

sometimes when they become emotionally aroused—and (b) cut costs to themselves by acting through a lobbying organization, which is likely to represent them fairly well on some issues though poorly on many other issues. Such behavior by voters is translated into a poorly representative set of pressures on government officials. Moreover, congressmen, senators, officials, and other governmental personnel are frequently afflicted by their own free rider problems, further aggravating the tendency for government to be of the people, by a few of the people, and for some of the people.

Utility-Maximizing Models

Other models of government emphasize not the voting process but the various costs and rewards that confront personnel as they try to maximize "utility." The general idea is that anything that alters a person's abilities to capture net gains (nonpecuniary as well as pecuniary) will affect behavior: individuals, in government no less than elsewhere, will shift toward activities that become more rewarding or less costly to those individuals and away from activities that become less rewarding or more costly to them.

In government, however, the ability of officials to appropriate gains from increasing the nation's wealth or the municipality's wealth is extremely limited. No voter or politician or official can buy and sell shares or assets and capture increments in present values. No one has exclusive claim to residual annual income from wealth-increasing programs. Indeed, the rights even to use assets are assigned by the political and bureaucratic processes, and those rights of use cannot be traded freely even though trades might be mutually advantageous.

Given this rights structure, it seems unlikely that politicians will be moved to cater to individuals' wishes in quite the way business entrepreneurs do. The wealth of public officials comes through the political and bureaucratic processes—chiefly through promotions or elections (or future private-sector alternatives). Through these processes also come most nonpecuniary rewards and setbacks: changes in power, prestige, ability to do good for others, convenience, and security. Moreover, these processes involve bargaining, in which a legislator or official can sometimes exchange for reciprocal favors the benefits he generates and must often pay penalties for inflicting costs on others. Does this bargaining mechanism work out so that government personnel are rewarded after all for giving due weight to the tastes of *all* citizens? It seems unlikely that bargaining guides society with any exactness in this direction.[10] Again one of the basic obstacles is the free rider status of individual voters and legislators in so many situations. Many people's preferences and bids do not influence the bargains that are struck. Thus the bargaining process—as well as the voting process per se—leaves room for social irresponsibility.

I wish to underline the importance of this free rider problem in government. In economics it has been discussed mainly with respect to the private sector; and, as mentioned before, profit-seeking enterprises cannot be expected to produce public goods like lighthouses. What I want to stress is that many kinds of "lighthouses," and socially responsible designs of the "lighthouses," cannot be expected from government either, because no participant in the political process can exclude nonpayers, "market" the output, and capture net benefits. The free rider phenomenon sends us to government for action but then threatens the success of that action.

Though not incorporated into existing models, prevailing ethical and behavioral codes help shape behavior in the public sector. A strong sense of duty to inform ourselves and monitor government, a strict work ethic, a tradition of conscientious public service, strong widespread belief that certain practices are unethical and wrong—such codes affect public-sector performance and our ability to rely on "trust" instead of expensive monitoring arrangements. As discussed in the next section, however, the free rider difficulty constantly threatens erosion of such ethical rules. They are as vulnerable in government as in the rest of the society. Atmospheres of honesty and public service are public goods. Why should I as a public servant pull my weight if failure to do so produces no noticeable consequence? Moreover, if others are violating the work ethic, any sense of duty—about the only counterbalance to free rider status—will diminish.

Information, Monitoring, and Enforcement Costs

Another weakness in the public sector results from information costs, monitoring costs, and enforcement costs within government. The diffi-

---

10. For a more detailed consideration of some of these issues, see Roland N. McKean, "Property Rights within Government, and Devices to Increase Governmental Efficiency," *Southern Economic Journal,* Vol. 39 (October 1972), pp. 177–86.

culties underlying these costs exert decisive influences on the way public programs really turn out. The problems of acquiring information, detecting aberrant performance, and enforcing desired behavior help shape, for example, the incentives of government personnel. Such considerations are crucial and deserve more emphasis than they usually get.

These difficulties too stem in part from the free rider problem. Why should lower-level personnel provide accurate, relevant, unbiased information about program performance if no one individual's action perceptibly affects his (or the overall) benefits? The individual employee's accuracy or candor costs him inconvenience and perhaps friction with co-workers yet gains nothing. (Accurate information transmitted by all would make a big difference, yet any one person's contribution would make essentially no difference.) Or, consider monitoring subordinates' behavior or enforcing desired performance. Individually, middle-level and even top officials can rarely make a dent in the overall implementation of public programs, partly because of pervasive incentive problems. Again, therefore, *careful* supervision looks to each official like an activity that would cost him something and change nothing. The outputs of monitoring and enforcement, like the production of information, become to a considerable extent public goods. In addition, on the other side of the coin, the awesome difficulties of collecting relevant information and enforcing desired performance make it difficult for any individual in government to affect most programs, intensifying and extending the public goods character of intermediate government outputs. Thus free rider phenomena both generate part of the monitoring difficulties and are further exacerbated by those difficulties.

Because of such factors, "fine-tuning" regulation is often not as effective as the uncritical expect, and meat-axe methods may at times be preferred.[11] For example, if enforcement costs are low, one might prefer, for municipal garbage pickup, charges per pound rather than lump sum fees; but if enforcement costs for the direct approach are high, it may be economical to retreat to the "clumsier" approach. Moreover, user charges and monitoring of lower-level personnel may be less efficiently managed within government than by firms, for the reasons just discussed. If one is realistic, therefore, the "fine-tuning" techniques may be less attractive than at first glance they appear to be. It will sometimes be better to have public disposal of abandoned automobiles or spillover-

11. Regulation of the private sector is examined in detail by James Q. Wilson in Chapter 6. I wish only to emphasize monitoring difficulties as they affect *any* government program, including regulatory activities.

abatement programs instead of spillover-deterrence programs, just as it is ordinarily better to have free sidewalks instead of allocation by user charges.

We walk a tightrope, however, and should not neglect the contrasting troubles that may accompany indirect regulation. For instance, instead of trying directly to reduce the ill effects of congestion and pollution, some have urged the ham-handed approach of stopping economic growth —sacrificing many gains for the sake of retarding, to an unknown and varying extent, the undesirable side effects. It is conceivable that this would be better than directly attacking the undesired effects, but a moment's reflection suggests that this is unlikely: it would be rather like cutting the power supply of a city in order to diminish neon lighting, prostitution, and noise. To repeat, implementation difficulties influence the kind of action the government should take as well as the amount of social benefits we can anticipate. These difficulties afflicting government action generate pervasive social costs—not just a few administrative costs.

Realistic Expectations about Government

Compared with some ideals, the public sector may seem unpromising as a producer or elicitor of responsibility toward others. Along this line, the preceding discussion has emphasized the shortcomings of government choice, partly to counteract naive models of government. People often appear to think of government as some sort of half-drugged servant: if one can only get him to act, he will of course do exactly what one has in mind. Or they sometimes feel that public choices would be fine if only we had good men in office instead of accidentally having evil or incompetent officials. Without exception, though, serious effort to think systematically about the public sector suggests that there are numerous inherent shortcomings.

We should, however, strive to see things in proportion. The glass is half full as well as half empty. The nature of public choice should give pause to those who automatically think, "There ought to be a law," but it does not mean that worthwhile actions can never be expected from government. Citizens and governments do make adjustments when tastes or conditions change so that situations persistently look improvable. Suffrage and political participation have gradually been extended over the centuries, fewer modern governments throw opponents into "the

Tower," and public choices do respond to unmistakable shifts in demands for public goods (though a fundamental condition for enduring change appears to be an enduring alteration of citizens' views). Furthermore, people have at times recoiled from permissiveness and introduced Victorian rules. Thus effective rules do change. People may evolve new traditions calling for us to inform ourselves, discuss issues, search for appropriate lobbies, and serve as witnesses.

The theory of collective action does not have reassuring implications; yet it reveals some of the sources of difficulty and therefore suggests in a general way what we must adjust to and what sources of trouble might be manipulated. Also the theory has some hopeful implications. Like exchange in the private sector, bargaining and compromise in government results in an invisible hand in the public sector. It is afflicted with a distressing case of palsy but nonetheless reduces the ability of officials to inflict social costs on others and offers some rewards to officials for generating benefits for citizens. Even with the crude monitoring that occurs at present, government can be expected to produce some socially responsible outputs and, though haltingly, an environment that is in some respects conducive to responsible behavior by firms and households. And, if a heightened sense of civic duty induced more individuals to ignore their free rider status, closer monitoring of government might improve public choices considerably.

The Economics of Ethical Codes

Before we ask what businessmen should do, in view of the prospects for government choice, we should examine another way in which people make collective decisions—namely, the adoption of ethical and behavioral codes. These precepts do not come into being as suddenly and dramatically as, say, the Clean Air Act, yet they sometimes constrain behavior as powerfully as formal legislation. In Japan, the hara-kiri of the Forty-seven Ronin (a dramatic incident that occurred in 1703) and many other such episodes illustrate the power of behavioral codes.[12] Less dramatic but no less important, honesty has been sufficiently prevalent in some cultures that doors never had to be locked.

12. Will Durant, *The Story of Civilization*, Pt. 1: *Our Oriental Heritage* (Simon and Schuster, 1954), pp. 847–50.

Ethical Codes and Public Goods

Such traditions and ethical codes can be used, as formal laws can be used, to overcome free rider difficulties and produce public goods (or public "bads"). Indeed, for some items—e.g., widespread trust or friendliness—such codes are the only way to produce them or are at least an essential supplement to formal laws. For purposes of discussion, such ethical and behavioral rules are examined here purely as instruments to achieve other ends—not as ends in themselves. (Similarly, formal regulations are usually analyzed as means toward other things rather than as ends in themselves.)

Most of the desirable results of ethical codes, such as honesty among strangers, are public goods, for the same consequences are available to any one individual whether or not he makes his contribution. (In close, enduring relationships, the free rider problem is less acute. If I am untrustworthy around habitual associates, I do suffer a penalty—namely, retaliation.) Directly coercing people to be honest in all transactions—if they were always ready to cheat when they would not be punished by the law—would entail prohibitive monitoring costs. Hence communities turn to ethical codes enforced by the indoctrination of children, by religious precepts, by social pressure such as competition for approval, and in business dealings by competition for customers. Where severe nuisance or damage is attributable to violations, the threat of lawsuit is an important last-resort deterrent. Thus the collective action that appears to be economical in many instances involves, at least in part, the use of voluntary "social contracts." The accompanying sense of duty or moral obligation can introduce penalties for not doing one's part and help inhibit free rider behavior.

Ethical and behavioral rules clearly influence business behavior. Managers make, and stockholders condone, charitable contributions—partly to buy goodwill in the light of the prevailing ethic. They cannot go too far, or competitors will gain an advantage and stockholders will bid down the stock or apply pressures in other ways. As long as the prevailing ethic causes all or most competitors to engage in designated profit-sacrificing actions, however, each can afford to do it. Similarly, businessmen may in certain industries provide better working conditions or less air pollution than profit maximization would call for. In order for this to happen, however, the customary practice must be widely accepted, so as to affect all major competitors similarly, and relatively clear-cut, so that violations can be detected and punished by social pressure.

It should be emphasized that such social contracts are always vulnerable to erosion. If the supplementary enforcement mechanisms are weakened, a sense of duty, or social pressure arising from others' sense of duty, is then the only factor that offsets the free rider motivation. If just this once I don't bother to take my garbage can to the rear of the house, it won't affect the decisions of the others, and I can still depend on seeing an attractive block. Since all will tend to reason in this way, though, a number of cans may be left out "just this once." If the rule begins to erode, the probability of complete collapse soars. If on any given day one can expect to see three garbage cans left out on the block, the rule no longer provides much benefit to anyone, and in addition the sense-of-duty basis for supporting the rule is undermined. Similarly, in the business world, an accepted ethical obligation to employ more older workers or more noise-reduction techniques than was consistent with maximum profits could go to pieces rapidly if some firms broke the rule and most persons who perceived the slippage said to themselves: "Why should I complain? It just means all trouble and no gain for me personally, and in fact my complaint won't yield any gain for anyone. The situation will be the same whether I make any sacrifice or not." Unless the rule becomes virtually compulsive, producing social responsibilities in this way is precarious—like producing national defense on the basis of voluntary contributions.

Nonetheless, in the aggregate, the impact of a society's ethical and behavioral principles is great. Much of the impact is desirable. Many rules, such as "Don't cheat on unwritten contracts" or "Don't bribe government officials," may impose short-run sacrifices on many businessmen but, if nearly all adhere to the rule, yield net long-run benefits to most. Habits of trust, friendliness, neatness, fairness, generosity, and nonviolence are to some extent public goods that are produced by the observance of behavioral traditions. Some of these are extremely important to the functioning of a private enterprise economy. Social contracts about honesty can save extra burglar alarms, time clocks, monitoring devices, legal actions, hours spent checking up on each other's statements, time wasted when appointments and promises are broken, energy and good humor squandered on bitterness and reprisal, and gains from trades that would otherwise not take place. Business and households find it advantageous to save contracting costs by relying heavily on trust and on tacit, rather than written, understandings.[13] (Fortunately

13. Stewart Macaulay, "Non-contractual Relations in Business: A Preliminary Study," *American Sociological Review,* Vol. 28 (February 1963), pp. 55–67.

the statement attributed to Sam Goldwyn, "An oral promise isn't worth the paper it's written on," is not always true.) Lack of basic moral codes and mutual trust aggravates material as well as spiritual poverty. Consider the amoral community in southern Italy described by the Banfields or the primitive society of the Ik, in which parents and children are said to steal from each other.[14] In the Italian setting people had ethical codes for dealings within families but little or no trust outside the family. The Ik apparently had no ethical rules or trust within families—an even less economical system.

Needless to say, however, the results of social contracts are not always good. Traditions and behavioral tenets, like formal laws, can serve undesirable as well as desirable ends. For instance, as seen in the traditional treatment of women and blacks, behavioral codes may dispense great injury to some groups. (Strong ideologies can sometimes make even the injured believe they are being rewarded—or will be rewarded in the hereafter.) Tacitly agreed-upon conventions and customs are important "resources," capable of making life much pleasanter or less costly to nearly everyone—or vice versa. They are capable of supporting institutions like caste systems or slavery, on the one hand, or institutions like organized charity or tribal peace and trade, on the other hand.

In sum, ethical and behavioral codes constitute an important type of collective choice. The need for such rules and, at the same time, their fragility stem from the free rider problem. Such principles influence the process through which formal public choices get made and help determine the social climate in which businessmen must operate.

Realistic Expectations about Behavioral Codes

To appraise future possibilities, it may help to examine several types of rules and the conditions for their effectiveness. For a country to rely on these informal, inexpensive means of enforcement, the precepts must be widely accepted—approved by more than just a majority. As a consequence, the circumstances in which they can be effective are restricted. Some social contracts are so obviously beneficial to oneself as well as to others that no auxiliary enforcement measures are needed. For instance, it does not require policemen to keep businessmen setting their clocks on eastern time if they are in that zone. Most will keep their

14. Edward C. Banfield and L. F. Banfield, *The Moral Basis of a Backward Society* (Free Press, 1958); Colin M. Turnbull, *The Mountain People* (Simon and Schuster, 1972).

word about engagements, not because of general social pressure, but because unreliability in social or business intercourse brings direct retaliation by specific associates. Even in the short run virtually everyone can anticipate gains to himself from adhering to, or losses to himself from violating, these "contracts." In effect there is no free rider difficulty. Tacitly agreed-upon rules will arise and survive in many such situations.[15]

Other behavioral rules, such as ones forbidding "unreasonable" arm-twisting or noise-making, may yield net benefits to most persons in the long run if everyone adheres to them; yet the gains to each individual may not depend on his individual contribution.[16] In these circumstances, the free rider appears, and the behavioral codes need extra support from indoctrination, general social pressure such as frowning on violations by persons other than those directly and immediately affected, or closely related religious precepts. In the competition for personal approval, social pressures such as village or colleague ostracism can be powerful reinforcements. Similarly, in business the competition for customers' approval is an invaluable enforcer of ethical behavior, especially for recurring sales by established firms. Often, in fact, the only force it is economical to rely on is the struggle for social or client approval, which makes a degree of honesty, fulfillment of unwritten contracts, and "fair dealing" operate in the selfish interest of almost everyone.

In addition, many aspects of behavioral codes are ultimately backed up by the threat of lawsuit. If noise, cheating, violations of oral contracts, carelessness, or callousness result in serious damage to others, laws against nuisance, or liability laws, or even criminal law may come into play. (These backup forces are extremely important. Even for driving on the right side of the road and obeying traffic signals, which must be in the enlightened selfish interest of everyone, policemen are apparently a worthwhile supplementary enforcement device, helping elicit "voluntary" compliance.) Finally, if fundamentalist religion can be brought to bear, the free rider problem is solved, for the violator is unfailingly caught by God and in the event of important violations is personally threatened with eternity in hell, whether or not his own transgression is just a drop in the bucket.

What are the prospects today for employing moral and behavioral

15. Thomas C. Schelling, "On the Ecology of Micromotives," *Public Interest,* No. 25 (Fall 1971), pp. 61–98.

16. Ordinarily, as a child grows up, he learns from specific situations what is considered to be "unreasonable."

rules to expand desirable activities? Trends are hard to perceive. On the one hand, less brutal treatment of people, modern welfare programs, and perhaps more honesty in business dealings today than existed a century ago suggest that the possibilities for desirable ethical rules are expanding. On the other hand, many particular rules are eroding. (Or are values simply changing?) Guilt feelings about damaging others may be declining; and attitudes of "I'm all right, Jack," and "That's *his* problem" seem widespread. On balance, the evidence about what is happening is inconclusive.

The economics of the matter, however, suggest that certain factors always threaten the effectiveness of this form of collective choice. Whatever the trend, these factors surely make behavioral codes less promising than they would otherwise be. First, rapidly changing values, technology, and acculturation make it less clear what rules would in fact yield net social gains. In a relatively stable society, one in which technology changes slowly and people remain in one location for long periods of time, what people mean by fair play, reasonable noise levels, the Golden Rule, or civic-mindedness may become fairly clear. As the same people confront repetitions of the same events, unambiguous rules pertaining to specific situations can evolve. With accelerated change, the rules become relatively ambiguous. Thus in several ways change makes people less certain about what the social contracts are or what reciprocal benefits to anticipate. Also in these circumstances a sense of duty toward any particular code is weakened.

Second, in a mobile society one is less certain that he will have the same neighbors or colleagues for long periods of time and for that reason too is less certain that in the long run he (or others) will receive reciprocal benefits from adherence to the rules or social disapproval from violations of them. The individual's violations become less costly to him, and in any case existence of the rule becomes less valuable. Sense of duty—the principal reason for adherence—crumbles. Third, sheer growth in the number of persons in any group, other things remaining the same, aggravates the free rider problem. Fourth, if these larger numbers are concentrated in modern "automobile cities," friends are dispersed, people go from place to place in isolated metal capsules, and kinship with any particular neighborhood is reduced. Social pressures from people that one knows and concern about what the neighbors will think or say diminish.

Fifth, with the decline of old-fashioned religion, the threat of eternity in hell or even guilt feelings lose force as deterrents against free riding in connection with many behavioral codes. In part this may be good, for religion, mythology, and superstition were often employed to produce public bad, e.g., inequities and exploitation, even human sacrifice. In the future it seems less likely that these mechanisms can be used to elicit such social irresponsibilities. At the same time, however, diminished credulity regarding religion raises questions about man's future ability to maintain valuable ethical codes. The past impact of Confucius suggests that ethics without religion *can* be strong; yet if each person is highly rational and sophisticated, he may behave increasingly like the free rider that he really is.

In any event, as far as these factors are concerned, each individual may have a weakened incentive to support rules regarding honesty, fairness, littering, queuing in an orderly fashion, using chain saws on Sunday mornings, purchasing political influence, squeezing every bit of hijacking potential from every decision, adopting dubious trade practices, issuing false advertising, attending to civic duties, monitoring government, or caring about others—in short, a weakened incentive to support codes about behavior toward others. It could conceivably turn out that the only effective ethical codes left will be those customs (such as rudimentary politeness) which bring obvious short-run gains at very low cost to virtually all participants—i.e., in situations where violators do suffer and there is no free rider problem. As with government choice, however, the glass is also half full. When people perceive high stakes for the group, they do at times sacrifice their selfish interests for the sake of others—sometimes even when their individual action by itself promises no perceptible impact. They may then converge on a widely accepted rule. People may move in this direction. It is not foreordained that we must converge on universal hijackery.

Government, its own performance influenced by traditions and ethics, in turn affects the functioning of behavioral codes. Government may exhort people to observe selected rules—e.g., turn down thermostats or engage in reverse racial or sex discrimination—and this may have some influence if circumstances are propitious and especially if the threat of additional government action is sensed. Through educational programs, governmental units can encourage or discourage rules about fair play or the role of the family. One should remember, though, that the specific rules a particular government propagandizes for—what it defines as socially responsible behavior—depend on the political process and have often turned out to be vicious. Note in this connection that the free rider syndrome can sometimes dissolve resistance to a new code much as it can erode adherence to an old one. The two phenomena are opposite sides of the same coin. As Ionesco's play *Rhinoceros* stressed in an entertaining way, each person's failure to resist viciousness reduces the expected sense-of-duty payoff to others from resisting.[17] In just the same way, each person's failure to support a help-your-neighbor custom reduces the anticipated payoff to all from having the custom and reduces any feeling of obligation to support it.

Governmental programs can sometimes make it either more rewarding or more costly to businessmen to follow desirable conventions. Moreover, government sets an example. If government officials fail to "take in their garbage cans," their failure reduces the anticipated benefits from the rules and also any sense-of-duty payoff to the rest of us individually, from taking in "our garbage cans." Sometimes it seems almost comical for government officials to be exhorting businessmen to shoulder more social responsibility. Why should one incur costs to reduce his polluting or his use of energy if reciprocal observance of minimal ethical codes by public personnel is not forthcoming—e.g., if high officials in one's Department of *Justice* appear to be involved in things like Watergate?

What Business Can Do about Social Responsibilities

To recapitulate, the logic of collective action warned us to expect little social responsibility, wherever the free rider problem existed, from voluntary action unaided by devices to coerce individuals. Subsequently, that logic warned us further not to expect too much from either government or ethical codes as such devices. Despite these formidable difficulties, however, mankind has squeezed out some extra social responsibility through both ethical rules and government.[18] People have on occasion been deterred from homicide, unfairness, and cheating by moral codes alone, quite apart from the threat of legal punishment. They have been further deterred in other instances, and induced to accept other programs to promote well-being, by formal laws and penalties. Ad-

17. Eugene Ionesco, *Rhinoceros and Other Plays* (Grove Press, 1960).
18. As far as private goods are concerned, mankind has arranged a great deal of social responsibility; with respect to goods and services that can economically be marketed, each of us is greatly concerned about what he can do for others.

herence by a large number of businessmen to ethical codes in reaching specific decisions can improve the ethical climate and formal public choices.

An implausible kind of behavior in view of the forces at work? Perhaps so, but even Adam Smith, realist that he was, assumed the maintenance of ethical standards, tracing out the virtues of voluntary rather than arm-twisting relationships. Indeed, Smith emphasized the crucial role of socially responsible behavior.[19] Moreover, the alternative to strengthening such codes may be their erosion and our descent into worldwide hijackery—a world in which interdependencies multiply and each person exploits every interdependency to the fullest. In that world, an executive would be evaluated mainly on the basis of his loyalty to particular persons (not to principles), his willingness to lie to protect them, his vulnerability to blackmail, and his political beliefs and political leverage. No ethical principle would say, "This choice should be decided on its merits—separate from the fact that Action A would provide a job for the mayor's brother-in-law and afford me an embezzlement opportunity."

If many people adopt the morality of a hijacker, most people will, and we must either tolerate this jungle or turn increasingly to government—to dossiers, inspections, civil service rules, and pervasive restrictions. Heavy policing costs, an oppressive atmosphere, and even more corrupt arbitrary inequities are bound to result. It seems that the only way to produce a decent society involves fairly heavy use of voluntary social contracts. Hence acceptance by businessmen (and others) of certain responsibilities amounts to a fundamental issue in the structure of society.

General Climate

Business conduct has a significant impact on people's attitudes and thence on political and ethical standards. According to 1974 polls, people's attitudes could use some uplifting, for they have become highly cynical about ethics in business, government, and most other organizations. This cynicism in turn causes further deterioration in our tacit social contracts. How, if at all, should businessmen shoulder responsibility for

---

19. Adam Smith, *The Theory of Moral Sentiments* (6th ed., Dublin: J. Beatty and C. Jackson, 1777).

stopping this deterioration? In trying to answer this question, we must remember that businessmen, like other individuals, are free riders with respect to public goods. If one businessman violates generally accepted ethical rules, he loses nothing—unless the violations are flagrant and publicized, resulting in a loss of customer goodwill or employee morale. If one businessman purchases political influence, he sacrifices nothing (assuming no legal penalty), for he still faces a political process having essentially the same quality as before. That quality will change markedly under the cumulative effect of numerous violations but not as a result of any one decision.

It is especially unrealistic to expect a businessman to ignore his free rider position unless something makes his competitors do likewise. For if he does not buy "protection," or take all possible steps to increase profits, yet his competitors do, the result is a reduced likelihood that his business will survive. Perhaps all one can ask is that each businessman resist the free rider motivation as long as there is a reasonable chance of reciprocity by competitors. He can, out of a sense of duty, refrain from *initiating* erosion of ethical codes or help block whatever erosion is threatening to occur. Maybe he can, out of a sense of duty, refrain from *initiating* purchases of political influence or even help discourage such purchases. Businessmen (as well as government officials) might realistically be expected to twist and squirm to avoid undermining principles instead of squirming to find profitable opportunities to do so.

Legal support is needed to back up the well-intentioned businessman, of course—antinuisance and antifraud laws, tort and contract law, libel and liability laws, new campaign financing laws, and heavy allocations of resources to enforcement. To produce wholesome public choices and effective ethical codes, two things appear to be essential: a widespread sense of duty and supplementary formal enforcement devices.

Relationships with Customers and Employees

Contributions to the general ethical climate must come, of course, through specific decisions about specific issues. Hence, wherever businessmen foster an improved "climate," they also promote particular social responsibilities. Often these pertain to relationships with consumers or employees.

In many industries, competition for customers and employees already reinforces any desire on the part of management to behave responsibly toward these groups. Where transactions are infrequent, however, as in the purchase of houses or durable items, or where competition for customers is weak (e.g., fly-by-night firms or some local monopolies), or where uncertainties are inherently great (automobile maintenance), there is much scope for ethics either to function or fail to function. Despite the laws (partly because of court costs), firms can often get by with false advertising, misleading information, and products that have lower quality or greater hazards than indicated to customers. Most of these practices boil down to cheating on tacitly understood contracts or even on written contracts. Competition may also permit discrimination in hiring or promoting and exposure of workers to unusually hazardous working conditions, as in mining or asbestos processing, that most persons believe are unjust or uneconomical in the long run.

From the standpoint of the whole economy, frequently even from the standpoint of businessmen as a group, alleviation of these practices would often be advantageous. The individual manager, however, will look upon any effort by *him* as a drop in the bucket, yielding essentially no benefits yet jeopardizing his survival. As noted above, perhaps all we can realistically expect is that each person squirm to be ethical instead of squirming to find profitable unethical opportunities. In making his decisions, perhaps each person, instead of assuming that others will be guilty of social irresponsibility unless proved otherwise, could start assuming that others will in plausible circumstances be socially responsible until proved otherwise. If, just from a sense of obligation, more businessmen refused to initiate sharp practices or unethical discrimination, business might ratchet itself (and society) toward stronger ethical codes instead of ratcheting us toward lower standards.

Jawboning people to do "good in general" is usually ineffective, but it is possible sometimes to develop wide support for unambiguous rules. I conjecture, for instance, that few businessmen would directly kill people to reduce the chances of bankruptcy (even apart from the laws against homicide). Or at least their price to commit murder would be high. Each can accept the prohibition against killing and yet stay solvent because almost everyone accepts, from a sense of moral obligation, this social responsibility. A reduction in the range of circumstances in which we would cheat—an increase in our price for cheating—may also be viable. The specific rules or applications would depend on the industry and circumstances, just as what is fair play depends on the game; but in all cultures people can identify numerous actions that constitute cheating.

Experience clears up most ambiguities regarding what is "honest." Even modest changes in many people's behavior could make quite a difference in the quality of life, including the extent to which we resort to oppressive government restrictions.

Businessmen often find it in their long-run interest to organize to maintain standards of conduct. For example, they would have had to police false advertising through some kind of association—in order to gain credibility for anyone's advertisements—if the Federal Trade Commission had not years ago taken on this chore (in part, incidentally, because of requests by businessmen). Firms might be able to use trade associations to monitor other business practices more effectively than at present. (This would facilitate collusion, of course, and safeguards against the use of associations for cartelization would need to be bolstered.) They might be able to develop a *better* Better Business Bureau. Unfortunately the bureau or trade association would have to offer some by-product service, perhaps pooled information, that was valuable to firms and from which any firm could be excluded if it failed to pay its dues.[20] Otherwise firms would gradually decide to "let George support the association."

Thus one can conceive of businesses following certain unambiguous rules relating to customers and employees or supporting advantageous trade associations. To the cynical, the former possibility may appear to be like the old suggestion that the Arabs and Jews solve their difficulties by following good Christian principles. Nonetheless, a sense of obligation has sometimes been a potent force.

Another way to be responsible to consumers is to preserve a desirable degree of competition and freedom of exchange. An invaluable mechanism for achieving socially responsible behavior—for inducing people to take into account what they are doing to others or what they could do for others—is voluntary exchange. (Indeed the principal reason for social irresponsibility is the failure of transactions to occur. People often have damage thrust upon them without anyone purchasing their voluntary consent, and at times they are unable to obtain conditions or goods that they would be willing to sacrifice something for.)

It would be naive to ask businessmen to encourage, in all possible ways, competition that would operate against them. The "rule" would be unclear, the sacrifice severe. Certainly we could not rely solely on firms'

20. Olson, *The Logic of Collective Action*, pp. 132–41.

voluntary efforts to reduce oligopoly or trade barriers that favored those firms. The most effective and injurious shelters from competition, however, have been those worked out with the aid of government. Frequently governmental restrictions on trade serve mainly to help some producer group. The ban on importing Mexican tomatoes favors U.S. growers, for example, and taxes on the sale of food substitutes like margarine, price supports, certain features of building codes, and many governmentally sanctioned barriers to occupational entry serve similar purposes. Deals between business and government may be a growing threat, for big conglomerates, though they do not directly impair competition, offer economies of scale in dickering for government favors. It may not be completely naive to ask enterprises (including unions) to refrain from warlike maneuvers to "buy" trade barriers for themselves. If each group goes all out—no holds barred by ethical guidelines—for legal expropriation of others' wealth, a stable, nondictatorial society may be impossible. At best the Antitrust Division of the Department of Justice and other public policing agencies can help only if they themselves are not captured. Like it or not, we are ultimately dependent on some voluntary restraints if a (semi) voluntarist society is to be preserved. In this connection, a moral resolution *not to buy government help* in blocking entry and exchange would be valuable. Scruples against procuring governmental favors once prevailed in some segments of society and therefore may not be too fanciful. The specific applications would vary, but the rule need not be impossibly vague. Though there are borderline situations, most businessmen know when they are trying to influence government out of civic-mindedness and when they are negotiating for favors. In addition, as noted before, voters should seek backup antitrust policies and improved campaign financing laws, with careful even though costly enforcement. Morality is easier, the fewer the rewards from immorality.

Relationships with Others

Business has many relationships, sometimes through "Rube Goldberg" repercussions, with "bystanders"—that is, with persons other than customers, employees, and competitors. For instance, decisions by businessmen can affect urban congestion, air and ocean pollution, employment, job training, technological change, poverty, and community development. Indeed, much discussion of social responsibility has focused on the possibility of business doing something to secure community or national well-being. Ideally, since appropriate action taken voluntarily would be very economical, one might like businessmen to assume broad responsibility. However, it is difficult to determine, especially in a rapidly changing society, what is the appropriate action in each instance, and it is difficult to imagine unambiguous rules that could be a basis for "social contracts." In addition, rules that convey benefits to some but sharp losses to others (even if the aggregate benefits exceed the losses) are unlikely to survive. Many precepts concerning environmental quality, for instance, are vague. If admonished not to pollute the river "too much," nobody knows what the social contract is. Even if specific, an environmental code does not bring reciprocal benefits; it inflicts heavy costs on the very persons (stockholders and personnel in the polluting industries) who would have to take action and is unlikely to survive.

Some steps to improve the community will be profitable to a firm—donations of executives' time to the United Fund, contributions of money to other charitable endeavors, financial participation in a downtown mall project. The gains to businesses might come from increments in land values, extra goodwill and sales, a better labor force, greater stability, maybe even reduced crime rates. We need not worry about businessmen perceiving and seizing such opportunities. Without tacit or explicit agreement among most businesses, however, these steps will not amount to much. Moreover, the rapidity of change nowadays and the resulting uncertainties may shorten businessmen's time horizon, making goodwill investments look less profitable than they used to. Agreement among local businesses could make additional "investment" in the community profitable, but negotiation costs might prevent much action. Also, agreement to support community projects invites collusion to achieve monopoly power and unwholesome deals with government.

Beyond the profitable community investments, one can imagine some profit-sacrificing charitable efforts based on a general sense of duty among businessmen. Some fairly clear-cut and relatively inexpensive (to business) benign practices might survive—e.g., do not use high-sulphur coal in cities; contribute x percent of profits to Alcoholics Anonymous, the Boy Scouts, and the Mexican-American Legal Defense Fund. There would be no test, of course, as to whether these actions yielded more social benefit than cost. Also, if the scale of such activities was large, political issues would arise. To consider an extreme example, voluntary price controls would yield benefits for some persons but would redistribute income promiscuously and cause inefficiency and net losses to the nation. (It becomes terribly inefficient, by the way, to allow impacts on income distribution to swing every government decision, let alone every private decision.) The political system would be derelict if it allowed any Tom, Dick, and Harry to shape community programs; so the exercise of these social responsibilities would be tantamount to a government program after all. The scale of corporate community activities, however, is almost certain to be small. It would be too difficult to develop either explicit agreement among businesses or a sense of duty among all firms about "worthwhile" welfare programs. Yet no one firm could go it alone on large profit-sacrificing ventures.

In connection with such endeavors, therefore, the chief social responsibility of businessmen may have to be in their relationships with government. In connection with the environment, for example, instead of pressing for *no* regulation of side effects from ocean mining or asbestos production, businessmen could channel their efforts toward devising new ways for market transactions to embrace these side effects. Or, where market exchange is too costly, they could put their efforts into devising and supporting sensible governmental regulations. Positive steps of this sort are in the long-run interest of most firms as well as of the economy. Central regulation will often be the least bad way to deal with these growing interdependencies, and heel-dragging may result in impulsive, exceptionally ill-advised regulations. Again a major moral responsibility of business should be to improve—not subvert—governmental processes.

Summing Up

In thinking about the social responsibility of business, we should keep in mind the climate provided by government (formal law) and by prevalent ethical codes (informal "law"). Both are collective choices— choices that cannot be determined by any one decision maker alone and that affect many members of the society. A basic fact of life, the free rider problem, causes the monitoring of government by citizens to be imprecise and unreliable, permitting government officials often to be irresponsible toward many persons and to provide a poor climate for the exercise of social responsibility by business. Recent models of several parts of the public choice process highlight the major difficulties and limitations. The same free rider problem keeps ethical codes vulnerable to erosion, again offering a somewhat inhospitable environment for the exercise of social responsibility. We should be keenly aware of these difficulties rather than being naively optimistic or complacent.

The glass is half full, however, as well as half empty. Clearly we need the help of businessmen (and all individuals), but, despite the difficulties, the public sector and ethical codes do offer more than zero hope of producing and eliciting social responsibility. In this context, perhaps businessmen can, through a sense of duty, overlook their free rider positions more often and give more support to ethical precepts governing relationships with customers, employees, and bystanders. They may be able to follow certain moral guidelines, from a sense of duty, governing their relationships with the political system. In these ways, they may also contribute at the same time to a climate that favors social responsibility. Adherence to precepts is always precarious, yet they have been powerful forces at times. And even a semivoluntarist society is ultimately dependent on voluntary observance of *some* ethical constraints by individuals even if they realize that their actions individually will have no effect.

CHAPTER SIX

The Politics of Regulation

JAMES Q. WILSON

WHENEVER government in the United States has sought to introduce social objectives or constraints into the management of business enterprise, it has usually done so by administrative regulation or regulation combined with direct or indirect cash subsidies.[1] The public authorities have largely forgone the major alternative device for altering business behavior—namely, changing the structure of the economy by means of public ownership or management. Though experiments have been made from time to time with varying degrees of ownership or control over railroads and atomic energy production, and though there are at the local and regional level a substantial number of publicly owned utilities, the United States, more than almost any other advanced industrial society, has left the ownership and management of enterprise in private hands even in those industries—transportation, broadcasting, and telephone and telegram communication—that have been most frequently nationalized in other countries.

It is increasingly recognized that the U.S. public regulatory agencies do not select optimal regulatory policies.[2] This may be because in the nature of things no such policy can exist. It is impossible, for example, to devise a "correct" or "optimal" criterion by which to choose among

1. For help in gaining an overview of American business regulation, I would like to acknowledge the research assistance of Frances Francis, Marc Landy, and Paul Quirk and the useful comments on earlier drafts of this paper by Richard A. Posner and Suzanne Weaver, by my colleagues in the Faculty Seminar on the Politics of Regulation at the Institute of Politics at Harvard, by members of the Workshop on Industrial Organization at the University of Chicago, and by my associates in the Brookings project on the social responsibilities of business.

2. See, for example, Paul W. MacAvoy (ed.), *The Crisis of the Regulatory Commissions* (Norton, 1970).

competing applicants for a broadcast license if the choice depends on measuring the value of what an applicant will broadcast; for that is largely a matter of taste over which consumers will differ. Or the difficulty may arise because a legislature has required that an economically inefficient policy be pursued, as when Congress enacted the Federal Water Pollution Control Act Amendments of 1972 requiring that the discharge of all effluents into the nation's waters end by 1985, whatever the cost (it will be vast) and however illusory the benefit (many waterways can easily handle, at no significant loss of water quality, some effluent discharge). Or the problem may result from the constellation of political forces in which the agency is caught. Strong arguments have been made, for instance, that cable broadcasting deserves at least a reasonable chance to compete in large cities with over-the-air broadcasting, but the political influence of the television stations and networks is so great and that of the cable companies and allied consumer groups so weak that the cable rules adopted by the Federal Communications Commission (FCC) are prohibitively restrictive.[3]

That regulation is subject to these difficulties does not mean there should never be regulation. We often prefer the imperfect benefits of a regulatory system to the imperfections of the market, as when we ask the government to determine the prices that can be charged by "natural monopolies" such as the telephone company. It is remarkably difficult to decide what those prices should be and to revise them in a timely and equitable way as costs change, but the alternative is to allow the company to set its own monopoly prices or to place it under government ownership.

Much, probably most, regulation in the United States is not concerned with avoiding the evils of monopoly, however. Various levels of government regulate railroads, trucking companies, airlines, broadcasters, pharmaceutical firms, dry cleaners, savings banks, and automobile manufacturers, not because these industries are immune from effective competition and thus in a position to charge monopoly prices, but because we wish them to serve objectives other than, or in addition to, the objective of selling their products at the lowest possible price. In some cases we regulate them to ensure that they will *not* engage in price competition, because we believe the "health" of the industry (and presumably, the

3. Roger G. Noll, Merton J. Peck, and John J. McGowan, *Economic Aspects of Television Regulation* (Brookings Institution, 1973), Chaps. 6–7.

well-being of the country) is served by prices being set higher than market forces would allow. In other cases we regulate to protect the consumer from fraud, misrepresentation, or hazard. In still other cases we regulate to prevent market transactions from imposing uncompensated costs on third parties, as when a factory pours noxious fumes into the air or a household sends untreated sewage into a river that cannot absorb it.

Some of these regulatory objectives, such as that of avoiding price competition in the transportation industry, are questionable; others, such as that of reducing pollution, unexceptionable. And some laudatory objectives could perhaps be served as well or better by nonregulatory devices, such as negotiating contractual agreements, levying appropriate taxes, or imposing compensatory charges for wear on the environment. It is not the purpose of this chapter, however, to evaluate the worth of a regulatory objective or to consider alternative means to reach a given objective. Rather, the purpose here is to explain, insofar as available facts permit, the circumstances under which regulation becomes politically possible, the pattern of regulation that is likely to emerge from a given political context, and the forces that will influence how a regulatory agency does its job.

The reason for this approach is simple. Whenever we want business to act in ways other than as self-interest would require, we rarely content ourselves for long with urging businessmen to examine their consciences or to attend conferences on their social responsibilities. If the problem is sufficiently bothersome or a political constituency opposed to a certain practice can be readily mobilized (not necessarily the same thing), we ask the government to direct businessmen to stop doing certain things and to start doing something else. Often businessmen themselves are in the forefront of those making these demands. If we turn so often to government regulation to achieve what self-interest cannot, we ought to have a better understanding than we do of what is necessary to enact such regulatory legislation and how the process of its enactment and the imperatives of agency management will affect the regulatory policy that emerges. Such an analysis may help us decide under what circumstances government regulation is an efficient and fair means to realize public objectives and under what circumstances it is not, and therefore it may help us decide the larger question of when the imperfections of government action are preferable to the imperfections of the market and when they are not. The world being as it is, a choice between imperfect alternatives is usually the best that can be hoped for.

The Sources of Regulation

The political circumstances under which business regulation occurs must be distinguished from those economic factors that may or may not make such regulation desirable. Sometimes, to be sure, the economic reasons for regulation are so compelling that, sooner or later, the political capacity for regulation is developed. The existence of "natural monopolies" is usually regarded as a case in point: when a firm, such as a telephone company, can realize substantial returns to scale because of continuously falling average costs, it has a powerful incentive to drive out or buy up competitors. Only by government regulation or government ownership can such a firm be prevented from charging a monopoly price (assuming there are no ready substitutes for its services). Every country places such natural monopolies under some form of public control.

But in most cases, there is no overwhelming reason why business regulation must occur—it may be desirable or undesirable, but it is not inevitable. For example, instead of regulating drug companies to prevent them from making harmful medicines, the government might facilitate the recovery of damages by injured parties.

There have been, in general, two main theories of the political causes of regulation. According to the first one, regulation results when legislators, mobilized by a broad social movement or energized by a dramatic crisis, enact laws designed to prevent a firm or industry from carrying on certain practices. This is the "public interest" theory of regulation. The other, currently more in fashion among many scholars, is that regulation results when an industry successfully uses its political influence to obtain legal protection for itself or to impose legal burdens on its rivals. This is the "self-interest" theory of regulation. The origins of many regulatory laws are hotly disputed between adherents of the one theory and adherents of the other. The act that created the Interstate Commerce Commission is believed by some scholars to have been in large part a governmental response to the interests of farmers and other shippers who were aggrieved by monopoly rates being charged on short-haul railroad lines. Other scholars contend, on the contrary, that the creation of the ICC was a response to the demands of railroad companies eager to reduce price competition and create or preserve cartel arrangements.[4]

The view taken here is that regulatory laws can have a variety of

4. Compare Gabriel Kolko, *Railroads and Regulation, 1877–1916* (Princeton

political causes and that it is necessary, in order to understand why regulation occurs, to specify the circumstances under which one or another cause will be operative.

These circumstances can be classified by examining the distribution of the perceived costs and benefits of the proposed regulation. A cost may be perceived to be widely distributed (as when it is paid for through a general tax levy or a general price increase) or narrowly concentrated (as when it is met with a fee or impost charged to a particular industry, firm, or locality). Similarly a benefit, real or imagined, may be widely distributed (as with lower prices or taxes, improved products and services, or reductions in the degree of fraud and deception tried on the public); or a benefit may be narrowly concentrated (as when a subsidy is paid to a particular industry or occupation or a license is granted for the operation of a particular valuable facility). Not everyone will agree on the distribution of costs and benefits, opinions about any particular distribution often change over time, and occasionally beliefs can be made to change by skillful political advocacy.

The distribution of costs and benefits affects regulatory politics in two ways. First, individuals and groups are politically more sensitive to sudden or significant *decreases* in their net benefits than they are to increases in net benefits. That is, they are more sensitive to, and thus more easily mobilized for political action about, circumstances that make costs seem likely to go up or benefits to go down than they are when they foresee a chance to reduce costs or enhance benefits. They are, in short, more *threat*-oriented than opportunity-oriented.

This is, of course, a sweeping generalization, but it is on the whole consistent with such evidence as we have regarding how persons compare expected utilities and expected disutilities in experimental situations.[5] It fits with what we know about the behavior of economic organizations in legislative struggles over tariff legislation.[6] It is in line with the circumstances under which various trade associations have emerged.[7]

University Press, 1965), with John A. Garraty, *The New Commonwealth, 1877–1890* (Harper and Row, 1968), and Edward A. Purcell, Jr., "Ideas and Interests: Businessmen and the Interstate Commerce Act," *Journal of American History,* Vol. 54 (December 1967), pp. 561–78.

5. Howard Raiffa, *Decision Analysis: Introductory Lectures on Choices under Uncertainty* (Addison-Wesley, 1968), pp. 91–94; Frederick Mosteller and Philip Nogee, "An Experimental Measurement of Utility," *Journal of Political Economy,* Vol. 59 (October 1951), pp. 371–404.

6. Raymond A. Bauer, Ithiel de Sola Pool, and Lewis Anthony Dexter, *American Business and Public Policy* (Atherton, 1963), pp. 139–42.

7. James Q. Wilson, *Political Organizations* (Basic Books, 1973), Chaps. 8, 10.

Most of the governmental regulatory agencies designed to control the behavior of single industries or organizations were created in response to serious economic instability in that industry: price wars among long-haul railroads and price increases to shippers served by short-haul railroads contributed to the creation of the Interstate Commerce Commission; acute signal interference led to the formation of the Federal Radio Commission (later the Federal Communications Commission); depressed conditions in the coal industry gave rise to the National Bituminous Coal Commission (later abolished); the financial crises of the airlines and accompanying scandals with respect to the awarding of subsidies for carrying mail by air led to the creation of the Civil Aeronautics Authority (later the Civil Aeronautics Board); extreme fluctuations in the money supply stimulated the organization of the Federal Reserve Board; the insecurity of labor organizations gave rise to demands for the Wagner Act and the establishment of a National Labor Relations Board; the uncertainty of the congressional licensing system for hydroelectric power plants led to the creation of the Federal Power Commission; and the competition of foreign shipbuilders and the sudden increases in the cost of shipping occasioned by World War I led to the formation of the Shipping Board (superseded by the U.S. Maritime Commission).

Interest-group activity intensifies when the associations confront a visible, direct, and immediate threat to their values. The National Association of Manufacturers (NAM) has typically waxed (in size, budget, and energy) during "anti-business" Democratic administrations and waned during "pro-business" Republican ones. The AFL-CIO has been more active in attempting to defeat the Taft-Hartley Act, to repeal section 14(b) of that act after it was passed, and to defeat state "right-to-work" laws than in arguing for new wage-and-hours legislation. Conservation groups are more easily mobilized by a threat to an existing forest or a particular marshland than by proposals to create new forests or new bird sanctuaries.

In addition to serving as a source of assumed threats or deprivation, there is a second way in which costs and benefits affect regulatory politics, and that has to do with the extent to which they are concentrated. When the cost to be avoided or the benefit to be maintained is specific to a certain sector of society conscious of its special identity, political action is easier to stimulate than when costs or benefits fall on a large, diverse group with no sense of special identity and no established patterns of interaction. Partly this is simply a matter of size: in a small group each member's contribution is sufficiently significant so that it may help to attain the organization's goal and sufficiently visible so that its presence will be noted and rewarded by other members.[8] As a result, members of small organizations often find it more satisfying to contribute time, money, and effort to a common cause than do members of a large one. By itself, a feeling of deprivation does not necessarily lead to a political effort.

The greater ease of organizational activity in response to concentrated costs and benefits is also the result of the greater homogeneity of interest and belief among sectors of society that are clearly defined along lines of occupation, industry, or locality. People are less likely to be divided by a proposed policy that serves their common interests as members of an organization than they are by a policy that cuts across their various interests either as individuals or as members of society in general. For example, an organization representing firms making watches will be more aroused by a proposed tariff reduction on imported watches than will an organization representing businessmen generally, some of whom buy and others of whom sell watches. Of course, organizations purporting to speak for very large sectors are often active in regulatory politics, but in many cases the positions they take are either highly general (so as to avoid antagonizing any element of a diverse membership) or unrepresentative (because they are responsive to the interests and beliefs of an activist minority rather than to those of a broad constituency).

So far as degree of concentration is concerned, costs and benefits may fall into any of several distribution patterns. The main patterns are worth looking at one by one for their different consequences.

Concentrated Benefits, Diffused Costs

Any proposed policy that confers highly concentrated costs or benefits will be more likely to stimulate organized activity by a fully representative group than will a policy that confers widely distributed costs and benefits. When the benefit is entirely concentrated on a single group but the cost is diffused, an organization will quickly form to propose a regulatory arrangement to institutionalize the benefit; and that proposal, except under special conditions to be noted below, will not be seriously challenged. At the behest of the Florida Dairy Products Association, the Florida Milk Commission was created in 1939 to eliminate "overproduc-

8. Mancur Olson, Jr., *The Logic of Collective Action: Public Goods and the Theory of Groups* (Harvard University Press, 1965), pp. 48–50, 126–28.

tion" and "predatory" price-cutting. The benefits to the producer of a guaranteed minimum price were great; the cost to the average consumer was relatively small.[9] Over seventy-five occupations in the United States require state licenses; there is an average of twenty-five such laws per state. A typical one is the 1939 law that created the Oklahoma State Dry Cleaning Board, charged with many duties, including the prevention of fires, but over the years concerned chiefly with eliminating price competition.[10] The regulation of, and limitations on, the number of taxicab licenses in cities is a well-known example of a competitive industry using legal enactments, usually defended in terms of eliminating fraud, enhancing safety, or maintaining quality of service, in order to restrict entry and set minimum prices.[11]

Thus regulatory constraints often arise out of a political situation in which a small, relatively homogeneous beneficiary group can make substantial gains by imposing unobtrusive costs on large numbers of others. Constraints arising under such conditions tend to have the following characteristics: (1) they will involve the elimination or reduction of price competition within the affected industry; (2) entry to the industry will be restricted or at least made more expensive; (3) the organized beneficiary will strongly influence the regulatory agency that administers the policy; (4) the industry and its agency will strive to maintain a position of low visibility to avoid stimulating the formation of an organization representative of those who bear the costs of the regulation; and (5) should the regulation become controversial, it will be defended by attempting to show that eliminating price competition is an appropriate means for ensuring safety, ending fraud, and promoting amenity (correcting evils allegedly caused by price cutters, who will be termed "fly-by-night operators").

Concentrated Benefits, Concentrated Costs

Some regulatory constraints arise, not out of the unopposed aggrandizement of a single beneficiary, but out of competition between two or

9. Harmon Zeigler, *The Florida Milk Commission Changes Minimum Prices* (University of Alabama Press for the Inter-University Case Program, 1963).

10. Charles R. Plott, "Occupational Self-Regulation: A Case Study of the Oklahoma Dry Cleaners," *Journal of Law and Economics,* Vol. 8 (October 1965), pp. 195–222.

11. Edmund W. Kitch, Marc Isaacson, and Daniel Kasper, "The Regulation of Taxicabs in Chicago," *Journal of Law and Economics,* Vol. 14 (October 1971), pp. 285–350.

more organized opponents. This occurs when a historical development or a proposed policy creates both concentrated benefits and concentrated costs. The struggle between labor and management over union recognition and union security agreements is the most obvious instance. The conflict between wholesalers and retailers and between large chain stores and small independent ones over resale price maintenance is another, and the battle between the railroads and the truckers when the former were regulated and the latter were not is a third. The union-management issue led to three major federal laws (the Wagner Act, the Taft-Hartley Act, and the Landrum-Griffin Act) and the creation of a regulatory body (the National Labor Relations Board) which has been a cockpit for continuing organized struggle. Resale price maintenance issues were won by the small retailers who obtained passage of the Robinson-Patman Act (1936), the Miller-Tydings Act (1937), and the McGuire Act (1952). The transportation conflict was temporarily resolved, not by deregulating railroads but by extending rate regulation, through the Motor Carrier Act of 1935, to truckers.

Regulatory constraints arising out of a political situation in which two clearly defined, undifferentiated sectors of the economy contend over the allocation of costs and benefits tend to have these characteristics: (1) a "charter" will be adopted that contains a definition of the competing rights and obligations of each party; (2) no one organized sector will be able to dominate permanently the administrative arrangements created to implement the charter; (3) there will be continuing efforts to renegotiate or amend the charter; and (4) the visibility of the issue will be relatively high because there is conflict, because each party to it will attempt to enlist allies (for example, business groups will try to enlist the American Farm Bureau Federation against labor, while labor will try to enlist the National Farmers Union), and because there will be frequent appeals to the courts.

Diffused Benefits, Concentrated Costs

Finally, regulatory constraints may impose highly concentrated costs on some in order to obtain widely distributed benefits for others. Politically, this implies that a small group, faced with the immediate prospect of increased burdens, is unable to defeat a proposal brought on behalf of large numbers of (inevitably unorganized) persons, each of whom may benefit, if at all, only in the future. Such an eventuality strikes some political scientists as so unlikely that they have argued that it will almost

never occur barring a major crisis (a depression or a war) or a fundamental political realignment. In fact, regulatory constraints embodying
concentrated costs and distributed benefits have been imposed, and with
increasing frequency in recent years. The Sherman Antitrust Act of 1890,
the Pure Food and Drug Act of 1906, the Meat Inspection Act of 1906,
the Food, Drug, and Cosmetic Act of 1938, and the Public Utility Holding Company Act of 1935 are familiar examples from the early decades
of this century and before. In the 1960s, the number of such laws, especially in the consumer and environmental protection fields, increased dramatically. Congress passed twenty consumer bills between 1962 and
1970—bills aimed against postal fraud, flammable fabrics, unwholesome
meat and poultry, radiation, automobile and highway dangers, unsafe
toys, exploitative credit practices, deceptive package labeling, and inadequate testing of drugs. In the ecology area, Congress enacted the Water
Quality Act and the Motor Vehicle Air Pollution Control Act in 1965,
the Clean Water Restoration Act of 1966, the Air Quality Act of 1967,
the National Environmental Policy Act of 1969, the Water Quality Improvement Act of 1970, and the 1970 amendments to the Clean Air Act.

Some of these bills were the products of major scandals: the early
food and drug and meat inspection acts followed upon public exposures
of unsavory conditions in these industries; the 1938 drug laws were
prompted by the deaths caused by elixir of sulfanilamide; the National
Traffic and Motor Vehicle Safety Act of 1966 was helped along by public
disclosure of a General Motors investigation of Ralph Nader; and the
1962 amendments to the drug laws were aided in their passage by the
thalidomide disaster. Similarly, the crisis conditions of the Depression
facilitated public utility and stock exchange control legislation. Yet it
is easy to exaggerate the importance of any one set of critical events.[12]
The Kefauver drug probe leading to the 1962 legislation was under way
well before thalidomide was a public issue. Most of the environmental
legislation was unrelated to any particular crisis or disaster, and the
"truth-in-lending" and "truth-in-packaging" bills developed slowly in
Congress without benefit of scandal.

One of the striking aspects of the politics of consumer and ecology
legislation is the important role Congress—or, more accurately, key
congressmen and congressional committees—plays in their initiation. The
usual assumption (an assumption increasingly questioned by scholars)

12. I draw here on Mark V. Nadel, *The Politics of Consumer Protection*
(Bobbs-Merrill, 1971), pp. 18, 143.

that the executive proposes and the legislature disposes seems not to hold for consumer and environmental bills.[13] Senator Abraham A. Ribicoff formulated the auto safety bill, Senator Estes Kefauver the 1962 drug amendments, Senator Paul Douglas the truth-in-lending bill, Senator Phillip A. Hart the truth-in-packaging bill, and Senator Edmund S. Muskie most of the water and air pollution bills. Furthermore, even when a president has submitted his own bills in these fields, consumer and ecological activists have usually judged them to be "weaker"; and when a president has endorsed an existing bill, his support has been slow in coming. President John F. Kennedy, for example, was reluctant to support the truth-in-lending bill until several years after it was first introduced, and he backed a prescription drug bill less stringent than that initiated by Senator Kefauver. President Lyndon Johnson moved more cautiously on auto safety than Senator Ribicoff. President Richard Nixon opposed much of the pollution legislation emanating from the so-called Muskie subcommittee and offered several alternatives.

The importance of Congress in issues of this sort is in part a result of the relative newness of consumer and environmental enthusiasms: the White House, along with much of the rest of the country (including, to their chagrin, auto manufacturers, credit institutions, and other affected industries), at first underestimated the salience and appeal of these legislative initiatives. Had a president guessed sooner that such issues were politically important, he no doubt would have acted sooner and by so doing preempted the field. But legislative leadership has also been the result of the symbiotic political relationship between certain congressmen and various "public interest" activists. As Paul Halpern observes in his study of auto safety legislation, many congressmen are continuously surveying their political horizons in search of issues with which they can become personally identified and which can become the basis of subcommittee chairmanships, highly publicized hearings, and state or national visibility.[14] This is especially true of senators, who not only must appeal to larger, harder-to-reach constituencies but who, unlike representatives, can take advantage of televised hearings. Senators Ribicoff and Warren G. Magnuson, for example, deliberately sought out auto

13. See ibid., pp. 242–43; Ronald C. Moe and Steven C. Teel, "Congress as Policy-Maker: A Necessary Reappraisal," *Political Science Quarterly,* Vol. 85 (September 1970), pp. 443–70; John R. Johannes, "When Congress Leads" (Ph.D. dissertation, Harvard University, 1970).

14. Paul J. Halpern, "Consumer Politics and Corporate Behavior: The Case of Automobile Safety" (Ph.D. dissertation, Harvard University, 1972).

safety as an issue with which they could make their mark, as Senator Kefauver before them had done, first with organized crime and then with prescription drugs. In becoming the source of regulatory legislation, a senator of course does not act alone: he is only the central figure in a constellation of staff assistants, newspapermen, organizational representatives, and political celebrities (such as Ralph Nader).

Regulatory proposals emerging from this process are likely to have certain distinctive features. First, in order to ensure vital publicity and develop political momentum in the competition for attention in and around Congress, the bills will focus attention on an "evil," personified if possible in a corporation, industry, or victim. Second, the proposal will be "strong"—that is, there will be little incentive in the developmental process to accommodate conflicting interests and thus little incentive to find a politically acceptable formula which all affected parties can live with. (To compromise the proposal would be to sacrifice the capacity of the bill to mobilize support by its moralistic appeal.) Third, though few *substantive* bargains will be struck, many procedural ones will, especially ones that recognize the central structural fact of the American Congress—namely, that it is a federal institution based on state and district representation. Concessions will often be made to recognize existing state programs or to provide incentives for states to develop new programs. Finally, the proposed solution to the problematic business practice will be shaped as much by the political process by which the proposal is generated as by an analysis of the problem itself. The consequences for a regulatory strategy of the political gestation it undergoes is discussed in the next section. It should be recognized, of course, that the tendencies latent in congressionally initiated regulatory programs with widely distributed benefits and concentrated costs are only tendencies: the final shape of the bill will be affected by the legislative struggle itself. It is worth noting, however, that many of the major consumer and environmental bills were passed by extraordinary majorities, especially during the 1960s, and that the number of floor amendments adopted was typically rather small.

The Nature of Regulation

Economists and others frequently complain that the regulations imposed on American business are not optimal and in some cases may even be unnecessary. Academic journals and books are filled with detailed analyses of why much regulatory policy is wrong and how it might be corrected. Few of these suggestions are acted upon by the government.

This political indifference to professional opinion may in part result from the arcane language in which the professionals address each other, but in large part it is the result of the imperatives of the political and administrative processes. When government regulation fails to compel businesses to serve socially desirable objectives, it is not usually because of the incompetence or venality of the regulators but because of the constraints placed on them by the need to operate within the political system. When the regulation arises out of the desire to alleviate widely distributed burdens (say, auto accidents, water pollution, hidden interest charges), then assigning blame becomes virtually a political necessity in order to get the issue on the public agenda and move it through the legislative obstacle course. If the regulation arises out of a desire to confer highly concentrated benefits (stabilized prices, lessened competition, restricted entry), then the "needs" of the industry must be dramatized, the "failures" of the economic system emphasized, and an administrative alternative to that system devised. If the regulation is the result of the momentary political supremacy of one organized interest over another (as with the victory of labor over management or retailers over wholesalers), then the constraints employed will be devised to protect the politically stronger group from the politically weaker. The protection conferred, however, will rarely be complete, for the adversary will look for new ways to organize for political action. As the political tides change, counterattacks occur, and new constraints are imposed to redress the effects of old ones.

In all three cases, the result is the multiplication of detailed constraints, sometimes in the form of rules, sometimes by way of the exercise of ad hoc administrative discretion undefined by rule. In the case of a widely shared burden such as pollution, the administrative agency charged with alleviating that burden will (provided it retains the capacity for independent action, a matter discussed in a later section) consider that it was created to constrain the wicked or self-seeking behavior of a firm, industry, or group and thus that it has a mandate to do whatever it legally can to eliminate abuses (and not merely the particular abuse to which it owes its existence). In the case of concentrated benefits such as reducing price competition, the agency will believe that it has general responsibility for ensuring the health and well-being of a firm, industry, or group and thus will seek not merely to eliminate a particular problem but generally to reduce uncertainty and protect firms against failure. In the case of organized interests struggling for political advantage over each other, rules will multiply and discretionary authority expand as a consequence of the seesaw battle for agency domination between two or more organized sectors of the economy whose interests are at stake.

These tendencies can be illustrated with a few important examples. Many economists argue that the control of noxious effluents from fixed sources, as with the discharge of sewage from a pipe into streams or the emission of gaseous pollutants into the air from factory smokestacks, is best handled by forcing those who discharge undesirable wastes to bear the cost of doing so. This can be accomplished by levying an effluent tax or discharge fee that increases with the amount emitted. The result is to increase the cost to the producer of using the heretofore "free" environment as a dump and to induce him to economize by finding ways of reducing his output of effluents, by recycling his waste products in order to use them in the productive process, or by reducing his production of high-waste products in favor of producing more low-waste products.[15] Such a strategy would lead the producer to find the least-cost solution to a waste problem but would leave him free to select among various technologies for achieving this. If technology is unavailing, the producer will be led either to pass the cost of effluents on to the consumer, thereby reducing demand and thus production, or, if competitive conditions do not permit him to increase prices, to accept lower profits, which would discourage new investment in the industry.

The actual legislation aimed at air and water pollution uses quite different strategies—generally a combination of fixed standards (regarding the absolute level of pollutants that may be discharged) with financial incentives (such as accelerated depreciation of investment in anti-pollution equipment or cash subsidies to municipalities building sewage treatment plants). The most extreme form of what might be termed a directive strategy, as distinct from an incentive strategy, is the Federal Water Pollution Control Amendments of 1972 that would ban *all* effluent

---

15. A. Myrick Freeman III and Robert H. Haveman, "Clean Rhetoric and Dirty Water," *Public Interest* (Summer 1972), pp. 51–65. See also, in Selma Mushkin (ed.), *Public Prices for Public Products* (Urban Institute, 1972), the chapter by Allen V. Kneese, "Discharge Capacity of Waterways and Effluent Charges," pp. 133–51, and Paul H. Gerhardt's chapter on "Air Pollution Control: Benefits, Costs, and Inducements," pp. 153–71.

discharge into the nation's waters by 1985, however great the cost of achieving the ban and however small the benefits from preventing the last quantum of discharge.

A second example is in the area of air pollution caused by motor vehicles. The Motor Vehicle Air Pollution Control Act of 1965 set some emission standards; the 1970 amendments to the Clean Air Act made the standards more severe. They required auto manufacturers to reduce hydrocarbon emissions by 90 percent by 1975 and nitrous oxide emissions by the same amount by 1976. Though some may disagree with these standards as inadequate, the chief difficulty with the approach is that any such standards, imposed within a short time, almost certainly require the industry to commit itself to seeking improvements in the present technology (namely, the internal combustion engine) and provide no serious incentive to explore theoretically more promising alternatives involving other technologies (for example, external, continuous combustion engines, as in steam engines, gas turbines, or electric drives).[16] Adapting the internal combustion engine to minimal-pollution operation is quite difficult, and maintaining such an engine in proper tune or inspecting it to ensure that it remains in tune would be expensive and easily evaded by both motorists and repairmen. Furthermore, without a major development of alternative technologies, the government agency enforcing the 1975/1976 emission standards was forced to choose between stopping auto production (politically unthinkable) or relaxing the standards to accord with whatever level of improvement the industry has been able to attain. So far, the government has been inclined to relax the standards marginally.

A third instance of political rather than economic solutions can be found in the area of consumer credit. Various studies have suggested that "the poor pay more" for various items, especially furniture and major appliances.[17] Some part of these higher prices results from steep finance charges. The upshot is that a significant proportion of the poor in the city are heavily in debt as purchasers of low-quality household furnishings, and many of these persons have their wages garnisheed when they

16. I am indebted here to Henry D. Jacoby and John Steinbruner, "Salvaging the Federal Attempt To Control Auto Pollution," *Public Policy*, Vol. 21 (Winter 1973), pp. 1–48, and to Steinbruner, "Toward an Analysis of Policy Implementation: The Case of Mobile Source Air Pollution" (paper prepared for the 1971 annual meeting of the American Political Science Association; processed).

17. See, for example, David Caplovitz, *The Poor Pay More* (Free Press, 1963).

default on the payments. Ostensibly to deal with this problem, the Consumer Credit Protection Act of 1968 (the "truth-in-lending bill") was passed, providing that there must be full disclosure of all interest and finance charges in consumer transactions, that "loan sharking" is a federal crime, and that wages can be garnisheed only up to 25 percent of a person's weekly paycheck after exemption of the first $48 earned. Interest-charge disclosure, the most hotly debated of the bill's provisions, has apparently had almost no effect on the evils it was intended to cure and probably cannot even in principle have much of an effect. The prior Massachusetts truth-in-lending law was reportedly without impact, and this fact was known before the federal law was passed.[18] The ineffectual nature of such regulatory devices arises from the nature of both the demand and the supply of consumer goods. Poor persons are not comparison shoppers and display little interest in the size of a finance charge, though considerable interest in the size of the total weekly or monthly payments. If these latter figures are kept small enough, the consumer will buy with little regard for interest rates. And those firms that supply such persons can, if regulation lowers finance charges, recapture profits by either raising the price or lowering the quality of the merchandise sold. Furthermore, owing to the higher cost of doing business in poor neighborhoods (resulting from credit losses, theft, and the like), retailers in these areas, though they have higher markups, do not have higher profit levels than similar retailers in middle-class areas.[19] If the "problems" of consumer credit can be solved by government at all, easier access to chain stores that sell good merchandise at reasonable prices might be arranged for the poor (which in turn would require investment subsidies and credit guarantees to induce such stores to locate in the poorest neighborhoods); or else the amount of debt low-income persons can run up might be restricted (by, for example, requiring large down payments such as were in effect during the Second World War). Throughout the debate on the truth-in-lending legislation, the discussion of the problems of poor consumers bore almost no relationship to the provisions of the bill.

A fourth example concerns the regulation of prices in competitive

18. Homer Kripke, "Gesture and Reality in Consumer Credit Reform," *New York University Law Review,* Vol. 44 (March 1969), pp. 7–9.

19. This is the finding of Federal Trade Commission, *Economic Report on Installment Credit and Retail Sales Practices of District of Columbia Retailers* (1968).

industries. Most economists who have examined the air passenger and freight transport industries have concluded that prices charged to most (though not all) consumers by federally regulated airlines and truckers are higher than they would be without regulation and that deregulation would not substantially affect other important values (such as safety).[20] There is substantial evidence that the regulation of the field prices of natural gas, though it may have kept gas prices down for some present-day consumers, will eventually lead to higher prices owing to the absence of any market incentive to explore and develop additional gas reserves.[21]

In these four cases, the government sought either to protect an industry (as in the regulation of air fares and truck and rail rates) or to set for industry a standard that was impossible of attainment (as with the ban on effluent discharges into waterways), irrelevant to the objective being sought (as with the disclosure of finance charges), or likely to produce unwanted side effects (as with the auto emission standards). These examples are not necessarily representative of all regulatory policies, but they are important cases that affect the behavior of thousands of firms and the expenditure of many millions of dollars. To obtain any regulation at all, it was necessary in each case to get legislators to take the problem seriously, to forge a winning coalition among legislators with diverse interests and perceptions, and to overcome the arguments and influence of opponents. Accomplishing this in a representative government requires the recitation of powerful arguments, the evocation of horror stories, or the mobilization of a broad political movement. Political inertia is not easily overcome, and when it is overcome, it is often at the price of exaggerating the virtue of those who are to benefit (a de-

20. Regarding the airlines, see Richard E. Caves, *Air Transport and Its Regulators: An Industry Study* (Harvard University Press, 1962), Chap. 18; William A. Jordan, *Airline Regulation in America* (Johns Hopkins Press, 1970). On freight transportation, see John R. Meyer et al., *The Economics of Competition in the Transportation Industries* (Harvard University Press, 1959); Merton J. Peck, "Competitive Policy for Transportation?" in Almarin Phillips (ed.), *Perspectives on Antitrust Policy* (Princeton University Press, 1965), pp. 244–72. A synthesis of much of the recent evidence on both industries can be found in William A. Jordan, "Producer Protection, Prior Market Structure, and the Effects of Government Regulation," *Journal of Law and Economics,* Vol. 15 (April 1972), pp. 151–76.

21. Paul W. MacAvoy, *Price Formation in Natural Gas Fields: A Study of Competition, Monopsony, and Regulation* (Yale University Press, 1962), Chap. 8; MacAvoy, "The Regulation-Induced Shortage of Natural Gas," *Journal of Law and Economics,* Vol. 14 (April 1971), pp. 167–99; Edward W. Erickson and Robert M. Spann, "Supply Response in a Regulated Industry: The Case of Natural Gas," *Bell Journal of Economics and Management Science,* Vol. 2 (Spring 1971), pp. 94–121.

frauded debtor, a sick industry) or the wickedness of those who are to bear the burden (a smog-belching car, a polluting factory, a grasping creditor).

These political constraints on economic regulation may exist in all governments, or they may be especially pervasive in American government. Without a study comparing regulation in several regimes, that question cannot be answered, and scarcely any such studies exist. It is a plausible hypothesis, however, that American government is not powerful enough to impose radical solutions for problems of business behavior (by nationalizing firms or sectors); but neither is it powerful enough to ignore demands for political solutions (by deliberately choosing free market arrangements). In short, the U.S. government may own fewer businesses but regulate more business practices than most other democracies. This is because political power in the United States is sufficiently localistic in its sources to be responsive to demands for change and sufficiently diffuse in its institutional forms to be incapable of extreme actions. The result is piecemeal regulation made possible by either quiet bargaining on behalf of benefited interests or populistic appeals on behalf of larger publics.

Regulatory Administration

Business regulation is affected not only by its political origins but by its administrative embodiment. Sometimes this takes the form of rule making, as when the Federal Reserve Board sets the discount rate, the Environmental Protection Agency sets allowable automotive emission standards, or the ICC sets freight rates. Sometimes administration consists of adjudicating claims, as when the FCC awards a television license or the National Labor Relations Board (NLRB) hears a complaint about employment practices. Sometimes administration takes the form of attacking an alleged ill, as when the Department of Justice Antitrust Division prosecutes under the Sherman Act or the Federal Trade Commission (FTC) orders an advertiser to cease and desist.

For all agencies with less than precise standards for their actions and conspicuous boundaries to their authority, regulatory management will consist of efforts to enlarge the domain and specificity of regulation. One reason for this is the continuing effort of the agency to decide, in the absence of a clear standard, what it wants to accomplish. If "public interest, convenience, and necessity" cannot guide automatically the licensing process of the FCC, the FCC will begin elaborating, on a case-by-case basis, an opinion, not always consistent or enduring, as to what this phrase entails. It will suggest, for example, that the phrase requires local ownership of broadcast stations, a limit on the number of stations under a single ownership, and a commitment to "public service" broadcasting at least some of the time. A case can be made for these rules, though they are hardly without drawbacks (for example, local ownership inhibits the development of regional broadcast services with some attendant economies of scale) or always mutually consistent (the smaller the ownership interest, the fewer the resources for public service broadcasting). But these standards, detailed though they seem, are insufficient to settle all contests for licenses or even to narrow the field down very much. Hence further criteria, generally a good deal less plausible and even less likely to remain intact from one case to the next, are invented —whether the prospective licensee is of "good character," whether he will conduct a survey of "community groups" to ensure that he is meeting their "needs," and so on. One does not have to go very far down this road before one has enough "standards" to permit one to make virtually any decision one wants—which is to say, to act arbitrarily. The result is a state of affairs that both outrages the critics of broadcasting (who find the FCC too close to the regulated industry) and dismays the broadcasters themselves (who find the FCC constantly meddling in decisions about the content of broadcasting and generally keeping them on tenterhooks).

A second reason for the efforts to enlarge the domain of regulation can be found in what James W. McKie has called the "tar-baby effect."[22] This occurs when an agency applies a regulation, perhaps a quite clear and defensible one, to some single aspect of an enterprise (for example, the rate a utility may earn) only to discover that the effect of its regulation is not what it hoped; as a consequence, it then seeks to regulate additional aspects of the enterprise in order to make the initial regulation "come out right." Suppose, to use McKie's example, one sought to regulate the rate of return on investment to prevent a utility from making monopoly profits. Theoretically, such a strategy meets most of the requirements of an economizing approach: a single key variable is regu-

22. McKie, "Regulation and the Free Market: The Problem of Boundaries," *Bell Journal of Economics and Management Science,* Vol. 1 (Spring 1970), p. 9.

lated; the regulation takes the form of an unambiguous quantitative constraint; and the public purpose is clear and easily justified. But once the rate of return is set, the utility's managers lose much of their incentive to keep costs down and produce efficiently: they will get their allowable earnings whatever the costs. (One appealing way to let costs go up is to inflate managerial salaries.) If the allowed rate of return is higher than the cost of capital, there may be a tendency to overinvest in capital-intensive innovations (the so-called Averch-Johnson effect, the empirical existence of which is debatable). The utility may charge very high prices to customers whose demand for the utility's product is inelastic and much lower prices for the same product to those whose demands are highly elastic, and all this will appear to be unjust price discrimination. In response, the regulatory agency will endeavor to issue new directives controlling executive salaries, licensing new capital investment, and setting prices for various classes of users. In counter-response, the utility may let the quality of its service deteriorate to those customers for whom the agency has set prices lower than what the utility would have charged. In counter-counter-response, the agency will issue quality-of-service directives. And so on.[23] This sort of friction occurs even if the regulated monopoly faces no competition. Competition frequently exists, however (as between electricity and gas as a source of power), and of course multiplies the problems.

An especially interesting example of the unintended effect is found in the attitude of public utility commissions toward the charitable contributions of regulated utilities. Because the commissions see their task as keeping rates down, they typically will not allow utilities to charge as business expenses any educational or charitable contributions. These must instead be shown as deductions from net income. As a result, utilities contribute, on the average, a much smaller percentage of their before-tax income to charity than do industries not subject to rate regulation. Here, the existence of regulation, designed originally to achieve one social objective, prevents the development of "social responsibility" among businessmen.[24]

23. The work of the New York Public Service Commission serves as a case in point. At one time that agency had under way eight separate investigations into the pricing and service levels of the New York Telephone Company. *New York Times,* August 24, 1972.

24. Council for Financial Aid to Education, *Educational Contributions by Public Utilities and Other Regulated Industries as an Allowable Operating Expense for Rate-Making Purposes* (New York, 1972), p. 15. The figures used by the CFAE

A third reason for the tendency to increase the domain of regulation arises out of the fact that a regulatory agency is a *public* body and thus is the natural locus for public expectations that "problems" involving the affected industry will be solved. If a group feels that television programs are silly or dull or show too much violence, it is only necessary that there be an FCC for it to become the object of a campaign aimed at requiring broadcasters to show programs that are sophisticated, entertaining, and nonviolent (by somebody's standards). Never mind that the FCC has no idea how to achieve these results and, given the economics of over-the-air broadcasting, that perhaps they cannot be achieved at all. The agency will either resist the demands (a risky course now that plaintiffs increasingly obtain court orders compelling action), or it will conduct studies and issue notices of proposed regulations. In due time new rules will emerge—for example, restricting the number of hours of prime time that can be preempted by networks—but who can say whether the programs will improve?

If passenger rail service is declining in quality or appears on the verge of going out of existence altogether, it is only necessary that there be an ICC for suburban middle-class commuters, in their own interest, to find a plausible target. If two small cities wish to acquire air service between them, it is only necessary that the Civil Aeronautics Board (CAB) exist and have the power to award air routes and approve fares; in time Jonesville and Toonerville will get air service, and the cost of this uneconomic arrangement will be passed on to those who fly on self-sustaining routes. Richard A. Posner has offered a theory that summarizes many of these tendencies: regulation has, as one of its functions, the performance of taxation and subsidization chores normally (but with greater difficulty) performed by the legislature.[25] Other examples of this process include the requirement that auto insurers accept high-risk drivers at rates that produce a loss to the company, that AT&T provide free interconnections for the National Educational Television network, that electric utilities give discounts to hospitals, and (until recently) that magazine publishers be allowed to mail at rates below the postal service's marginal cost.

---

are from 1967 tabulations of corporate income tax returns. See also Henry G. Manne, "The Social Responsibility of Regulated Utilities," *Wisconsin Law Review*, No. 4 (1972), pp. 995–1009.

25. Posner, "Taxation by Regulation," *Bell Journal of Economics and Management Science,* Vol. 2 (Spring 1971), pp. 22–50.

Some of these subsidies may be desirable, others may not be. But all create great difficulties for the rational management of public regulation inasmuch as there is neither a criterion for balancing costs and benefits nor any incentive to reveal publicly who is getting how much from whom. There are also difficult questions of equity. For example, even if one ought to subsidize uneconomic air or train service, should the cost fall wholly on other passengers or shippers? Finally, if the cost of the subsidy is not fully recovered by the affected industry, it will have a powerful incentive to cheat by allowing service to deteriorate. This, of course, produces more consumer complaints and a further round of regulatory intervention.

A fourth reason why regulation expands is that an agency may wish to increase its power over an industry. The agency may wish to improve its prospects for accomplishing its substantive objectives, perhaps by increasing its bargaining power so as to get better settlements than the rote application of policy would produce. Or (a motive rare among federal agencies but not so rare among state and local ones) the agency may wish to increase its nuisance value and thus what its members can charge the industry in graft or favors. The Antitrust Division brings many cases it probably cannot win but through which it may influence business behavior via consent-decree proceedings. The Securities and Exchange Commission (SEC) can use its right to approve or disapprove new security registrations to exact changes in corporate arrangements. The FCC can use the vagueness of its policies and the fact that broadcast licenses are issued for only three years at a time to get changes (or promises of changes) in broadcast content even though in the end hardly any license is ever revoked and despite the fact that the governing legislation specifically forbids the regulation of content.

Finally, as a matter of bureaucratic politics, agency officials often wish to hold the initiative. The existence of an unchanging policy or set of substantive rules makes more predictable the behavior of an agency in various circumstances; the more predictable the behavior, the more it can be taken for granted, and the less discretionary influence the agency can wield.[26] Furthermore, as studies of bureaucratic administration have shown, if a rule specifies the minimum expected behavior for a person, then his actual behavior will tend to conform to—and in some cases

26. Michel Crozier, *The Bureaucratic Phenomenon* (University of Chicago Press, 1964), pp. 156–59; James Q. Wilson, "The Dead Hand of Regulation," *Public Interest,* No. 25 (Fall 1971), pp. 39–58.

decline to—that minimum.[27] Thus recurrent changes are necessary to break the pattern.

We have no direct and systematic measure of the extent to which an agency's domain of directive regulation expands for the reasons suggested here. Roger G. Noll has argued, after reviewing historical data on selected agency budgets, that many agencies use additional money to increase regulatory domain rather than to improve performance.[28] In any event, the argument that expansive tendencies cannot possibly prevail because the regulatory agencies are always starved for funds is clearly false. After World War II and again in the late 1950s and early 1960s, agency appropriations increased dramatically (in the latter period, they tripled). George J. Stigler has observed that "economic regulation is clearly a prosperous calling: the average federal regulatory agency doubles its dollar expenditures each eight to ten years."[29]

There will, of course, be exceptions to the general tendencies discussed above. Some agencies administer legal rules so exact and under grants of authority so inflexible that reinterpreting those rules or extending the boundaries of that authority is virtually impossible. The minimum wage and maximum hours legislation enforced by a bureau of the Department of Labor seems to be of this character. To many readers, however, the chief defect with the expansion theory offered here is that it neglects the principal determinant of the growth and function of business regulation—the interests and preferences of the regulated businesses.

Business "Capture" of Regulatory Agencies

Commentators as otherwise different as George Stigler and Gabriel Kolko have argued that administrative regulation will not succeed in constraining business firms to act in accordance with socially valuable objectives because the agencies that administer these regulations will be "captured" by or otherwise serve the interests of the affected industries. Professor Stigler in particular has offered as a general theory the proposition that government regulation is "acquired by the industry and is

27. Alvin W. Gouldner, *Patterns of Industrial Bureaucracy: A Case Study of Modern Factory Administration* (Free Press, 1954), Chap. 9.

28. Noll, *Reforming Regulation: An Evaluation of the Ash Council Proposals* (Brookings Institution, 1971), p. 88.

29. Stigler, "The Process of Economic Regulation," *Antitrust Bulletin*, Vol. 17 (Spring 1972), pp. 216, 218.

designed and operated primarily for its benefit."[30] Beneficial regulation can take several forms: direct money subsidies (as for airlines or the merchant marine), control over entry (as with airline certification, bank charters, protective tariffs, or oil import quotas), the control of substitute products and processes (as with restrictions on oleomargarine to benefit butter producers or on labor-saving devices to protect the craft unions), and price fixing (as with freight rates).

To the extent regulation takes this form, its use as a means of inducing business to serve socially desirable objectives is obviously quite limited, even trivial, unless one can argue that the anticompetitive interests of a particular industry are coincident with the broader interests of society.

The analysis earlier in this chapter regarding the political sources of regulation should provide some clues as to the circumstances under which the regulated industry will become the client of the regulatory agency. When a potential government policy promises to confer concentrated (i.e., high per capita) benefits on a small, organizable sector of society and impose only widely distributed (i.e., low per capita) costs on a large, hard-to-organize segment of society, then (a) the proposed policy will probably be adopted and (b) those who implement the policy will seek to serve the group requesting it. It is now generally understood, for example, that those agencies which have in the past been most solicitous of the welfare of the industries they regulate—the CAB and the airlines, the FCC and the broadcasters—were not "captured" by those industries but were created at the industries' request or at least with their active support. To serve these industries was only to obey a clear legislative mandate. Domestic airlines complained of the "chaos" caused by "destructive competition," and broadcasters confronted acute problems of signal interference. Both turned, with varying degrees of unanimity and enthusiasm, to the government for help.[31]

---

30. Stigler, "The Theory of Economic Regulation," *Bell Journal of Economics and Management Science*, Vol. 2 (Spring 1971), p. 3.

31. On the airlines, see Robert Burkhardt, *The Federal Aviation Administration* (Praeger, 1967); on railroads, see Kolko, *Railroads and Regulation,* and Garraty, *The New Commonwealth;* on broadcasters, see Robert E. Cushman, *The Independent Regulatory Commissions* (Oxford University Press, 1941), and *Regulation of Broadcasting*, a study for the House Committee on Interstate and Foreign Commerce, 85 Cong. 1 sess. (1958). After a period in which public interest theories of the origins of regulation were unquestioningly accepted, we have now entered a period in which self-interest theories are uncritically substituted. In most cases, the matter is more complex than either theory admits. Railroaders

Regulatory agencies that were created out of the conflict between two organized sectors of society under circumstances such that the benefits to one were costs to the other are less likely to adopt a serving-the-client attitude. If favoritism develops, it will represent an unstable equilibrium of forces, and the balance will shift from time to time. The National Labor Relations Board began as the patron of organized labor, became pro-business under the Eisenhower administration, shifted back toward labor under Kennedy, and so on. The railroads' position as the favored clients of the ICC declined after the truckers were brought under ICC control in the 1930s.

Regulations created to impose costs on organizable sectors of the economy in order to obtain diffused benefits for the society offer the key test of the "capture" hypothesis. When government attempts to prevent restraint of trade, to keep impure food and harmful drugs off the market, to improve auto safety, to eliminate unsafe toys, to end false and misleading advertising, to reduce air and water pollution, or to maintain a minimum wage, it is in effect defying an industry or even all of industry. There are two ways industry can fight back: block passage of the legislation or (failing that) influence its administration.

In the past, blocking legislation entirely has been the most successful strategy, though in truth little "strategy" was involved because until fairly recently legislators did not take most "consumer" bills seriously. Today, the advent of consumer and ecology movements, combined with the publicity rewards and the increased opportunities for presidential nominations now available to senators who can find and capitalize on a popular issue, have reduced significantly (but not eliminated) the chances of industry blockage of such legislation.

Such legislation can be emasculated. The case most frequently mentioned (though the accounts thus far available have scarcely been dispassionate) is that of the Food and Drug Administration (FDA), which allegedly adopted for many years a solicitous and benign attitude toward the pharmaceutical manufacturers. This attitude was rewarded, it is claimed, by giving lucrative or prestigious jobs in the drug industry to

---

were divided about the Interstate Commerce Act. Furthermore, the act specifically denied the railroads what they most wanted—legally binding "pooling" (i.e., cartel) agreements. The Radio Act of 1927, strongly supported by the broadcasting industry, was also supported by spokesmen for a public that was upset by poor radio reception. A full discussion of these matters is beyond the scope of this paper.

former members of the agency. Assuming that the worst was true, what is striking is how easily the situation was reversed by the appointment in 1966 of a new, more vigorous administrator. A comparable degree of activism was instilled in the Federal Trade Commission by the appointment of new commissioners. Whether these new ways of acting will persist remains to be seen. And the behavior of the newer agencies in the fields of auto safety and pollution abatement is too recent to be assessed.

Before one supposes that the laxity of the old Federal Drug Administration and perhaps of the old FTC was entirely the result of industrial capture, it is important to consider other explanations consistent with the same facts. The Department of Agriculture must inspect every piece of meat slaughtered for shipment across state lines; under the Wool Products Labeling Act of 1939, the FTC examined in a recent year 25 million products in 12,000 establishments, thereby discovering 14,000 violations. Postal inspectors are supposed to prevent the mailing of materials intended to defraud, the amount of which must be staggering; the FDA is empowered to inspect any establishment processing or storing foods, drugs, or cosmetics, but there are 85,000 such establishments, the total output of which is vast. The FTC is charged with preventing false and misleading advertising, an ambiguous criterion that must (in theory) be applied to hundreds of thousands of commercial announcements.[32] In short, part of the problem of using regulation to confer widely distributed benefits is that the transactions to be regulated are almost as numerous and as widely distributed as the benefits to be had from them. This often means that what is in fact controlled is not all such transactions but a sample of them somehow drawn—by lot, by complaint, or by design. And where in fact all such transactions are controlled, as is the case in meat inspection, the number of persons who must be employed is very large and the circumstances under which they work give little visibility to, and thus impede control over, their activity.

Regulation on behalf of consumers creates very large problems of discretion among lower-ranking personnel, just as attempts to enforce traffic laws and vice laws create such problems for police departments.[33] How the members of a large organization will manage that discretion depends on a number of factors, of which influence from the affected

32. See Clair Wilcox, *Public Policies toward Business* (rev. ed., Irwin, 1960), p. 204.
33. See James Q. Wilson, *Varieties of Police Behavior: The Management of Law and Order in Eight Communities* (Harvard University Press, 1968), Chap. 2.

industry is only one, and may not be the most important. We know very little—indeed, next to nothing—about the day-to-day management of these regulatory tasks. (By comparison, assessing the behavior of the more industry-oriented agencies is relatively easy: each year the FCC handles six hundred to seven hundred commercial broadcast license applications, and the CAB takes on perhaps five thousand or six thousand economic enforcement cases.) We can here only speculate on the factors that will make for better or worse agency discretion.

One is the extent of the sampling problem. Bias can enter into any situation in which one can claim he "didn't have time" to consider a particularly nettlesome problem. The FTC has been in this position, to its great regret. The Antitrust Division of the Justice Department, by contrast, is in the happy position of being able to investigate *every* plausible case presented to it. As Suzanne Weaver has shown, clues as to possible violations of the Sherman Act arise in manageable numbers each year, and the division has enough lawyers to look closely at all but the most farfetched or trivial.[34]

Another factor behind agency performance is the presence or absence of an external, more or less objective measure of success. For the Antitrust Division, this is found in the decisions of judges before whom Sherman or Clayton Act cases are brought: the division does not *decide* cases; it *prosecutes* them. Requiring conformity to an explicit monetary figure is the essence of wage regulation in the Labor Department.[35] On the other hand, there is no objective measure or third-party judgment for the FTC or the FCC.

Sometimes there is no objective test of the rightness of an agency decision but there are strong professional norms maintained by outside reference groups which can serve much the same function. Suzanne Weaver's research suggests the importance to the lawyers of the Antitrust Division of the good opinion of the "antitrust bar," and not merely because a number of division lawyers will someday join that bar on the side of the defense—the respect of professional colleagues, earned by bringing "good cases," is valued even by those attorneys who spend their lives

34. Suzanne Weaver, "Decision-Making in the U.S. Antitrust Division" (Ph.D. dissertation, Harvard University, 1973).

35. See Peter M. Blau, *The Dynamics of Bureaucracy: A Study of Interpersonal Relations in Two Government Agencies* (University of Chicago Press, 1955), Chaps. 7–11. The agency analyzed by Blau is not identified by him, but I have it on excellent authority that he in fact studied the office in the Department of Labor that administers the Fair Labor Standards Act.

in the division.[36] By contrast, examiners who conduct hearings for some of the regulatory agencies may have to make important decisions without generally accepted and professional norms to guide them. And the meat inspectors of the Department of Agriculture, though they perform semiprofessional tasks for which one might be expected to know a good deal of medicine, anatomy, bacteriology, and law, are in fact low-paid civil servants with a rudimentary knowledge of such matters and are required to work in the unpleasant, sometimes hostile environment of a slaughterhouse. Recently several inspectors went on trial in Boston for allegedly accepting gratuities from a meatpacker (though the facts of the case do not indicate clearly whether there was any substantial wrongdoing).[37] Meat inspectors are in a situation very much like big-city policemen: the wonder is that they can do their jobs as well as they do. The about-face in the posture of the FDA came about, it seems, in large part because a new administrator was able to hire new personnel and instill in the old personnel a sense that the governing standards of their work in drug testing should be those of academic and research-oriented chemists and doctors rather than those of medical practitioners and commercial chemists.

The existence of strong professional norms is not an unmixed blessing. What is a desideratum to some will be a bias to others. The Antitrust Division, for example, has succeeded in institutionalizing the ethos of the lawyer, or more exactly of the prosecuting attorney, in a field in which one might wish for the application of economic analysis as well. From time to time economic guidelines have been suggested for antitrust work (in order, for example, to gauge the likelihood of workable competition or predict the market effect of a divestiture order), but these have been ignored. Few organizations, and especially few successful ones, can tolerate having more than a single governing ethos: the need for morale, for a sense of mission and of distinctive competence, and for standard operating procedures means that competing norms will be suppressed, ignored, or isolated.[38]

A partial and temporary substitute for professional norms is missionary zeal. An agency in its formative years, especially one created on a

36. Weaver, "Decision-Making in the U.S. Antitrust Division."

37. Peter Schuck, "The Curious Case of the Indicted Meat Inspectors," *Harper's*, Vol. 245 (September 1972), pp. 81–88.

38. The perspective is that of Philip Selznick, *Leadership in Administration* (Row, Peterson, 1957).

wave of public expectations or as a result of an ideological struggle, will attract as pioneer staff members persons who believe in the cause and who are adventurous enough to attract public attention during the early years. This was true of the Bureau of Chemistry (predecessor agency of the FDA) under Dr. Harvey Wiley and of the National Highway Safety Bureau (predecessor of the National Highway Traffic Safety Administration—NHTSA) under Dr. William Haddon, Jr. The zeal of the FDA soon began to decline, a slowdown caused as much by presidential opposition as by industry "capture" or internal complacency: Wiley made the mistake of describing saccharin as perhaps harmful to health at a time when President Theodore Roosevelt was using it every day. Roosevelt retaliated by appointing a board to review (and in effect to overturn) many bureau decisions.[39] The fate of the NHTSA remains to be seen.

The nature of the rules being administered will influence the exercise of discretion and the degree of industry compliance. If compliance with a rule is highly visible, costs little, and entails no competitive disadvantage, that rule will be more easily enforced than one with the opposite characteristics. Thus scarcely any administrative effort will be required to get cigarette manufacturers to print a health warning on their packages: the printed message costs little, its absence would be quickly noted, and no brand is likely to sell better because the warning is left off. By contrast, great effort will be needed to ensure proper meat inspection: it is expensive and arduous work, the consumer cannot readily detect falsely certified meat, and meat packaging is so competitive and the profit margins so thin that the sale of substandard or adulterated products could be quite profitable.

There is evidence that compliance is more readily obtained from large, prosperous firms than from small, marginal ones. This was the conclusion of Robert Lane in his study of the economic regulation of New England businessmen, and there is some support for this in George Katona's study of business observance of wartime price controls.[40] If this difference between firms exists, one reason may be that large firms are more visible and politically more vulnerable (i.e., they make more inviting targets for critical politicians) than smaller ones. The New York

39. Nadel, *Politics of Consumer Protection*, p. 24.
40. Robert E. Lane, *The Regulation of Businessmen* (Yale University Press, 1954), pp. 95, 103; George Katona, *Price Control and Business: Field Studies among Producers and Distributors of Consumer Goods in the Chicago Area, 1942–44* (University of Indiana Press, 1946), p. 241.

City Department of Consumer Affairs, for example, has found that large retail stores will often yield to adverse publicity whereas the smaller stores must be taken to court to achieve the same result. Another reason may be that a big firm is likely to have a large, specialized bureaucracy to handle compliance with rules just as it has specialized bureaucracies to handle other aspects of its business.

Finally, solicitousness toward industry is sometimes promoted by the requirements of due process. As Richard E. Caves observed in his study of air transport regulation, a perfectly autonomous and (from an economic point of view) efficient regulatory agency would be one that was free to act without constraint—which is to say, to act without giving notice, holding hearings, considering evidence, receiving petitions, or rendering opinions.[41] Not only does political reality often conflict with an economizing approach to regulation; so also do the rule of law and the requirement of adversary proceedings. The interests of the producer are often taken into account because, at a hearing, he makes a persuasive case that they *ought* to be. And when an adversary hearing is held—for example, when two airlines are competing for a particular route—the agency's attention is inevitably drawn away from fundamental issues. (Should the route be regulated at all? What service would competition produce?) From the start, the question is narrowed down to that of who should provide a given service. In any case, how could an agency *not* be "industry-oriented" when the only parties to hearings are *firms*.

Constraints versus Conscience

Most discussions of the social responsibilities of business firms focus on the "soul" of firms, have as their object persuading firms to do as conscience dictates, and proceed along hortatory, if not evangelical, lines. It would be easy to dismiss these exchanges, and the voluminous literature and endless conferences in which they are to be found, as mere rhetoric. Easy, and in part justified. Most such discussions never address seriously the question of by whom, or with what authority, a firm will be instructed in its social duty; how the consequences of a conscience-inspired act will be made known and, when necessary, modified; who

41. Caves, *Air Transport and Its Regulators*, p. 297.

will bear the costs of conscience-serving acts; and, above all, by what means competing consciences will be reconciled. These difficulties are so patent and yet so commonly ignored by those who discuss social responsibility that one is tempted to infer that such discussion is mere verbal posturing designed to deceive the onlooker into supposing that something is happening when in fact nothing is intended.

That inference, though true in some degree, is misleading, for the striking fact is that government programs to change corporate behavior in allegedly beneficial ways increase in direct proportion to the amount of discussion about the need for corporate social responsibility. As conferences multiply and books on corporate responsibility appear in growing numbers, laws regulating corporate activity are enacted in comparably growing numbers. If any vice president for community relations thought that by talking about his firm's social responsibilities he would avert public regulation, he has by now been thoroughly disabused. It is almost as if the exercise of private conscience leads to the imposition of public constraints.

This is, perhaps, the most important finding from a review of the politics of economic regulation. For various reasons—a shift in the national mood, the increasingly critical posture of the mass media, the appeal that consumer and ecological issues have for presidential hopefuls, the changing attitudes of the business elite itself—the conventional theory of interest-group politics seems no longer adequate as an explanation of economic regulation. That theory was, in simplified form, that political power was sufficiently diffused and interests sufficiently organized that any interest seriously threatened by a proposed policy could force supporters of the policy to bargain with it and make substantial concessions. Policy making, where there were two or more affected interests, was supposedly based on consensus building. Where there was only one affected interest (that is, where the costs of a program were diffused among many unorganized citizens), policy making would, according to the conventional theory, lead to government programs serving a single interest (i.e., to the "capture" of an agency).

To the extent that a large political market exists for programs with diffused benefits and to the degree that the interests which must bear the cost of such programs can be defeated through the skillful use of the media, American politics has lost one of its principal characteristics—the capacity of an organized interest to "cast a veto" on policies that affect it powerfully and adversely.

It is premature to conclude that any lasting change of this sort has occurred. The capacity to mobilize support for consumer and environmental legislation may be short-lived, as these enthusiasms wane or as interests that are both harmed by the program and possessed of public legitimacy (e.g., organizations of workers, blacks, etc.) raise objections. But it is equally risky to dismiss the symbolic changes already made as having no effect in "real politics."

The creation, reaffirmation, and institutionalization of symbols is a vitally important and easily neglected causal factor in politics. Adopting policies that provide largely symbolic gratifications for demands may achieve little of substance in the immediate case but constitute nonetheless a positive reinforcement for the demands themselves and the legitimation of a governmental role in dealing with these demands. The decisive stage in the ebb and flow of social conflict is control over the public agenda: what government may or may not do is chiefly determined by what people have come to believe is properly a "private" or a "public" matter. Thus a series of consumer, environmental, or drug-testing programs constitute, whatever may result in the particular instance, an assertion of governmental jurisdiction over matters once left to private arrangements. Furthermore, regulatory efforts, once institutionalized, are rarely abandoned; indeed, they usually expand.

Even the creation within government of a "Department of Consumer Affairs" that had only advisory and hortatory powers might have a significance that extended well beyond the initial grant of authority. It would constitute a formal repudiation of the rule of caveat emptor, and, depending on who ran the department, it could be a rallying point for forces in and out of the government seeking to hold the behavior of manufacturers and merchandisers to principles other than that of selling whatever anyone can be induced to buy. Consumer efforts will wax and wane with the rising and falling of tides of popular concern and the linkage between these efforts and political ambitions, but their secular trend will be in the direction of enhancing the status and powers of the proposed agency.

Some Preconditions of Effective Regulation

The administrative management and economic effect of regulatory agencies vary with the kind of rules enforced and the kind of industry regulated. Other things being equal, a program adopted as the result of the successful effort by one organized economic interest to impose constraints on another organized interest will be more effective than one adopted in response to efforts to confer benefits on large numbers of diverse and unorganized beneficiaries. The reason for this is that in the former case market power reinforces political power. For example, legal requirements to disclose the composition and quality of insecticides, fungicides, seeds, animal serums and toxins, caustic poisons, fabrics, and wool products are ordinarily obeyed because the "consumers" to whom the information is disclosed are to a significant degree not individual users but economic producers—farmers, clothing and furniture manufacturers, and importers. They purchase in large quantities and by specifications rather than by brand names, and they have trade associations that monitor business behavior and report violations.

If the beneficiaries of a regulation are large numbers of individual consumers, the regulation is most likely to be obeyed when compliance is readily visible and no firm suffers a competitive disadvantage by obeying (e.g., by printing proof numbers on liquor bottles or health warnings on cigarette labels). When noncompliance is easily concealed in ways that confer an economic advantage, compliance will be greatest among the largest firms and least among the smallest: a few large firms are easier to inspect than many small ones, and large firms are more likely to be internally bureaucratic to a degree that leads to the routinization of compliance. For example, compliance with many of the requirements of the Occupational Safety and Health Act or with various mine safety regulations seems to be greater among large firms that have the specialized competence to devise, acquire, and maintain the necessary equipment and for whom monetary costs of compliance represent a smaller proportional increase in overhead.

Regulations that stipulate a clear and timely standard for compliance such that all improper behavior can be specified or reasonably inferred in advance will be more effective than those that do not. A package-labeling requirement that calls for a full statement of the contents of the package will be routinely obeyed; a regulation barring "false and misleading advertising" will not. Though some advertising statements clearly contrary to fact can be made the subject of effective administrative actions, the myriad ways by which claims, including false ones, can be suggested or implied can never be anticipated in advance nor ended before there has been an opportunity for economic gain from their use.

Furthermore, claims proscribed from nationally circulated advertising can be shifted from the media to the point of sale and from printed statements at the point of sale to oral representations made by store clerks responding, perhaps, to special rebates or other incentives.

The institutional arrangements defining an enforcement agency's powers and jurisdiction will influence its effectiveness. An agency monitoring all commerce will be less influenced by industry claims than one monitoring a particular sector. An agency that prosecutes suspected offenders will be inclined to judge its own performance by how many cases it wins; an agency with the power to examine goods or investigate conditions will judge its behavior by how many inspections it carries out and at what cost. Neither test may be meaningful in terms of larger social objectives. In the first instance, the cases won by the agency's prosecutors may be trivial rather than important, have adverse rather than beneficial economic effects, and represent empty victories if there is no means for ensuring continuing compliance among the parties to the proceedings. In the second instance, the number of inspections executed tells one nothing about the fairness and propriety of the inspections, the existence or absence of corruption among the inspectors, or the value to the consumer of the inspected as opposed to the uninspected product. At a minimum, prosecutorial agencies seem less likely to be "captured" by an industry than inspectional ones.

Both business firms and regulatory agencies act on the basis of a common principle: maintain the organization. For the firm, that means creating and managing an income stream in a way that pleases union leaders, boards of directors, and institutional investors. For the public agency, that means creating and managing services (or a public image of services) that please key congressmen, organized clients, and the news media. From time to time that pattern is interrupted by an Upton Sinclair or a Ralph Nader, but there are not yet grounds for concluding that the functions of the crusader and the watchdog can be institutionalized.

CHAPTER SEVEN

The Consumer

MARTIN BRONFENBRENNER

It is not from the benevolence of the butcher, the brewer, or the baker, that we expect our dinner, but from their regard to their own interest. We address ourselves, not to their humanity but to their self-love, and never talk to them of our own necessities but of their advantages.
—Adam Smith, *The Wealth of Nations*, bk. i, chap. 2

A large part of the critics' strictures on the existing system comes down to protests against the individual wanting what he wants instead of what is good for him, of which the critic is to be the judge; and the critic does not feel himself called upon even to outline any standards other than his own preferences upon a basis of which judgment is to be passed. It would be well for the progress of science if we had less of this sort of thing and more serious effort to formulate standards and to determine the conditions under which free contract does or does not promote individual interests harmoniously and realize social ideals.
—Frank H. Knight, *Risk, Uncertainty and Profit* (1921)

THIS DISCUSSION of relations between business and the consumer combines normative and positive economics. In theory, a firm is behaving responsibly toward consumers when it sets prices and specifications for its products as it would set them if five conditions held perfectly:

1. *As if* the firm were a pure competitor with no monopoly or oligopoly power whatever, either in the short run or (especially) in the long run.

2. *As if* the firm's "economic horizon," meaning the horizon of its management, were sufficiently "long" to subordinate short-term concerns.

3. *As if* the firm's externalities, positive and negative, were all internalized, with no spillover. That is to say, as if the firm could not gain or lose indirectly by the activities of other firms—and vice versa.

4. *As if* accurate information as to product prices and quality were available to all consumers free of charge.

169

5. *As if* the law of agency operated, with sternness and certitude, to make the firm liable for the lapses of its officers, salesmen, technicians, workers, dealers, and subcontractors vis-à-vis the consuming public.

But of course neither the business sector nor the consuming public is composed of economic theorists. Consumers often see themselves as victims of restrictive and deceptive business practices. The extent to which that view can be justified is one of the issues here. Consumer groups have adopted certain strategies to advance their cause. Are these likely to succeed? What if they produce unintended results such as higher prices and the disappearance of "poor man's goods"? Finally, there is the issue of whether an adversary model provides the best guidance in this case. It may be more useful to focus upon ways to make a pro-consumer stand more profitable for a wider group of corporations.

The Consumer as Hero

Every economic interest group has its ideology, updated whenever the group feels put upon by comparison with some Golden Age or with what some rival group is getting. A usable ideology makes one's own group both the epic hero of economic development and the noble victim of exploitation in the marketplace. The businessman has at various times adopted the congenial doctrines of laissez-faire, Social Darwinism, rugged individualism, "Less government in business and more business in government," and "What's good for General Motors is good for the country." He tells dread tales of the confiscatory tax collector and the predatory trade unionist. The farmer, for his part, has relied on doctrines of physiocracy and agricultural fundamentalism. To hear the farmer tell it, the city slicker "chisels on his board bill" and doesn't know what hard work is. In a similar vein, organized labor has not only gloried in the labor theory of value but has pictured the unorganized worker as the ultimate victim of deflationary "higgling" of the market at less than full employment. Labor has also emphasized economic theories of maldistribution as the root of business recession and depression.

Economists, journalists, and social critics have contributed to all these images by treating the business, agricultural, and labor interests of a country as more unified than the facts warrant. (Witness, for example, the conflicts between export industries and import-competing ones with regard to tariffs and quotas.) Probably to an even greater extent, distinctions are obscured by the blanket term "consumer."[1] We assume, however, the existence of a common range of issues on which it is realistic to speak of "the" consumer being represented with reasonable accuracy by "consumer" spokesmen. We assume further that in the overall conflict between broad interest groups the scattered and diffuse consumer interest has come out on balance less well than the others.

In this sense we recognize that consumerism, too, has an ideology and a history. For centuries religious and social philosophers classified the businessman as a quasi criminal. Even Adam Smith, alleged spokesman for the bourgeoisie, made hostile remarks along those lines. "People of the same trade," he wrote, "seldom meet together, even for merriment and diversion, but the conversation ends in a conspiracy against the public, or in some contrivance to raise prices."[2]

In terms of economics, the easiest argument for the consumer as representing the public interest in a special sense that producer pressure groups cannot match is that the consumer spreads his income over a broad spectrum of goods and services, whereas the typical producer concentrates on a few items. According to Henry C. Simons, "One gets the right answers usually by regarding simply the interests of consumers, since we are all consumers."[3] A different but allied argument was put forth as early as 1845 by Frédéric Bastiat, who in *Sophismes Economiques* held that consumers and the public as a whole are interested in abundance of all goods, whereas any producer benefits by scarcity of whatever he himself supplies.

The tradition of identifying the public welfare with the consumer's interest has been particularly strong in pronouncements on international trade. The case against protective tariffs and quotas is argued in terms of abundance versus scarcity, in the spirit of Bastiat and Simons. (The abundance or scarcity involved is that of imports; the fact that free trade decreases the domestic abundance of *exports* is neglected except in inflationary emergencies.)

Going beyond the simple identification of the public good with the

1. A cogent presentation of this point is made by Ralph K. Winter, Jr., *The Consumer Advocate versus the Consumer* (Washington: American Enterprise Institute for Public Policy Research, 1972), pp. 14–15.

2. Smith, *Wealth of Nations,* bk. i, chap. 10, pt. 2. On prices, however, recall the observation attributed to John Ruskin: "There is hardly anything in the world that some man cannot make a little worse and sell a little cheaper."

3. Simons, *Economic Policy for a Free Society* (University of Chicago Press, 1948), p. 123.

consumer's interest, the so-called utility economists have offered a more recondite argument.[4] They begin by implicitly assuming fixed and fully employed stocks of the fundamental productive factors—land and labor. Given this assumption, one can reduce the cost and the supply of any good x to the marginal utilities of whatever quantity of other goods y, z, . . . must be sacrificed for x production. On this basis, one can allege that the consumer is and should be sovereign in allocating an economy's resources—ultimately determining by his choices in free markets what should be produced and in what quantities, by what methods it should be produced, how not only consumer goods but also other goods should be evaluated. This amounts to indirectly deciding the distribution of income and wealth and the social provision for growth and change. Such is the economic gospel of consumer sovereignty.

It is always admitted in the abstract that any consumer's tastes and choices are determined largely by his social milieu and can therefore be affected by producer devices such as advertising and salesmanship. In practice, however, producer influence on demand and utility is downgraded by utility economists as ephemeral.

The consumer sovereignty doctrine involves acceptance, at least as a satisfactory starting point, of the existing distribution of income and wealth, on the basis of "one dollar one vote." Particularly in Great Britain the doctrine in recent decades has been diluted in the direction of the parliamentary-democratic "one man one vote."

A neglected macroeconomic implication of the consumer sovereignty doctrine is that buyers' strikes against high prices should be regarded with benevolent neutrality if not absolute favor by the public authorities, even at the cost of bankruptcies among producers and unemployment among workers. As a matter of fact, however, the independent gospel of full employment has led to inflationary fiscal and monetary policies which look very like consumer strikebreaking. That is to say, govern-

---

4. The term "utility economics" refers to the demand-centered theory of value introduced in the 1870s. Reacting strongly against the labor theory of value, the early utility economists argued that value and price depend solely upon marginal utility and that prices determine costs through a process of imputation, rather than costs determining prices. Sometimes known as the "Austrian" theory of value, this view achieved its widest and most one-sided acceptance among Austrian economists during the period from 1870 to 1914. Most of these economists were highly conservative in their social outlook, their best-known spokesman being Eugen von Böhm-Bawerk. Ludwig von Mises and Friedrich von Hayek have presented "modernized" versions of the theory.

mental concern with consumer prices is replaced by concern for employment as soon as buyers' strikes cut into sales.

Since this particular historical and ideological underpinning for consumer sovereignty conflicts with other welfare doctrines and since the doctrine is said to exaggerate the likelihood of true competition, a newer theory carries more credibility. This newer line of thought presents the consumer as the potential victim of what might be called organizational slack.

The typical large corporation most of the time accrues what economists call net profit, accountants call net income, and operations researchers call organizational slack. Some portions of this slack can be concealed by the accounting mechanism in the short run. The remainder, however, is divided by decision or default among four broad groups of claimants: (1) the managers—in salary increments, bonuses, perquisites, and fringe benefits; (2) the stockholders—directly by way of higher dividends or indirectly by way of internal investment and capital gains; (3) the workers and the suppliers of productive inputs (on occasion including farmers and landlords)—in higher than competitive wages and other higher input prices; and (4) the consumers of the product—in lower output prices and/or higher output quality.

A natural tendency of corporate management, in the presence of organizational slack, is to arrogate a large fraction to itself. Since the management cadres of other prosperous companies do the same, interfirm competition for managerial talent provides a plausible reason for such arrogation. Stockholders and workers, for their part, must be "lived with" on a periodic if not a daily basis. Particularly if organized, they can and do bargain for substantial shares in the prosperous firm's organizational slack. The same can be said for suppliers of other productive inputs, including raw materials and intermediate goods. (Textbook treatments of the theory of the firm sometimes suggest that the stockholders are entitled to the entire amount, in discounted capital gains if not in dividends. The world usually runs on different lines.)

This leaves the final consumer—as distinguished from the large corporate buyer—characteristically devoid of bargaining power and organization, close to the end of the line, and a presumptive net loser in consequence of the imperfections of competition. It was not always thus; it is not thus today for small and medium-sized independent neighborhood retailers and service entrepreneurs who live with their consumers no less closely than with their suppliers, workers, or stockholders. But within J. K. Galbraith's "new industrial state," the consumer lives anonymously "off there in Endsville" far from centers of corporate decision making and outside the expensive suburbs where decision makers dwell.

The various movements of disaffected consumers may be looked on as attempts to readjust accumulated imbalance in the allocation of organizational slack. They operate by propaganda ("negative advertising" for the business firms attacked), by lawsuits, by legislation, by support for consumer-owned stores and factories.

American consumerism, drawing on various economic theories at one time or another, has gone through three phases. First came the consumer cooperative movement, dominated by immigrants and especially immigrants from Scandinavia. Second, protest against the business abuses of the 1920s, expressed most forcefully in the writings of Stuart Chase, led to the formation of watchdog groups, on guard against shoddy products and misleading advertisements. The principal organizations have been the Consumer Research Institute and Consumers Union, which specialize in testing products, evaluating advertisements, and reporting the results to the consuming public.[5] The third and current wave of consumerism dates from Ralph Nader's 1965 volume *Unsafe at Any Speed,* critical of the dangers of automobiles in general, General Motors automobiles in particular, and the Chevrolet Corvair *über alles.* Naderism, as this movement has been called, is still in progress and still widening.

Complaints and Strategies

In the ordinary sense, the major complaints of consumers and consumer advocates fall into five categories. (In terms of the economist's theoretical construct of perfect competition, the five may be reduced to two: high information costs and high transaction costs, rising to infinity for information impossible to come by and transactions impossible to make.) Those categories are: (1) deceptive advertising; (2) hidden

5. *Consumer Reports,* published monthly by Consumers Union, claimed a circulation in the neighborhood of 2 million in 1972. That same year, in a departure from tradition, the organization moved toward political activism by opening a consumer interest law division in Washington. See Judith Miller, "A Bolder Consumers Union," *Progressive,* Vol. 36 (September 1972), pp. 9–10.

Also located in Washington, the Consumer Federation of America represents about 200 organizations—national and local—concerned with particular commodities.

charges, primarily for financing purchases in installments; (3) meaningless warranties, inferior service, built-in obsolescence; (4) unsafe or impure products, failing to meet reasonable standards; (5) assorted fraud (misbranding, short weighting, and so forth).

Better Business Bureaus and similar business-supported consumer agencies do a more or less efficient job of protecting the middle-class customer against foul play at the hands of the price cutter, the door-to-door salesman, the out-of-town or mail-order interloper, and the desperate submarginal entrepreneur. They are not so effective against the large corporation and the well-established local business or on behalf of the consumer whose income and command of standard English are low.

Four strategies are usually advocated to reduce imbalance between consumer and producer interests. Given the subject of the present book, it is interesting to note that only one of these (employing the term "corporate soulfulness") emphasizes voluntary sacrifice by business itself.

Increased competition is the first of the strategies. To Andrew Jackson is ascribed the assertion that the remedy for the evils of democracy is more democracy. In the same way, the remedy for the evils of impure and imperfect competition may be more competition.[6] Proposals to increase the competitiveness of the market economy usually begin and end with a call for more vigorous, better-funded, and less "political" enforcement of antitrust and antimonopoly legislation already on the books, both federal and state. They sometimes advocate the closing of loopholes left open for trade unions and farm cooperatives. Too little is said about allowing greater scope for international competition by lowering or repealing tariff protection against imports and by loosening or removing import quotas.

Consumer self-help, a second strategy advocated, takes several forms. In some areas, primarily the upper Midwest and the campus communities, confidence in the consumer cooperative movement remains stronger than elsewhere. In most middle-class circles, however, the major

---

6. "Pure," "perfect," and their correlates are technical terms. Pure (atomistic) competition involves no loftier morality than its alternatives, but only the assumption that no competitor or group of competitors acting collusively is strong enough to affect the prices of any outputs it sells or inputs it buys. Perfect competition involves a number of other attributes in addition to purity; the most important of these, for our purposes, is the absence of information or transaction costs.

vehicle of consumer self-help has been the privately published consumer guide, often an antibusiness agency of negative advertising. Best known of these is the monthly *Consumer Reports,* which also publishes annual buying guides and occasional monographs on particular industries (food additives, cosmetics, patent medicines, etc.). A wider appeal has suddenly accrued to the complex of antibusiness information agencies and political action agencies associated with Ralph Nader and "Nader's Raiders."[7] (One wonders whether this network will survive Nader's own activities or instead whether Ralph Nader will be to twentieth-century consumerism what Henry George was to nineteenth-century tax reform.) Finally, consumer self-help can operate through class-action lawsuits against offending companies. In these suits, plaintiffs seek recovery of damages not only for themselves as individuals but for all similarly damaged consumers, most of whom do not participate actively in the suits themselves.[8]

Government regulation is a third strategy favored by consumer groups. Some forms of regulation make no distinctions among industries, as under the FTC penalties for fraud and deception in interstate commerce. (These are imposed not only in aid of consumers but primarily to protect "ethical" businessmen against allegedly "unfair" competition.) Or the regulation sought may involve the setting and enforcement of specific standards on specific products, as by the FDA or the Agricultural

7. Beginning with *Unsafe at Any Speed* in 1965, the Nader movement has gone on from exposure of the defects of the Corvair automobile to scrutinize the activities of regulatory agencies like the Federal Trade Commission (FTC) and the Food and Drug Administration (FDA), the banking business, monetary and fiscal policy, the operations of Congress, water pollution and air pollution, nursing homes, and land use. Two useful summaries are Ralph Nader, "A Citizen's Guide to the American Economy," *New York Review of Books,* Vol. 17 (September 2, 1971), pp. 14–18, and Charles McCarry, "The Public Ways of the Private Nader," *Saturday Review,* Vol. 55 (February 12, 1972), pp. 32ff.

Some part of the groundwork for Nader and his ombudsman-like activities was laid in Jessica Mitford's exposé of the mortuary industry, *The American Way of Death* (Simon and Schuster, 1963).

8. A detailed analysis of class action suits in the consumer area is found in American Enterprise Institute for Public Policy Research, "Consumer Class Action Legislation" (Washington: AEI, 1972; processed).

No legislation smoothing the way for such suits passed the Ninety-second Congress. Ralph Nader ascribes this outcome to White House intervention, in "Consumer Bills Blocked by Nixon," *Minneapolis Tribune,* October 28, 1972.

A secondary aspect of class-action suits may be the formation of "anticorporations" to finance them. (The anticorporations are themselves to be financed by the public sale of their securities.)

and Marketing Service of the Department of Agriculture.[9] Certain standards and tolerances are matters of public record; others remain confidential.

Inducing firms to act in a benign way—to do business in the spirit of what is sometimes called the "soulful corporation"—constitutes a fourth strategy for consumer groups. The ostensibly pro-consumer activities of the "soulful corporation" may indicate primarily a lengthening of the time horizon within which a particular corporation is maximizing or otherwise projecting its profit position. In such a lengthening of a firm's planning horizon, short-term losses are expected to be at least balanced by the longer-term gains in profit margins, sales, market shares, growth rates, and so forth that are supposed to result from improving the company's image and goodwill. Alternatively, the short-term losses may be regarded as insurance premiums to ward off hostile regulation or unsympathetic enforcement of regulation already in effect. Or the short-term losses may be deliberately written off. The compensation is to lie in the conscience of the losers, be they corporate executives or corporate stockholders. They can contemplate their altruism and its consequences—and presumably die happy. (Only the corporation whose sacrifice of short-term profit results from pure altruism is truly worthy of the title "soulful corporation," coined by Carl Kaysen. All other kinds are sham, more or less, but are lumped together here. Not only does skimmed milk masquerade as cream, but the economist possesses no effective separator.)

The pure strategies listed above can be combined into mixed strategies. As they stand, they are both complementary and competitive. Certain of the complementarities are obvious. For example, the activities of the Antitrust Division of the Department of Justice involve "increased competition" and "government regulation" simultaneously. Likewise, the effectiveness of consumer class-action suits under "consumer self-help" would be increased substantially by changes in the Federal Rules of Civil Procedure; these changes themselves fall under "government regulation."[10]

9. "Regulators look at, say, the spice processor they regard as the nation's most efficient and determine that the best he can do is keep the number of whole dead insects in each lot at four. Therefore, four or less is tolerable; more than four is illegal." "U.S. Food Inspection: Is a Bug in Thyme a Bent Guideline?" *Christian Science Monitor,* November 22, 1971.

10. Under Rule 23 of the existing Federal Rules, no private consumer class-action suit has standing in court until after a related suit by a public agency has

Competition among the four strategies arises mainly because consumer movements have limited time, personnel, and finances and because of the desirability of alliances with other pressure groups. Money, people, and time used to induce a grocery chain to provide unit pricing and open-code dating are lost for lobbying against higher tariffs or quotas on shoes, or for reduction of the lead content of gasoline, or for stricter inspection of nursing homes. There are not enough money, people, and time to go round. Indeed, a weakness of the consumer movement has been a tendency to scatter its shots in de minimis complaints whose main effect may be to raise business costs and eventual selling prices.

In lobbying for pro-consumer legislation, consumer advocates feel a need for more support from organized labor. This is not surprising, given the number of working-class families that are consumers. To judge by the official organ of the Industrial Union Department of the AFL-CIO, such support is generously available.[11] It would hardly remain so if the consumer movement encouraged the undercutting of domestic textiles through imports or publicized employee responsibility for defects in automobiles. (In 1972, for example, Chevrolet charged that sabotage had been committed by workers at the Vega plant in Lordstown, Ohio.)

The Consumer as Villain

To this point in the discussion, the consumer has been presented in his favorite role of economic hero. However, the numerous instances when he plays the role of economic villain should not be forgotten—for example, as exploiter, as thief, as vandal, or as homeowner.

The *consumer as exploiter* has an interest, often unconscious, in the monopsonistic exploitation of workers, farmers, the Organization of Petroleum Exporting Countries, and other producers, by reason of his

---

proceeded against the specific defendant on the precise point at issue and has received *final* determination. A consumer class action bill (H.R. 5630) was introduced into the Ninety-second Congress by Representative Bob Eckhardt (D. Tex.) to liberalize these provisions but was strongly opposed as encouraging harassment of business firms. See Eckhardt, "Consumer Class Action: Defense against Fraud," *Viewpoint*, Vol. 1 (Fall 1971), pp. 22–25.

11. This journal, *Viewpoint*, called its Fall 1971 issue "Voice and Value—The Consumer's Concern" and devoted the entire issue to six pro-consumer essays, one of them cited in the preceding note.

overt interest in lower prices.[12] Monopsony, or buyer's monopoly, results in systematically lowering the price of an input below the value of the input's marginal product. Fear of monopsony has stocked intellectual armories in support of trade unionism, minimum-wage laws, farm parity, fair trade, and price stabilization schemes with upward biases. Under average-cost or markup pricing, monopsony holds down the cost of labor and raw materials per unit of output, to which the markup is applied. Hence the consumer interest in monopsony. Under marginal-cost pricing of outputs, the "textbook" system deducible from short-run profit-maximizing behavior, the problem is more complex. Here it is in the consumer's interest to hold down marginal *input* cost. Marginal input cost can be held down in two ways: (1) by lowering average input cost, as monopsony does; (2) by lowering the differential between average and marginal input cost, which monopsony raises. In addition, the lowering of average input cost by monopsonistic exploitation, as in (1) above, lowers employment and output. It may therefore be reflected more commonly in an increased profit margin than in a lowered output price.

The *consumer as thief* triggers much of the hostility vented by business interests toward their own customers and toward the "holier-than-thou" approach of organized consumers. (The eventual sufferers when consumers steal, of course, are usually other consumers rather than businessmen, taking account of the shifting and incidence of the costs involved. The putative loss to other consumers takes the form of higher prices to compensate for higher costs from theft or from its prevention. An additional loss may be the waste of time and effort that results when stores shut down in high crime areas and residents must shop at distant or otherwise inconvenient locations.)

When one thinks of the consumer as thief, the immediate examples which come to mind are shoplifting and "ripoffs" in retail establishments. Their cost in the United States is estimated at over $9 million a day—$3.5 billion a year as of 1971.[13] Such consumer theft is nothing new. Neither is its extension to outright looting in emergency situations—fire, flood, earthquake, riot, or power failure. Neither are its rationalizations. What appears to be new is a rise both in the magnitude of the activities involved and in the extent of the apparently frank and sincere acceptance

12. See M. Bronfenbrenner, "Monopsony and the Consumer Interest," *Indian Economic Review*, Vol. 2 (February 1954), pp. 1–20.
13. See Curtis J. Sitomer, "U.S. Crackdown: Shoplifters, Beware!" *Christian Science Monitor*, November 16, 1972.

of the rationalizations by intelligent people as corollaries of one or another set of social principles. The most familiar rationalization is that since a private business corporation—or, for that matter, a university, hospital, housing project, public agency, or similar large, bureaucratic organization—is not itself a natural person, no natural person is injured when it is "ripped off." Theft—like gambling, pot smoking, overtime parking, and extramarital consensual sex—becomes a crime without victims and hence not a crime at all. Alternatively, senior corporation executives or principal shareholders are malefactors of great wealth, imperialist racist pigs, or what have you. They won't miss what is taken; or even if they do, so the story goes, their wealth was stolen from the people in the first place.

While shoplifting and looting are the major incursions of the consumer as thief, minor manifestations should not be overlooked. These include such tricks as "skipping" on unpaid bills and loan contracts. They also include concealment and disguising of defects of used property offered as part payment or "returned" as still new.

Vandalism often accompanies theft and looting. During the American student protests at the end of the 1960s, the *consumer as vandal* was widely publicized. "Trashing" committed by the student subclass of the consuming public against financial institutions, computer facilities, school buildings, and assorted retail establishments in campus communities from Harvard Square to Telegraph Avenue was rationalized as an outlet for the "political frustration" brought on by events in Indochina, sub-Saharan Africa, or the inner city, as well as by high campus-area prices. On a chronic or day-to-day basis, however, the most significant example of consumer vandalism is the continuous and systematic spoliation and respoliation of low-grade rental housing, both public and private, by the tenants. Neither Hitler nor Stalin is easier to denounce than the urban slumlord. He makes no repairs, his properties stink to high heaven and are unfit for human habitation. When permitted a plea in his own defense, however, the slumlord will maintain that the tenants have wrecked the property themselves and sold the fixtures for liquor or drugs. Were he to repair it, the same tenants would do the same thing again.

The *consumer as homeowner* is unavoidably an investor at the same time. The consumption and investment are joint products in fixed proportions.[14] If Jones owns Blackacre, his interests as consumer of Black-

14. Owned housing is assumed here to be a consumption good for many home-

acre's amenities are seldom separable from his interests as custodian of Blackacre's future value. For Jones is simultaneously consuming an indefinitely long stream of Blackacre's housing services—the length of the stream distinguishing him from a mere tenant—and investing (speculating) in real estate.

Assume that Blackacre is indeed an inflation hedge. That is to say, its real as well as its nominal value moves in the same direction as the general level of prices. Thus home ownership propels Jones's views and votes in an inflationist direction, particularly if, like most of his neighbors, he has incurred fixed money debt to acquire Blackacre.

Since the continually promised and continually postponed housing revolution might simultaneously lower Blackacre's market value and devalue its amenities in utility terms, Jones, if the choice were given to him, would be pushed to the side of delaying technical progress in construction. Conversely, whatever raises building costs on newer houses may further Blackacre's own value and utility to Jones—unless of course Jones plans to move or remodel in the near future. This consideration gives Jones a potential economic interest in keeping building costs forever rising.

On similar grounds, Jones is a potential opponent of subsidized public housing of any sort if it would lower housing costs in an important segment of the housing market. He is less likely to oppose an equally costly public subsidy of the moderate-income home buyer (or even renter) who might otherwise be unable to enter the market for Blackacre on terms acceptable to Jones.

Jones is no racist. Some of his best friends, and none of his worst enemies, belong to whatever minorities are currently attracting sympathetic attention. Yet Blackacre's amenities and property values may depend on distance from "tacky," crowded neighborhoods. It follows that Jones will probably in the final analysis support some combination of snob zoning and restrictive covenants to keep the poor, and therefore the minorities, far, far away from Blackacre's green lawns and inflation hedges.

Public services, epitomized by the schools, present another problem.

---

owners. In addition, its value enters explicitly into its utility as an item of conspicuous consumption. It is for this reason that the consumption and investment aspects of home ownership are more difficult to disentangle than for most other goods.

In the Blackacre enclave and wherever Jones, his neighbors, and other "desirable" home buyers work, shop, and amuse themselves, Jones is surely all for public services. Only the best is good enough, in his opinion, and benefits usually overbalance costs. For the farther and lower reaches of the city, county, school district, or other taxing jurisdiction, however, the situation is different. Jones accepts a theory relating property tax rates and property values inversely, in the absence of clearly offsetting benefits. And so the total combined effect of the homeowning syndrome on Jones's position toward public services is apt to be negative for however long taxes on real property (including improvements) continue as the backbone of the local tax system. And what of Blackacre's home enclave? Jones and his friends may be able to bargain for a larger share of the smaller pie of tax receipts, and if not, it may be cheaper after all (considering capital gains on Blackacre along with income and expenditures) for Jones to rely on private schools and hospitals altogether while the public ones unfortunately deteriorate.

Strategic Pitfalls

Having found a less flattering side to the consumer despite legitimate claims in his behalf, we ought also to look critically at the strategies chosen to advance consumer interests. Do they work? Do they benefit the economy?

Consumer self-help, one of the standard strategies identified above, has been hampered by concentration on the problems and interests of the well-to-do and the highly educated. Snobbery toward the prosaic business of managing retail stores has held back the consumer co-op, for example, by lessening the co-op's willingness to pay market rates for managerial talent. Outside of a few campus communities lucky enough to find a combination of altruism and practical intelligence, only submarginal managerial talent has been available with any regularity at the prices co-ops have been willing to pay. A number of co-op stores have failed by choosing submarginal sites (inconvenient or even dangerous), by operating with submarginal inventory (inadequate and sometimes stale) and submarginal protection (open to high shoplifting losses) and by picking the wrong competitors (the big food chains). One reason the co-op has seldom made headway against the chain stores is that it has seldom (outside centers of Scandinavian ethnicity) attracted ordinary working people.

The consumer press, represented by *Consumer Reports,* has concentrated largely on products consumed by the middle class and has used a vocabulary with little "common touch." The January 1972 issue, chosen at random, may be an extreme example. It features reports on color TV consoles, genital deodorants, hair dryers, frozen shrimp, rosé wines, compact refrigerators, five new models of compact cars, life insurance for college students, and an alleged "anti-pollution engine economizer" for automobiles. These are real items of consumption, and they are treated in a lively as well as an authoritative manner. The most fascinating articles to any individual consumer deal with markets in which he has himself recently been burned or which he proposes to enter in the near future. But the items covered in that issue are hardly crucial to the problems summarized as "the poor pay more," which most critics consider the central consumer issues of the American economy. Can the consumer movement not expand its journalistic activities to meet the poor man's needs more directly?

Naderism may be a long-term strengthening of the feeble consumer lobby. It may implant more backbone in consumer protection agencies and secure new agencies with wider powers and better funding. Probably more important, it may arouse sufficient consumer interest to render consumer protection more profitable for business firms. It may even remove the short-run profit from consumer disservice and enforce responsible behavior by lowering consumer information costs. On the other hand, Nader's Raiders scatter their shots widely and threaten to submerge consumerism in Nader's personal grand design for reforming American society.

By and large, the consumer movement has remained "respectable" in its tactics even while other movements were through militance enlisting consumer support for essentially nonconsumer causes. Raising agricultural wages in California was one such cause, and increasing the proportion of blacks employed in nonmenial jobs by Chicago retailers was another. Business might see its responsibility differently if consumer organizations were militant enough on their own behalf to picket individual stores for extensive periods against unsafe or unsanitary products, deceptive financing and advertising, and price gouging.

Advocating the "soulful corporation" is another consumer strategy mentioned above. Here the effort is to convince firms that sacrificing short-term profit in the public interest is "good business" in the long run (and in some cases that with proper planning recoupment would be feasible). Several questions arise as to the persuasiveness of this argument.

Why are firms not already planning as far ahead as consumer advocates say they should? Primarily, one supposes, they are averse to the risk, the disproportionate uncertainty of the distant future. Why should corporate management go out on a limb when national economic plans are customarily limited to five years even in socialist countries? Furthermore, the individual manager or executive can usually expect potential outside bidders for his services, as well as his present superiors, to judge him in terms of short-term results. Each member of a management team is under pressure to adopt a strategy called "end-gaming," which makes him look good at his successor's expense. With a certain bias toward end-gaming in every branch of a firm's operations, can the firm as a whole be far behind? In addition, the prevalence of externalities, spillovers, and what is called "free riding" rationalizes strategies biased toward the short run. An oil company contemplates spending millions to reduce pollution from its refinery and tanker operations. Will an advertising campaign about "trying to make things better" cut its losses in the long run, by appealing to car owners for its particular brand of gasoline and lubricants? Not if rivals can use its research results without sharing its research and development costs. And not if its advertising campaign brightens primarily the image of the entire oil industry rather than its own.

Can corporate planning horizons be expected to lengthen in the relatively near future? The answer is probably affirmative, primarily because of increased use of electronic computation, particularly "simulation" applications to "total systems."[15] These methods are already increasingly used by sophisticated managers to detect not only the longitudinal scheme of end-gaming but the parallel sin in cross-section—namely, improving the record of one's own division or "profit center" at the expense of the corporate whole and in disregard of the "systems ap-

15. An additional reason for an affirmative forecast is the presumed ability of U.S. firms to learn from their short-sightedness of the 1950s, when their failure to maintain a technological lead over European and Japanese competitors had unpleasant results for both their aggregate international competitive position and the U.S. balances of trade and of payments.

proach."[16] These changes imply a wider scope for "soulfulness"—sacrificing present profits for later recoupment—at once a gambit and a gamble.

Can corporations ever be expected actually to make altruistic decisions in the public interest (as they see it) at their own long-term expense? Yes, on occasion; it is, however, easier and more natural to make believe. Let us view large, established corporations as maximizing or at least "satisficing" not profits but some mysterious entity of which profits and public service are two components. It lies well within the boundaries of belief that consumer protests, like voluntary controls and jawboning, may shift the relative importance of these components so that some potential profits will be traded for service—in this case, service to consumers.[17] On the other hand, a reading of business history suggests that few successful corporations have acted altruistically for long periods. Rather, corporations disguise motivations skillfully, attributing to themselves benevolence whenever they change strategies, even though the change also increases long-term gains or reduces inevitable long-run losses.

What is the likelihood that corporate "soulfulness" (in the sense of short-run sacrifice) will select the consumer as its beneficiary? Not very great, if our conclusions on organizational slack and the consumer as villain are valid and relevant. We suggested that concessions are "financed" out of corporate organizational slack, that a corporation's organizational slack is tapped most readily in favor of those with whom the management must live from day to day, that corporate contacts with consumers are generally distant and indirect, and that some consumer activities are both ethically reprehensible and positively abrasive to the representative corporation. Therefore, the primary beneficiaries of corporate responsibility, when it exists, are more likely to be workers, suppliers, subcontractors, and minority stockholders than the invisible consuming public.

---

16. All this improvement, of course, is expensive. The most obvious expense is sophisticated computer hardware with rapid obsolescence. The training cost of programmers and other computer technicians must be included. Nor should we overlook the indirect effects on middle management, possibly driven to neurosis by the constant threat of computerized discovery of little end-games they may be playing for the sake of quiet lives and rapid promotions.

17. In "A Guidepost-Mortem," *Industrial and Labor Relations Review,* Vol. 20 (July 1967), pp. 637–49, I use a multiple-goal utility function as an argument for the possible effectiveness of voluntary guidelines and guideposts.

Whatever happens to "soulfulness," government regulation remains a perennial strategy favored by consumer groups. In recent years a number of legislative proposals have emerged for adding a consumer protection agency in the Executive Office of the President (or as an independent department in the Cabinet). It is presumed that representatives from such an agency would appear regularly as "witnesses" at hearings conducted by other federal agencies. Receiving and transmitting consumer complaints, carrying out research, and publishing the results in a federal "consumer register of information" (with safeguards for trade secrets) are also envisioned. Making grants to state, local, and private agencies in aid of their own consumer protection programs is also a possibility.

It is unlikely that such an agency could accomplish anything commensurate with its initial ballyhoo. For one thing, the abuses most cited as justification for a vigorous consumer agency would be the hardest for it to reach. These typically involve the sale of shoddy merchandise or useless services at high prices to the inner-city poor. But the firms that engage in these practices tend to be small, highly competitive, indifferent to social esteem, and evasive.

In opposition to the generalized consumer protection agency approach, another form of legislative enactment has its advocates. Of these, Ralph Winter is representative. He suggests five priority areas for government regulation:

First, safety regulations [are needed] where parties other than the buyer or seller may reasonably be expected to suffer injury. . . .

Second, government must play a role in suppressing false advertising. . . .

Third, the government ought to establish uniform standards where objective rules can be imposed, for instance, weights and measures. . . .

Fourth, where there is high risk of serious harm, the government can seek out and provide information to consumers if that information is unlikely to be available to competitors or independent testing organizations. . . .

Fifth, when a product is by its nature either dangerous or addictive and there are no close substitutes . . . some role of government may be justified . . . because there is less expectation that competitors will inform consumers about safer alternatives.[18]

Winter, like many other commentators, would prefer (p. 13) "identifying areas of market failure and *carefully tailoring* [italics added] the role of government to them" to setting up an organization with latitude as wide as that of the consumer protection agency often proposed. But

18. Winter, *The Consumer Advocate versus the Consumer*, pp. 11–13.

"careful tailoring" smacks of the counsel of perfection, exceedingly utopian against the background of current and recent American governmental policies. Surely the tailoring Winter proposes is to be modeled neither on the Interstate Commerce Commission's rate books nor on the tariff schedules contrived by Congress. Does he have any actual model in mind?

It is not clear in many industries that enough is known to make "tailoring" possible. With respect to food, drugs, and chemicals, for example, the courts and the administrative agencies have for decades been receiving voluminous and inconclusive testimony. The experts seldom agree on what if anything the association of mouse cancer with heavy doses of Preparation X implies as to the carcinogenic properties of smaller doses of Preparation X in human beings.[19] As for regulation of advertising, it is not clear that "tailoring" would give the consumer much return for his tax dollar. Should administrative talent be used to deliberate, say in the case of a misrepresentation of pickles by a food processor, whether to affix a warning for the consumer on all the firms' products or only on the pickles? It may well be a waste of high-grade human resources to start a massive game of enforcement versus avoidance.

Over and above the drawbacks just discussed for each strategy, the consumer must beware that his efforts of whatever kind do not push business in the opposite direction from the one intended. Four sorts of backlash in particular may surprise him.[20]

1. The most probable consequence of ostensible business altruism is cartelization and price fixing, often combined with restrictions on entry, so that existing firms can "afford" to fulfill their social obligations. One flagrant example has been barbering in Japan. After the postwar inflation of 1945–48, the price of haircuts remained approximately stable for ten years at 90–100 yen (25–30 cents). Work was done on an assembly-

19. On the subject of testing and sales moratoria, see American Enterprise Institute for Public Policy Research, "Consumer Product Safety Bills" (AEI, 1972; processed). This publication concentrates on products *other than* "automobiles, foods, drugs, cosmetics, cigarettes, firearms, insecticides, radiological hazards, and some flammable fabrics . . . already subject to some safety regulation by the federal government" (p. 21).

20. The subject of the unanticipated anti-consumer backlash is discussed in M. Bronfenbrenner, "The Spectrum of Current Protest Movements," in George A. Steiner (ed.), *Contemporary Challenges in the Business-Society Relationship* (University of California Press, 1972).

line basis by the master barber, his wife, his children, and sometimes an apprentice or two, in an atmosphere of animated conversation, with television added after 1955. But, alas, the barbershops lacked something in sanitation as compared with those in the United States, and the equipment was often prewar. Why shouldn't Japanese barbershops be as clean and neat as American ones? The barbers were willing, if only prices were raised enough and trade restricted to those already in the business. In the next ten years, the price of haircuts rose six- or seven-fold.

2. A related consequence of business "reform" is the elimination of poor man's goods. The second-hand items, the economy models, the stripped-down items are almost always the ones which turn out to be unsafe (or at least uninspected), or which fall short of some arbitrary standard of this or that costly desideratum. The Model T and the Volkswagen fall under suspicion, but the market is made safe for Cadillacs, armored cars, and Sherman tanks. The exemplar here is the broad field of building and zoning regulations. The cumulation of standards, none unreasonable by itself, in most cities adds up to a set of codes so tight as to preclude new housing for the poor except under subsidy from the taxpayers. (In New York City, a side effect is $125 million a year in bribes to city building inspectors, clerks in various city agencies, and union representatives.[21] This amounts to perhaps 5 percent of total construction costs.)

3. A third consequence is increased protectionism—ruling out the distantly produced item which has the unfair competitive advantage of exemption from local inspection procedures. This is the way milk inspection works. To ensure that milk comes from inspected farms, none is admitted to the major urban markets from the Wisconsin-Minnesota milk shed, outside the inspection range of local health departments. And let no one forget the longstanding exclusion of Argentine beef from the United States because of occasional hoof-and-mouth disease; it has done so much for U.S. relations with Latin America!

4. A final consequence of unreflective consumerism is the vulnerability of a cooperative management to loss of control. When industries give away too much in terms of profit—whether to consumers, workers, minorities, charity, or the environment—stockholders protest. Some sell their securities and buy those of less socially minded companies. Most

---

21. Harlow Unger, "Bribery Is Major Headache for New York Contractors," a *Washington Post* news story reprinted in the *Durham Morning Herald*, September 3, 1972.

will retain their securities, contemplating with mounting horror the evaporation of paper capital gains or the accumulation of paper declines. Individual, corporate, and conglomerate raiders will hover about, soliciting proxies against the responsible, benevolent management. A new management team may be voted in; or the existing management may be compelled to change its ways. In either case, the business of the company will once more be business rather than charity. If the stockholders are fortunate, they will be little if any worse off than they were before their company embarked on social responsibility. If the successful raider is also a looter, their company may have been crippled or even killed by the adventure.

Consumer Surrogates

The one consumer strategy mentioned earlier in this chapter but not criticized for its shortcomings is the strategy of encouraging competition among producers. It is hardly the perfect solution for all consumer problems, let alone all economic problems. Nor is it always attainable in the face of political and social pressures. Nevertheless, freer competition among producers, including freer trade across national frontiers, remains the consumer's best defense. Under the necessity of meeting competition, business often in effect acts as the consumer's friend, proxy, or surrogate.

The most obvious and powerful consumer surrogates have been the price cutters, chiselers, market disrupters, and private branders. Included among them are chain stores, mail-order houses, and discounters. They are often unpopular with liberals, being chargeable with exploiting workers and subcontractors, neglecting the environment, stressing ugly and flimsy merchandise (including imports from low-wage countries), and ignoring local charities.

At another extreme, catering to more affluent consumers, a quite different group of consumer surrogates emerges. These are the quality-firsters, from the Rolls-Royce manufacturer to the local gourmet shop. Their efforts are often marred, however, in some economists' opinion, by reinforcing the wealthy consumers' propensity to judge quality by price.[22]

22. The economists' text here is Tibor Scitovsky, "Some Consequences of the Habit of Judging Quality by Price," *Review of Economic Studies*, Vol. 12 (1944–45), pp. 100–05. Two caveats may be in order. First, the propensity to judge quality by price may be entirely rational, as a device for saving valuable time. Second, the propensity may be balanced by other consumers' antibusiness pro-

Consumer surrogation is a form of short-run responsibility, particularly in an inflationary environment. It has been downgraded precisely because it is short run and is expected to pay for itself in the longer period as a form of advertisement and image improvement. It may also pay for itself as an insurance premium against looting, vandalism, expropriation, and punitive regulation. These dangers are not yet serious domestic problems for U.S. corporations, outside ghetto areas and academic slums. Overseas, especially in less developed countries, it may be vital for the foreign-owned corporation to change its image from that of imperialistic exploiter to that of consumer's friend. Yet the foreign firm in the less developed countries plays the consumer surrogate at its peril if its success drives too many domestic rivals out of business. Sears, Roebuck is learning this lesson in its Latin American operations—including, for example, a Caracas, Venezuela, establishment facing the main gate of the Universidad Nacional. There are indeed situations—primarily abroad, but also in domestic small towns—where the foreigner or chain store can do nothing right. If a firm cuts prices, it is driving local businessmen into bankruptcy. If a firm does not cut prices, it is exploiting native consumers. It had best stay away or get out.

As suggested earlier, an important contribution of Nader and Naderism may be to arouse the sort of consumer interests which make the consumer surrogate strategy more profitable to a wider group of corporations.[23] This would require somewhat more stress on lower price for a given quality, as against the existing stress on higher quality for a given price. If the consumer surrogate strategy can be made to serve corporation goals, such as faster growth, larger market share, or higher security valuation, the gap between responsibility to the firm and responsibility to the consumer will narrow.

---

pensity to treat quality as uniform and to ascribe all price differentials to fraud. It is, however, conventional on balance for economists to look on "cheap junk" with some favor, as adding to the range of rational choice, particularly for poor consumers.

23. At least four "social responsibility" mutual funds have been established, which limit their purchases to the securities of companies whose social attitudes are approved by the funds in question. It is hoped that such mutual funds can eventually operate to raise the relative security valuations of "responsible" firms. (This seems dubious on conventional financial grounds, but see Harvey Shapiro, "Wall Street's New 'Social Responsibility' Funds," *Saturday Review,* Vol. 55 [August 26, 1972], pp. 43–45, for an optimistic view.) These funds' concepts of social responsibility extend to ecology, peace, minority employment, and safety rather than the "your-money's-worth" aspects of consumerism.

CHAPTER EIGHT

The Physical Environment

JEROME ROTHENBERG

ENVIRONMENTAL degradation is not a new thing. It is not new in the United States; it is not new in the world. Marshall I. Goldman points out instances of water pollution in Rome before 100 B.C. and of air pollution in England as early as the fourteenth century.[1]

Moreover, in broader terms, the sociophysical environment of large cities in Europe, Asia, and the United States have been generally appalling—noisy, filthy, dangerous—for centuries. Yet, although many of these conditions were deplored at the time and sometimes even dealt with through public policies, deterioration of the environment was rarely looked upon as a crucial problem. It represented a local concern—and only one of many concerns, some of them more urgent.

Growth and Destruction

Environmental degradation holds a different place today. For one thing, it is considerably worse and affects more people. For another, we notice it more and are less tolerant of problems of this sort. Finally, it raises the whole question of man's place on Earth.

Environmental degradation is found today in many different forms, in many different places, and in some cases in greater degree than ever before. It is roughly proportional to the scale and variety of production and consumption. The recent huge increase in the population on Earth, the manyfold expansion of production and consumption activities per capita, and the physical consequences of technology—all these have

1. Goldman (ed.), *Controlling Pollution: The Economics of a Cleaner America* (Prentice-Hall, 1967), especially p. 4.

radically increased the scale, pervasiveness, and variety of environmental degradation in the United States and elsewhere.

Moreover, Americans are prone to notice it now because problems of hunger, exposure, and disease have been largely solved for the mass of the population. Second-order problems come to the fore and are deemed less permissible than they were earlier.

A feeling of perplexity and disappointment is also on the rise. Is there some intrinsic barrier to human advancement after all? Is economic growth pressing man against the ultimate ceiling?

The carrier of the virus of growth is the business firm. Thus concern with the environment has created a kind of crisis of confidence in business enterprise. Traditional incentives and the workings of the market are suspected of destroying environmental values. In some quarters the expansion of the gross national product and other conventional standards of "growth" are no longer regarded as creditable.

This chapter is concerned in particular with air pollution (which can include noise) and water pollution (which can include heat). Two critical points to make are that both forms of pollution involve a variety of substances and processes and that many different kinds of polluters are responsible. Business firms pollute. Government agencies and nonprofit institutions pollute. Households pollute. Everyone who drives a car pollutes. If the object is to determine business responsibility, the assessment must be sophisticated.

Just as the responsibility that the business sector shares with other sources varies for different forms of pollution, so too firms differ widely among themselves in their responsibility for each kind of damage. Some firms contribute to several types of damage, others predominantly to one. Some are heavy polluters; others approach complete innocence. Moreover, the degree of damage per unit of economic activity is less related to size of enterprise than to type of productive process. Business pollution is a problem not of big business but of polluting business. The traditional ideological stereotypes about economic heroes and villains have to be jettisoned for any serious examination of the role of business in environmental degradation.

It is not the purpose of this chapter to measure the size and distribute the blame for pollution damage done by business firms. It is enough to grant that business firms do considerable damage. The purpose here is to examine how and why the damage is created, what problems this gives rise to in the society as a whole, and what can and should firms do about it either on their own or in conjunction with the public sector.

The Meaning of Pollution

Some kind of pollution is bound to occur as long as human beings exist and carry on economic activity. The problem comes with the wrong amounts and kinds: "suboptimal pollution." In arriving at the concept of "optimal pollution" and in analyzing the discrepancy between optimal and suboptimal conditions, one can discover the materials necessary for an appropriate delineation of the proper role of business firms.

Waste and Pollution

Almost every production and consumption activity generates waste products. Differences among them are great, much more within each branch than between production and consumption. The pollution potential of a pleasure ride downtown in an automobile is closer to the production of electric power than it is to shooting at a target with a bow and arrow in the back yard; while that of the latter is closer to a sales representative's meeting than is the production of electric power.

Whether classified as production or consumption, there is usually no fixed, proportional relationship between levels of the primary activity and levels of waste (residuals). Different inputs or input combinations, or choice of techniques, or simple change in scale of operations can change the ratio between them. The recent interest in low-sulphur petroleum as an input in power generation shows this clearly.

Pollution is, however, more closely involved with the disposal of wastes than with their generation. If all wastes were, for example, solids that accumulated where they were generated, each waste producer would be required to incur the cost of disposing of them or suffer their growing interference with his other activities. The cost of doing so would be like any other cost associated with production or consumption. As such, it would have to be explicitly considered in deciding what to produce or consume and at what levels. Moreover, the cost would consist in using up resources (say, labor and land for dumping or filling).

In reserving land specifically for the disposal of wastes, one *expects* that specialized use to preclude its use for other activities. The preemption of land by pollution, by contrast, is unintended and unwanted. The resource taken over by pollution is in principle the physical environment. The pollution situation is one in which a common domain or resource is being expropriated in fact but not in legal status through its use as a disposal medium. The common "owners" of the resource find their nondisposal rights tainted. This resource—the physical environment— is degraded (not "specialized").

Whoever has quantities of waste to dispose of is subject to a double temptation. First, air and water are the natural media for disposal. Second, there is no owner to charge for their use. As a result, spatial disposal via these media is financially far more advantageous than recycling of wastes.

The Damage Done

The chief property of air and water as waste removal media is their dilutive capacity. Pollution occurs when the waste discharged exceeds the medium's dilutive capacity. The amount of damage that results varies by type of pollutant, types of other users (polluters and victims), and "functional distance" of these users from the source of pollution. The farther the distance in time or space, the greater is the dilution of toxicity and the less the damage. Beyond a certain boundary the medium regains its unpolluted state. Dilutive capacity is thus really assimilative capacity.[2]

An important and recently highly visible class of exceptions remains to be noted, however. These are substances that are not ultimately dispersed, diluted, or transformed within the medium; substances that actually build increasing concentration in the medium over time; substances that above some low threshold level create a relatively constant amount of damage per unit regardless of their concentration in the medium. Nonbiodegradable substances such as plastics, cumulatively dangerous products such as DDT and mercury, and radioactive wastes (which cannot be decontaminated) belong to this category. These are all substances which have intrinsically obtrusive or toxic effects when discharged at levels reached or exceeded by many of them since the recent past.

2. Most studies in the economics of pollution and pollution policy, including the present one, owe a heavy debt to the many writings of Allen V. Kneese. Three representative ones are: Kneese, *Water Pollution: Economic Aspects and Research Needs* (Washington: Resources for the Future, 1962); Allen V. Kneese and Blair T. Bower, *Managing Water Quality: Economics, Technology, Institutions* (Johns Hopkins Press for Resources for the Future, 1968); Kneese, "Environmental Pollution: Economics and Policy," in American Economic Association, *Papers and Proceedings of the Eighty-third Annual Meeting, 1970* (*American Economic Review*, Vol. 61, May 1971), pp. 153–66. See also Jerome Rothenberg, "The Economics of Congestion and Pollution: An Integrated View," in American Economic Association, *Papers and Proceedings of the Eighty-second Annual Meeting, 1969* (*American Economic Review*, Vol. 60, May 1970), pp. 114–21.

Thus the central feature of the pollution situation is that from a number of parties making free use of a common resource come wastes sufficient to decrease the quality of the resource to at least some of the users, because the wastes exceed the assimilative capacity of the medium. The polluters thereby cause damage—costs—to others (and perhaps to themselves) which do not arise out of voluntary market transactions between them. Such costs are called "negative externalities." Polluters' calculations about their primary activities which generate pollution take into account gains and losses to themselves but not these external costs.

The chief rationale of a market system's efficiency in allocating resources is that it supports only actions whose overall gains exceed overall costs to the system. Each decentralized decision maker supposedly balances his own prospective gains from proposed action with the costs he would thereby incur. Where the gains and costs that are recognized truly reflect the overall gains and costs in the system as a whole, decentralized decision making allocates resources efficiently. But where private actions generate significant externalities, the decentralized decisions are warped. Severe pollution represents a breakdown in the ability of the market to prompt efficient resource decisions.

Pollution as a Variable: The Alternatives

The kinds and degrees of pollution are subject to many variations. Assimilative capacity varies with the medium into which waste is discharged and with actions taken to augment assimilative capacity. On the other side are the effluent flows of waste products. These can be altered by varying the rate and composition of the primary consumption and production activities that generate the wastes, by changing inputs or techniques, or by adopting measures to recycle, modify, reduce, or "denature" residual discharges.

Relative to the situation established through a free market, by how much, if at all, should pollution be decreased and by which methods? In answering these questions, the following facts are crucial:

1. Every method of decreasing pollution incurs some social costs. To decrease the level of the primary activities that generated the wastes means losing the net social advantage of the primary output or consumption involved. To substitute "cleaner" inputs for pollution-rich inputs means using either a more costly or less productive combination of inputs than was freely chosen and therefore a greater total use of resources to produce the same primary output. To adopt private treat-

ment investment shifts resources away from other forms of primary production by the offending agent. To make public assimilative capacity investment would likewise shift resources away from primary production into mitigation of the burdens of present production. All these modifications and investments lower total primary production below the level that is achievable without them. This total output discrepancy is their real social cost.[3]

2. Disposal of wastes into the common environment is not a rare phenomenon. Quite the contrary. Businesses both large and small resort to it, in many different industries; households of all socioeconomic levels; agencies at all levels of government.

3. Pollution is not the intended goal of the polluters: it is the *unintended, unwanted by-product* of the primary activities of consumption and production which are their real purposes. Moreover, pollution comes into being as decision makers attempt to choose activities, techniques, and inputs "optimally"—that is, apart from pollution, so as to maximize the overall net advantage to the community from total resource use. Pollution is the intimate accompaniment of efficient private resource management as well as inefficient management. It is *not* a social penalty for privately irresponsible behavior.

These three facts should modify the popular stereotype that the polluter is a villainous corporation executive. The "villainy" is predominantly a breakdown of market signals which results in systematically distorted choices. The "villain" is for the most part a cross-section of producer-consumer-government decision makers. Thus the social wrongdoing is of a special, nonsadistic, amoral kind. Furthermore, curtailment of pollution entails real social costs. The problem of pollution is not simply one of reducing it to zero at any cost.

Pollution is the other side of the coin of engaging in those activities of production and consumption which are deemed to be the proper goals of economic activity. Indeed, it is probably the unavoidable and not totally eradicable accompaniment of those desirable activities. It should be thus considered an inescapable type of cost of carrying on these activities. Once it is looked on in this way, instead of as some special

3. The recent controversy over Alaskan petroleum pipelines is a good illustration of these issues. Protection of two highly vulnerable environments—the Alaskan tundra and the Pacific coastline—calls for no pipeline or, at best, an Alaskan-Canadian route which excludes an ocean shipping link (to avoid tanker oil spills). A presumed urgent energy shortage calls for early and heavy exploitation of Alaskan oil finds via a cross-Alaska pipeline with tanker linkage. Some conflict of ends is unavoidable here.

category of absolute corruption (or, at the other extreme, as something that can be disregarded when making resource choices), a fundamental principle for dealing with it stands out: when different uses for resources are being considered, social costs resulting from pollution should be treated like any other costs associated with those uses. A use should be deemed attractive only if its prospective benefits exceed *all* the costs associated with it—including pollution costs. The following rules, derived from this principle, would lead to efficient overall use of society's resources and result in the "right amount and kind of pollution": (a) any degree of pollution abatement aimed for should be carried out at the lowest possible social cost; (b) the proper amount of abatement is that for which the minimum cost of an extra unit of abatement is neither more nor less than the damage decrease achieved by the extra abatement (costs below that line would warrant more abatement, costs above that line less abatement).

Abatement and Self-Interest

In the last section pollution was described as arising out of a set of negative externalities connected with the disposal of the waste products of consumption and production activities. As a result of "externality," market incentives are distorted to favor too high a level of pollution. In pondering the social responsibilities of business in this area, it is natural to speculate that much might be done through private transactions based on conventional market motivations. These are well within the legal and economic capabilities of businesses and require no collective actions at all. Perhaps the present laws of property, of contract, and of torts would suffice to regulate the transactions.

Market Contracting by Affected Parties

The sheer existence of pollution is nearly inevitable. The social problem lies in its character and magnitude—the wrong amount of pollution, the wrong sort, and in the wrong places. How might market adjustments come about to confine pollution to relatively the "right" amount, the right sort, and the right places?

The first answer that comes to mind is adjustment through voluntary market agreement among the parties affected by pollution.[4] Suppose the

4. The seminal contribution along this line is R. H. Coase, "The Problem of

disposal of wastes from the business managed by A (a paper mill beside a river) threatens the livelihood of B (a fisherman who lives downstream). Suppose further that B can calculate the extra damage caused by each additional unit of A's activity; also that A can calculate the additional net gain that accrues to each additional unit of activity. We begin with A selecting that level of activity that maximizes company gain. Since the firm is unconstrained by concern for the damages to B, this will typically be a high level and result in considerable damages to B. At such a level, if B could afford to pay A to operate at a lower level, both would be better off, since the bribe would exceed the loss to A of cutting the activity level. By calculating incremental gains and losses to both, the most advantageous bribe to be offered is that which reduces A's activity to such a level that any further gains to B from an even greater reduction would be more than matched by higher losses to A, and any further gains to A from a lesser reduction would be more than matched by higher losses to B. This most advantageous bribe, if acted upon, would make both better off *and* most efficiently balance the opposing interests of the two decision makers.

It has been argued that each such private market adjustment would elicit a uniquely most efficient use of resources by generating just the right amount and kind of pollution relative to other commodities. But the supposed optimality is seriously deficient from a normative point of view, and the whole presumption that private adjustments like the one described would occur with any frequency is highly suspect.

Bargaining in such instances would not be restricted to technical calculations of externality but would reflect the relative market power of the participants and include the question of who held a legal right to certain uses of the environment. Potential polluters might even deliberately increase the by-product obtrusiveness of their primary activities to elicit more favorable offers from victims to desist. Moreover, most pollution problems involve many participants, usually as victims but often as polluters. The same river in which A dumps waste and B fishes is also affected by sewage, auto exhaust, and a power plant, for example. It is unlikely that uniform measures of externality for all the interests involved *can* be calculated. In any event, organizing voluntary agreements itself carries a high cost. Strong incentives for most participants

Social Cost," *Journal of Law and Economics,* Vol. 3 (October 1960), pp. 1–44. See also James M. Buchanan and Wm. Craig Stubblebine, "Externality," *Economica,* n.s., Vol. 29 (November 1962), pp. 371–84.

to let the burden and cost of action fall upon others dooms most such presumed opportunities. It is doubtful that firms can or will clear up pollution by contract.

Judicial Rectification through Claims

By suing polluters for damages victims can sometimes force abatement and often compensation. Thus polluters are faced in these cases with direct costs that are a function of damages. Moreover, they are *required* to abate. But the combination of abatement and compensation is not based on any balance of incremental benefits to polluter and incremental damages to victims. It may fall short of or exceed the optimal mix, since it will be based on the sheer existence of damages and relative legal bargaining power.

The adjustment, though not optimal, might nonetheless go far toward resolving the problem. But here too the likelihood of successful court outcomes, and of suits even being brought, is very low. Present laws do not grant unambiguous rights against pollution damages.[5] Indeed, in the question of water pollution, riparian laws grant rights to polluters which may protect them against such suits (although new interpretations of the application of riparian laws might reverse this). Court processes are quite expensive for claimants, and the burden of organizing effective action in the typical multiparty situation is as great as for the voluntary market-type adjustments discussed above. Not much is to be expected from this route.

Property Rights

Some of the inadequacies of both adjustment by contract and judicial rectification would be allayed if property rights were clarified. Two relevant areas of improvement, for example, would be to stipulate who has the right to engage in what activities (whether polluting activities or activities that would be damaged by pollution) and in what quantities.[6]

5. The recent growth of public interest ecology organizations like the Sierra Club, of consumer protection groups such as Ralph Nader has formed, and of public interest law firms makes conceivable a more far-reaching and circumspect legal attack on environmental degradation. But these agents so far have had little more than marginal, episodic impact on the problem.

6. The path-breaking work here is that of John H. Dales, *Pollution, Property, and Prices: An Essay in Policy-Making and Economics* (University of Toronto Press, 1968).

A decrease in information costs and a decrease in transaction costs might be expected to follow.

Mere spelling out of rights would not resolve the difficulties, however. It would still matter who received the rights at the start, even if they were initially distributed by the government through an auction process. Second, the number of rights issued would matter. For optimal resource use, the number should be such that the incremental damage incurred as a result of the last unit of use employed by a polluter just equals the incremental benefit of that use. The problem is that if conditions change over time, as they should be expected to, and the original holders sell rights to a second generation of polluters, this will disturb the original balance of incremental gains and losses, since even here private transactions will fail to heed externality effects. Continuing balance will require the continuing active participation of government, issuing, buying and selling, or otherwise directly controlling the transactions in rights. Such continuing governmental action is not really a process of "privatizing" pollution rights.

The problem can be generalized as follows. A private market in pollution (effluent) rights would differ from a normal private market in that every transaction between a pair of participants (after the initial sale by the government) would produce substantial and variable spillovers affecting numerous other parties because the "rights" refer not to pollution effects but to intervening processes (effluent emissions) whose damage effects vary with the number and identity of the polluters as well as the victims. The pollution impacts of any trade invariably depend on who buys what from whom and what everyone else is doing.

In sum, extension and clarification of property rights might somewhat increase the scope of market adjustments but would not of itself create an adjustment process capable of operating flexibly and pervasively to keep an efficient balance on the claim for scarce resources among polluters and between polluters and victims.

Business Altruism

If private market incentives, operating through the institutions and structure of free market transactions, fail to provide environmental protection, can private business initiatives which operate outside the normal market nexus work? Perhaps business "altruism"—a strong sense of social responsibility by individual businessmen (or at least a feeling for long-run consequences)—can bypass the perverse vectors of market forces and constraints to make significant improvement.

Forms of Altruistic Behavior

Three types of business behavior can be called altruistic in this broad sense. First is self-policing by the firm of its own waste removal activities. Second is the application of pressure by the firm on other firms to police their emissions, pressure applied by manipulating transactions with those other firms in the market. Third is the taking of initiatives in social, nonmarket activities in the community—say, organizing community cleanup campaigns and campaigns to compensate victims damaged by abatement programs.

A self-policing firm can directly decrease pollution in a number of ways discussed earlier: reducing its activity levels; substituting low-pollution inputs for high-pollution inputs; switching production techniques to reduce emissions; recycling or denaturing pollution-causing residuals. Many smoke-producing plants have voluntarily installed stackscrubbers and electrostatic precipitators to decrease the offensiveness of their airborne wastes. Managers of nuclear power plants generally plan to install —on their own initiative—cooling towers to lessen thermal pollution of waterways from their emissions. The main London airport has set up self-operating rules for takeoffs and landings to mitigate noise disturbance to neighboring households. Through such acts, firms seek to allay or prevent public hostility and fend off governmental intervention.

Interfirm pressure starts with the "altruistic" firm identifying heavy polluters among its suppliers and customers. It then threatens withdrawal of business to obtain the promise from these firms to decrease their polluting effects. Examples are harder to find here. A form that approximates this is the exercise of stockholder voting rights in one firm by officers of other firms. More broadly, concerned citizen groups sometimes employ whatever stockholder rights they possess in banks and other enterprises to influence these firms to boycott certain other firms with which they have business relations, these other firms being deemed flagrant offenders. The initiative in such cases stems from outside the enterprise but attempts to capture its market power for use as leverage against the targeted offenders.

"Altruistic" social initiative involves the firm in social and political rather than strictly economic activity. For example, a company may try to persuade a community to invest in improved treatment of municipal wastes; or it may take the lead in exposing especially dangerous polluting activities; or it may lobby for new legislation to apply collective action against pollution; or it may help to finance direct or ancillary aspects of community cleanup programs. One frequently sees corporations displaying their public conscience in ringing advertisements about the environment. Corporation officials are often noticeably in the vanguard of community pressure for new local regulations or cleanup projects.

All three types of action cost the firm something. With self-policing, since we assume that before its altruistic actions the firm had found a level of output that maximized profits, to deviate from this level, by modifying techniques or by other means, decreases profits. Interfirm pressure raises the cost of production by altering input purchases from what they would have been if determined on cost-productivity grounds alone or such pressure necessitates selling output less advantageously than before. Social initiative entails either contributions of money by the firm or expenditure of its personnel's time, energy, and attention. The sacrifice of profits and the change in the firm's relations with other firms and with the community mean that the firm must obtain understanding and approval from those who have decision-making authority—its managers, directors, and stockholders, perhaps even its workers.

The Uncertainty of Results

Because of the cost, some of the firm's veto authorities may disapprove of business altruism. In particular, since both market sanctions and freewheeling community initiative may damage the profit situation of large polluters, employment of these means will arouse resentment against the firm, in part within the business community. It could well be felt that the firm should mind its own business.

But suppose the broad objectives of the program *are* approved. Then the more difficult problems begin. By how much should pollution be abated? Which polluting clients should be threatened? How much money and effort should be contributed to community cleanup or other programs? The basic fact is that there are no intrinsic quantitative goals on which to lean, such as profit maximization or optimal size. The targets, the means, and the goals are all judgmental, open to the momentary discretion of the firm's decision makers.

Presumably, judgments will be based on the tradeoffs between abatement and losses to the firm in profits and goodwill. Yet because voluntary initiatives are not linked to other firms by efficient signals, their repercussions are unpredictable. Costs to the altruistic firm may differ from overall social costs, and anticipated gains may differ from actual gains. The firm's perceived criterion of action is likely to distort the requirements for overall social balance, even assuming a company's willingness to gather more information than its market-oriented self-interest warrants.

The social consequences of business altruism depend not only on how any one altruist behaves but on the impact of all of the altruistic activities concurrently at work in the market. Will several companies or industries each setting its own initiatives have coherent, consistent, and mutually augmenting effects, or will they sometimes show inconsistent, competitive, mutually diminishing efforts?

The same question can of course be posed about the market-oriented behavior of the multiplicity of economic entities interacting in the market. But there is an important difference. The market is a mechanism that induces mutual coherence and consistency by generating sequences of public signals that point the way to continuous mutually adjustive behavior when there are disharmonies. The extra-market system of altruistic behavior lacks such a system of public signals with dependable directions for correct mutual adjustments by decentralized agents. It is distinctly possible for well-wishers to bestow on society "improvements" that cancel each other out—as in O. Henry's story "The Gift of the Magi."[7]

Prospects for Socially Efficient Altruism

What are the prospects for altruism to mount a significant assault on pollution? The foregoing discussion leads one to doubt strongly that such private extra-market adjustments can succeed. The prospects rest on the willingness of equity holders to sacrifice income and other goals; on the

7. For example, a switch by some firms from a high-polluting to a lower-polluting input may be frustrated when the makers of the less harmful input switch to some other product to decrease their own pollution. Mutually contradictory behavior in production decisions is likely to be embedded in relative price movements and therefore to be obscured. The more striking cases are likely to involve locational decisions, where a number of partcipants voluntarily absent themselves from, say, a highly congested road only to find that their substitute route has become congested because of the coincidence of their partly altruistic choices. Much the same happens if a number of firms coincidentally stagger their work hours the same way to avoid the height of the rush hour and thereby contribute to creating a new congestion mode.

ability of managers to formulate consistent rules of behavior; on the amassing of very sizable amounts of difficult and intrinsically ambiguous information beyond what is required for each firm's own operations; and on the ability and desire of numbers of altruistic firms to coordinate their efforts. All of these are questionable.

Thus self-policing and interfirm pressure are not likely to be taken up in most companies or to reach a degree of coordination sufficient to substantially reduce pollution. The prospect for social initiative is more hopeful, however. Since cleanup campaigns are open and public, they are visible to a widely affected audience. Their coherence is a matter of public display, since they are organized in the first place as multiparty coordinated ventures.

Business altruism which takes the form of social initiative does not generally call for a great deal of direct action in the firm as such, and some public-sector involvement is usually expected. Thus benefits of social initiative are proximate, not ultimate—an increased probability of effective public action. How such benefits are "cashed in" depends to a great extent on public policy.

Public Policy

What we have argued above is that private, decentralized approaches fail to control environmental degradation. Some coordination is clearly needed: to promote recognition of responsibility, to orchestrate separate actions into compatible wholes, to guarantee action on a scale large enough to make real inroads into problems and therefore to promise overall rewards more than commensurate with costs.

Pollution is a social problem precisely because polluters do not have to heed damages to others in making their decisions about how to use resources. This suggests that if such damages were made a financial responsibility of such polluters, the social problem would disappear, even though pollution itself might not. For such explicit responsibility would mean that each firm, in contemplating some resource-using activity, would have to balance its own prospective gains against damages to others. Those damages would be counted as a genuine cost of production —in other words, internalized by the polluters. Internalization would lower pollution by altering business choices across industries, locations, technologies, inputs, output levels, and recycling and waste treatment processes. Since firms differ markedly with respect to these pollution dimensions, the optimal compromise would typically call for quite different degrees and measures by different firms: unequal treatment is required for efficiency; equal treatment would result in waste.

Not all pollution results from the day-to-day activities of individual firms attuned to a market that fails to signal certain costs. Some of it results from the rather discontinuous, lumpy effects of aggregate behavior. Thus, for example, the overall welfare of the population might be enhanced if one river were kept in pristine condition for special uses while other rivers were frankly regarded as open sewers—this division being an alternative to having all rivers just a bit less polluted. Incremental adjustments by individual decision makers will not bring about the large-scale specialization necessary to keep a wilderness wild and a city urban rather than achieving an average smear of equal density for both. Specialized land use on a large scale is something like national defense: no small adjustment of individual behavior will do the job; deliberate collective action involves what economists call public goods. A high degree of coordination and mobilization is called for to achieve the desired results.

Aggregate patterns of resource use must be subject to public discernment and preferences. The public must have mechanisms for monitoring the overall configuration resulting from private and governmental actions and for effecting decisive changes in such configurations.

However, the fact that purely private action is insufficient does not mean that public coordination is guaranteed to succeed. We shall examine various forms of public action against pollution for their potential for achievement and for what they imply about the nature of social responsibility for business in this area. Clearly, it is beyond the scope of this chapter to offer an extensive examination of public policies. But a brief evaluation of different approaches is important to indicate the kind of partnership between business and government that may be called for. The different governmental approaches considered here are: (1) direct government treatment of wastes; (2) public subsidy for private waste treatment; (3) regulation and prohibition; and (4) effluent charges and subsidies.

Government Treatment

Public handling of wastes means public investment to increase the assimilative capacity of common property resources. To the extent that such activities are worthwhile, they check pollution by direct government action. They do not require any particular pattern of private business behavior. There is no significant partnership between government and business, no distinct social responsibility for business firms.

How heavy a reliance should be placed on government treatment of wastes? On the one hand, it has been the dominant mode of action for limiting water pollution. The federal government has made grants to local governments for constructing municipal treatment plants. For denaturing liquid-borne wastes and incineration of solid wastes, economies of scale may be achieved through concentration and joint processing. In addition, certain operations can be performed on the conveying medium, the common property resource itself, which improves its assimilative capacity. An example is river flow augmentation by use of upstream reservoirs. On the other hand, public treatment facilities depend on a small subset of pollution abatement methods, totally ignoring the considerable range of other methods available and inefficiently treating all waste dischargers equally—not influencing them to change their activities in any way. The big government "plant" simply ratifies the existing pattern of resource use by polluters.

Thus public treatment is poorly adapted to be the mainstay of public policy toward pollution, even toward water pollution. It bypasses the many short- and long-run individual private adjustments that are called for and freezes resource uses in status quo configurations. But it could be a *partner* with other methods in achieving well-balanced abatement. Its centralizing calculation and mobilizing of resources on a large scale smooth the way for critical changes in overall resource use patterns.

Public Subsidy for Private Treatment

Government has the option of offering funds to firms to modify the volume and noxiousness of the wastes they discharge. The subsidy is paid to meet part of the capital costs of investing in equipment to subject wastes to recycling or denaturing treatment. In some variants, the subsidy is markedly less than the total capital cost of the equipment, say, about 50 percent; in other variants, it is as much as 80 to 90 percent of the cost.

The trouble with partial subsidization is that it is not likely in fact to elicit substantial private effort, since in almost all antipollution activity the gains fall preponderantly on outsiders while the costs must be borne by the would-be abater. Subsidies short of nearly complete cost coverage would probably leave firms as net losers and therefore unwilling to act.

Is this, however, an area where business altruism should be encouraged? Is private financing of the unsubsidized cost margin a good social investment? For two reasons, the answer must be no. First, the private actions involved are restricted to one mode of abatement and therefore would hardly ever constitute the least-cost way of achieving any overall lowering of pollution. Second, offering subsidies to private applicants on a come-one, come-all basis does not allow the government to select the projects that will yield the greatest abatement per public dollar spent or even to decide whether a given degree of abatement is worth its cost.

So public subsidization of private treatment facilities has serious weaknesses as a mainstay program to improve environmental quality. It may be useful as part of a package program that has other components.

Regulation and Prohibition

Governments are prone to resort to prohibition of various activities as their first line of defense against pollution. Such acts as burning leaves, discharging wastes into navigable waterways, or putting phosphates into detergents come to be forbidden.

When enforced, prohibitions may achieve abatement. But they are clumsy instruments, covering in blanket fashion a very wide variety of circumstances, without regard for cost or for the relative seriousness of one kind of damage as compared with another. There is no provision to ensure—or even to determine roughly—whether the overall reduction is worth the cost.

Prohibitions do, however, have one attractive application: for pollutants such as lead, mercury, arsenic, asbestos, DDT, and radioactive substances that reach dangerous levels of concentration rather than dispersing in the environment. Provided the best estimate of expected damage over time is reasonably close to the presumed cost stemming from prohibition, a reasonably strong case can be made for the prohibition approach, since a healthy margin for error is prudent if there is a risk of toxic conditions.

The setting of ambient standards and emission standards is another device resorted to by government through regulatory agencies. Ambient standards are stipulations by the controlling agency about the quality levels below which the relevant common property resource will not be allowed to fall. For instance, rivers in Category I must contain dissolved oxygen at least equal to amount x, those in Category II at least equal to amount y, etc. Airsheds over Class A cities may not exceed amount w

of sulphur dioxide in any 24-hour period; over Class B cities the level may not exceed amount z. Emission standards likewise set a quality level, or "floor," below which environmental resources may not drop, but they cannot be implemented without regulations on individual users. If a specific ambient standard is the policy goal, then individual regulations are simply a means of achieving it. If a specific emission standard is the goal, the regulations on individuals take priority, and the resulting ambient quality is derivative.

If a policy of setting standards is compared with a policy of levying charges on effluents, standards come off poorly. Efficient application of standards entails an enormous information burden very much larger than that entailed in levying charges. "Standards" are much more vulnerable to obsolescence. The enforcement burden is much greater. Moreover, there is almost invariably an administrative emphasis on nondiscriminatory treatment, and this makes the mistake of treating unequals (among polluters) as equal. Finally, standards do not readily permit the weighting of prospective gains and losses in determining what abatement is proper and how to achieve it at lowest cost.

An interesting illustration of these and other issues concerning direct regulation is the policy expressed in the Clean Air Amendments of 1970 toward automobile emissions before the 1973–74 gasoline shortage. The idea was that the problem would be solved by simply forbidding the emission of harmful wastes from autos. While such a dictum might well result in significant abatement, apparently little thought was given to total auto usage and its distribution over time and space or to cost. Because production of autos is concentrated in a handful of companies, a policy emphasis on industrywide technological change is at least feasible, but blanket changes do not fit well into the enormous range of pollution conditions under which autos are actually used. Regulation imposes a single abatement mode regardless of circumstances. To impose a solution aimed at Los Angeles on auto use in Montana may result in heavy economic waste.

Despite the defects and difficulties of the regulatory approach, it does possess two important advantages over the levying of charges on effluents. We noted above that efficient resource use may sometimes require large, decisive adjustments in resource use—not a little more or less pollution in a given river, but a system of specialized and separated facilities: one river to be cleaned up for recreation or drinking, another allowed to carry massive wastes. To accomplish this, charges are inefficient. But the establishment of appropriately differentiated ambient standards can set the stage for the desirable transformation.

The other advantage concerns an aspect of pollution that we have only touched upon. The pollution damage from a given set of activities depends on situational characteristics. Some of these are random events occurring in the environment with some frequency—like wind or rainfall. When a particularly unfortunate random event occurs that creates a pollution crisis (as has in fact occurred in a number of communities in the United States and elsewhere), ambient standards and the rough and ready direct action injunctions of the accompanying individual implementation procedures serve better than effluent charges for emergency relief.[8]

Effluent Charges

Ideally, a system of charges is the public policy analogue to correcting the market system by imposing financial responsibility for pollution damages on those who cause the damage. In effect, it sets prices on the using-up of the hitherto nonpriced assimilative capacity of the common property resources. Charges are imposed on every user in the amount of the incremental pollution damage which one extra unit of that use causes in the system. This charge means that any diminution in that incremental damage saves the user an amount of money equal to the charge per unit. Reduction can be accomplished by any of the types of adjustment spoken of earlier: in the case of the firm, by technological change, input substitution, waste treatment, output variation, or recycling. All can be invoked, and each to the extent that its effect on the value of damages is no less than the cost of achieving the reduction. In principle, the result is a combination of adjustments that gives the best compromise abatement (and at the lowest cost). The focus is on minimizing the net damages from pollution, not on environment quality for its own sake. Fairness becomes a principle of responsibility for

8. See William J. Baumol and Wallace E. Oates, "The Instruments for Environmental Policy," in Edwin S. Mills (ed.), *Economic Analysis of the Environment* (National Bureau of Economic Research, 1975).

The famous pioneer study attempting to compare the actual social costs of a standards versus a charges approach is the Federal Water Pollution Control Administration, *Delaware Estuary Comprehensive Study: Summary of Preliminary Report and Findings* (1966).

damages produced rather than of equal treatment. Such considerations are important for political implementation.

An important contrast between the charges approach and the standards approach is that the existence of a charge keeps the firm interested in reducing its damages further if profitable opportunities arise, regardless of the level of damage reduction already achieved. Since the charges approach makes *every* profitable damage reduction relevant, a variety of experiments with general technological change and input substitution may be tried, as well as new forms of recycling.

Prospectively, therefore, effluent charges are an attractive instrument of public policy. Basic to implementation is the ability to measure incremental damage by each polluter. Because of unknown or incommensurable effects it is infeasible in practice to estimate accurately all the information needed. Nevertheless, polluters could be sorted into groups, and a limited number of damage situations could be estimated for each. By the same token, monitoring damage flows would be difficult, but at least the burden of proof of damage reduction could be placed on the polluters.

An alternative to measuring damages would be to specify certain environmental quality goals and attempt to achieve them by the least-cost level of effluent reduction. The charge mechanism could be used either directly or indirectly. In its direct use, an ambient quality standard is established, and a sequence of emission charges (not *damage* charges) is tried until one is reached that elicits the desired ambient quality.[9] In the indirect use, the ambient standard is set, and the total level of emissions compatible with that standard is determined. Then fixed-term licenses, each permitting emission of one unit but together adding up to the number corresponding with the standard, are auctioned off to private bidders. Buyers can subsequently buy and sell such licenses within that term from private holders within the same pollution situation group as themselves. Here too the desired ambient quality level is achievable at lowest total cost.[10] Both methods, but especially the second, reduce information requirements considerably.

9. William J. Baumol and Wallace E. Oates, "The Use of Standards and Prices for Protection of the Environment," *Swedish Journal of Economics,* Vol. 73 (March 1971), pp. 42–54.

10. J. H. Dales, "Land, Water, and Ownership," *Canadian Journal of Economics,* Vol. 1 (November 1968), pp. 791–804.

In sum, the damage-pricing approach looks best for fine-tuned environmental policy. Implementation would require compromises involving measurement of damages and enforcement of compliance. Integrating prices with ambient standards and other components having the special advantages noted above would help.

Public Responsibility and Business Responsibility

I conclude that a public policy package should be tried that places major weight on pricing damages caused and/or effluents discharged but also makes selective use of government treatment of wastes, prohibitions, and ambient and emission standards. With this package would come a good deal of interaction between government and business. Much is to be hoped from government setting signals and business responding in predictable ways.

I have argued that a substitution of altruism for self-interest on the part of business enterprises is not called for in resolving environmental problems—indeed, that an attempt at such substitution might have mischievous consequences. Self-interest is not simply to be left intact; it is to be relied on. The responsibility of the public sector is to enact policies that do elicit socially responsible behavior from firms that are following self-interest.

The task for public administrators is to induce firms to act in ways that are in the aggregate socially desirable.[11] In doing the job, three facets of business behavior must be kept in mind: (1) information, (2) short-run operations, and (3) long-term investment and innovation.

The flow of information between business and government in both directions is crucial. The flow from government to business is essential to transmit the intention of the public program, its relation to each particular firm, and the terms of the regulations, controls, or charges imposed. The ability of the firm to act responsibly depends on its understanding unambiguously what is expected of it. Regulations must specify precisely what constraints must be heeded, or charges or penalties paid, or subsidies obtained. Lack of regulatory precision can lead to serious distortions and extensive litigation.

11. I am indebted to an anonymous reader of an earlier version of this chapter for emphasizing this aspect of the social responsibility issue.

The reverse flow of information is critical in two respects. First, to formulate the program the public authority may need very substantial information about emission technology, prospects of individual treatment and recycling, and various forms of pollution damage. Second, to enforce the program it will need information about the degree of individual conformity to regulations, activity levels, and composition.

In worrying about aggregate resource allocation, government must take care not to exploit the more able firms merely to make the target figure. If firms with better-than-average efficiency in treating or recycling wastes are called upon to make *greater* than average decreases in emissions and firms with less-than-average efficiency are called upon to make *lesser* decreases, business self-interest will encourage misinformation flows, or decreasing treatment efficiency, or both. Critical surveillance of these responses would impose impossible burdens on the public authorities.

An emission standards policy is more likely to set up a conflict between self-interest and required behavior than is a policy of emission charges or subsidies. For the latter policy, the preliminary reporting necessary to establish appropriate levels is much less demanding: detailed data on technology and costs do not have to be collected. Moreover, the regulations bring about a tilting of relative gains under which it is the firm that decides its own subsequent action. This decision can well be based on self-interest; but it is a self-interest in which differential efficiency in treatment and recycling is rewarded and not punished, inefficiency is punished and not rewarded. With a standards policy, by contrast, the only way to avoid creating a conflict between company interests and the public interest is to jettison the attempt to differentiate treatment of unequals; and the foregoing discrimination leads to a different form of distorted outcomes.

Much the same analysis holds for business adjustments in short-term operations. Where a centralized determination of individualized constraints or emission standards is judgmentally based on firms' own production situations, two important dysfunctional responses may occur. First, there may well be a heavy resort to private litigation, whereby firms contest the soundness or equity of bureaucratic regulations applied to them. The spread of litigation is itself part of a defensive business strategy in which successful business litigants must not be allowed thereby to obtain competitive advantages over other firms. Widespread litigation can easily impose inordinate delays on a program, even paralyze it, since tolerable administration costs depend on general acceptance and uncontested compliance.[12]

A second response is a slackened search for treatment efficiency within current technology. There is some incentive for firms to establish an observable record of high treatment cost, although this is likely to be weaker than the disincentives mentioned above, especially if adjustment of bureaucratic standards to changing conditions is not prompt (the size of the administrative burden in such programs is likely to prevent prompt bureaucratic responsiveness).

Again, the disincentives are milder under a system of charges or subsidies, since: (1) the level of charges (subsidies) is based not on the secretive *internal* situation of firms but on their *external* impacts—something about which the polluting firms are not nearly so proprietary; (2) efficiency advantages are not penalized but are rewarded in differential profits.

Long-term investment and innovation tell this same story, but even more strikingly. Although maintenance of an achieved level of efficiency in handling residuals on a current basis may cost little (most of the expenses being fixed costs), investments in additional treatment capacity and for new technology to decrease obtrusive waste are inherently costly. If reward for successful activity of this sort is simply to shift upward the required quality standards, then efficiency is even more dramatically being punished. So standards based on a firm's own *achieved* efficiency will tend seriously to discourage any such activity.

The same cannot be said about standards based on *achievable* technological improvements. Such regulations can induce considerable investment and even innovative action toward improved treatment. But the effect is not all salutary—it may be far from wise in overall resource terms over the long run. Three important problems are: (1) forced attention to a limited set of technological options may foreclose much more promising directions; (2) differences in circumstances among firms and their customers are generally disregarded; and (3) little opportunity is given to achieve the most appropriate degree of technological improvement by balancing prospective gains and costs.

The case of automobile emission standards is again a good example. By stipulating a short period in which to lower pollution the government

12. Consider administration of the prohibition of liquor in the United States from 1919 to 1933, when automatic widespread compliance could not be counted on.

precluded industry attention to radically new directions, directions which some experts believe far superior to those actually being explored. All firms, moreover, were pushed into the same limited range of alterations. Where significant improvements are sought, diversity of effort is a useful strategy for a system as a whole.[13] The matter of government-fostered directions precluding others is important because investment in innovation, especially involving capital-intensive processes, tends to commit an enterprise's resources for considerable periods of time. Given the inertia of heavy commitment in one direction, the firm is unlikely to be able to readjust to even substantial changes in market opportunities for extended periods. Thus ineffectual innovations can be serious for the economy. Finally, and for reasons already advanced, the program directed at auto emissions does not permit easy calculation of what is the appropriate level of standards, since it does not facilitate the balancing of incremental overall gains minus losses from different emission standards, let alone different ambient standards. The matter of alternative measures for curtailing emissions in actual use rather than by vehicle design ought to be investigated too. Yet these considerations seem absent from the formulation and administration of this kind of program.

Once again, an emission charge (subsidy) approach avoids many of these problems. The disincentive to innovation is cleared away, since improved efficiency with residuals is rewarded by lower charges and/or higher production. Indeed, this approach gives a continuous incentive to technological improvements. Moreover, the improvements can be tailored to the differing opportunities and constraints of differently situated enterprises. A wide variety of improvements can be tried, and notable successes imitated where appropriate. And technological improvements can be coordinated with short-term adjustments for individual firms. Last, because charges represent an implicit valuation of social benefits to be obtained from each additional unit of improvement, the decentralized calculations of firms as to how to adjust to them represents a balancing of prospective gains and losses which can lead the system as a whole to an appropriate degree of overall adjustment.

13. The Clean Air Amendments of 1970 stipulated emission-control devices that raised gasoline consumption. Then the 1973–74 petroleum crisis developed, making such devices impractical and thus wasting the research that had gone into them. If a wide spectrum of options had been encouraged originally, measures for achieving gasoline economy (including engines that use other fuels) might now be well along.

What I have been arguing is that business firms that want to act responsibly may be inadvertently induced by public policy into irresponsible behavior. Given the failure of purely decentralized behavior to solve the problem of environmental quality, public action must provide an appropriate framework to induce business behavior that *is* responsible.

But an appropriate framework and business self-interest do not guarantee a successful program. If businesses see in the various rigors of compliance an arbitrary governmental interference or competitive disadvantage, their response could be defensive, evasive, or legally obstructive. The program I have sketched is especially vulnerable to such noncooperation, since it depends on substantial flows of information and a largely self-enforcing posture from business. To understand the requirements of reasonable public policy, to grant that it may succeed with cooperation (and fail without), and therefore to act as a genuine partner with government instead of as an adversary to make it succeed—these seem part of the social responsibility of business. At the least, exploration in good faith of public programs to check pollution implies compliance with the requirement for full and accurate information.[14] It also implies that the necessarily differentiated impact of the program will not be misunderstood as unwarranted discrimination and opposed by evasion and obstructive litigation. Active partnership with government, essential to the success of public policy, is not the only conceivable expression of business self-interest, but it is one such expression. By deliberately choosing it instead of other possible stances, business becomes socially responsible and a true agent of society.

14. One further aspect of information should be mentioned. The public program must operate over time, during which many changes take place. Though most changes would impose only modest requirements for adjustment on the program, some critical ones might impose great strain on a system designed to adjust by incremental amounts. Some of these are associated with technological change. It has been argued that much technological change is both sought and applied by firms on the narrowest of perspectives (see Barry Commoner, *The Closing Circle: Nature, Man, and Technology* [Knopf, 1972], especially Chap. 9). Business firms can show a further exercise of social responsibility by broadening their focus on the likely range of consequences of each new technical advance they either seek or are ready to apply. Once acted upon, some such "advances" represent advance only in that they are in practical terms irreversible. It is much easier to stop them before they begin.

CHAPTER NINE

Urban Problems

JOHN F. KAIN

FOUR FACTORS may be identified as contributing in major ways to most of the diverse problems that have been popularly termed the urban crisis. Racial discrimination and poverty are the two most important factors—in particular the concentration of the poor and of the victims of discrimination inside the central city and their virtual exclusion from other localities. The outmoded institutional arrangements for providing and financing public services in metropolitan areas constitute the third factor. The difficulty of modifying the obsolete stocks of private and particularly public capital in old cities to accommodate changing tastes, incomes, and technology is the fourth factor, completing the list. Co-operative action to correct these four conditions would eliminate or reduce to manageable proportions most urban problems as they now manifest themselves in U.S. metropolitan areas.

A few years ago, when each summer seemed to bring worse riots in the nation's largest cities, solutions to the urban crisis were demanded from business. Indeed, corporation executives themselves were among the most active in urging an enlarged role for business in dealing with urban problems.

The arguments used by these business leaders to justify a greater role by business appealed to public and private interests in varying degrees.[1] Some businessmen claimed to see attractive and unexploited possibilities for growth and profits in various public-private programs for dealing

---

1. A good selection of these diverse justifications for business involvement is contained in Neil W. Chamberlain (ed.), *Business and the Cities: A Book of Relevant Readings* (Basic Books, 1970).

with urban problems. Others justified business efforts to deal with urban problems as pure acts of corporate philanthropy. Most business advocates of a larger role for private enterprise in solving urban problems, however, contended that efforts to ensure a stable and orderly urban environment are in the interest not only of private enterprise as a whole but of individual businesses. They pointed out that nearly all firms own property or serve markets in major urban areas, and they argued that long-term profitability depends on the stability and order of the urban society. Business efforts to help resolve the urban problems were depicted as a kind of disaster insurance that no enlightened corporation should do without.

Neither the motives nor the actual accomplishments of business in helping with the problems of the cities went unchallenged. The most frequent criticism was that business was doing too little. Conservatives, on the other hand, continued to argue that business should limit itself to the search for profits. A few liberals voiced concern over the then rampant enthusiasm for business involvement because they feared that exaggerated claims about what business might accomplish would make it more difficult to obtain acceptance for the large government programs they believed were needed.[2] The far left had still other objections to business participation. The socialist Michael Harrington was quoted as saying that "whatever other qualifications they may have, businessmen are not competent to design a new civilization . . . [and] have no democratic right to do so."[3]

Urging an enlarged role for business in solving urban problems is somewhat out of style today. But the underlying social and economic conditions that spawned the "urban crisis" during the 1960s still exist. Indeed, in some respects these conditions have worsened. Thus this chapter begins with the presumption that businesses and businessmen will again be compelled either by their consciences or by external pressure to address the host of social, economic, and physical problems of the nation's cities.

2. For example, see "Statement of Chester Hartman," in *Urban America: Goals and Problems,* Hearings before the Subcommittee on Urban Affairs of the Joint Economic Committee, 90 Cong. 1 sess. (1967), pp. 192–94, and Hartman, "The Private Sector and Community Development: A Cautious Proposal," in *Urban America: Goals and Problems* (materials compiled for the same committee, 1967), pp. 272–82.

3. Quoted in Robert C. Albrook, "Business Wrestles with Its Social Conscience," *Fortune,* Vol. 78 (August 1968), p. 90.

The Four Problem Areas

The four factors named above are examined here with the aim of identifying those areas where private enterprise can help directly and those where it should support actions by the public sector. It would be a tragedy if a resumption of large-scale violence was required to cause businessmen to consider what they might do to reduce the inequities and inefficiencies that continue to threaten the stability of our society and undermine the quality of life in our largest cities.

Racial Discrimination

Racial discrimination, the most intractable of the four factors, takes many forms. In the labor market, it is a major cause of the low incomes of minority groups. Otis Dudley Duncan estimated that $1,430 of a measured gap of $3,790 in 1962 between the earnings of native Negro and white men twenty-five to sixty-four years old with nonfarm background was attributable to income discrimination.[4] Similarly, Bradley R. Schiller concluded that approximately half of the $3,000 difference in the average earnings of *all* white and black male workers in 1970 could be attributed to prior (nonmarket) discrimination in the schools, one-fourth to past market discrimination (work skills and experience), and one-fourth to current labor market discrimination.[5]

The lower money incomes of blacks are further reduced by pervasive discrimination in consumer markets. Black occupants appear to pay 5 to 10 percent more in rents and house prices than do whites for comparable housing.[6] Since poor blacks may spend 40 percent or more of

4. Duncan defines income discrimination as "the difference between Negro and white incomes that cannot be attributed to differential occupational levels, differential educational attainment . . . differences in size of family of origin, or differences in the socio-economic status thereof." Duncan, "Inheritance of Poverty or Inheritance of Race?" in Daniel P. Moynihan (ed.), *On Understanding Poverty: Perspectives from the Social Sciences* (Basic Books, 1969), p. 100.

5. Schiller, *The Economics of Poverty and Discrimination* (Prentice-Hall 1973), pp. 125–26. Paul M. Siegel, using similar methods, estimated that labor market discrimination cost the average black worker roughly $1,000 in 1960. "On the Cost of Being a Negro," *Sociological Inquiry*, Vol. 35 (Winter 1965), p. 47.

6. A. Thomas King and Peter Mieszkowski, "Racial Discrimination, Segregation, and the Price of Housing," *Journal of Political Economy,* Vol. 81 (May–

their incomes on housing, a 10 percent markup would be equivalent to a 4 percent reduction in the family incomes of black households.

The higher price nonwhites must pay for comparable housing is only a small part of the welfare loss imposed on them by housing market discrimination. A nonwhite wishing to rent or buy outside nonwhite residential areas must spend far more time house hunting than a similarly situated white would; he must be prepared to accept frequent humiliation; and, if he succeeds, both he and his family must be prepared to face a hostile, if not violent, reception when they move into their new home. These psychic and transaction costs may loom far larger than out-of-pocket costs for blacks considering a move out of the ghetto. As a consequence most blacks limit their search to the ghetto. Since many types of housing are unavailable in the ghetto at any price, the bundles of housing services consumed by black households differ in important respects from those they would consume in the absence of housing market discrimination.

Housing suitable for homeownership, for instance, is generally in short supply in the ghetto. As a result, blacks are much less likely to be homeowners than are whites of similar characteristics. A bar to homeownership has more substantial and far-reaching implications than are evident at first. Homeowning is usually cheaper than renting for families that live more than three years in the same urban area. Indeed, a de facto limitation on homeownership can increase housing costs for blacks by over 30 percent, even assuming no value appreciation.

De facto segregation, rooted in racial discrimination in urban housing markets, has displaced de jure segregation as the principal cause of segregated schooling and the inferior education it typically provides. Blacks who buy homes in the ghetto must pay more for theft and fire insurance than the cost of similar coverage in suburban communities or are unable to obtain it at all. Mortgage financing is more difficult and more expensive to obtain. Ghetto residents, in addition, usually must pay more for auto insurance than suburban whites pay.

Housing segregation and discrimination reinforce more direct forms of employment discrimination.[7] If nonwhites ever hear about and man-

---

June 1973), pp. 590–606; John F. Kain and John M. Quigley, "Housing Market Discrimination, Homeownership, and Savings Behavior," *American Economic Review*, Vol. 62 (June 1972), pp. 263–77.

7. John F. Kain, "Housing Segregation, Negro Employment, and Metropolitan Decentralization," *Quarterly Journal of Economics*, Vol. 82 (May 1968), pp. 175–97.

age to obtain distant jobs, their real wages (subtracting the money and time outlays for commuting) will be less than those of comparable white workers. Frequently they do not learn of available jobs far from the ghetto or else do not bother to apply because of the cost and difficulty of reaching them. They may accept low-paying jobs near the ghetto or no job at all, choosing leisure and welfare as a rational alternative to low pay and poor working conditions.

No section of the country has a good record in terms of equal treatment of its minority population. The extremes of segregated housing, however, are reached in metropolitan regions where the suburbs remain closed to nonwhites even though minority populations have been growing rapidly. Those metropolitan areas that rank highest in keeping nonwhites bottled up inside the old central city are nearly synonymous with the urban crisis: Washington, D.C., Newark, Hartford, St. Louis, Detroit, Baltimore, and Cleveland.

It would be a mistake to conclude that all of the costs of racial discrimination fall on minorities. Commuting costs of whites employed in the central city are appreciably higher than they would be if housing segregation did not exist. The steady growth of central city ghettos has led high- and middle-income whites to move farther and farther from their places of employment. The intense pressures for expensive high-speed highway and transit links to declining central employment areas is one of the consequences.[8]

Racial discrimination and the steady growth of central city ghettos have discouraged private renewal actions and have doomed ambitious urban renewal schemes by local governments. If it were not for racial discrimination, a large fraction of blacks employed at suburban workplaces would have chosen housing near their places of employment, just as white workers employed at these locations have. The dispersal of employment, rising incomes, and transport costs would have induced a decline in the demand for dwelling units in central residential areas.[9] Centrally employed middle- and high-income households would have been encouraged by bargain prices to buy and renovate older dwellings. In neighborhoods where individual units were structurally unsound and

8. A more complete discussion of the social costs of racial discrimination in urban housing markets is presented in John F. Kain and Joseph J. Persky, "Alternatives to the Gilded Ghetto," *Public Interest* (Winter 1969), pp. 74–87.

9. See John F. Kain, "Effect of Housing Market Segregation on Urban Development," in United States Savings and Loan League, *Savings and Residential Financing: 1969 Conference Proceedings* (Chicago: U.S. Savings and Loan League, 1969), pp. 89–113.

unsuitable for renovation by individual buyers, still lower prices would have encouraged private developers, perhaps assisted by government programs, to carry out more comprehensive renewal schemes.

But the rapid growth of central ghettos eliminated the bargains in most U.S. cities. In central residential areas, housing discrimination created a market only loosely related to accessibility advantages. The demand for central housing by entrapped minorities maintained central land prices, and relative housing prices more often favored suburban locations even for those employed in core areas. The poverty of minority and other disadvantaged populations ensured that central city housing would deteriorate. The result was a steady expansion of slum housing, deterioration of urban services, and an expectation that the process would continue until the entire central city became a black slum.

Poverty

There is a tendency to use the terms "poverty" and "discrimination" as though they refer to identical problems. Although current and past discrimination is clearly the principal cause of the poverty endemic to black Americans, the problems are by no means identical, for two-thirds of the poor in 1970 were white.

Poverty is at once a symptom and a cause of the interrelated problems that have been termed the urban crisis. It is a symptom of the low skill levels, discrimination, infirmities, and lack of family stability that afflict nearly all poor persons or households. It is the principal cause of substandard housing, inadequate health care, and low educational achievement for a significant share of the urban population. Moreover, the pressure on central cities and low-income suburbs to provide decent levels of housing, health care, police and fire protection, schooling, food, clothing, and other private and public goods and services for their residents is *the* urban crisis as it is perceived daily by mayors and other public officials.

Urban poverty is very unequally distributed among communities within each metropolitan area. Of the 12.3 million poor persons living in metropolitan areas in 1969, 7.8 million lived in central cities, and a large fraction of the remainder were concentrated in a few suburban communities.[10] The ratio of poor people to total population in central cities and suburbs is a more meaningful measure of this imbalance: 13.4 percent

10. U.S. Bureau of the Census, *Statistical Abstract of the United States, 1971,* p. 324, Table 518.

of all persons living in central cities in 1969 were poor, as contrasted with 6.3 percent of persons living in the suburban rings.

The unequal spatial distribution of poverty ensures that the burdens of coping with the seemingly endless list of poverty-related problems fall disproportionately on a few local governments. The heavy dependence on local tax sources to finance local governments typically means that these units of government lack resources to deal with the problems without resort to levels of taxation that accelerate the flight of both high-income households and nonresidential taxpayers from the city. The adequacy of existing metropolitan fiscal mechanisms is considered at a later point in this chapter. But it can be safely asserted now that these mechanisms are not fully responsive to the different needs and resources of local government within metropolitan areas. The predictable consequences have been frustration of the poor, a shortening of the political careers of many mayors, serious distortions in the pattern of metropolitan development, and a continued crisis atmosphere.

For a variety of reasons, including the different effects of racial discrimination, poverty is more prevalent in the central cities of some metropolitan areas than others. Shown in Table 9-1 are several measures of this unequal distribution of poverty for the thirty U.S. metropolitan areas with the highest percentage of their poor residents confined to the central city. Newark and Hartford share the dubious honor of ranking highest by this criterion; both have a proportion of low-income residents that is two and one-half times that of the surrounding suburbs. Newark also has the largest ratio of poor persons to total population of the area. Miami, which ranks twenty-fifth in terms of relative poverty, ranks second in terms of absolute share. This large discrepancy raises the question whether relative poverty or some absolute standard is more suitable in evaluating the seriousness of poverty in urban areas.

Both common sense and an extensive body of scholarly evidence make it clear that poverty is very much a relative concept.[11] As long as there continue to be large differences in earnings and family incomes among regions and metropolitan areas, perceptions of minimum living standards will vary. Among people at the same absolute poverty level, those indi-

11. Lee Rainwater deals extensively with this question in a report on the relation between poverty and personal well-being prepared for the Joint Economic Committee. He found that in surveys the responses to the Gallup poll question "What is the smallest amount of money a family of four needs to get along in this community?" bore a virtually constant relationship to family disposable income and workers' earnings. The "get along" standard matches very closely the U.S. Bureau of Labor Statistics' lower standard budget for an urban family. Between

viduals feel most deprived who believe that the remainder of the community is much better off. It does not follow, however, that individual communities can solve their poverty problem in isolation. Although differences already exist in employment opportunities, welfare, and public services among metropolitan areas and between metropolitan and nonmetropolitan areas, if a single area made an exceptionally bold attempt to solve its poverty problem without comparable efforts in other regions, it would undoubtedly attract large numbers of disadvantaged persons. Corporations, when they consider policies to alleviate poverty in the city, must consider both local imbalances and the need for national efforts.

Obsolescence of Urban Capital

Private and public stocks of capital in old cities were developed to serve populations with different tastes and incomes and firms with different technological alternatives and costs than now prevail. Some of this capital can be modernized at reasonable cost. More often, although it could be maintained in good physical condition, business allows it to depreciate, because the old plant would become functionally obsolete even if maintained in good physical condition.

The decline of manufacturing, wholesaling, and other goods producing and handling employment in the central city and the departure of many firms to the suburbs reflect the obsolescence of much nonresidential capital.[12] Current production techniques and relative factor prices lead firms

---

1959 and 1970 per family consumption and the Gallup poll "get along" figure both increased by about two-thirds, while the consumer price index and the low-income budget which is tied to it increased by only 27 percent. Rainwater, *Poverty, Living Standards and Family Well-Being,* prepared for the Subcommittee on Fiscal Policy of the Joint Economic Committee of the Congress, Working Paper 10 (Joint Center for Urban Studies of the Massachusetts Institute of Technology and Harvard University, 1972), pp. 44–46.

12. For a discussion of these trends, see Raymond Vernon, *The Changing Economic Function of the Central City* (New York: Area Development Committee of the Committee for Economic Development, 1959); Edgar M. Hoover and Raymond Vernon, *Anatomy of a Metropolis: The Changing Distribution of People and Jobs within the New York Metropolitan Region* (Harvard University Press, 1959); John R. Meyer, John F. Kain, and Martin Wohl, *The Urban Transportation Problem* (Harvard University Press, 1965); John F. Kain, "The Distribution and Movement of Jobs and Industry," in James Q. Wilson (ed.), *The Metropolitan Enigma* (Harvard University Press, 1968); Roger Noll, "Metropolitan Employment and Population Distribution and the Conditions of the Urban Poor," in John P. Crecine (ed.), *Financing the Metropolis* (Sage Publications, 1970).

Table 9-1. Measures of Intrametropolitan Income Inequality for Large Urban Areas Ranked by Relative Central City Poverty in 1970

Standard metropolitan statistical area (SMSA)	Ratio of poor people in central city to poor people in SMSA[a]	Percent of persons below poverty level, 1970			Ratio of median family income in central city to median family income in the SMSA	
		Central city	Suburbs	SMSA	1970	1950
Newark	2.47	22.5	5.6	9.1	.65	n.a.
Hartford	2.46	17.0	3.8	6.9	.74	.90
Paterson-Clifton-Passaic	2.19	12.7	4.1	5.8	.77	n.a.
Washington, D.C.	2.05	17.0	5.3	8.3	.74	.89
Cleveland	1.92	17.3	4.3	9.0	.80	.91
Boston	1.91	16.2	6.3	8.5	.80	.92
St. Louis	1.86	20.3	7.6	10.9	.78	.95
Dayton	1.78	14.2	5.6	8.0	.85	1.00
Detroit	1.75	14.9	4.9	8.5	.83	.99
Atlanta	1.74	20.4	7.0	11.7	.79	.91
Rochester	1.68	12.4	4.8	7.4	.84	.96
Cincinnati	1.67	17.7	7.2	10.6	.87	.96
Buffalo	1.67	15.2	6.0	9.1	.84	.97
Minneapolis-St. Paul	1.64	11.0	3.7	6.7	.87	n.a.
Baltimore	1.63	18.4	5.8	11.3	.83	.98
Chicago	1.56	14.5	4.3	9.3	.86	.97
Louisville	1.54	17.4	6.7	11.3	.87	.99
Philadelphia	1.54	15.4	6.4	10.0	.87	.96
Youngstown-Warren, Ohio	1.54	12.8	5.5	8.3	.91	n.a.
Grand Rapids	1.52	12.5	5.7	8.2	.94	1.02
Albany-Schenectady-Troy	1.49	13.0	6.5	8.7	.90	n.a.
Richmond, Va.	1.49	18.0	6.7	12.1	.86	.97
Salt Lake City	1.49	14.2	7.4	9.5	.89	n.a.
Syracuse	1.48	14.1	7.5	9.5	.88	1.00
Miami	1.45	20.6	11.9	14.2	n.a.	.96
Milwaukee	1.44	11.4	4.2	7.9	.91	.97
Seattle-Everett	1.39	10.4	5.6	7.5	.94	n.a.
Gary-Hammond-East Chicago	1.38	12.1	5.2	8.8	.92	n.a.
Akron	1.37	11.8	6.3	8.6	.91	.99
Allentown-Bethlehem-Easton	1.37	10.3	5.4	7.5	n.a.	n.a.

Sources: U.S. Bureau of the Census, *Census of Population, 1970: General Social and Economic Characteristics*, Final Report PC (1)-C (1972), Tables 89–90 in relevant state reports; *Census of Population, 1950*, Vol. 2, *Characteristics of the Population* (1952), Table 37 in relevant state reports.
n.a. Not available.
a. Ratio of percent of poor people in the central city to percent of poor people in SMSA.

to employ more physical space in production activities and in most instances to demand spacious single-story structures. Additional space is required for the parking of employees' cars as growing numbers shift from public transit to automobile commutation.

Some firms with relatively new or specialized plants or with especially strong linkages to nearby suppliers or customers obtain the additional space required by these changed technological and economic circumstances through expansion of their existing facilities. But expansion within built-up central cities is usually difficult and expensive. The supply of vacant land is limited, of poor quality, or inconveniently located. The limited supply of vacant land, the expansion demands by existing firms and households, and the cost of acquiring and clearing occupied sites maintains central city land prices at levels well above competitive suburban sites.

A useful survey by the Boston Economic Development and Industrial Commission of central city and suburban manufacturing firms illustrates these propositions clearly. The survey determined that 42 percent of the firms in the sample that were located inside Boston proper and 29 percent of suburban firms were considering a change in location. Only a fourth of the in-town firms and 1 percent of suburban firms considering a move listed the city as a proposed location. When asked their reasons for leaving or staying, the sampled firms clearly indicated the importance to them of space requirements and the availability of skilled labor.[13]

Obsolescence of public capital may be an even more serious problem for old cities. Modernization of urban transport systems, in particular, remains a major challenge for the governments of those urban areas. Old, dense central cities have too little street space to accommodate the large numbers of trucks and automobiles which crowd into them during morning and evening peaks. These physical inadequacies are aggravated by unwise policies governing the allocation of this scarce street space among competing users. Irritating and costly delays to commuters and shoppers and the decline of public transit systems are the uniform results. Congestion, generally a highly inefficient allocation mechanism, is disastrous in old cities.

The sunk capital located in central cities often has an acquisition or use cost that is a fraction of the cost of new capital. In the case of resi-

13. See Andrew M. Hamer, *Industrial Exodus from Central City* (D. C. Heath, 1973), Tables 1-7, 1-8, and 1-9.

dential capital, the depreciated capital stocks located in central cities may be more suitable for the production of low-income than of high-income housing services. But if racial discrimination ceased and if the structure of urban government were suitably modified, the modest concentration of low-income households that might arise would not be a cause for alarm. A deteriorated and substandard housing stock is not an inexorable result of the passing of time. Generally, the housing stock in central cities is in poor repair not because of its age or basic structural defects but because too little has been spent to maintain it. Poverty is unquestionably the principal cause of this undermaintenance. Elimination of urban poverty would largely eliminate underinvestment and housing deterioration in central cities.

Fiscal and Governmental Structures

The outmoded arrangements for producing and financing government services in metropolitan areas differ in an important respect from racial discrimination, poverty, and obsolescence as a cause of the urban crisis. It is nearly impossible to imagine policies that could quickly undo the debilitating effects of racial discrimination and poverty, and the obsolescence of public and private capital is a feature of some urban areas that simply must be taken as a given fact in the design of urban policy. But the structure of governments within metropolitan areas, and to an even greater extent the arrangements for financing urban services, could be quickly modified to correct the most serious inadequacies of present fiscal structures.

That existing governmental structures tend to magnify the effects of poverty, discrimination, and obsolescence should come as no surprise. Existing arrangements of local governments in urban areas allow high- and middle-income households to escape the city's problems. They in fact permit a degree of discrimination in the provision of urban services within metropolitan areas that would be considered unconstitutional if it took place within a single political jurisdiction.[14]

Local government expenditures in metropolitan areas are financed by

14. Michael Harrington shows less restraint in describing these considerations. "Suburbia was Balkanized as a conscious strategy of a white middle class which wanted to flee big-city problems. This tactic allowed the suburbs to build comfortable, Federally financed and lily-white Shangri-las." Harrington, *Toward a Democratic Left* (Macmillan, 1968; Pelican, 1969), p. 121.

a variety of grants-in-aid from state and federal agencies and by an assortment of fees and taxes, especially local property taxes. Local taxes influence the locational and investment decisions of firms and households. Areas with unusually heavy demands for poverty-related services typically have high tax rates, a factor which discourages investment and the location of certain types of economic activity within their boundaries. The geographic concentration of low-income populations in central cities and some low-income suburbs and the corresponding concentration of high-income populations and industry in other suburban communities create differences of this kind, particularly in the older metropolitan areas. When these differences become large enough, they may foster an inefficient arrangement of economic activities.

Table 9-2 lists the thirty large metropolitan areas found to be worst in terms of central city tax burdens. Central city tax burden in this case is measured by the ratio of per capita revenue collected from local sources to per capita income for each city. Newark and Washington, D.C., rank worst by this index, which reflects differences in local demand for public services, differences in nonresidential tax sources, and the extent of assistance by other levels of government. The second column in Table 9-2 provides the same measure of tax effort for suburban governments. The difference between these two measures may be the best single indicator of the distortions to urban growth produced by the metropolitan fiscal structures.

Some segregation of households by income within urban areas is not new and is characteristic of cities throughout the world. But in American cities until the past few decades most poor, average, and rich neighborhoods were located in the same political jurisdiction, i.e., the independent city. Around the turn of the century, particularly with the advent of commuter railways, urban areas began to develop separate residential suburbs, and central cities began to acquire disproportionate numbers of low-income households. Until the end of World War II, however, the fragmented structure of urban government in metropolitan areas worked reasonably well. Central cities had a disproportionate share of low-income households, but they also had most of the nonresidential tax base, which could be used to subsidize services for low-income populations. High-income bedroom suburbs were able to do without nonresidential tax revenues because of the high per capita value of residential property.

The rapid growth and the suburbanization of metropolitan areas following World War II shattered this fragile arrangement. Industry and

Table 9-2. Fiscal Imbalance between City and Suburbs, 1970

Area	Tax burden (local tax levy as percent of per capita income)[a] Central city	Suburbs	House value per capita (dollars) Central city	Suburbs	Population in annexed area (1950–70) as percentage of 1960 population in city
Newark	15.6	7.8	3,100	6,300	b
Washington, D.C.	15.1	6.7	4,700	6,800	b
Cincinnati	14.6	5.7	3,600	4,000	1.7
Boston	13.7	n.a.	3,400	5,000	b
New York	13.1	9.3	3,600	6,600	b
San Francisco-Oakland	12.9	n.a.	6,300	6,900	0.1
Cleveland	12.6	7.4	3,300	5,900	b
Hartford	12.5	n.a.	4,000	6,100	b
Miami	11.7	7.1	4,100	5,300	c
Dayton	11.3	5.7	3,900	4,600	13.6
St. Louis	11.1	6.6	2,900	4,100	b
Atlanta	10.9	5.8	3,700	5,100	35.9
Milwaukee	10.9	6.9	3,800	5,300	17.6
Rochester	10.4	7.3	3,800	5,200	c
Detroit	10.2	7.2	3,700	5,200	b
Philadelphia	10.2	6.5	2,900	4,200	b
Portland, Ore.	10.0	6.1	4,500	4,400	7.1
Baltimore	9.9	6.5	2,900	4,200	b
Louisville	9.8	5.8	3,200	4,000	19.2
Buffalo	9.8	8.2	2,400	4,200	b
Los Angeles-Long Beach	9.8	10.2	6,000	5,600	3.0
Jersey City	9.4	8.6	2,900	3,200	b
Gary	9.1	n.a.	3,200	4,000	2.8
Pittsburgh	9.0	6.7	3,200	3,800	c
Akron	8.9	6.9	4,100	4,500	0.2
Kansas City	8.7	n.a.	3,900	4,300	23.5
Memphis	8.7	8.5	3,200	2,600	41.3
Grand Rapids	8.6	6.4	3,900	3,700	22.3
New Orleans	8.4	5.5	3,400	4,200	b
Tampa-St. Petersburg	7.6	6.8	3,700	3,900	34.3

Sources: U.S. Bureau of the Census, *Local Government Finances in Selected Metropolitan Areas and Large Counties, 1969–70*, GF70–No. 6 (1971), Tables 2, 4; *Census of Population, 1970: General Population Characteristics*, Final Report PC(1)-B1, *United States Summary* (1972), Table 66; *Census of Housing, 1970: General Housing Characteristics*, Final Report HC(1)-A1, *United States Summary* (1971), Table 17; *Census of Population, 1970: General Social and Economic Characteristics*, Final Report PC(1)-C (1972), Table 89 in relevant state reports.

a. County revenue data are distributed between central city and suburbs on the basis of population.
b. No populated areas were annexed during the period.
c. Less than 0.05 percent.

middle-income households joined high-income households in the suburbs, and low-income households steadily replaced middle- and high-income households in central cities.[15] As a result, demands for locally provided services grew rapidly while nonresidential and residential tax bases shrunk or failed to expand with these growing demands.

Central cities would have been bankrupt years ago if the institutional arrangements for financing local services had remained unchanged. Since the end of World II, central cities have never seemed to have enough resources to cope with their growing array of problems, and an atmosphere of crisis has accompanied each budget cycle. Even so, changes in fiscal structure have been continuous and remarkably similar among states and metropolitan areas. Federal and state governments have assumed responsibility for an increasing number of "city" functions—particularly welfare, health care, and other poverty-related services—and have provided numerous categorical grants-in-aid to assist municipalities with specific problems.

In general, the best approach to intrametropolitan imbalance would be to redistribute funds to communities with large low-income populations and to remove existing fiscal incentives for firms and households to locate in one community rather than another because of differences in tax rates.[16]

Business and the Urban Crisis

The preceding discussion should clarify the way in which racial discrimination, poverty, obsolete capital stocks, and outmoded fiscal mech-

15. One measure of these changes is the widening gap between median family income in the city and median family income in the total metropolitan area to which the city belongs, shown in Table 9-1.

16. Firms and households might continue to choose one community over another because of differences in the types of services provided, but these choices would have far different welfare implications than choices rooted in differences in tax prices or real tax rates.

Much of the resistance to metropolitan government arises from those who value the closeness and diversity of local government. If financing of poverty-related services were moved entirely to state and federal levels, some balkanization of central cities might be desirable to provide these real or imagined benefits. The "little city halls" and the community school districts in some large cities are efforts to accomplish some of these objectives. Released from the need to be concerned about redistribution, a larger number of communities would be able to provide a greater variety of public goods appealing to households of different incomes and tastes.

anisms distort metropolitan growth and combine to create the collection of interrelated problems popularly referred to as the urban crisis. It is now time to consider what business can and should do to help eliminate these factors or to ameliorate their adverse effects.

That business does have some of the necessary power and influence appears indisputable. Businesses are "prominent citizens" in many communities and exert considerable influence over the actions of local officials and governments. Firms often use their economic and political power to extract tax concessions and to obtain favored treatment from local officials. This influence, which may be greatest when firms are choosing a new location, can be exerted to discourage local governments and officials from policies that, though efficient as defined by the narrow self-interest of the individual community, are inefficient from the viewpoint of the metropolitan area and nation. Large firms similarly influence the actions of a great many smaller firms and individuals such as suppliers, real estate agents, and local retailers. They seldom hesitate to use this power to advance the firm's interest; they may wish to use it to pursue a broader interest.

Furthermore, business has a powerful voice in state capitals and in Washington. Political contributions, paid lobbyists, and trade associations ensure that both the executive and legislative branches of government know of, and are influenced by, business views on pending legislation. In many circumstances business support or opposition will make the difference between the acceptance or rejection of legislation that would contribute to the solution of urban problems. Many of the causes of the urban crisis do not lend themselves to direct action by business. In these situations business can obtain improvement only by supporting governmental action. Unfortunately, business has often opposed measures that would produce major improvements in the urban crisis.

Business and Racial Discrimination

Racial discrimination, the most important of the four basic causes of the urban crisis, is one problem business can do something about. Business is directly responsible for many of the past and current practices of employment discrimination. Business managers could take the lead in making changes by seeing to it that official equal opportunity policies are implemented by subordinates. Business should use its influence to foster equal employment policies by suppliers and unions.

Racial discrimination in urban housing markets places a particularly heavy burden on suburban businesses. Firms are choosing suburban locations in increasing numbers. A consequence of these private location decisions is that more and more workplaces are located at sites inconvenient or inaccessible to the ghetto. Distance and lack of information will keep minority workers from applying if suburban businesses merely follow passive equal employment opportunity policies.

At the height of business concern about the urban crisis, a number of firms sought to respond to this challenge by locating branch plants or suppliers in the ghetto.[17] The experience of these social activists, though not fully documented, has not caused a stampede of private firms to follow their lead. This reinforces the impression that there were valid reasons for the choice of suburban locations by private firms. These reasons appear to have been translated into higher costs, lower profits, or even losses for those firms that attempted to overcome the labor market effects of housing discrimination by moving jobs to the ghettos.

A policy of locating jobs in the ghetto, whether entirely private or motivated by public subsidy, is probably an inefficient means of attacking the separation of ghetto housing markets and suburban job markets.[18] There are less costly ways of dealing with the isolation of the ghetto from growing employment centers in the short run. *In the long run,* a satisfactory solution to the problem must take another form and one, moreover, that a successful program of locating jobs in the ghetto could hinder.

Rather than locating unprofitable branch plants in the ghetto, a policy that is in any case impractical for all but a few giant firms, suburban employers should make special efforts to recruit and hold minority workers. These efforts should include ambitious recruiting programs in the ghetto, training programs to give disadvantaged ghetto workers the skills needed to earn enough to justify the long trips between home and work, and transport subsidies and programs to assist minority job seekers and workers in obtaining and holding jobs. Transportation programs

17. See Jack Chernick and Georgina Smith, "Employing the Disadvantaged," and Edward C. Banfield, "An Act of Corporate Citizenship," both in Peter B. Doeringer (ed.), *Programs To Employ the Disadvantaged* (Prentice-Hall, 1969), pp. 14–23 and 26–57; Sar A. Levitan, Garth L. Mangum, and Robert Taggart III, *Economic Opportunity in the Ghetto: The Partnership of Government and Business* (Johns Hopkins Press, 1970), pp. 46–60; William K. Tabb, "Government Incentives to Private Industry To Locate in Urban Poverty Areas," *Land Economics,* Vol. 45 (November 1969), pp. 392–99.

18. See Kain and Persky, "Alternatives to the Gilded Ghetto."

may be particularly crucial during the job-hunting period and the first few days or weeks of employment. After a short period most minority workers, if they have good-paying jobs, are able to solve their own transportation problems by buying a car, by working out carpooling arrangements with fellow employees, or, less frequently, by moving to locations more convenient to their jobs. These arrangements require time, however, and firms wishing to provide equal employment opportunities to minorities may have to provide unusual transport services to these workers during the first few days or weeks of employment and during other periods when their private transport arrangements break down.

Above and beyond these short-range measures, a lasting solution to the ghetto problem will require that minority workers have the same opportunities as their white co-workers to live near suburban job locations. Private firms should take the lead in ensuring that current and potential minority employees are able to obtain housing near their jobs. The instruments available to them in accomplishing this object are numerous and well tested. First they should make perfectly clear to local officials their opposition to measures that would directly or indirectly make it more difficult for their employees, of all races, to find housing convenient to their businesses. If insufficient housing exists in nearby communities, they can take the leadership in developing housing through the provision of seed capital and organizational manpower. Suburban firms should similarly make it clear to real estate agents, mortgage lenders, and other agents in the housing market that they expect them to provide the same courteous, efficient, and enthusiastic assistance to all company employees as they provide to white executives. Suburban firms might add an individual or office to their personnel department to assist new and old minority employees in finding housing convenient to their jobs and to monitor the performance of the agents.

A recent book by James L. Hecht surveys the actions and inactions of suburban firms in combating discrimination in suburban housing markets and outlines a kind of how-to-do-it manual for firms willing to make efforts to overcome these barriers to equal employment opportunity.[19] As an example of effective employer action to combat housing discrimination, Hecht cites the experience of a black IBM employee in

19. Hecht, *Because It Is Right: Integration in Housing* (Little, Brown, 1970). Chapter 8 is called "The Employer."

Lexington, Kentucky. The employee searched fruitlessly for housing for two weeks. Then IBM's vice president for manufacturing wrote a letter to the president of the First Security National Bank and Trust Company of Lexington, informing him that "IBM's policy is to utilize only those Realtors who provide their services to prospective purchasers without discrimination . . . because of race."[20] Within two days the black IBM employee who had been making no progress received nine phone calls from brokers. IBM has a policy similar to that of many other large national firms of guaranteeing the sale of employees' homes when they are transferred. These sales were allocated to members of the Lexington Real Estate Board by IBM's agent, the First Security National Bank and Trust Company. In 1967, IBM by virtue of this personnel policy was responsible for the turnover of $4 million in real estate in the Lexington area.

Private firms have maximum leverage in these matters when they first move to a new community, but there is no doubt they have a great deal of influence at any time. An anonymous reader of an earlier draft of this chapter underlined the scope for business action of this kind. "I know of several corporations (ours included)," he wrote, "which, when signing a contract for a new building, insisted on a certain percent of building labor coming from minority groups. It is amazing how contractors can at one moment say they have no power over unions and, when a $30,000,000 job is involved, find that indeed they can meet your requirements." Finally business should support all reasonable measures to deploy the powers of federal, state, and local governments to ensure nondiscrimination in employment, housing, education, and other spheres of life.

Not all efforts by the private sector to aid in the urban crisis are to be commended, however. Well-intended efforts based on a faulty understanding of the causes of the urban crisis can do more harm than good. The ill-fated BBURG (Boston Banks Urban Renewal Groups) program in Boston is a clear example of misdirected private efforts. BBURG was a cooperative effort by several Boston banks to provide mortgage credit to high-risk minority borrowers. By itself this is clearly a laudable objective, for, as pointed out previously, difficulties in obtaining mortgage financing and the limited availability of suitable housing in the ghetto have kept homeownership among black Americans low, thereby increas-

20. Ibid., p. 192.

ing their housing costs and their opportunity to accumulate wealth. But eligibility for the BBURG programs was limited to properties within the ghetto and in a few boundary neighborhoods. The results were completely predictable. Channeling black demand for homeownership into these few neighborhoods simply contributed to the more rapid growth of the ghetto.

Business and Urban Poverty

In contrast to opportunities for combating racial discrimination, the scope for direct action by the private sector in eliminating poverty or reducing its geographic concentration is far more limited. Vigorous efforts by business to reduce employment discrimination, to increase black access to suburban jobs, and to reduce housing discrimination will, of course, have a significant impact on both the extent and the geographic concentration of urban poverty. Moreover, business can make important contributions to reducing the poverty of the working poor and of households headed by unemployed male heads by participating in programs to employ and train disadvantaged workers. Often a careful review of testing and hiring standards will reveal practices that exclude disadvantaged workers but cannot be justified in terms of higher worker productivity.

After the Detroit and Watts riots, business devoted considerable energy and resources to programs to train and employ disadvantaged workers and the hard-core unemployed both with and without subsidy.[21] Serious questions have been raised about the efficiency and effectiveness of these programs, and recently business interest in programs of this kind has all but disappeared. Many persons have concluded from this experience that the private sector cannot or will not employ the hard-core unemployed and have proposed a variety of public programs that would use government as the employer of last resort.

Another approach might well be preferable, however, and that would be to replace all or most public-private manpower training programs with a simple wage subsidy program for bringing the long-term unemployed into the work force. This program would be operated as part of a modernized U.S. employment service. Experience with manpower

21. Doeringer (ed.), *Programs To Employ the Disadvantaged;* Levitan, Mangum, and Taggart, *Economic Opportunity in the Ghetto.*

training programs indicates that the job training for specific jobs is most cost-effective and that costs are higher for persons with the least recent job experience.[22] This suggests the use of a variable wage subsidy to employers to defray the extra costs of training the long-term unemployed. Because these extra costs are presumably greatest for those who have been without a job longest, the subsidy might be made to increase in dollar amount as the number of weeks a person has been unemployed increases. The subsidy should be reduced as the formerly unemployed acquire more skills and presumably could be eliminated after a time.[23] It is possible, however, that some workers might require a perpetual subsidy to remain employed at legal or traditional minimum-wage levels. In recognition of both the greater difficulties faced by suburban employers in recruiting and holding minority workers and the social benefits of encouraging racial integration at suburban workplaces, such a program might provide larger payments per worker hired for suburban firms than for firms located near the ghetto.

A wage subsidy program of this kind, which could be administered as part of the unemployment insurance program, would be an effective complement to a negative income tax and would help minimize possible adverse employment incentive effects of such programs. It would, moreover, regularize the participation of private enterprise in training and employing disadvantaged workers. Employers best able to train and use disadvantaged workers would participate in the program, and economic efficiency would replace the complex set of criteria that have determined business participation in these programs in recent years. Business support of fiscal and monetary policies maintaining full employment would be a logical accompaniment to the program.

Unfortunately, a large fraction of the urban poor belong to households without a member in the labor force. Nearly 20 percent of the poor residents of metropolitan areas belong to households headed by a person over sixty-five years old, and 6 percent belong to households headed by a disabled male.[24] Another 28 percent belong to households headed by

22. Lester C. Thurow, "Raising Incomes through Manpower Training Programs," in Anthony H. Pascal (ed.), *Thinking about Cities* (Dickenson, 1970).

23. A program of this kind is outlined in John F. Kain, "Coping with Ghetto Unemployment," *Journal of the American Institute of Planners*, Vol. 35 (March 1969).

24. Anthony Downs, *Who Are the Urban Poor?* (New York: Committee for Economic Development, 1968), p. 24.

females, and child-care responsibilities of course severely limit the employability of a large fraction of the adult members of these households. Businessmen have no effective way of reaching households without a member in the labor force, but they can support fundamental and far-reaching measures to transfer income and resources to the poverty population.

To maintain work incentives and overcome equity problems, the President's Commission on Income Maintenance Programs and many private individuals have proposed some form of negative income tax. These proposals would provide a minimum cash income for all households and would allow all working households to keep some fraction of their earnings to provide an incentive to work.[25]

The Ninety-first Congress nearly enacted a negative income tax closely resembling the Family Assistance Plan (FAP) proposed by President Nixon.[26] The measure was approved by the House of Representatives by a two-to-one vote but was defeated in the Senate by a coalition of liberals and conservatives.[27] Business leaders and business organizations divided sharply on the merits of FAP. The Committee for Economic Development and the National Association of Manufacturers supported the measure. The Chamber of Commerce lobbied strongly against it.

Virtually all the controversy about FAP and other income maintenance proposals centers on the issue of whether replacement of existing

25. The commission estimated that a negative income tax that would provide all households with a minimum income equal to poverty levels then current would have cost $27.5 billion in 1971. Considering a program of this magnitude impractical in the light of budgetary realities, the commission proposed the immediate enactment of a more modest program which would guarantee for a family of four an income of $2,400 a year and recommended that the minimum guaranteed income be increased as rapidly as possible to the poverty level. This more modest proposal could have been substituted for then current welfare payments at an additional annual cost of $5.9 billion. President's Commission on Income Maintenance Programs, *Poverty amid Plenty: The American Paradox* (1969), pp. 57–61.

26. See *The President's Proposals for Welfare Reform and Social Security Amendments, 1969,* prepared for the House Committee on Ways and Means, 91 Cong. 1 sess. (1969).

27. Liberal opponents, though generally supportive of the concept of welfare reform and a negative income tax, were dissatisfied with the proposed benefit levels and certain work requirements included in the bill. Conservative opponents were, in contrast, opposed to the concept of a minimum income for those able to work. A detailed, if not completely objective, account of efforts to enact FAP is presented in Daniel P. Moynihan, *The Politics of a Guaranteed Income: The*

welfare programs with a generous negative income tax would increase or decrease labor force participation and employment.[28] No conclusive evidence exists, but studies by David H. Greenberg and Marvin Kosters and by Leonard Goodwin and findings from the New Jersey-Pennsylvania income maintenance experiment all suggest that the disincentive effects, if any, would probably be small.[29] Moreover, it is clear that the most vociferous opponents of such programs implicitly compare them with an imaginary and nonexistent situation in which anyone can easily find worthwhile work. The current patchwork of welfare and other forms of assistance to low-income persons and households, of course, is laced with employment disincentives. A negative income tax would eliminate many of them.

Whatever the merits of opposing views about income maintenance, it

---

Nixon Administration and the Family Assistance Plan (Random House, 1973). An excellent critique of Moynihan's interpretation of events is contained in a review of Moynihan's book by Abraham Ribicoff in the *New Republic,* Vol. 168 (February 17, 1973), pp. 22ff.

28. A careful and scholarly critique of efforts to reform the welfare system and an excellent discussion of the problems of replacing the existing system with a simple income maintenance program is contained in Henry J. Aaron, *Why Is Welfare So Hard to Reform?* (Brookings Institution, 1973).

29. David H. Greenberg and Marvin Kosters estimate from survey data that FAP would cause households headed by married males under sixty-two years of age to reduce their man-hours worked by about 1 percent and that the plan proposed by the President's Commission on Income Maintenance Programs would cause them to reduce their man-hours worked by 1.5 percent. Greenberg and Kosters, *Income Guarantees and the Working Poor: The Effect of Income Maintenance Programs on the Hours of Work of Male Family Heads* (RAND Corporation, 1970), pp. viii, 60.

Leonard Goodwin concluded as follows from a careful social-psychological study of the work orientations of more than 4,000 persons: "Excessive concern that a relatively low level of guaranteed income—around the poverty level—would cause people to drop out of the work force reflects a misunderstanding of the life and work orientations of the poor. They are no more likely to settle for this meager income and cease working than are middle-class people." Goodwin, *Do the Poor Want to Work?* (Brookings Institution, 1972), p. 117.

Analyses of the Graduated Work Incentive Experiment in New Jersey and Pennsylvania, initiated by the Office of Economic Opportunity in 1968, have been summarized as follows: "[The results] clearly indicate that a negative tax type plan with a basic benefit as high as the official poverty line will not trigger large-scale reductions in work effort among male heads of families. Indeed, there is no evidence here that even a small proportion of male heads would drop out of the labor force completely." William A. Morrill, "Introduction" (to a symposium on the Graduated Work Incentive Experiment), *Journal of Human Resources,* Vol. 9 (Spring 1974), p. 157.

is apparent that a large fraction of urban problems are directly traceable to the concentration of low-income populations in central cities. A national program of income maintenance would provide for low-income households and the communities in which they reside the resources needed to break out of the poverty cycle. By removing the financial and organizational burdens of many existing welfare and poverty programs, a negative income tax would allow city governments to breathe again.

Metropolitan Fiscal Reform

A negative income tax would have a major impact on the existing causes of fiscal imbalance in metropolitan areas. Central cities would be released immediately from some of their expenses. In the long run, increased expenditures for housing by central city residents (better provided for than formerly) would improve the city's residential property base and reduce the gap between suburban and city tax bases. Lower expenditures for poverty-related services and the greater taxpaying ability of the city population would ease the pressure on the nonresidential tax rates.[30]

Because the effects of discrimination and poverty would take time to remove, however, there remains a strong rationale for a sharply progressive grant-in-aid program for low-income communities. This concept should not be confused with President Nixon's revenue sharing plan, which transfers revenues to states and cities but does almost nothing to reduce the current fiscal imbalances between low-income and high-income communities.

As long as the current fiscal structures remain, businesses will continue to be confronted with a number of difficult decisions. Should they ignore the differences in property taxes among communities in choosing where to locate new facilities? Or to pose an even more radical question, should they swim against the tide and purposely locate their facilities in

30. For example, the House version of the Family Assistance Plan proposed in 1969 would have increased the income of Atlanta residents by an estimated $27.5 million and the income of Detroit residents in the same year by $58.1 million. A negative income tax with an income guarantee set at the poverty level would have increased the income of Atlanta residents by $102.2 million and the income of Detroit residents by an estimated $230.9 million in 1969. See John F. Kain and Robert Schafer, "Effects of Income Maintenance on Urban Fiscal Problems," Harvard University Program on Regional and Urban Economics, Discussion Paper 83 (Harvard University, 1974; processed), pp. 24, 28.

high-tax, low-income communities? Few businesses are likely to follow the latter course, and even the former may depart too far from the search for profits. It is perhaps not unreasonable, however, to ask that business show restraint in seeking special treatment from communities with inadequate tax bases. In addition, business may be able to use its influence with local officials to curb some of the excesses fostered by existing institutional arrangements.

To eliminate the unwise arrangements themselves, business should support radical changes in the methods of financing local government. In addition to a generous negative income tax and a sharply progressive program of grants-in-aid to low-income communities, business would be well advised to use its influence in Washington and in the fifty state capitals to remove any residual variations in tax rates among metropolitan communities that are attributable to difference in tax bases.[31] A scheme recently enacted in Minnesota, which involves the redistribution of taxes from all new nonresidential properties, is an example of a practical technique that, over time, would eliminate the present incentives for communities to pursue beggar-thy-neighbor policies injurious to the well-being of the metropolitan population as a whole.

Policies for Old Cities

To create the right climate specifically inside the older central cities, business should press for an additional and distinct set of policies. In particular, old cities must achieve substantial changes in their physical and economic structures to make them more consistent with new technological and economic circumstances. It is unlikely that old cities will be able to reverse the relative national decline in goods producing and handling employment. This suggests they should accept a future made up of fewer jobs and fewer residents and develop policies to make the necessary adjustments less painful and more orderly. An improved fiscal base would enable mayors to take a more dispassionate look at the benefits and costs of extensive development and perhaps enable them to consider policies that would imply lower employment levels, greater specialization in service industries, and smaller but wealthier resident populations.

31. Tax rates might still vary somewhat among communities because some communities are more efficient than others or because some communities decide to provide more or better services than others.

Until some form of income maintenance becomes law, and even perhaps afterwards, there may be pressures for specific housing programs. There is a growing agreement among housing analysts that in old cities, at least, low-income housing programs should be reoriented from their current emphasis on production subsidies and should instead concentrate on conserving the stock of structurally sound residential units.[32] Some form of housing allowance or a program involving the leasing of existing units may be the best way of accomplishing these objectives. Such programs would provide sufficient income to property owners to allow them to maintain the city housing stock in good condition.

It is crucial that leased housing or housing allowance programs of the kind referred to above be accompanied by vigorous enforcement of open occupancy laws and programs of counseling and education for both the minority and majority populations. Some individuals have opposed housing allowances and similar proposals because they fear the supply of good housing available to minorities will not increase. This argument deserves to be taken seriously, but a housing allowance program with adequate counseling and strict enforcement of open occupancy laws offers the greatest hope for improving housing conditions for minorities and increasing their access to the suburbs.

Redevelopment of blighted residential areas, however, may require public subsidy or participation. Individual structures in good neighborhoods can be improved by the actions of individual property owners. But where the units are structurally unsound, where the entire neighborhood is blighted, or where the density or physical arrangement of the neighborhood is unsuitable, it may be necessary to redevelop large tracts.

These considerations were used to justify the controversial urban renewal programs of the 1950s and 1960s. Without attempting a post mortem of these programs, it may be that conditions in the next few decades will be more favorable to urban renewal programs. Urban renewal failed largely because the demand for city properties, fed by the growth of the ghetto and the increased space demands of firms already located in central cities, was too great. Widespread concern recently with the abandonment of "sound" properties in many cities, rising vacancy

---

32. Arthur P. Solomon, "Housing and Public Policy Analysis," *Public Policy,* Vol. 20 (Summer 1972), pp. 443–71; Ira S. Lowry, "Housing Assistance for Low-Income Urban Families: A Fresh Approach," paper prepared for the Subcommittee on Housing of the House Committee on Banking and Currency, 92 Cong. 2 sess. (1971; processed).

rates, and other fragments of evidence suggest that the forces of demand and supply for central properties and the prices of central real estate may be shifting in a way that makes large-scale renewal efforts more feasible in many cities.

It is in the interest of business to perceive that new urban renewal programs will succeed only if suburban housing is opened to racial minorities, if urban poverty is eliminated or dispersed, if obsolete capital stock is improved or replaced, and if more suitable metropolitan fiscal mechanisms are developed. The adverse effects of each of the four basic causes of the urban crisis reinforce one another in today's urban environment. Similarly, improvement in any one area would tend to produce improvement in the others. For example, reductions in housing discrimination would reduce the extreme segregation by income characteristic of today's metropolitan areas. Elimination of urban poverty would at once reduce the need to make extreme changes in fiscal structures. Physical changes in the urban environment would change the view of investors and house buyers about the city and modify their expectations about its future. Business would discover emerging opportunities near central workplaces.

There may be some scope for a nonresidential renewal program to help current and future city businesses to assemble land needed for expansion and to install their plant and equipment. The potential for abuse in such a program is considerable, but modest public subsidies to old cities for these purposes probably are justified, particularly in the short run when the legacy of past structural deficiencies remains strong.

Accessibility is another consideration in the revival of the city, and frequently a program of capital grants for transit is suggested as the answer. Such a program is conceived of by many of its advocates solely as a tool to enable central cities to extend existing rail transit or to build entirely new rail rapid transit systems. This preconception about how to improve transit service in U.S. cities is most unfortunate, since it virtually ensures that billions of dollars will be wasted without greatly improving the accessibility of central cities. John Meyer, Martin Wohl, and the present author demonstrated several years ago that the market for conventional rail rapid transit is exceedingly limited in U.S. cities and that a better and far cheaper approach to improving transit service to the older central business districts would be to exploit the potential of existing and proposed urban expressways.[33]

33. Meyer, Kain, and Wohl, *The Urban Transportation Problem.*

If congestion on urban expressways were eliminated, an objective that could be achieved cheaply and quickly, and if transit vehicles were allowed priority access to these uncongested facilities, an extensive system of rapid transit could be provided in nearly all U.S. metropolitan areas within a few months.[34] The performance of these rapid transit systems could be improved further through the application of road pricing principles to the entire surface system. Appropriate tools include the development of efficient parking policies and the use of tolls, special licenses, and traffic engineering principles that favor public transit vehicles. Retail merchants and owners of downtown property have generally resisted suggestions of this kind, because they incorrectly perceive such policies as not being in their self-interest. Central-area property owners generally have supported the construction of radial expressways, radial rail rapid transit links, and subsidized parking facilities. These expenditures to increase transport capacity serving central areas have no doubt benefited some central property owners and users in the short run. But as an overall urban transportation policy such measures must be considered costly failures. The competitive advantage of central locations depends on their aggregate accessibility: the appropriately weighted time and money costs of moving people and goods during various parts of the day by private and public transport. Accessibility will be maximized only when the high cost of adding vehicular capacity to central areas is recognized and policies implemented to ensure that this limited capacity is allocated to those users for whom it provides greatest benefits.

Conclusions

In this chapter four factors have been named as major contributors to the seemingly endless list of problems popularly referred to as the urban crisis. These four factors were identified as racial discrimination; poverty (particularly its unequal distribution among local political jurisdictions); archaic institutional arrangements for providing and financing public services in metropolitan areas; and, in old cities, obsolete stocks of private and public capital. If those factors could be eliminated or significantly ameliorated, mayors and other officials would still face real difficulties, but the seemingly intractable web of interrelated problems that they confront today would assume manageable proportions.

34. See John F. Kain, "How To Improve Urban Transportation at Practically No Cost," *Public Policy*, Vol. 20 (Summer 1972), pp. 335–58.

The prescriptions for business offered here follow directly from the analysis of the nature of the urban crisis. In addition, the assumption is made that business will not willingly undertake actions that are not in the interest of its owners, managers, or workers. There is plenty of room for debate about what individual businesses seek to maximize, but there is abundant evidence that business leaders are exceedingly reluctant to engage in ventures that are clearly unprofitable or that are likely to fail. In response to public opinion and governmental pressure, individual businesses have engaged in both under the banner of social responsibility. Still, it is doubtful, to say the least, whether business will or should be expected to engage in such actions on a sustained basis. Therefore the only rational course is to identify those areas where constructive action is not costly or, better yet, where it is in the interest of individual firms or the business community as a whole.

The private and social consequences of business decisions diverge because of market imperfections or because the distribution of opportunity and income provided by our mixed economy is offensive to many people. It is in the interest both of individual businesses and of the business community as a whole to use their prestige, political power, and influence to bring about fundamental changes in the nonmarket institutions that produce these outcomes. Fortunately, numerous opportunities exist to change these institutional arrangements in ways that would ensure that private and public interests become more consistent. Until these structural improvements are accomplished, however, private firms will often find that actions which would be in their interest conflict with the public interest. Prudent businessmen would be well advised to avoid the most blatant conflicts of this kind and to be sensitive to opportunities to help resolve the urban crisis in the normal exercise of their prerogatives.

Individual businesses by themselves can do very little to correct the deficiencies of current fiscal and governmental arrangements. But individual businessmen, individual businesses, and the business community as a whole can make major contributions to resolving the urban crisis by placing their prestige and political power behind the development of more suitable fiscal and governmental arrangements for metropolitan areas. These reform efforts should focus on the development of fiscal mechanisms that would provide a more equal distribution of the burden of servicing low-income households. If central cities and other low-income communities did not have to carry such an unequal portion of the burden, a major source of economic inefficiency would be eliminated, and business would less often be asked to weigh nonmarket considerations in making location and investment decisions.

Individual businesses can make a more direct contribution to the elimination of urban poverty through private programs to train and employ disadvantaged workers and through participation in joint government-industry subsidy programs to increase the skills and earnings of these individuals. Indeed, business has made important contributions of this kind in the past. But, even in this area, business would make a larger contribution if it persuaded Congress and the Executive to maintain full employment and to enact national wage subsidies and income maintenance. As noted, manpower and income maintenance programs are not urban programs in the usual sense, but it is hard to imagine any measures that would relieve the urban crisis to the extent these would.

A well-articulated wage subsidy program for low-skilled workers and a minimum income for all as part of a negative income tax plan would appear to provide the best compromise between the often conflicting objectives of equity and efficiency. With programs of this kind in existence, business would less often be asked to compromise private interests in the name of social responsibility and, when asked, could with greater justification decline. If businesses and businessmen are unwilling to support collective measures of this kind, they will be in a weak position to avoid demands that they accept individual responsibility.

Vigorous efforts to combat racial discrimination in all aspects of life provide the best opportunity for business to make a large contribution to resolving the urban crisis. One reason is that equal opportunity is so difficult to ensure by governmental or legislative means. Individual businesses and individual businessmen, as important community leaders, possess great influence and political power. If they are willing to use these levers to combat racial prejudice and discrimination, there is reason to believe they can be more effective than any other institution or collection of individuals, including government.

CHAPTER TEN

Regional Development

BENJAMIN CHINITZ

PLANT LOCATION may affect profits as much or more than most business decisions. The choice of location may also entail important social consequences through the effect on income and employment in local areas. Nevertheless, for most of America's history, the calculations underlying plant location decisions have not encompassed social costs or social benefits. Only recently have various units of government begun to try to influence such calculations via taxes and subsidies.

The authors of this volume have wrestled individually and collectively with the meaning of social responsibility in an effort to put it on a firm conceptual foundation. Since no easy consensus has emerged, I should like to explain what I mean by social responsibility for purposes of this chapter. I mean calculating how income and employment in the relevant communities and regions would be affected by a given choice of plant location. Furthermore, I mean asking how, when, and where modifications of the private pursuit of profit should be encouraged (on either a voluntary or an involuntary basis) as a result of what the calculations indicate.

For example, in the United Kingdom, there is a law which prohibits the location of certain kinds of facilities in the Greater London area, and substantial subsidies are available to companies which locate in or move their operations to such places as Scotland, where the demand for labor is sluggish. The rationale for this policy, to put it briefly, runs in terms of the social costs of further growth in the London area and the social benefits of "fuller" employment in Scotland. Some firms which want to locate in London must, by virtue of the law, take these social effects into account. Other firms have the option of behaving in accordance with the spirit of the law even if their specific circumstances leave them outside the letter of the law.

This is not a chapter about Britain. It is about the exercise of corporate social responsibility in the United States. But the example of Greater London raises the kinds of questions we need to address. What is the nature and extent of local and/or regional economic distress in the United States? How do plant location decisions affect local economic conditions? What kinds of laws and incentives do we have in the United States for broadening the plant location calculation to include social costs and benefits? What is the rationale for such public policy, and is it sound? Is there any evidence of the voluntary exercise of social responsibility in regard to plant location? Should it be encouraged?

Local and Regional Economic Indicators

The 1970 census reported that the population of the United States had increased 13.3 percent over the decade between 1960 and 1970, that the median income for American families was $9,590 in 1969, and that 4.4 percent of the labor force was unemployed in 1970. But different parts of the nation differed radically in the figures they contributed to these national measures of economic performance.

Even if we divide the country into just four broad regions (Northeast, North Central, South, and West), we observe great disparities on all counts. For example, the western population increased 24 percent while the population of both northern regions increased by only 10 percent. Unemployment was significantly higher in the North Central region at 7.6 percent. Median income was significantly lower in the South at $8,079.

The perception of local economic distress usually centers on unsatisfactory values of one or more of these three national indexes: growth, per capita income, and rate of unemployment. The welfare implications of these indicators depend very much on one's place in the social scale. Low per capita income reflects the hardship of the poor, for their meager incomes account for the low per capita figure in the community. The very rich may actually be better off with a low average per capita income if this means low wages for local labor. On the other hand, the local merchant may wish that more of his customers had greater purchasing power.

Similarly, a high unemployment rate means suffering and deprivation for the unemployed. Employers may prefer a soft labor market. Merchants wish that more of their customers could afford to buy more of their products. The employed may or may not feel threatened by the potential competition of the unemployed.

Slow growth may be seen as a virtue by those who worry about crowding and the deterioration of the environment. Others may want to accept those costs in exchange for the benefits of a vibrant local economy which continually expands their range of opportunities for both work and leisure. Those who have committed their capital to the local area in land, buildings, or enterprises catering to the local market have an obvious stake in growth.

When and where slow-growing or declining areas register satisfactory values for income and unemployment, the "problem," if it is perceived as such, is best left to the local Chamber of Commerce, which typically represents the interests of those who have committed their capital to the local area. One can hardly make a case in such circumstances for intervention either by government or by the exercise of corporate social responsibility to accelerate growth.

One should acknowledge, however, that in recent years the fate of lagging areas has become part of a larger set of issues relating to population distribution trends and the pattern of settlement, which includes the shift from rural to urban, from small towns to big cities to big metropolitan areas, and from cities to suburbs within these metropolitan areas. The question has been raised whether the benefits in economic progress associated with these shifts exceed the costs of decline at one end and the costs of growth at the other. Could the country not achieve a geographic pattern of population which would yield a better ratio of benefits to costs, perhaps a smaller gross national product as conventionally measured but a lot less pain in terms of unemployment, poverty, pollution, congestion, crime? Through such a pattern, could the costs for public services be lowered?

In this context, programs to accelerate growth in lagging areas are part of an overall strategy to influence the geographic distribution of population. Before, more jobs and higher incomes in distressed areas were the ends of policy; now, they are the means to serve the end of a more desirable pattern of population distribution.

But the country has by no means achieved a consensus on this issue. Many social scientists believe that "distribution" is a smoke screen, an escape from having to face up to the nation's domestic ills wherever they occur. They see little reason to expect substantial relief from a redrawing of the map. Economists in particular tend to be very skeptical and emphasize the losses in efficiency which might result from a serious diversion of market forces. Others are skeptical about the ability of any public body to identify concrete alternatives and to formulate policies which can be implemented to achieve any desired distribution of population.

Much of the dialogue boils down to a plea for greater consistency in public policy. Awareness is the key word—be aware of the geographic implications of existing policies and take steps to avoid conflicting results.

Given the unresolved state of thinking on this larger issue, it would be premature to explore notions of social responsibility of business enterprise in this context. No clear and widely agreed-upon vision exists as to where the balance lies between local interests and overall social interest. Agreement is much more pronounced with reference to equal opportunity and the reduction of poverty, for example. If most people who studied the matter were certain that the further growth of, say, the New York metropolitan region was socially undesirable, we could at least raise the question whether a business enterprise should, as a matter of social responsibility, avoid locating or expanding in that region. Clearly the majority of commentators are not ready to make statements of that kind.

On the other hand, regional and local poverty and unemployment, whether or not they are accompanied or caused by slow growth or decline, should be and have been on the agenda of public policy. By the formal criteria of the federal legislation addressed to these problems since 1960, the number of counties in which poverty conditions prevail has varied from one-third to one-half of all U.S. counties, embracing more than 25 percent of total U.S. population.

I have elsewhere attempted a topology of disadvantaged areas by suggesting seven prototypes.[1] They may be described as follows:

Model I: The "Rich" and Rapidly Growing Distressed Area. Nothing illustrates more dramatically the tremendous range of "distress" embraced by U.S. legislation than the inclusion of areas in California where per capita income is very high, growth very rapid, but the rate of unemployment is also high, thus providing a basis for eligibility.

Model II: The Well-to-Do Mature Distressed Area. Localities conforming to this model are what Senator Douglas had in mind when he first designed "relief" legislation in the mid-1950s. Such places combine average or slightly above average per capita income with very slow

1. Benjamin Chinitz, "The Regional Problem in the U.S.A.," in E. A. G. Robinson (ed.), *Backward Areas in Advanced Countries* (St. Martin's Press, 1969).

growth or absolute decline, generally in a highly urban setting. A classic example is Pittsburgh. The downward trend is intensified and leads to serious unemployment during national slumps. The basic cause is one of secular decline in the area's historically important industries, with only moderate compensation in other sectors of the economy.

Model III and Model III(A): The Not-So-Poor Depressed Rural Area. Here I have in mind the upper reaches of the Great Lakes region, the Pacific Northwest, and northern New England. Unemployment is high, income is moderately below national averages, and the setting is basically rural, although there are small towns dispersed throughout these regions. The difficulty is caused by a decline in employment opportunities in extractive industries: agriculture, mining, fishing, timber. In the Model III areas proper, population is declining, with heavy migration from rural to urban areas. However, in the Model III(A) areas the large natural increase in population is not offset by a net migration loss.

Model IV: The Poor Depressed Rural Area. Model IV takes in the type of low-income area which meets the very rigorous standard of a median level of family income less than 50 percent of the national average. This model is confined to the southern sections of the United States where the classic characteristics of underdevelopment still prevail.

Model V: Appalachia (The Special Case of Model IV). Model IV areas generally do not suffer from high unemployment as it is normally defined. (Underemployment is a different story.) And they generally have large Negro populations. The core of the Appalachian region— eastern Kentucky and neighboring areas in Virginia, West Virginia, North Carolina, and Tennessee—contains a large proportion of poor and unemployed whites. Here the liabilities of Model II and Model IV areas are compounded. The earlier exploitation of the region's mineral resources has left a heritage of liabilities and no assets. The land is ravaged, the waters are being poisoned by acid mine drainage, the miners are unemployed and unsuited for alternative occupations, there is no indigenous entrepreneurship, and public capital is almost totally lacking. I do not know of any other episode in American history which offers a better example of exploitation in its most derogatory sense.

Model VI: The Big-City "Ghetto"; and Model VII: The "Indian Reservation." John Kain, in Chapter 9 of this volume, considers the role of business regarding urban areas formed by racial discrimination and poverty, and I will omit them, along with rural counterparts, from the present discussion. In Models I through V, the actual and potential impact of business location decisions on the problem and/or the solution is fairly obvious. The decision to abandon a plant altogether or to cut back operations substantially is at the heart of the problem of the Model I and Model II areas. The absence of industrial development, on the other hand, or the failure to favor such areas with new or expanded capacity, is at the heart of the problem of Model III, IV, and V areas. In all areas, a more vigorous demand for labor on the part of business enterprise would obviously reduce unemployment and/or raise wages and incomes.

National Policy for Depressed Areas

Except for TVA in the 1930s, which had a regional focus with multiple objectives, it is only since the 1960s that the United States has had specific legislation to assist lagging areas. In May 1961, President Kennedy signed the Area Redevelopment Act, which created the Area Redevelopment Administration (ARA).

The Area Redevelopment Act authorized four kinds of expenditures by the federal government in distressed areas. Long-term, low-interest loans to industrial and commercial enterprises locating in eligible areas were the core of the program. Such loans could be made only to firms which were planning to establish new plants or expand existing plants in these areas. In further support of such activities, funds were made available to communities to assist in the financing of a public facility, such as an access road or a sewer system, which would help to attract new plants or ease the expansion of existing ones. Grants for public facilities were to be made only if a substantial benefit could reasonably be expected. To round out the package of subsidies, the Area Redevelopment Act also authorized the expenditure of funds for the training of workers in new skills required by local industry and for technical assistance to help alleviate or prevent unemployment.

It soon became apparent that the ARA approach to area distress was not producing tangible results. The cards were stacked against success both because the national economy was in recession and by the terms of the legislation (which called for the attraction of industry or the expansion of industry within the eligible area and primarily through the subsidization of capital costs). At a time when industry in general was operating substantially below capacity and the rate of new plant construction was low, there were few takers for the capital subsidy under the terms of the act.

Impatience with the slow progress of ARA gave impetus to two major pieces of legislation which differed strategically from ARA and from each other. The 1962 Public Works Acceleration Act (APW) provided large sums of money to build public projects in depressed areas as a way of putting more people to work quickly. Success was to be measured by the number of jobs created in the process of construction, although it was also hoped that the resulting infrastructure would facilitate further industrial development later on.

In the meantime the governors of Kentucky, West Virginia, Virginia, Tennessee, and other states which had large Model V pockets of poverty and unemployment had organized themselves into an effective lobby for a federally financed program to develop Appalachia. They argued that ARA had provided too few dollars and the wrong strategy to cope with the vast needs of their region, and they struck a responsive chord in a President who had scored a critical political victory in their region during the 1960 primary campaign. (John Kennedy defeated Hubert Humphrey in West Virginia.) Kennedy appointed a committee in 1963 to recommend a program, and the requisite legislation was ultimately enacted under Johnson in 1965.

The Appalachian Regional Development Act (ARDA) called for the creation of a new institution, a federal-state regional planning commission, which would develop and review plans designed to upgrade the physical, social, and human capital of the region. There was to be no explicit subsidization of industry. Human needs were to be attended to wherever they occurred, but infrastructure projects were to be concentrated at places which had the best potential for development (so-called growth centers).

But the time had now arrived to formulate new legislation for the national area development program. ARA was due to expire in June of 1965. In the meantime, the national economy had long since turned the corner and was continuing to expand at a very rapid rate. Unemployment had dipped below the 5 percent level and was still heading downward. The new thinking and the new conditions were reflected in the new legislation which was signed into law by President Johnson on August 26, 1965.

In the Public Works and Economic Development Act of 1965 (PWED), the county-by-county approach of ARA was retained, as well as the direct subsidization of industry through long-term low-interest loans. But new features were added, reflecting the influence of APW and ARDA.

Grants were made available to cover up to 75 percent of the cost of organizing and staffing an Economic Development District planning unit. A district would normally consist of at least two redevelopment counties or communities and embrace contiguous areas that had strong economic ties with the redevelopment areas. The district would also include an economic development center. This would be an area of considerable growth potential that could serve as a focus for development efforts in the district.

The programs were to be administered by one new agency, the Economic Development Administration (EDA), replacing ARA. EDA was also authorized to create in other lagging parts of the country regional planning bodies modeled on the Appalachian Commission. Since then, commissions have been created in seven regions: New England, the Ozarks, Upper Great Lakes, Coastal Plains, Four Corners, Old West, and Pacific Northwest. None has yet achieved the financial or legislative status of the Appalachian Commission, although their ties with their creator—the Economic Development Administration—have been loosened.

The sums available for business loans from EDA were held close to their former levels under ARA; the amount authorized for infrastructure investment was substantially increased as compared to ARA but substantially reduced as compared to APW. Now public works projects were to be evaluated not in terms of the jobs created directly by the construction process but rather as a prerequisite for industrial development in the spirit of the Appalachian legislation.

None of the acts—ARA, APW, ARDA, PWED—made an issue of corporate social responsibility. Nothing suggested that business was ethically obliged to favor depressed areas by locating there or that location decisions ought to be regulated to further social objectives. On the contrary, it was assumed that choice of location could be tilted in favor of depressed areas only through subsidies which would lower capital and/ or operating costs. And in order to assure a majority vote for these modest subsidies it was necessary to include provisions specifically forbidding the relocation of existing plants and the construction of new plants in industries with excess capacity.

There is only one possible interpretation of the implicit rationale of federal policy toward depressed areas and regions during the thirteen years between 1961 and 1974. County, district, and regional programs were aimed at the reduction of unemployment and the raising of incomes in distressed areas and regions. They were not conceived of as parts of an overall strategy to bring about a preferred geographic pattern of population growth. Success was not to be measured in terms of a reversal of migration trends. But why economic development and not outright relief? And can economic development in particular areas be achieved without serious costs in terms of economic efficiency?

Economists differ among themselves as to the dynamics of regional economic growth. The "majority" view is that the momentum of national growth is independent of its regional distribution, that regions participate more or less in this growth in proportion as they attain a cost advantage in the provision of certain goods and services demanded by the nation's consumers, producers, and government organizations. The market is said to guarantee that employers will seek out locations which generate the highest profits. Thus a region's destiny is ultimately determined by the free play of market forces. A rich and growing region is one which is preferred by rich and growing enterprises. A poor and declining region is one which is less attractive in these terms.

An alternative view of the process of regional development places considerably more emphasis on internal influences. This view looks inward to the sources of growth as they are manifested in a particular region. It assumes that regions contribute unevenly to the pool of ingredients which make for economic progress in the nation as a whole. A region fails to develop in part because it cannot seize upon opportunities in the national economy, but it also fails to develop in part because it contributes less to the flow of opportunities in the national economy. A nation is as much the sum of its regions as a region is a part of a nation.

This view at least offers the possibility that efforts to develop particular areas can be consistent with efficiency criteria. But it is also possible to defend economic development efforts on equity grounds. This is how I put the case elsewhere:

The unique aspect of an economic development program is the encouragement of private enterprise in the community. One should not have to argue too hard that the presence of a vigorous private sector is valuable, even if the vigor can only be generated through subsidy. All the beneficiaries—the local government which collects property taxes, the local industries which supply the new firm, the workers who are employed there—can legitimately have the normal feeling of economic achievement which would prevail in the absence of the subsidy, and this carries with it a greater assurance that the forward momentum will be sustained. To put it somewhat cynically, a "derived" subsidy is not as bad for morale as a "direct" subsidy. The normal processes of growth can be stimulated better by the stimulation of private enterprise than by direct transfers either to people or to local governments.[2]

If a national policy to stimulate economic development in depressed areas makes sense, then it also makes sense to ask whether business corporations can assist in the implementation of that policy. We can ask whether there are opportunities for business enterprises to decide upon location in a way that is both socially beneficial and consistent with their viability as profit-making producers.

Plant Abandonment

One crucial decision a firm could take to assist a depressed area is a negative one: not to close down a plant. Plant closings are not always unwelcome. If the plant generates a lot of dirt and smoke, employs few people or pays low wages, is seasonally or cyclically unstable, and the area is otherwise thriving, then the announcement of a plant closing might actually be greeted with a celebration. Normally, however, a plant closing, especially in a small community, hits like a natural disaster. Workers lose their jobs, sales drop off in local shops, municipal revenues decline, and there is a general atmosphere of gloom. In many areas, it is precisely the repeated closings of plants, or what we might call the process of abandonment, which creates the condition of distress.

The firm making the abandonment decision, unless it is very small, is aware of the impact of its decision on the community. Management may be more or less sensitive to the hardship caused by such an action, but rarely is the decision motivated by the desire to strike back at an unfriendly community. Typically, the decision reflects the workings of the profit motive. The plant is operating at a loss or at a rate of profit substantially below its rivals or other plants of the same firm at other locations. Survival or maximum profit dictates the abandonment decision.

Is there any scope for the exercise of social responsibility in such circumstances? Later, we shall consider what the firm might do in the

2. Benjamin Chinitz, "National Policy for Regional Development," in John F. Kain and John R. Meyer (eds.), *Essays in Regional Economics* (Harvard University Press, 1971), p. 26.

way of compensation, having made an irrevocable decision to abandon. For the moment, we want to look at the decision itself. Can we reach for a definition of social responsibility which would bring the decision itself into question? Clearly, a lot depends on the underlying situation.

When the sales of a plant decline because of changes in consumption and production patterns in the national economy, the only way to keep the plant alive is to create an artificial market for the product. Such policies are hard to justify against the alternative of simple transfer payments and inducements to out-migration. However we judge the merits of these alternatives, there seems to be no foundation for raising issues of social responsibility. How can a firm stay in business if there is no market for its product?

Where abandonment reflects pursuit of maximum advantage through a change of location, rather than the decline of the industry, the diagnosis is likely to be much more complex, and the door is opened wider to questions of social responsibility. Here, withdrawal implies a search for higher revenues or lower costs or some combination leading to higher profits. What has happened to alter the relative profitability of different locations?

A pervasive shift in the relative attractiveness of various locales results from factors operating on the industry rather than on areas. That any particular area suffers economic distress is incidental to the process. When technical change confers further savings on volume production, there will be a tendency to reduce the number of plants, and some locations must lose out in the process. In the nineteenth century, both production technology and transport technology operated to create vast concentrations of industry on an interregional basis. In the twentieth century, the truck and the auto, along with further developments in production technology, operated mainly to create patterns of concentration on an intraregional basis. The nineteenth-century developments were more relevant to heavy industry (e.g., steel and machinery), whereas the twentieth-century developments were more relevant to light industry and distribution (e.g., bread and warehousing). The nineteenth-century developments changed the map in broad geographic terms, shifting the locus of growth away from the East Coast to the middle of the country. The twentieth-century developments operated on a microscale to alter the spatial distribution of economic activity within broad regions, generally in favor of the big metropolitan areas and against small towns and rural areas.

I do not see a viable role for either public policy or social responsibility in blunting this kind of locational change in the private sector. Ironically, on their own behalf and strictly within the political domain, local governments have been very successful in withstanding the pressures of centralization and consolidation that undermined locally controlled business. Here and there they have surrendered functions to larger units—the state, a special authority, a regional school district—in response to the twin forces of scale and improved mobility, but they have, on the whole, managed to preserve the jurisdictional structure in the face of these powerful forces. In the private sector, by contrast, the quest for lower costs and higher profits prevails. We love the corner grocer, but in the end he goes. If it were a question of where to locate the corner grocery, he might have a chance. But when it is the corner grocer's stock and prices and general backing versus the supermarket, he generally loses out.

Another kind of locational shift which is broad-based but of a different character is that which leads to the decline of one pattern of concentration and the emergence of another. The classic example is textiles moving from New England to the South, presumably in search of lower labor costs. Many communities in New England depended heavily on textile employment and experienced decline along with high unemployment rates as a consequence. The wage differential was of long standing, and so it does not provide a sufficient explanation for the timing of the migration. Other things happened to make the wage differential operative as a locational force. Nevertheless, the wage differential is still viewed as the prime cause.

Between 1950 and 1960, textile employment fell sharply in such places as Providence, Lawrence, Lowell, and Fall River, declining by two-thirds or more in the first three cities. The resulting drop in total employment was substantial, for textiles had provided from 8 to 40 percent of total employment in 1950.

Once again, we find it difficult to conceive of policies, public or private, which could have prevented such declines or mitigated their severity. Furthermore, it is not at all obvious that policies to prevent these shifts would be in the national interest. There can be cases of robbing Peter to pay Paul when *both* Peter and Paul are in need. The area to which the industry migrated needed the additional jobs as a stimulus to its development. Textile wages may have been lower in the South than in New England, but, for the South, they represented progress in raising incomes.

I have thus far cited three broad reasons for abandonment: decline of an industry, decline in the number of locations, and a shift in the locus of concentration. These causes of abandonment do not seem to be amenable to treatment by public policy or by private action motivated by social responsibility. But it would be a mistake to assume that all cases of abandonment can be traced to one of these three causes. Often, the pressures which motivate abandonment in a particular situation are not mere reflections of pervasive national trends but are rather specific to that situation. A conscientious effort to resolve the difficulties may alter the circumstances which underlie the abandonment decision and avoid the dislocations caused by the closing, to both the firm and the community. It is tempting to assume that rational management, even leaving social responsibility aside, would always make that effort in the interests of the firm. Reason suggests, however, that the effort is more likely to be made if there is a keen sense of social responsibility within the firm. This is particularly likely to be the case if the joint action of a number of firms in cooperation with other local authorities is required to resolve the difficulties.

For example, the problem may be one of inadequate space, either to accommodate expansion or to permit redesign of the plant in response to certain technological developments. If there are strong profit pressures favoring the existing location, the firm will typically work out these problems on its own. Conversely, if strong profit pressures have built up in favor of other locations, the immediate space problem will precipitate the inevitable abandonment. But, in a situation in which inertia could tip the balance in favor of the existing location, a sense of social responsibility could make the difference in motivating the firm to work diligently with local authorities to obtain the space needed. The answer might lie in the creation of an industrial park in cooperation with other firms and the local authorities.

Similarly, a firm may face severe handicaps on account of inadequate rail freight service. Perhaps other plants have closed down or shifted their business to trucking firms, resulting in a decline of business to the railroads, which, in turn, causes them to reduce their service to their remaining customers. Left to itself, this kind of adverse dynamic sequence is potentially disastrous to an area, more so than the simple multiplier process whereby a decline of purchasing power in one sector spreads to other sectors.

We normally think of the community where the plant is located as having the greatest vested interest in reversing that process, and of course it does. But the firm which acts in a socially responsible manner is more likely to join the community in its effort to halt the downward spiral, while the firm which is insensitive to these issues may take the rail service deterioration as given and move that much closer to a decision to abandon.

Perhaps this is the crux of the matter, whether a firm takes things as "given," an assumption fundamental to the classic theory of the firm in competitive markets. Swings in national demand patterns, technological developments which alter the optimal scale of production, and severe wage pressures arising out of large regional differences may indeed be treated as "givens," although some radical economists have attributed even these seemingly powerful forces to the exercise of market power. But you do not have to be a radical to discern situations in which the firm, in relation to the community in which it operates, can exercise a significant influence on the parameters which affect the health and the vigor of the local economy.

The notion that there is enough slack in the location choices of firms to allow for the exercise of social responsibility finds support in the concluding statements of two landmark studies of industrial location. The first study states:

The survey clearly demonstrates that location decisions are governed only partly by the distribution of economic resources and population. To be sure, cost and demand factors exclude certain locations from the list of possible alternatives, but they seem to leave many firms with a considerable range of choice. Within that range, location decisions reflect in part historical accident, in part they are governed by locational factors which are "man-made" and can be altered. These include community factors such as housing, schools, and recreational facilities. They also include feelings of satisfaction and dissatisfaction on the part of business executives with labor conditions, taxes, legal climate, and their evaluations of the industrial climate. Dissatisfaction with these matters often stems from lack of co-operation between labor, government, and business. It hardly needs to be pointed out that the economic growth of a state depends to an important extent on the innovation-mindedness of its businessmen, the energy which they apply to the development of new products, new markets, and channels of distribution, and new production processes. Finally, the study indicates that a community can improve its chances of interesting new firms in locating there by having suitable plant sites (or even plants) available and by being able to provide new firms with detailed information on local conditions and resources.[3]

3. Eva Mueller and James N. Morgan, "Location Decisions of Manufacturers," American Economic Association, *Papers and Proceedings of the Seventy-fourth Annual Meeting* (*American Economic Review,* Vol. 52, May 1962), p. 216.

The second study states:

But where more than one location would be almost equally satisfactory, the behavior and the reactions of the particular person making the decision are likely to be deciding factors.[4]

The objective of socially responsible business behavior should therefore be to exploit the "range of choice" in location decisions for the benefit of distressed areas. There is not, and there should not be, any pretense that the tilting of location decisions will resolve all the distress. Most "recovery" will be accomplished through migration in any case. Even with successful local development efforts, a large part of the overall residual problem has to be dealt with through various forms of transfer payments and other varieties of public expenditure. Favorable location decisions can only be part of a total strategy. But, if the sacrifice in productive efficiency and profits is not great, it is hard to argue that the benefits flowing from an increase in the demand for workers are not worth the cost.

New Plant Locations

The issue of abandonment, as suggested earlier, arises mainly in Model I and Model II areas where there is a history of industrial development in an urban setting. The problems of rural areas—Models III, IV, and V —arise mainly from the absence of sufficient industrial development to offset the decline of extractive industries such as agriculture, mining, and forestry. If there is a potential here for the exercise of corporate social responsibility, it must be seen in terms of favoring such areas with new plants.

The potential must be viewed in full recognition of the rather impressive rate of growth of manufacturing employment in rural areas in recent years. As shown in Table 10-1, between 1960 and 1970 manufacturing employment hardly increased at all in metropolitan areas but grew most rapidly in the most thinly populated nonmetropolitan counties.

This trend is even more pronounced in the South, where the problem of low income in rural areas is most prevalent (Model IV). The very rapid growth of manufacturing employment in the South as a whole is a familiar story. But the spread of manufacturing into eastern Arkansas,

4. Glenn E. McLaughlin and Stefan Robock, *Why Industry Moves South* (National Planning Association, 1949), p. 148.

Table 10-1. Growth in Manufacturing, Service, and Employment in Metropolitan and Nonmetropolitan Counties, 1960–70

Percent

Employment sector	Total	Metropolitan[a]	Nonmetropolitan					
			Urbanized[b]		Less urbanized[c]		Thinly populated[d]	
			Adjacent to SMSA	Not adjacent to SMSA	Adjacent to SMSA	Not adjacent to SMSA	Adjacent to SMSA	Not adjacent to SMSA
Manufacturing	7.8	3.7	15.6	14.3	28.1	25.4	34.3	34.5
Service	37.1	40.0	35.7	32.4	26.8	23.2	25.2	21.2
All sectors[e]	19.6	22.7	19.2	14.7	11.3	6.7	7.4	0.1

Source: *Rural Development Goals: First Annual Report of the Secretary of Agriculture to the Congress* (1974), Table 43, p. c-10.

SMSA = standard metropolitan statistical area.

a. All counties designated "metropolitan" by the federal government in 1973.

b. Counties with 20,000 or more urban residents.

c. Counties with urban residents numbering 2,500 to 19,999.

d. Counties with fewer than 2,500 urban residents.

e. Total for the United States, including sectors not shown in the table.

northern Mississippi, and northwestern Alabama constitutes a new phase. This process of rural industrialization, a highly significant new development, has been described by one observer as follows:

Since 1959 the metropolitan areas' total share of the region's manufacturing employment has been declining. Larger shares are being developed by smaller and intermediate sized communities. . . .

The most rapid growth in per capita incomes has taken place in selected non-metropolitan areas. . . . The key to this rapid income growth is the pace of industrial development in these smaller communities. . . .

Heavy capital investment is evidence of the significance of the move towards rural industrialization. . . .

Rural industrialization results from the simple fact that the pools of labor available in the "backwoods," though unskilled, are relatively cheap. . . . These "captive" labor pools provide the firm with a steady source of cheap labor and provide substantial cost savings as a result.[5]

Of course, if "development" were that simple, it would have occurred a long time ago. Be that as it may, the evidence is clear that the "invisible hand" is now working to convert the quest for higher profits into benefits for the poor and unemployed workers in some rural areas. Can the exercise of corporate social responsibility contribute still further to the alleviation of rural poverty?

Current national policy suggests that it would be unreasonable to expect industry to act in such a socially responsible manner without subsidy. I think this is realistic. In contrast to abandonment when the problem which is motivating the relocation can be identified and possibly solved, the firm making a fresh location decision, tempered by considerations of social responsibility, faces much more uncertainty in contemplating a move *to* a depressed area. The availability of subsidies may compensate and thus leave room for the exercise of social responsibility. But not just any subsidy. Amounts and conditions must be carefully worked out.

In this context I see a role for the exercise of social responsibility on the part of the business community apart from the actions of specific firms. From my own experience in this field of national policy, from my conversations with others, and from the literature, I have the strong impression that the seducers (i.e., the federal agencies) are not getting much advice from those they propose to seduce (i.e., the business firms) as to the relative effectiveness of different kinds of subsidy in accom-

5. John H. Zammito, *Dynamics of Southern Growth* (Memphis: Morgan, Keegan, 1972), pp. 56, 59, 60.

plishing regional development goals. Although a business firm may not always be able to articulate the calculation underlying a plant location decision, I find it hard to believe that the business community could not make a useful "input" into the design of subsidy programs which are aimed at influencing business location decisions.

Interestingly enough, EDA, like its predecessor agency, ARA, is housed in the Department of Commerce, a fact suggesting that government expected business to become involved in forming policy for the distressed areas. But the expectation, to my knowledge, has not been fulfilled. My own explanation for this failure is that business is not convinced that it would be in the national interest to tamper with plant location decisions. Nothing so inhibits the exercise of social responsibility as the nagging doubt that a specific action motivated by a sense of social responsibility may in fact be socially counterproductive.

Yet, despite thirteen years of less than dramatic progress, a conservative administration determined to get rid of ineffective, poorly conceived federal policies and programs concluded that federal subsidies should be used to:

A. Permit early and orderly adjustment to structural changes in regional or area economic conditions to minimize economic and social distress.
B. Stimulate employment opportunities for the unemployed of areas of persistent and substantial unemployment.
C. Stimulate more productive employment opportunities for the underemployed of areas with low average income.
D. Stimulate expanded employment opportunities in rural areas.[6]

Depressed Areas: Other Issues

So far we have cast the issue of corporate social responsibility in terms of plant location, and our eye has been on those companies which are not tied to the local market. Let us now examine the posture of a firm in a depressed area where the issue of location or relocation does not arise.

The firm is there, it is going to stay, but considerable latitude exists as to how much and in what ways it will contribute to the alleviation of local distress.

6. Department of Commerce and Office of Management and Budget, "Report to the Congress on the Proposal for an Economic Adjustment Program" (1974; processed), p. 1.

Akin to the location decision would be a decision to favor the local plant when the market calls for an expansion in output. Socially responsible behavior would call for a careful calculation of the relative profitability at the margin of expanding output at this location versus other locations where the additional jobs are not so crucial to the health of the local economy. A large and successful multi-plant firm with a comfortable profit margin might well sacrifice some profit to help alleviate some local unemployment.

EDA subsidies are in fact available in certain circumstances to encourage expansion of the local plant, but existing legislation is inefficient in exploiting such opportunities. What EDA offers is a capital subsidy to encourage expansion on the assumption that, despite the cheapening of capital, there will be a net gain in employment. A wage subsidy would be more effective in expanding employment and would relieve the firm of the uncertainty surrounding the expansion decision.

The firm can also contribute to the flow of purchasing power through the local public sector. Assuming the firm is in a comfortable profit situation, it should resist the temptation to drive a hard bargain on local taxes because it knows that the area sorely needs the industry. A benevolent approach to local government need not be incompatible with profit maximization when the feedback is taken into account. The quality of public services, especially education and health, may influence the productivity of the labor force and the availability of good management to the firm, assuming the firm intends to remain in the area.

The Pittsburgh renaissance of the 1950s and 1960s can be viewed in this light. Business leaders decided that, if they were not to abandon Pittsburgh altogether, they would have to broaden their concept of profit maximization to cover investments in the community to improve the physical and social environment and the quality of Pittsburgh's institutions.

Where the interests of an area and a firm may run counter to each other is in the attempt to attract other firms to the area. There are two sides to this coin. On the one hand, the firm may benefit from the higher level of commercial activity that comes from having additional enterprises in the vicinity. Transport services may improve, job opportunities may open up for spouses, the range of locally available specialized services may expand. On the other hand, the entry of additional firms may cut into the easy availability of labor and put pressure on the wage rate and the cost of other local inputs. Social responsibility would suggest a careful and realistic assessment of the gains and losses consequent upon a successful industrial promotion program.

The firm which derives much of its revenue from the local market faces much less of a dilemma in this regard. Banks, department stores, railroads, utilities, and the like have much to gain from an expanding local economy in the form of sales and are not likely to worry too much about rising costs. For them, the exercise of social responsibility harmonizes quite well with the profit motive. Not surprisingly, these firms are typically the most active in local economic development efforts.[7]

But, even with these firms, it would be a mistake to take their efforts on behalf of the local area for granted. The simple logic which equates the community's welfare with their own is limited to their fixed capital, the plants and the equipment already in place. With respect to their financial capital, they may behave very much like firms which are not oriented to the local market. Given the high mobility of money capital, they may look elsewhere for attractive investments, thus engaging in a process of "abandonment" analogous to the process we discussed earlier.

This process is most likely to occur when plants serving the local market are branches of large regional or national concerns. As the demand for their product or service in the local market declines, these firms will increasingly look to other markets for the profitable investment of profits and depreciation funds accumulated in the area now declining. With such opportunities readily available, there is again a divergence between private and communal interests. Instead of shoring up the local economy, the firm amplifies the downward trend by exporting its capital.

The exercise of social responsibility in this context calls for a careful assessment of investment opportunities in the local area, including those which may require cooperative efforts to bring them to the point of profitability. Financial institutions can play a crucial role in this regard. The visibility of profitable investment opportunities elsewhere may be greater than the visibility of opportunities in the local area. Outside,

7. In his autobiography, Ivan Allen, Jr., a former mayor of Atlanta, describes the business leaders of Atlanta who were active in promoting the area: "We were the presidents of the five major banks, the heads of the Atlanta-headquartered industries like Coca Cola, the presidents of the three big utilities, the heads of the three or four top retail establishments, the managers of the leading national-firm branches for the Southeast, the man in charge of the city transit system, the heads of the larger local businesses such as the Ivan Allen Company and the Haverty Furniture Company, and the leading realtors." Ivan Allen, Jr., *Mayor: Notes on the Sixties* (Simon and Schuster, 1971), pp. 30–31.

there is rapid growth, and the demand for capital is strong. Here, there is decline, and demand is sluggish. But a strong commitment to the local area will at least assure a fair shake for the local area and may serve to arrest a process of cumulative decline.

A national survey conducted by the Committee for Economic Development (CED) over a decade ago revealed a great variety of organized local economic development efforts in which business firms participated. Railroads, utilities, banks, airlines, shipping firms, and trucking companies operating independently accounted for over 600 programs. There were close to 5,000 programs run by local Chambers of Commerce and 2,000 by Community Development Corporations. Unfortunately, the CED was unable to provide objective measures of the effectiveness of these efforts, but, on a subjective basis, "nearly 60 per cent of the reporting organizations stated that in their own opinion their programs had been successful. . . . The most frequently cited drawback was insufficient funds and/or personnel, followed by lack of interest and participation by the general public and by business leaders."[8]

A firm operating in a distressed area or region can also help matters by the appropriate design of its explicitly charitable activities. Whether it be in the form of cash or executive time, the firm should balance the need of its own community against the prestige gained by contributing to national causes. As with the movement of capital for normal business purposes, the relative obscurity of the local community should not deter the firm from making an honest effort to find worthwhile things to do locally. If this dimension of social responsibility is taken seriously, then donations to local charities can serve two purposes, whereas donations to national charities can serve only one.

If we sum it all up—a firm expanding its work force, joining with local government to enhance the quality of life, participating in local economic development efforts, directing charity to local needs—we get a pattern of behavior which would unmistakably convey a sense of social responsibility compatible with the pursuit of profit. Obviously, not all firms could afford this posture, and not all depressed areas deserve it. Where the hard facts indicate that decline is irreversible and the downward momentum is strong, the firm must fend for itself and at best provide whatever it can in the way of relief but little or nothing for new

8. Donald R. Gilmore, *Developing the "Little" Economies: A Survey of Area Development Programs in the United States* (New York: Committee for Economic Development, 1960), pp. 19–20.

investments which are bound to fail. Even when the prognosis is more favorable, we cannot expect a firm operating on a thin margin in a fiercely competitive industry to do very much.

In a predictive sense we might expect the large single-plant firm with a comfortable profit margin to offer the best combination of capacity and motivation for socially responsible behavior. The multi-plant firm has the resources, but its frame of reference is larger than the individual community. It scans the horizon for the most "profitable" application of its capital, its managerial talent, and its charitable instincts. The nation is its oyster. In the jargon of economics, the supply of its resources to the local community is highly "elastic." It will tolerate no margin of disadvantage for very long. From the narrow perspective of economic efficiency, narrowly conceived, such behavior is consistent with Adam Smith's famous dictum on the invisible hand. But, from the contemporary, more eclectic perspective, the sense of place pervading a single-plant firm committed to its community would seem more benign. It would be ironical, indeed, if the trend toward merger and the creation of large conglomerates were to deprive distressed areas of the benefits that are supposed to flow from a greater assumption of social responsibility on the part of the big, modern, secure, sophisticated company.

Precisely where corporations ought to direct their efforts is harder to say than what efforts in general they ought to make. Federal policy has been ambiguous on this score from the beginning. On the one hand, there is the criterion of need. This criterion led at one stage in EDA's history to the pursuit of a "worst first" policy—i.e., a policy to give priority to areas with the lowest per capita income and the highest unemployment rates. On the other hand, there is the criterion of potential—i.e., where will the input of federal dollars accomplish the most in terms of raising income and/or reducing unemployment? This criterion is favored in the Appalachian legislation and in the development districts authorized in the Public Works and Economic Development Act, both of which emphasize the role of growth centers.

The risk that resources will be used ineffectively occurs at both ends of the spectrum. A "worst first" strategy poses the obvious risk of waste in the ordinary sense of that term. The investments will not in the long run produce enough jobs or any other kind of benefit to help the local area significantly. A "growth center" strategy runs the risk of using federal resources where they are not needed to stimulate further development. If the federal government is to operate by the same standards of profitability as the private sector, then we can hardly justify the use of public funds.

The private corporation which wants to be socially responsible faces a similar dilemma. There is no point in sacrificing private profits for local development purposes in a hopeless situation; nor does it make sense to do so where the natural processes of adjustment will work smoothly to compensate for the adverse impact of the firm's operations on the area.

The dilemma may be resolved at the federal level by a policy which gives priority to needy areas but minimizes the risk of failure by concentrating rather than scattering investments so as to capitalize on economies of scale. For the individual business enterprise the dilemma is not so easily resolved. Unless it can act in concert with other firms, it cannot avoid making a judgment as to whether a given action will be both necessary and sufficient to produce a positive effect in terms of sustaining the local economy. Hope and need may have little to do with the probability of success.

Socially Responsible Abandonment

When a decision to abandon a community cannot be reversed, there are still other ways to act in a socially responsible manner. The departing firm can assist the community by augmenting that community's physical and financial capability to attract other firms. One such action was reported in the *Wall Street Journal:*

Olin Corp. said it had signed an agreement giving this town of 2,500 people title to the company's plant and much of its other real estate holdings here plus $600,000 in cash. The agreement seeks to rescue the local economy following Olin's decision to close its salt-mining operations 23 months ago, putting 900 of the town's residents out of work.[9]

Another example occurred in New England:

The giant Firestone manufacturing plant in Fall River, which once provided jobs for hundreds of Rhode Islanders and was the city's major employer, will close idling some 800 workers.

Firestone said today it plans to offer the land, buildings, and water rights associated with the plant operations to the City of Fall River as a gift.[10]

9. *Wall Street Journal,* December 29, 1972.
10. *Providence Journal,* June 25, 1971.

Whether or not in these specific instances the actions taken were in fact also financially profitable, it would seem that this kind of socially responsible behavior would normally pose less of a threat to profits than the actions discussed so far. Unless a firm is continuously on the move, the cost of a gracious departure can be closely calculated and the move made on a once-and-for-all basis. There is no uncertainty of the kind associated with location decisions.

The notion of a severance payment may also be consistent with a corporate view of social justice and social responsibility. If one were to strike before-and-after balance sheets for the community, it might turn out that a firm, in the course of its operations in the community, had, on balance, depleted the community's assets and/or aggravated its liabilities. The obvious example, treated in Chapter 8, is pollution of a kind which is cumulative. But there are other, more subtle effects to consider:

1. How has the industry affected the quality of the natural environment?

2. How has the industry affected the quality of the labor force?

3. Has the industry added to or subtracted from the supply of private physical capital?

4. Has the industry added to or subtracted from the supply of social overhead capital?

5. What has been the impact of the industry on the range and quality of business services available to other enterprises in the area?

6. How has the industry affected the quality of public and quasi-public institutions in the area?

It is easy to see how an industry can score well on all these questions. The industry is not likely to enhance the natural environment, but it might have no perceptible negative impact on air and water quality. It could easily upgrade the labor force in terms of skill and experience. It could leave behind plants which are quite readily adaptable to other processes. It could, via generous tax payments to local government, upgrade the quality of public capital. Its demands could have expanded the supply of independent business service enterprises. By participating in local affairs, it might have improved the quality of local government and nonprofit institutions.

All of these positive effects would put the area in a better position than it had been before to develop and attract other kinds of industry. In a very real sense, the industry has made a permanent contribution to the development of the area.

But the other kind of tale is also familiar: the industry which pollutes heavily and destroys the landscape, which uses workers in a way which makes them unsuitable for other kinds of work, which leaves useless plants behind, which bargains hard for low tax rates and contributes little in charity, which is self-sufficient in business services and does not do much to upgrade the quality of local institutions. In short, the industry which is leaving may have depleted rather than enriched the natural, social, and economic environment.

The most dramatic example of such exploitation on a grand scale is the mining industry in Appalachia. Nobody tells it better than Harry Caudill:

> Even more ruinous than the loss of its physical resources is the disappearance of the plateau's best human material. Most of the thousands who left were people who recognized the towering importance of education in the lives of their children, and craved for them better schools than Kentucky afforded. Too many of those who remained behind were without interest in real education as distinguished from its trappings. If their children attended the neighborhood schools, the parents had done their duty. Too often they were far less ambitious and such ambition as they possessed was to evaporate in the arms of Welfarism and in the face of repeated failures.
>
> From the beginning, the coal and timber companies insisted on keeping all, or nearly all, the wealth they produced. They were unwilling to plow more than a tiny part of the money they earned back into schools, libraries, health facilities, and other institutions essential to a balanced, pleasant, productive, and civilized society. The knowledge and guile of their managers enabled them to corrupt and cozen all too many of the region's elected public officials and to thwart the legitimate aspirations of the people. The greed and cunning of the coal magnates left behind an agglomeration of misery for a people who can boast of few of the facilities deemed indispensable to life in more sophisticated areas, and even these few are inadequate and of inferior quality.[11]

In a very real sense we are now trying to repair with public funds the damage done in Appalachia by the pursuit of private profit. There can be no question but that by current standards of social responsibility the profit rate would have been lower, the damage much less, and the region would be in less dire straits.

Severance payments, therefore, may be viewed in such situations as lump sum allocations to a social cost account. Even when the firm scores well and really "owes" the community nothing in these terms, a payment

11. Harry M. Caudill, *Night Comes to the Cumberlands* (Little, Brown, 1963), p. 326.

to cushion the shock of its departure and facilitate a transition to other forms of employment fits well into my conception of social responsibility.

The departing firm can also express its sense of social responsibility to the community by assisting the displaced workers in their search for new employment. The firm is in a strategic position to perform this role for two reasons. First, if it is, in fact, relocating elsewhere, it knows first-hand of job opportunities which may be of interest to its current labor force. The investment in relocation may, in fact, be more than justified by profit considerations alone, since the management might very well put a high value on the retention of certain personnel. But, beyond such purely selfish motives, the firm can exploit its superior knowledge of the national labor market for the benefit of the workers about to be displaced by the plant closing. Here is an opportunity to share with the community some of the benefits of the process by which firms discover that they can operate at a greater profit at another location. The same channels which serve the mobility of capital can be used to augment the mobility of labor.

We should recognize, however, that in such situations there may be serious discrepancies between the interests of the community and the interests of the workers who are to be induced to migrate. The loss of highly skilled people may make it that much more difficult for the area to develop alternative sources of employment. The community may therefore resent rather than welcome the altruistic efforts of the firm on behalf of the workers in finding them jobs elsewhere.

Conclusion

The distress caused in a locality by an anemic private sector should be dealt with in part by deliberate efforts, both public and private, to enhance the demand for labor in the area. The private firm can and should act responsibly to meet this objective in a variety of ways. There are situations in which location decisions in pursuit of private profit can be tilted in favor of such areas by taking full advantage of public subsidies and complete information. The basic responsibility of the firm here is to avoid being influenced unduly by an image of cumulative comparative disadvantage and work hard to identify, instead, the potential advantages of operating in a soft labor market in cooperation with a community which is eager to have the firm in its midst.

The firm in the distressed area should seek to act responsibly by participating in local development efforts, by not exercising its monopolistic power vis-à-vis the local jurisdiction in tax negotiations, and by favoring the local area in its explicitly charitable ventures.

Finally, when abandonment is unavoidable, the firm should give serious consideration to severance payments in the form of cash and/or physical facilities and capital equipment. These may be justified in some instances by the cumulative costs inflicted by the firm on the community which were not "covered" by current tax payments. Assistance in relocating displaced workers is another way of manifesting social responsibility, although the community may not always welcome such assistance.

These suggested actions do not assume a coherent national policy to arrest urban crowding and rural decline or otherwise redirect the geographic pattern of population growth. They flow from the simple proposition that the private sector can and should help to ameliorate the distress which is caused in part by location decisions.

If and when the nation develops a clear consensus on desired population distribution patterns, the potential for making socially responsible location decisions will be greatly enlarged. But we are not at that point yet.

CHAPTER ELEVEN

Foreign Operations

RAYMOND VERNON

SOME ISSUES of social responsibility apply to all business enterprises, simply because they are engaged in business; but some apply mainly to enterprises that carry on extensive operations overseas. The great expansion of U.S. business abroad in the past two decades elevates the question of social responsibility in overseas operations to a major issue.[1]

The issue has its own special complexities. The social goals of certain nations in which multinational enterprises operate may conflict with the social goals of other nations. Countries compete for jobs, for foreign exchange, for military supremacy. To serve the ends of the home country may prejudice the objectives of the host country. To serve one host country may be to hamper the goals of another. Besides, even if each country is content, there is no assurance that global welfare is being aided. How, then, is the social performance of the multinational enterprise to be assessed?

Social Responsibility in the United States

American opinion has been going through such an agony of introspection in the past few years that it would be hard to say how the social performance of any U.S. institution should be measured. If the social responsibility of American multinational enterprises were measured simply by their propensity to move goods, money, people, and ideas across international boundaries, they would be rated very high as performers. Compared with mechanisms tried by other countries and at other times

1. This chapter draws heavily upon the research of the Harvard Multinational Enterprise Project, financed by the Ford Foundation through a grant to the Harvard University Graduate School of Business Administration.

275

to add to national affluence through international transactions, they are outstanding. The 10,000 or so foreign branches and subsidiaries of U.S. firms control assets on the order of $150 billion. U.S.-sponsored companies account for about 60 percent of Canada's industry; elsewhere they dominate key industries such as automobiles, chemicals, petroleum, and aluminum. About half the exports of manufactured goods from the United States directly involve the parent firm or the overseas subsidiary of a U.S.-based multinational firm. Over 80 percent of the long-term capital flow out of the United States and two-thirds of the recorded fees, dividends, and interest payments flowing in are generated by these enterprises.[2] It would be too much to assert that multinational enterprises always follow strategies that contribute to the growth of international trade and investment. There are industries—oil, aluminum, copper, and nickel among them—in which the objective of the leaders is to avoid any upset to a precarious equilibrium. Despite caveats of this sort, however, the record of U.S. enterprises in crossing national boundaries has been impressive.

In industries in which the market equilibrium is precarious, some special problems of social responsibility often appear. In such industries the leading firms find themselves from time to time plunged into the position of trying to manage world markets. In periods of surplus, the leaders may be seen holding down production through parallel patterns of restraint. In periods of shortage, they may be found engaged in informal rationing schemes.

It is hard to say what the canons of social responsibility, as interpreted by the values of the United States, would require in cases of this sort. A classic illustration of the difficulties entailed in defining social responsibility in such cases is offered by the role of the U.S.-based international oil companies during the crisis that began in 1970. The facts on their behavior in that period are not all in; perhaps they never will be. Several things are evident, however. One is that, with the blessing of the U.S. government, the companies played a key role in the management of the world's oil supply. Another is that the considerations which governed the oil companies in their pricing and distribution were complex. As business enterprises, the companies naturally favored markets with high profit margins over markets with low profit margins, customers with long-standing ties over buyers of opportunity, affiliates over indepen-

2. *Survey of Current Business*, Vol. 52 (March 1972), pp. 42–43.

dents, and so on. Accordingly, because German markets were free of price control, they were better supplied than U.S. markets. Because Ibn Saud seemed in a position to do the U.S.-based firms great hurt, his commands were carefully heeded. Because the companies saw themselves operating in the Japanese market on sufferance and saw their future as doubtful, they tended to place that market low on their list of priorities.

At the same time, however, there are some indications that the profit-making instincts of the U.S. firms were held in check occasionally so that situations involving special hardship or egregious unfairness or acute political sensitivity could be dealt with. As the principal officers and directors of these companies struggled with the crisis, it is a safe surmise that they saw themselves as having fulfilled their social responsibilities to the United States with dedication and commitment.

Was the self-perception of the oil companies justified? For some elements of U.S. opinion, it is plainly offensive whenever the private sector takes over the management of markets in a crisis and even more offensive when they seem to profit from the opportunity. The case grows more difficult, however, when the firms assume their quasi-administrative role by explicit default of the U.S. government and when they seem to be vested by the U.S. government with some of the powers of a public agent. In that case, it is a bit more difficult to conclude that the requirements of social responsibility are not being fully discharged. One can question the wisdom or the objectivity of the government in selecting an agency with such complex and divided motivations; but it is more difficult to be critical of the enterprises themselves.

But of course the social performance of U.S. enterprises is not gauged merely by their ability to manage the movement of goods and money across boundaries. Other criteria also have been applied. The charge has been made, for instance, that the operation of U.S. enterprises in foreign markets has had adverse social side effects by injuring the U.S. balance of payments.[3] The evidence on this question, as it turns out, is inconclusive.[4]

3. David W. Ewing, "MNCs on Trial," *Harvard Business Review,* Vol. 50 (May–June 1972), pp. 132, 134; Nat Goldfinger, "U.S.-Based Multi-national Companies and U.S. Foreign Trade," *Atlantic Community Quarterly,* Vol. 8 (Fall 1970), pp. 393–97.
4. For a macroeconomic approach to the problem, see G. C. Hufbauer and F. M. Adler, *Overseas Manufacturing Investment and the Balance of Payments,* U.S. Treasury Department (1968). The Hufbauer-Adler approach is updated in

The concern over the effects of the multinational enterprise upon the U.S. balance of payments is sometimes directed to short-term speculative effects, sometimes to longer-term effects. According to the prevailing assumption, U.S. parent companies are in an excellent position, whenever the dollar seems weak, to shuttle their liquid funds out of dollars into other currencies; their built-in connections overseas make it especially cheap and especially easy to effect the transfers. Indeed, all they need do is delay the anticipated receipt of currencies due from their subsidiaries abroad or expedite their ordinary payments to their overseas subsidiaries; small variations in leads and lags, it is assumed, will have a major effect on the U.S. payments position.

Though the evidence that U.S. firms engage widely in such practices is largely circumstantial, it does have a certain cumulative persuasiveness. Prudent and knowledgeable businessmen, alert to opportunities and risks, would normally be expected to take just such cautionary measures in time of crisis. And there is not much doubt that a small number of large enterprises, reacting in this manner to a common set of danger signals, would have a collective impact sufficient to precipitate or enlarge a crisis.[5]

The critical judgment, however, is to assess what would have happened if the multinational enterprise did not exist. The fact that foreign exchange markets are vulnerable to short-term capital movements goes without saying; the question is whether the operations of the multinational enterprise increase that vulnerability very much, as compared with some stated alternative. Probably the expertise and the sensitivity which are required to generate these speculative movements have by now developed to such an extent that the phenomenon would persist even if the multinational enterprise structure were liquidated.

The balance-of-payments problem is also seen, however, as one with

---

R. B. Stobaugh, P. Telesio, and J. de la Torre, "The Effect of U.S. Foreign Direct Investment in Manufacturing on the U.S. Balance of Payments, U.S. Employment, and Changes in Skill Composition of Employment," Center for Multinational Studies Occasional Paper No. 4 (Washington: Center for Multinational Studies, 1973; processed). For a microeconomic approach, see R. B. Stobaugh and others, "U.S. Multinational Enterprises and the U.S. Economy," in U.S. Department of Commerce, Bureau of International Commerce, *The Multinational Corporation: Studies on U.S. Foreign Investment* (1972), Vol. I; elaborated in Center for Multinational Studies Occasional Paper No. 4, cited above.

5. R. B. Stobaugh and S. M. Robbins, *Money in the Multinational Enterprise* (Basic Books, 1973), pp. 180–83.

a long-term dimension. It is often thought, for instance, that the disposition of U.S. firms to set up subsidiaries abroad injures the U.S. payments position in the long run by altering U.S. export and import patterns. Once more, the critical question is: what would have happened if multinational enterprises did not exist?

A number of studies suggest that the answer to the question may differ from industry to industry. In the highly competitive industries, such as shoes and consumer electronics, there are plausible grounds for assuming that a relatively rapid shift to foreign production was almost unavoidable —that producers operating in the United States were bound in any case to lose the bulk of their markets to facilities located abroad. In industries in which the U.S. producers enjoy an advantage based on product differentiation, however, such as machinery and chemical specialties, outside pressures are not quite so strong. In these industries, the assumption is that eventually the U.S. advantage in any given product line will be lost to producers operating elsewhere, because at some stage production costs abroad will be lower than those in the United States. Though the exact timing may entail a certain amount of choice, investment in overseas facilities at some appropriate time seems preferable to inaction, at least as measured in balance-of-payments terms.

Perhaps the most baffling part of the balance-of-payments analysis relates to the mature oligopolies. Many overseas investments of U.S. firms represent obscure moves aimed at buttressing the stability of an oligopoly or reducing the vulnerability of an enterprise within the oligopoly. It is hard to picture what would happen if these investments were not made. In all likelihood, the price discipline of such world oligopolies would not be nearly as strong in the absence of these investments. But what would that mean in terms of the balance of payments?

The misgivings expressed over the effects that U.S. multinational enterprises may have at home are not limited to the balance of payments; they are expressed even more strongly with regard to the employment and income goals of the United States. Whatever benefits the U.S. economy may derive from the foreign operations of U.S. enterprises are, according to one line of criticism, offset by the fact that U.S. jobs are lost. The same kind of issue arose several decades ago when many of the industries now moving abroad were migrating from the Northeast to the Midwest, and from the Midwest to the South. When domestic shifts of this sort were involved, the justification always seemed to be the same: the jobs were doomed at their original location anyway—

priced out of a highly competitive market by a relative rise in wages, a relative increase in economies of scale, or a relative decline in transport costs. However, the mitigating element from a social point of view was that what one part of the country lost, another gained. The responsibility for easing a transition of this sort, therefore, was in large part a collective responsibility of society, to be borne mainly by national social institutions.

Where foreign operations are concerned, however, that justification has less relevance. For in foreign operations, it is American workers who are displaced and foreign workers who take up the displaced activity. Worse still, the U.S. workers directly affected have sometimes been those who were already among the lowest paid in the nation—the last pockets of low-wage U.S. labor available to the industries involved. If a U.S. enterprise triggered the move, therefore, it could not so easily expect the social institutions of the country to shoulder the responsibility of easing the transition.

The studies that have been done so far on this issue indicate that the employment effects of the foreign operations of U.S. firms are far from simple. There is even a case to be made that the employment-generating effects of the investments are favorable on balance to the U.S. economy, not unfavorable. Many of the jobs lost would in any case have disappeared; and some new U.S. jobs created by the investment are superior in quality to the jobs lost.[6]

On the other hand, social gain and loss are not all that easily measured; society does not feel bound to do its calibrating by the taut calculus of Marshall and Pareto. The pain of an unskilled worker who has lost his job in an isolated textile town in the Mississippi delta may be regarded as entailing a social cost that is unrelated to the money value of his output; and the increased opportunities of some less needy member of the U.S. labor force may be assigned a very much smaller measure of social gain. To be sure, from the viewpoint of economists, sociopsychological measures of gain and loss appear vague and inelegant. But valuations of this sort may well reflect the collective social values of the country.

The fact that economic criteria may have very limited relevance in the assessment of social responsibility is illustrated even more strongly by

6. Stobaugh and others, "U.S. Multinational Enterprises and the U.S. Economy," pp. 30–31.

the protest of some Americans against investment by U.S. firms in countries whose political or social systems the protesters regard as objectionable. U.S. firms that set up enterprises in Yugoslavia or South Africa or Brazil are likely to be charged from some quarter with supporting political or social systems that are antithetical to the interests of the American people. In a few situations, a strong case can be made in support of such views. In most of these situations, however, the political implications of the behavior of U.S. enterprises abroad prove to be highly ambiguous. Still, whatever the facts in the individual case may be, political judgments deeply affect the way in which Americans look on the overseas operations of U.S. enterprises.

Social Responsibility in Other Advanced Countries

Political and social attitudes in the United States make up one "climate" to which American multinational corporations must conform. Their operations in other advanced countries must be adapted to a different "climate." Ironically, it is their responsiveness to U.S. norms of business responsibility that can cause tensions abroad.

The social criteria by which Americans tend to measure the performance of large enterprises are very far removed at times from the criteria used by other countries. Today that gap is particularly wide. Though large parts of U.S. society are deeply disturbed by the size and power of U.S. business, there are very few other countries in the advanced world which see the size and power of business enterprises as a threat to their social goals. To be sure, they may object to the size and power of U.S. enterprises in their economy; but they do not ordinarily fear large private enterprises as a class.

In the spectrum of national views on "big business," U.S. norms have always seemed a bit distinctive. It is hard to capture the essence of the difference in a few words.[7] Yet certain aspects of the American view merit mention here, even at the risk of oversimplification.

One of these is the enormous ideological importance of the boundary line between the public and the private sectors in the United States. To be sure, there are all sorts of complex ties in the United States between

7. Those who wish to pursue the subject may find it useful to read an elaboration in my *Sovereignty at Bay: The Multinational Spread of U.S. Enterprises* (Basic Books, 1971), pp. 204–30.

business leaders and government. These ties become visible from time to time in political contributions, in contract awards, and in job appointments. To some observers, these ties indicate the existence of a "deeply symbiotic relationship"; to others they suggest conspiracy.[8] Nevertheless, compared with the characteristic situation in most other advanced countries, the situations in which public and private power are openly combined in the United States are comparatively few.

Moreover, by comparison with most other countries, interactions in the United States across the boundary that separates the public and the private sectors are undertaken with a degree of formality, almost of rigidity, that bespeaks the deep ideological importance of the boundary. The formality often declines in Republican administrations, increases in Democratic regimes. But in all administrations it is relatively strong, and it imparts a special flavor to the relations between the public and private sectors.

Generally speaking, the public-private frontier can be crossed much more readily in other countries than in the United States. Britain, for instance, has nationalized its steel industry, then denationalized the industry, without anything like the ideological crises that similar developments would have provoked in the United States. The Italian government, operating through state-owned enterprises, has come to control the lion's share of Italy's industry, including the leading chemical and petroleum firms; continued acquisitions create no more than a ripple of ideological ferment. Similarly, the French government effectively controls practically every source of external capital that large French enterprises can tap; and as a matter of course it makes detailed "contracts" with such enterprises on pricing and production. The Japanese government has pushed relations of a similar sort to levels of detail and intensity almost without parallel in a capitalist country. Because the relations between government and enterprise in some of these countries are so intimate and continuous, some American reactions are close to incomprehensible from the viewpoint of foreigners. If ITT were British or French or Japanese, for example, the fact that it tried to enlist its home government in an effort to overthrow an unfriendly foreign govern-

---

8. For representative generalizations, see John Kenneth Galbraith, "Power and the Useful Economist," *American Economic Review,* Vol. 63 (March 1973), p. 5; J. F. Galloway, "The Military-Industrial Linkages of U.S.-Based Multinational Corporations," *International Studies Quarterly,* Vol. 16 (December 1972), pp. 491–510; and R. L. Thornton, "Governments and Airlines," *International Organization,* Vol. 25 (Summer 1971), p. 548.

ment would probably be taken as a matter of course. Protest there might be, but more probably on the merits of the situation than on the private-public tie. The protest in the United States, it is clear, drew some of its strength from the fact that the ITT proposal violated some relatively distinctive U.S. perceptions of the right and proper relationship between big business and government.

The distinction between U.S. norms and those of other countries, however, is not a difference in the degree of willingness to exercise public power; it is rather a distinction in the way in which public power is used. The United States has proved perfectly capable of breaking up and redistributing the ownership of $70 billion of assets in the public utility industry, of dissolving the Standard Oil trust, and of launching several new producers of aluminum to weaken the erstwhile aluminum monopoly. The U.S. government also has taken a much more aggressive hand than the Europeans in supporting industries that utilize advanced technology, by underwriting their developmental costs and offering assured markets for their output.[9] But the general approach in these cases has been to operate at arm's length, relatively speaking, with elaborate consideration for the distinction between public and private power.

This different approach contributes to the tension that the presence of U.S. enterprises abroad seems to engender. That tension is expressed in various ways. One author nicely summarizes the Japanese reaction:

The Ministries are apprehensive that foreign concerns would not accept the Government's extra-legal administrative guidance, thus endangering the politico-economic establishment. There is also doubt that the majority of Westerners would show adequate understanding of Japan's mores, and fear that they would eventually find themselves at odds with their employees, their bankers, their suppliers, their joint venture partners, their customers, their trade associations and the Government.[10]

Though the Japanese reaction is relatively acute, similar themes emerge repeatedly in other countries, even in culturally proximate Canada.[11] Officials often assume that if a U.S. firm were requested to cooperate with the host country's government by, say, reducing its use of foreign

9. Organisation for Economic Co-operation and Development, *The Conditions for Success in Technological Innovation* (Paris: OECD, 1971), pp. 46–47, 114.

10. H. F. Van Zandt, "Japanese Culture and the Business Boom," *Foreign Affairs*, Vol. 48 (January 1970), p. 354.

11. See Kari Levitt, *Silent Surrender: The Multinational Corporation in Canada* (St. Martin's Press, 1970), pp. 1–15; *Foreign Ownership and the Structure of Canadian Industry: Report of the Task Force* . . . (Ottawa: Queen's Printer, 1968); Andrew Shonfield, *Modern Capitalism* (London: Oxford University Press, 1965), pp. 385–417.

exchange, or slowing up its rate of hiring or firing, or placing a lid on price increases, the firm might be unable or unwilling to comply.

Contrary to the common assumption, many U.S. firms try to remain quite sensitive to the admonition "When in Rome . . ." To be sure, when the issue is one of real gravity to the multinational enterprise, imperiling the interests of the system as a whole, the autonomy of the local subsidiary inevitably goes by the board. But day-to-day policy is something else again. Close studies of various firms indicate that in areas of policy where they think it important to conform to local norms—notably in personnel administration and labor relations—considerable real autonomy is extended to overseas subsidiaries. Nationals of the local area almost always hold the key policy jobs; and nationals decide the day-to-day tactics to be followed.[12]

Still, the behavior of U.S. firms in foreign settings is commonly distinguishable from that of their local counterparts. In Britain, for instance, U.S. firms exhibit a relative reluctance to join employer federations as well as a relative reluctance to recognize unions. It is not clear whether the U.S. subsidiaries or the local firms come off more favorably in terms of social responsibility. U.S.-owned subsidiaries in England appear to have fewer labor disputes than comparable English firms, though in a parallel study for Scotland the opposite finding emerged.[13]

More broadly, U.S. subsidiaries come off fairly well by the usual measures of social performance that are applied in advanced countries.[14]

12. See, for instance, the unusual study by Duane Kujawa, *International Labor Relations Management in the Automotive Industry: A Comparative Study of Chrysler, Ford, and General Motors* (Praeger, 1971).

13. Max Steuer and John Gennard, "Industrial Relations, Labour Disputes and Labour Utilisation in Foreign-Owned Firms in the United Kingdom," in John H. Dunning (ed.), *The Multinational Enterprise* (London: Allen and Unwin, 1971), pp. 94–102, 118–30; D. J. Forsyth and K. Docherty, *United States Investment in Scotland* (Praeger, 1972), pp. 164–99.

14. The leading sources on performance are John H. Dunning, *American Investment in British Manufacturing Industry* (London: Allen and Unwin, 1958); A. E. Safarian, *Foreign Ownership of Canadian Industry* (Toronto: McGraw-Hill, 1966); R. S. Deane, "Foreign Investment in New Zealand Manufacturing" (Ph.D. dissertation, Victoria University of Wellington, 1967); Forsyth and Docherty, *United States Investment in Scotland*. See also D. T. Brash, *American Investment in Australian Industry* (Harvard University Press, 1966); John H. Dunning, "Technology, United States Investment, and European Economic Growth," in Charles P. Kindleberger (ed.), *The International Corporation* (M.I.T. Press, 1970); D. Van den Bulcke, *Les Entreprises Etrangères dans l'Industrie Belge* (Ghent: University of Ghent, 1971).

Governments that are interested in establishing higher standards of probity in the income tax field generally find the subsidiaries of U.S.-based enterprises relatively amenable, as compared with local enterprises. Insofar as the subsidiaries deviate from the local wage patterns, deviations on the up side seem the more common.[15] When governments try to promote investment in lagging regions, such as the Italian government has done in its backward south, multinational enterprises are prominent among those that respond.[16] Governments in the advanced countries find U.S.-controlled enterprises effective in the promotion of exports, especially in the relatively advanced industrial sectors.[17]

On all these points, one can explain the action of the subsidiaries on grounds that have nothing to do with a conscious desire to shoulder social responsibilities. But the fact remains that, despite the tension they seem to generate, these enterprises generally rate quite well in terms of such criteria.

One cause of tension is the appearance of relative mobility on the part of U.S.-owned enterprises. Firms capable of establishing points of supply all over the world, for instance, presumably use that capability when their interests require; otherwise, there would be little reason to develop it. One compelling corollary is that if the actions of local government or of local labor reduce the attractiveness of any country as a point of operations there is a possibility of rapid withdrawal.[18]

15. One of the few serious studies of the subject reports deviations in both directions, though higher wages predominate. Steuer and Gennard, "Industrial Relations . . . in Foreign-Owned Firms in the United Kingdom," pp. 134–36. See also Van den Bulcke, *Les Entreprises Etrangères dans l'Industrie Belge*, p. 26; Forsyth and Docherty, *United States Investment in Scotland*, pp. 121–27.

16. P. P. Fano, "American Investment in Italy," in A. Kamin (ed.), *Western European Labor and the American Corporation* (Washington: Bureau of National Affairs, 1970), p. 473; M. D. Steuer and others, *The Impact of Foreign Direct Investment on the United Kingdom*, U.K. Department of Trade and Industry (London: HMSO, 1973), p. 104.

17. R. D. Belli, "Sales of Foreign Affiliates of U.S. Firms, 1961–65, 1967, and 1968," *Survey of Current Business*, Vol. 50 (October 1970), p. 20 (Table 3). See also A. E. Safarian, *The Performance of Foreign-Owned Enterprises in Canada* (Montreal: Private Planning Association of Canada, 1966), pp. 29–30; J. H. Dunning, *The Role of American Investment in the British Economy*, PEP Broadsheet 507 (London: Political and Economic Planning, 1969), p. 148; André Raynauld, "La Propriété et la Performance des Entreprises dans le Québec," *Etudes Internationales*, Vol. 2 (March 1971), p. 103; and Brash, *American Investment in Australian Industry*, pp. 203–11.

18. Sensitivity on that score is illustrated by the wariness with which labor

Concern is likewise felt with regard to short-term movements of money, especially during periods when currencies appear unstable. This is the counterpart of the U.S. problem mentioned earlier. When currencies are under pressure, the press is generally filled with observations about the role of foreign-owned enterprises in exacerbating the difficulties. Though evidence is hard to come by, two factors support the view that U.S.-owned enterprises behave somewhat differently from their local counterparts in this regard. First, as noted earlier, a considerable part of the international money flows in which such enterprises are engaged consists of transactions with parents and affiliates, a fact that makes it relatively easy for the subsidiaries to accelerate or to slow up their international payments. Second, for various complex technical reasons, foreign-owned enterprises have more at stake in situations of exchange rate instability than do locally owned enterprises. When local enterprises fail to take action against the weakness of their own currency, the usual consequence is merely that they pass up an opportunity for a windfall profit in that currency. When U.S.-owned subsidiaries fail to hedge, however, they risk the possibility that their parent may be obliged actually to record a loss on its books in its own currency of account. The widespread assumption seems reasonable, therefore, that foreign-owned enterprises tend to hedge more readily than their local counterparts, thereby adding to the pressures on currencies that are under stress.

Nevertheless, in any summary judgment of the social performance of U.S. enterprises in the advanced countries, one would be bound to observe that the social benefits, especially those of an economic sort, are more evident than the costs. Where social costs do exist, they are usually costs of the kind associated with large enterprises as a class, rather than with enterprises whose parent firms are based in the United States. On the other hand, the multinational character of the enterprises concerned does seem to pose some special risks to the well-being of the economies in which they operate. Though the possible losses seldom materialize,

---

in General Motors' Belgian plant has measured its competitive position against General Motors' German plant with respect to manufacturing Opels for export to the United States. Kujawa, *International Labor Relations Management,* p. 176. Note, too, the Ford Motor Company's decision to discontinue the production in Britain of Pinto engines because of uneasy labor relations, despite the lower cost of production there. See *Forbes,* Vol. 109 (January 1, 1972), p. 25. Nevertheless, Steuer and Gennard find little evidence of actual shifts of this sort in Britain.

their very potential can be thought of as a social cost. The problem, therefore, can be seen as one of social accountability; as long as it lies in the discretion of the foreign-owned enterprise whether to exercise its reserve power substantially to affect the economy, the presence of the enterprise will always generate tension.

Social Responsibility in the Less Developed Countries

The record shows that when U.S. enterprises operate in less developed countries, there is a very high probability that they will be charged from some quarters with various serious failings in terms of social responsibility.

Defining the Charge

At times, the basis for the charge lies in the fact that they are business firms rather than in the fact that they are foreign. As enterprises, they have an overwhelming preference for predictability in the business environment, a preference that is usually based on mundane business considerations much more than on ideologies. This preference generally means that they support the forces that guarantee order in preference to the forces that promise change. There is no basis for assuming, however, that local enterprises have any greater relish than foreign-owned enterprises for accepting the uncertainties associated with change.

Neither is there any basis for assuming that foreign-owned enterprises which explicitly identified themselves with the forces of social change in a less developed country would thereby reduce their vulnerability to criticism. Though it would be hard to find many actual cases in which foreign-owned enterprises adopted a calculated policy of identifying with the forces of social change, there is indirect evidence to suggest that such an identification involves considerable elements of danger.[19] When for-

19. Two independent studies—one of Peru, another of Chile—conclude that the pressures for social change on the part of the U.S. government in the Alliance for Progress programs of the early 1960s measurably weakened the position of U.S.-owned enterprises. See T. H. Moran, "The Multinational Corporation and the Politics of Development: The Case of Copper in Chile, 1945–1970" (Ph.D. dissertation, Harvard University, 1970); A. J. Pinelo, *The Multinational Corporation as a Force in Latin American Politics: A Case Study of the International Petroleum Company in Peru* (Praeger, 1973).

eigners declare themselves against the established interests in any country, they breach the ancient doctrine that only a Turk can curse at a **Turk.**

Whatever the underlying objections to foreign-owned enterprises may be, the actual charges against them are exceedingly varied. One reason for the variety has to do with the great range of conditions that are found in less developed areas. These countries run the gamut from those where the average annual income equals no more than bare subsistence to those with an income of $500 or $600 per capita. Moreover, the internal social structure of less developed nations as a rule is disconcertingly diverse, with huge differences in income between rich and poor as well as great gaps in outlook between city and country. As a result, national spokesmen reflect a vast range of views. And as the political fortunes of different factions rise and fall, the spokesmen's views tend to shift dramatically.

The vulnerability of any definition of social responsibility in circumstances of this sort is pointed up by the case of Libya. When oil was discovered in Libya in the 1950s, the government was an anachronistic monarchy, with a structure irrelevant to a modern state; but it was the only government there was. Moreover, despite its anachronistic character, that government managed to extract some unusually favorable terms from the oil companies. One major reason for these favorable terms was the government's willingness to deal with a maverick firm in the oil industry—an outsider which had much less interest in maintaining the existing equilibrium of the industry than did the leading firms. On the other hand, there were strongly documented allegations that the maverick outsider company had managed to make its way into Libya partly by bribing government officials.[20] When a "revolutionary" government eventually seized power by force, it duly charged both the ousted officials and the oil companies with corruption and antisocial action. With the favorable terms already secured from the oil companies and unlikely to be reversed, this was an easy judgment for the revolutionary government to make.

Thereafter the policies of the revolutionary government added even further to the confusion over social responsibility. That regime proceeded to use significant amounts of its extraordinarily high oil revenues to subsidize guerrillas in the Middle East, support the military efforts of

20. *International Herald Tribune* (Paris), February 9, 1972.

the Egyptian government, finance a counter-coup in the Sudan, and support Pakistan's government against India. When Libya's present government is eventually succeeded by another, it is not unlikely that the oil companies once again will be charged with "social irresponsibility," this time perhaps for supplying revenues to a government that was frittering away the country's resources.

A similar sort of problem exists with regard to many of the so-called export enclaves that foreign-owned enterprises have created in the less developed countries. When foreign mines or plantations have been set up in remote and backward areas, the governments of the countries concerned commonly have been in no position to provide the infrastructure and social services needed for the operation. In such cases, governments have agreed—indeed, insisted—that the foreign enterprises provide schools, hospitals, roads, communications, and even police protection. Foreign investors have sometimes been reluctant to assume such responsibilities, sometimes eager, according to their judgment about the alternatives. Thereafter, some have performed efficiently, others less so; some have maintained their perspective as foreign private enterprises, while others have developed illusions of absolute sovereignty.

Enterprises that run company towns experience in microcosm all the conflicts of the social responsibility issue. When obliged to face the complex social problems of class and race discrimination, they seem to have handled the job about as poorly or as well as other institutions have done. Some have reinforced existing patterns of racial and occupational segregation; some have done the opposite. When they tried to think explicitly in terms of long-run social objectives, as a few have, they often blundered badly. Consider, for instance, the practice of segregating neighborhoods in company towns according to occupational level, a normal practice in less developed areas. A foreign enterprise that deviated from the policy and promoted integrated neighborhoods in its company town would almost surely find that its innovation was offensive to everybody concerned, at all occupational levels. Or consider some of the paternalistic, dependence-generating practices of local employers in the less developed areas, such as the practice of providing meals and amenities free of charge. Should the foreign firm abandon such practices by substituting equivalent cash payments; and, if so, how should it respond to the anguished protests of the employees?

If the record provided some indication of the way in which the policies chosen by foreign enterprises affected their chance of survival, the task of choosing might be eased; but no such indication is evident. In the last years of its operations in Peru, for instance, the International Petroleum Company reportedly followed "enlightened" policies in the operation of its Peruvian company towns—enlightened in two senses: it provided facilities that were unusually high by Peruvian standards; and it made some effort to break down paternalism and build up the sense of independence and dignity of its Peruvian employees. But there is no evidence that this had any bearing on the eventual nationalization of the enterprise in Peru. More generally, the tendency of U.S. firms to provide better amenities in the mining camps and oilfields of the less developed countries and to concern themselves more with social issues than, say, the British or the Italians has seemingly had little impact on their survival capabilities.[21]

The problem of defining social responsibility in less developed countries has been complicated by the marked heterogeneity of interests in these societies. Some degree of heterogeneity exists in all societies, of course, but in the poor countries the problem is particularly pronounced.

Take the situation in which foreign-owned enterprises operating company towns have been told by the host country to transfer quasi-public administrative functions back to national or local governments. In cases of this sort, workers in the foreign enclave have sometimes resisted the transfer, out of fear that public services would deteriorate and become more costly. Indeed, the clash between the private interests of the workers of foreign-owned enterprises and other interests in the less developed countries has drawn a great deal of attention from political philosophers. Though the documentation on the point leaves something to be desired, there is not much doubt that in most developing countries the workers in foreign-owned enterprises fare measurably better than their counterparts in locally owned enterprises. They generally get more training, are paid higher wages, receive larger fringe benefits, and even have greater opportunities for promotion than their counterparts in local enterprises.[22]

21. There are numerous sources that describe conditions in the camps and towns maintained in less developed countries by foreign-owned enterprises, but most such sources cannot claim objectivity. Accordingly, I have relied for these conclusions mainly on my own visits to such installations. A major contribution, however, is made to the literature by Charles T. Goodsell in *American Corporations and Peruvian Politics* (Harvard University Press, 1974). A. J. Pinelo's study of the International Petroleum Company in Peru, cited in n. 19, also is informative.

22. For instance, in a survey of seventy-four foreign-owned projects in less developed countries, twenty-nine firms reported paying local managers and pro-

What is uncertain, however, is whether the foreign-owned enterprises that are responsible for this performance can be regarded as making a social contribution.

The very question may prove disconcerting to some readers. But the fact is that there are many different views, both in the United States and abroad, on how best to achieve social and economic change in countries such as South Africa, Paraguay, and Ivory Coast. Groups in the United States that are oriented to social action have come to the conclusion that U.S.-owned enterprises should lead programs of social betterment in such countries. Others believe that these programs cannot be more than cosmetic palliatives, postponing the onset of basic change.

The idea that programs of social betterment are obstructive is well articulated in various quarters.[23] According to this view, social justice cannot be achieved in less developed areas without first cutting back the role of foreign-owned enterprises, because that role is inherently exploitative. The U.S. parent firm that improves the living conditions of black workers in its South African subsidiary is therefore engaged in a trivial, even an irrelevant, maneuver. Worse still, it is buying off protest cheaply, delaying the day when relevant action can bring about real reform. In an obvious extension of Lenin's views regarding the political unreliability of industrial workers, those who think in these terms see the local workers in foreign-owned enterprises as *malinches*— as potential sellouts to the foreigners and to the exploitative system they are thought to represent.

---

fessionals above the going rates, and thirty-two reported paying factory labor above the going rates. See G. L. Reuber, *Private Foreign Investment in Development* (Clarendon, 1973), p. 176.

23. See Teotonio dos Santos, "Foreign Investment and the Large Enterprise in Latin America: The Brazilian Case," in James Petras and Maurice Zeitlin (eds.), *Latin America: Reform or Revolution?* (Fawcett, 1969), pp. 431, 433–35, 453; A. G. Frank, *Capitalism and Underdevelopment in Latin America: Historical Studies of Chile and Brazil* (Monthly Review Press, 1967), pp. 115–19, 273; Celso Furtado, *Diagnosis of the Brazilian Crisis* (University of California Press, 1965), pp. 119–20; James Petras, "Revolution and Guerrilla Movements," in Petras and Zeitlin (eds.), *Latin America*, pp. 7–8, 330–31, 354, 358; P. M. Sweezy, "Notes on the Theory of Imperialism," in *Problems of Economic Dynamics and Planning: Essays in Honor of Michael Kalecki* (Warsaw: Polish Scientific Publishers, 1964), pp. 13, 14, 22, 24; Jeffrey Harrod, "Multinational Corporations, Trade Unions, and Industrial Relations: A Case Study of Jamaica," in Hans Günter (ed.), *Transnational Industrial Relations* (London: Macmillan, 1972), pp. 173–74.

Problems of Distortion

Foreign-owned enterprises have been charged with other types of antisocial behavior as well. Local consumers in the developing countries, it is often said, are being seduced and corrupted because of the introduction of Coca-Cola and Ford motor cars, products reflecting a culture that has no bearing on the value systems of indigenous life.[24] Apart from introducing the "wrong" products, foreigners are often charged with corralling the best talent in the country, sopping up the available supplies of local credit, and generally stifling the opportunities that otherwise would exist for local businessmen.[25] On top of that, they are accused of introducing the wrong techniques: steam shovels instead of hand carts; automatic lathes instead of manual grinders; and so on.[26]

The evidence itself presents a complex story. Take the much-debated issue of the production techniques used by foreign-owned enterprises. In many cases, the elasticity of substitution between capital and labor in less developed countries is very low and the choice of technologies very limited.[27] At times, labor-intensive techniques prove uneconomic, either because they require the use of scarce supervisory and maintenance personnel or because they place severe limits on the short-run elasticity of supply.[28] Even so, the substitution of labor-intensive tech-

24. Ivan Illich, "Outwitting the Developing Countries," *New York Review of Books,* Vol. 13 (November 6, 1969), p. 20.

25. P. B. Evans, "National Autonomy and Economic Development: Critical Perspectives on Multinational Corporations in Poor Countries," *International Organization,* Vol. 25 (Summer 1971), p. 691; Celso Furtado, "La Concentración del poder económico en los EE. UU. y sus proyecciones en America Latina," *Estudios Internacionales* (Santiago), Vol. 1, No. 3–4 (1968); Osvaldo Sunkel, "Big Business and 'Dependencia': A Latin American View," *Foreign Affairs,* Vol. 50 (April 1972), pp. 525, 527–29.

26. Frances Stewart and Paul Streeten, "Conflicts between Output and Employment Objectives in Developing Countries," *Oxford Economic Papers,* Vol. 23 (July 1971), pp. 148–49.

27. Jack Baranson, *Industrial Technologies for Developing Economies* (Praeger, 1969), pp. 15–20; Edwin Mansfield, *The Economics of Technological Change* (Norton, 1968), pp. 10–43; W. P. Strassmann, *Risk and Technological Innovation: American Manufacturing Methods during the Nineteenth Century* (Cornell University Press, 1959), pp. 46–52.

28. Jack Baranson, *Manufacturing Problems in India: The Cummins Diesel Experience* (Syracuse University Press, 1967), p. 112; Christopher Clague, "The Determinants of Efficiency in Manufacturing Industries in an Underdeveloped Country," *Economic Development and Cultural Change,* Vol. 18 (January 1970), pp. 192, 201–02; E. E. Hagen, *The Economics of Development* (Irwin, 1968), p. 421.

niques for capital-intensive methods by foreign-owned enterprises is not uncommon, especially when the means of substitution are readily apparent and when the adjustment is prima facie profitable.[29]

Nevertheless, a problem exists, especially where there is a social reason to substitute labor for capital but no private incentive for the shift. This situation can occur when industrial workers are paid more than their marginal social product because they are able to extract a portion of the employer's rent, or it can occur when the private cost of developing a new production process is higher than the expected private yield. It can also occur on occasion out of sheer inertia or ignorance of local conditions on the part of foreign-owned enterprises. A study of the production techniques in a large sample of manufacturing subsidiaries of foreign firms in Indonesia indicated that some firms were using techniques which made no sense even in terms of private profit. Evidently, in some of these cases, engineers had been allowed to select the technique with which they were most comfortable rather than the technique which was most profitable.[30] In the same vein, a study of the Sierra Leone diamond mining industry makes a case that the industry could efficiently revert to a decentralized pick-and-shovel operation, which would imply the end of large-scale foreign-owned operations.[31] Accordingly, one cannot say that concern regarding the production techniques used by

29. In the Reuber OECD study, mentioned in an earlier footnote, about one-third of 77 projects in less developed areas reported adaptations in production techniques, mainly to adjust to lower volumes of output. See also Baranson, *Industrial Technologies,* pp. 15–20; Clague, "The Determinants of Efficiency," p. 188; J. M. Katz, *Production Functions, Foreign Investment, and Growth: A Study Based on the Argentine Manufacturing Sector, 1946–1971* (Amsterdam: North-Holland Publishing Co., 1969), pp. 185–86; R. Hal Mason, "The Transfer of Technology and the Factor Proportions Problem: The Philippines and Mexico," UNITAR Research Report No. 10 (1971; processed); R. R. Nelson, *A Study of Industrialization in Colombia: Part I, Analysis* (Santa Monica: RAND Corporation, 1967), pp. 15–18; W. P. Strassmann, *Technological Change and Economic Development: The Manufacturing Experience of Mexico and Puerto Rico* (Cornell University Press, 1968), pp. 149–54. But see W. A. Yeoman, "Selection of Production Processes for the Manufacturing Subsidiaries of U.S.-Based Multinational Corporations" (D.B.A. thesis, Harvard University Graduate School of Business, 1968), who distinguishes cases in which substitution is likely from those in which it is not.

30. Louis T. Wells, Jr., "Economic Man and Engineering Man: Choice and Technology in a Low-Wage Country," *Public Policy,* Vol. 21 (Summer 1973), pp. 319–42.

31. Tony Killick and R. W. During, "A Structural Approach to the Balance of Payments of a Low-Income Country," *Journal of Development Studies,* Vol. 5 (July 1969), pp. 274–98.

foreign-owned enterprises is blatantly misplaced. But it can be said that there is an overwhelming propensity on the part of well-trained and well-informed critics to oversimplify the issue and to disregard the nonconforming evidence.

Balance of Payments

Something like the same point can be made with regard to the balance-of-payments consequences of the operations of foreign-owned subsidiaries. Conventional wisdom in the developing countries has it that such operations cause a major drain on the balance of payments of these countries. The demonstration is devastatingly simple: in a given period, for every $1.00 that is moved into such countries as fresh capital by U.S.-owned subsidiaries, according to official U.S. data, some $2.00 to $2.50 is remitted by subsidiaries to their parent firms.[32]

But perhaps this demonstration is simple in another sense. To conclude that foreign investment necessarily represents a balance-of-payments drain involves various fallacies of an elementary sort. The dollar that flows in is not the cause of the $2.00 or $2.50 outflow; that outflow is associated with all the foreign capital that previously was brought into the country. The dollars already at work in the country, however, have various balance-of-payments consequences, particularly effects on the imports and exports of the country in which the investment occurs. That point has been made repeatedly in the literature on the subject, and a number of major efforts have been made to measure the effects. Exercises of this sort are unavoidably complex. For one thing, the analyst is obliged to estimate what the balance-of-payments performance of the country would have been if the investment had not taken place. Beyond that he is obliged to decide how wide a net must be cast in order to capture the secondary balance-of-payments effects of the direct investment, effects that operate through income and price changes. Intuitively, one suspects that over any extended period of time such as ten or fifteen years the secondary effects may be more important than the direct consequences; and further that estimates of such effects are needed for intelligent policy analysis.

The difficulties of measurement are painfully evident as one reviews the most ambitious efforts to date, intended to capture the balance-of-

32. *Survey of Current Business* (March 1972), p. 43.

payments effects of foreign direct investment. Two elaborate efforts of this sort have been made so far. They use essentially similar concepts, though they apply somewhat different techniques in the implementation of the concepts. Both require heroic simplifying assumptions, under-lying the primitive nature of the estimates. In one of the models, for example, the output generated by any foreign investment is reckoned as a simple function of the capital involved; the exports generated by the investment are an unchanging proportion of the estimated output; the domestic component of the investment is assumed to have been diverted from productive uses elsewhere in the local economy; and so on. In short, the process of achieving an explicit method of estimation re-quires—probably unavoidably—gross distortions of reality.

Despite similarities in concept, the two approaches tried so far offer rather different results. One study covers all U.S. direct investments in manufacturing in less developed areas. Basing its estimates on the per-formance patterns of the early 1960s, this study produces results that suggest some net balance-of-payments gain for the less developed coun-tries, the size of the gain depending on one's choice among certain key alternative assumptions.[33] The other study, covering all foreign direct investment in India, the Philippines, Ghana, Guatemala, and Argentina for a five-year period in the mid-1960s, produces more heterogeneous results—but results, on the whole, that suggest balance-of-payments losses more often than balance-of-payments gains.[34] India, with a rigor-ous policy for selecting and policing its foreign investors, does no better in this respect—indeed, does a little worse—than the other countries with their more relaxed policies. All one can say in the end is that the available methods of measurement are too tentative to support any strong generalizations.

For a variety of technical reasons, studies of a similar sort for the raw materials industries are even more difficult; but it seems implausible prima facie that the less developed countries would have fared better in balance-of-payments terms if foreign investments in the major raw

33. Hufbauer and Adler, *Overseas Manufacturing Investment and the Balance of Payments.* Similar results are obtained from a study of 88 sample firms in India, Iran, Kenya, and Jamaica; see Sanjaya Lall, "Balance-of-Payments Effects of Private Foreign Investment in Developing Countries," TD/134/Supp. 1 (UN Conference on Trade and Development, April 1972; processed).

34. Netherlands Economic Institute, "A Quantitative Study on the Macro-Economic Evaluation of Private Foreign Investment in Less-Developed Countries" (Rotterdam, 1972; processed).

materials industries—oil, copper, bauxite, iron ore, and so on—had not been made.[35] In many cases, it is possible to envisage arrangements that might have yielded more positive balance-of-payments effects, assuming the arrangements could be agreed to; but that is a somewhat different question.

In addition to inquiries into the balance-of-payments effects of foreign direct investment, there have been studies of the effects of such investments on exports. Most developing countries give export promotion top social priority. The facts on the export performance of the foreign-owned subsidiaries are well known and adequately documented.

Foreign-owned enterprises currently have a high propensity to export manufactured products from less developed countries—higher than in their own past and higher than seemingly comparable national enterprises.[36] By 1968, for instance, U.S.-owned subsidiaries were responsible for about 40 percent of all exports of manufactured goods from the countries of Latin America. The annual exports of these enterprises amounted to about $750 million, of which more than $210 million went to the United States. Ten years earlier, exports of manufactured goods at that level would have been thought quite unattainable, and the figure would have appeared implausible as a likely development of the decade to follow.

Certain widespread reactions to the growth of these exports from less developed countries, however, underline how little the actual performance of the foreign investors can reduce the sense of dyspepsia with which their presence is received. The main effect of the growth of exports has been simply to change the nature of the questions being asked. The principal questions in the 1970s are these: (1) Are the exports of manufactured goods by foreign-owned subsidiaries in the developing areas, growing though they are, being held back from even higher levels by the restraints that parent firms place upon their subsidiaries in those areas?[37] (2) Is the rapid growth of exports from foreign-owned com-

35. Numerous studies of individual countries or individual commodities exist. For the most part these take a position consistent with the conclusion above. See, for instance, H. D. Huggins, *Aluminium in Changing Communities* (London: André Deutsch, 1965).

36. For a partial summary of the available evidence, see UNCTAD, "Restrictive Business Practices," TD/122/Supp. 1 (January 7, 1972; processed), pp. 26–34; Vernon, *Sovereignty at Bay*, pp. 102–06.

37. See Junta del Acuerdo de Cartagena, "Policies Relating to Technology of the Countries of the Andean Pact: Their Foundations," UNCTAD TD/107 (December 1971; processed), pp. 11–13, 16–17.

panies leading the less developed countries to a new state of dependence on the advanced countries?[38]

Questions such as these, of course, are not captious. They reflect some important concerns and suggest some substantial issues for analysis. The purpose in citing them here is not to cast doubt on their relevance. It is simply to dispel the illusion, if the illusion exists, that foreign-owned enterprises which behave in a manner that is consistent with the articulated social goals of a developing country can expect much easing of the doubts regarding their social performance.

An Unambiguous Abuse

There is one issue, however, on which most of the ambiguities and uncertainties are stripped away, exposing the foreign-owned enterprises to a thoroughly justified charge of abuse of social responsibility. When a U.S. enterprise demands the support of the U.S. government to sustain its operations abroad, it automatically moves into a delicate and difficult area in terms of social responsibility. If that move takes the form of importuning the U.S. government to use clandestine power to protect its private interests in a foreign country, such as the power of the CIA, the risk of social abuse is vastly increased. This, of course, is what ITT was accused of doing in Chile and United Fruit accused of doing in Central America. Even here, black cases can be recast in gray tones. What if the private interests of the enterprise and the public interests of the United States happen to coincide? What if the "pressure" from the firm consists simply of educating the U.S. government to the public implications of the position that the private enterprise is promoting? What if the foreign government itself is exploitative or its actions illegal? Nevertheless, possibilities of this sort still leave a basic point unchanged: a U.S. enterprise that tries to use the power of the United States to thwart the actions of another country in which the enterprise is operating takes on a heavy burden of justification in terms of social responsibility, whether that responsibility is weighed by U.S. interests or by the interests of the other country.

This is not to say that all cases of U.S. government pressure on less developed countries in the interests of a U.S. enterprise are equally censurable. A nation presumably has a right to protect its interests as it sees those interests—even when its actions would affect a less developed

38. G. K. Helleiner, "Manufactured Exports from Less-Developed Countries and Multinational Firms," *Economic Journal,* Vol. 83 (March 1973), pp. 21–47.

country. But some measures of pressure are more easily sanctioned than others. For instance, the Hickenlooper amendment explicitly links the continuation of U.S. foreign aid to any country with prompt and reasonable payment by that country for any U.S.-owned property that has been nationalized. U.S. policies in the international banks of which it is a member, such as the Inter-American Development Bank, often support the same sort of view. Though it may be bad policy, it represents an expression of U.S. will that is explicit and legitimate; its existence is known to any country that agrees to accept U.S. aid; and its application cannot be concealed from public view. A clandestine exercise of pressure without any visible basis of national legitimacy is quite another matter.

Once again, the need for a summary judgment carries us back to a core proposition. What U.S. enterprises actually do in the less developed countries seems generally constructive and socially useful. But their reserve power, as seen from within such countries, is disconcerting. From their viewpoint, large U.S. enterprises are seen as able to shut down installations, ship out capital, or call in the Marines. With the help of the U.S. government, it is thought, they can turn off foreign loans. And if they decide to exercise these reserve powers, as the less developed countries see it, no institution exists that effectively can call them to account.

A Guide for Action

From the point of view of the manager of the multinational enterprise, the issue of social responsibility generally arises in forms and contexts that seem unrelated to much of the discussion so far. For him, the issue usually takes more narrow and more explicit forms. Should a pharmaceutical enterprise label its exports to Latin America according to the stringent disclosure requirements of United States law; or should it follow the much more relaxed disclosure norms of its competitors in the Latin American market? Should a U.S. firm in South Africa conform to the apartheid practices of the country; or should it violate those practices?

The Manager's Dilemma

When the issue that arises can be judged by some universal standard of social responsibility—some standard acceptable to most people in most civilized societies—the problem is relatively simple. In those cases, managers are indistinguishable from anybody else. They follow the socially responsible course without much conscious thought. And if they do not, no purpose is served by simply asserting that they should.

But that is the easy case. In most situations, there is no such thing as a social standard that is universally acceptable. Conflicts over social responsibility generally arise between parties who are equally convinced of the social rightness of their positions. Muslims slew Christians as an act of social responsibility; Christians responded with the total conviction that they too were slaying for the public good. Doctrinaire communists are convinced that socialism is indispensable for a healthy society; doctrinaire capitalists that socialism is a threat to society.

The fact that social goals are not universally agreed upon has particular force when foreign operations are involved. For in those cases, the possibility that two sets of social norms may be in conflict is especially great. In these situations, where the question is one of personal or societal values, scholarship has very little to offer in the making of choices.

Where scholarship can help, however, is in identifying what some given course of conduct by managers is likely to do to the future of their enterprises. It matters to the manager whether the pursuit of some social objective in which he believes will be costly to his enterprise or, on the contrary, will leave the risks and opportunities of the enterprise little changed.

The preceding pages suggest a summary conclusion. Powerful enterprises that seem in a position to exercise choice are bound to create tensions wherever they operate. Whether the existence of those tensions will prove dangerous for the enterprise depends in part on how useful the enterprise appears to the country in which it is operating. Enterprises whose activities seem critical to the host country derive their basic survival strength from that fact; those that seem less critical to the fortunes of the country are more vulnerable. Conspicuous enterprises, such as public utilities, may be a little more vulnerable than those that are not; enterprises that deemphasize their foreignness a little less vulnerable than those that are egregiously foreign. But the primary factor in estimating the survival capabilities of the enterprise is the value that the host country places on it.

Generalizations of this sort are almost impossible to test in some objective way.[39] They frame themselves largely out of unstructured experi-

39. Essentially the same views, however, appear in United Nations, "Multi-

ence. Still, it helps to recall some of the cases that contribute to the formulation of the conclusion.

The case of the International Petroleum Company (IPC) in Peru, cited earlier, is pertinent. Though at times in its long history in Peru it was linked with some of the country's more notorious dictators, the company's social policies at the time of nationalization were in many respects a model of responsibility. The Achilles' heel of the company was the fact that it finally appeared to the Peruvians to have outlived much of its usefulness to Peru; its oil for the most part was being consumed inside Peru, and its exports were being sold in an international market where constant high demand seemed to eliminate the need for special marketing skills. As a purveyor of Peruvian oil to Peruvians, IPC was exposed to all the special disabilities of a public utility, including the need to raise its prices from time to time.

Illustrations of many sorts lead to the same conclusion. In 1964, Kennecott Copper Corporation startled the international copper industry by its offer to sell a majority of the equity in its Chilean copper mines to the Chilean government. A few years later, when the Chilean government felt itself in a position to nationalize, no distinction was made between Kennecott and the others. The Kennecott initiative, in fact, was widely interpreted in some Chilean quarters as a subtle device by which the company sought to prolong its exploitation of the Chilean economy. On similar lines, United Fruit's efforts to dispose of its landholdings in Central America has commonly invoked the response that it is trying to avoid its social responsibilities; so have the efforts of oil and mining companies when they sought to relieve themselves of quasi-governmental functions in the operation of company towns in Latin America.

On a more general level, the degree of progressiveness and modernity of concession agreements seems to have had little to do with the degree of vulnerability. The modern service contracts of foreign oil companies in Argentina during the 1960s suffered much the same fate as the old-fashioned concession agreements in that country in the 1950s. The relatively modern Libyan and Algerian concession arrangements in oil have proved no less vulnerable than more anachronistic arrangements in Iraq and Saudi Arabia.

There may be excellent reasons why foreign investors should attempt

---

national Corporations in World Development" (New York: UN Department of Economic and Social Affairs, 1973; processed).

to tailor their activities to what they believe to be the social requirements of the host countries; but there is no evidence to suggest that such efforts will greatly bolster their security in a country. If the host country is fundamentally concerned with the latent power of the foreign enterprise and if the host country reckons that the foreign enterprise is expendable, then the efforts of the enterprise to adhere to social norms will not change the situation very much. Such efforts may lead to nothing more than finding new grounds on which to charge the foreign-owned enterprise with failing in its responsibilities.

For example, if U.S. drug companies should decide to adhere to U.S. labeling standards in the sale of their products abroad, they would be unwise to assume that they could count on escaping criticism. Rather, they might be charged in the importing country with administering an implied rebuke to the local government for failing to protect its consumers adequately; or they might be charged with imperiling all sellers in the local market in ways that powerful foreign firms can afford but fledgling local firms cannot. Any U.S. company that decides to avoid apartheid practices within the limits of South Africa's tolerance must count on being charged from some quarters with holding back; and if such a company manages to get itself ousted, it must anticipate that it will be charged from other quarters with abandoning the Bantu.[40] If foreign enterprises raise local wages, they must be prepared to be accused of trying to hold local labor in thrall; if they increase local exports, of increasing the dependence of the local economy upon them; if they train local workers or give jobs to those that are trained, of monopolizing local talent.

There are occasional situations in which I feel convinced that, in the name of social responsibility, enterprises should conform to a standard of conduct more stringent than simple adherence to the law. But these are the easy cases, simple in their effects. Most cases are much too difficult for such unambiguous reactions; they involve impossible problems of projection, or they affect important social values in different directions. In those cases pressures on the enterprise are likely to come from one faction or another in the dispute, not from all. When an enterprise bends to pressure in such cases, the reason for bending can generally be found in the capacity of some group to pinch the enterprise

40. This is a familiar dilemma for those who wish to influence events through protest. See A. O. Hirschman, *Exit, Voice, and Loyalty* (Harvard University Press, 1970), pp. 120–26.

where it hurts, not in the intrinsic merits of their case. There is no reason to assume that businessmen who bend in these cases will be contributing to social welfare. The managers of the enterprise may decide to bend as a measure of expediency; they may even manage to persuade themselves that their response is motivated by a sense of social responsibility. But the outside observer is likely to find the tie much more ambiguous.

Still, men will often have to make choices in circumstances that are muddy and complex; and the choices they make can be of considerable importance both to themselves as individuals and to certain kinds of social values. In these cases, scholarship can rarely justify one choice over another either by demonstrating some objectively superior set of social values or by demonstrating an increased chance for survival. On the other hand, there is a more modest objective to which scholarship can make a contribution. Exacerbating the problem of social responsibility is the fact that the presence of powerful multinational enterprises generates a high level of tension. If it can be presumed that a reduction in the tension associated with the presence of the multinational enterprise is a useful step, what measures will contribute to that end?

The Standard Proposals

There have been numerous proposals for reducing the tensions associated with the presence of U.S. enterprises overseas. Some of them have been aimed precisely at increasing the accountability of the enterprises.

One such approach is the voluntary "code of good behavior." Proposals vary, but in general they bind foreign enterprises to do what presumably they are already doing of their own accord: obey the law, behave like modern employers, and contribute to good works. As noted earlier, U.S. enterprises operating overseas appear to pay their taxes, train and promote their employees, and keep out of local politics. Where side payments to government officials are unavoidable as part of the normal process of doing business, one has the impression that these enterprises make the necessary payments reluctantly and without joy. But, despite occasional anti-corruption rhetoric in less developed countries, that is not where the main concern of these countries lies; their main concern is with the potential impact if the full reserve powers of the multinational enterprise or of the parent firm's government were ever put in play. Accordingly, although the sentiment behind codes of good behavior is probably helpful, their content is close to irrelevant to the issues that concern us here.

Another common proposal is that foreign enterprises should set up their subsidiaries as joint ventures with local interests. There are some good reasons why managers should consider joint ventures. The best of these reasons is that, at the present stage of history, many countries prefer such arrangements to firms owned wholly by foreigners. But that preference does not stem from any solid evidence that joint ventures are superior in economic and social terms.

The most careful studies of joint ventures to date lead to a number of fairly explicit conclusions.[41] One is that the choice of joint ventures by foreign enterprises has been quite rational and systematic as a rule and has depended on the strategic problems of the industry, as well as certain characteristics of the firm and the country involved. Another conclusion is that the economic benefits to the country receiving the enterprise are indeed affected by the choice between joint ventures and subsidiaries owned entirely by outsiders—but that the benefits to the country are not necessarily higher if the subsidiary is jointly owned.

Moreover, the assumption that the presence of a local partner increases the social responsibility of a foreign-owned operation is exceedingly vulnerable. Local private partners often have less concern for the social objectives of a country than do their foreign associates, perhaps because local partners feel less exposed to the threat of sanctions. When such partners do have an active social concern, it may be expressed in goals that are oriented to a given social class or regional area; local partners may, for instance, be far more concerned with national growth than with national income distribution. Even if their social concerns coincide with those of the nation for the time being, those concerns run a major risk of being rendered obsolete by changes in the country itself. In some countries, including India, Pakistan, and Chile, local partners have already come under attack as native robber barons.[42] In short, the case for joint ventures—as a mechanism of survival or as a channel of social accountability—is dubious.

Still another suggestion that has been made from time to time is that foreign-based enterprises would be more conscientious about social responsibilities if they agreed from the very beginning to sell off their equity interests over some stated number of years.[43] As a matter of fact,

41. The most definitive studies so far are found in J. M. Stopford and L. T. Wells, Jr., *Managing the Multinational Enterprise* (Basic Books, 1972).
42. Sunkel, "Big Business and 'Dependencia,'" pp. 525, 527–29.
43. A. O. Hirschman, *A Bias for Hope: Essays on Development and Latin America* (Yale University Press, 1971), pp. 243–48.

that principle has been explicitly incorporated in a treaty among the countries of the Andean bloc.[44] Divestiture may well be a way of increasing the social accountability of an enterprise, especially if good marks in the actual operation of the enterprise will mean a postponement of the date when divestiture occurs. Still, though the divestiture approach does have certain possibilities, it also has some very distinct limitations.

For one thing, a policy of divestiture generally operates on the implicit assumption that there is an assured time when a country will want to be rid of the foreign enterprise. That assumption is not always consistent with the facts. In some of the mature oligopolies, especially those characterized by very large economies of scale and by a considerable degree of vertical integration, a fruitful interdependence between the multinational enterprises and the countries in which they operate can last for long periods. The importance of that tie is illustrated repeatedly and in different contexts. For instance, socialist Guinea decided to turn to the leading aluminum companies for help in developing its bauxite resources.[45]

Practically all oil-producing countries have used the oil shortage with outstanding success to play off the international oil companies against one another. But none has gone so far as to cut its marketing ties to the major oil companies. There is still the latent concern, probably well justified, that those ties may yet be needed. Because of disconcerting experiences with selling in a free copper market, Chile apparently continues to use some of the channels of distribution that existed before nationalization.[46]

More generally, divestiture smacks at times of a policy of throwing out the baby with the bath water. The more promising approach is to try to achieve the advantages of multinationality while avoiding its tensions. One has to face the fact, for instance, that a local facility established by an international producer of automobiles or of electrical equip-

44. Resolution No. 24 adopted by the Andean Common Market. For a summary of substance and implications, see R. A. Diaz, "The Andean Common Market," *Columbia Journal of World Business,* Vol. 6 (July–August 1971), pp. 22–28.

45. Philip Farin and G. G. Reibsamen (eds.), *Aluminum: Profile of an Industry* (New York: Metals Week, 1969), pp. 10, 27.

46. Moran, "The Multinational Corporation and the Politics of Development: The Case of Copper in Chile, 1945–1970"; Alan Angell, "Allende's First Year in Chile," *Current History,* Vol. 62 (February 1972), pp. 76–78.

ment is rarely efficient as a self-contained entity; its position as a member of a multinational enterprise generally implies that it is reliant on others in the system for some critical resource—a flow of technology, a scarce intermediate product, access to markets, or some other critical factor. Otherwise, there would be no particular advantage in the creation of a multinational structure.[47]

The divestiture formula, however, may well apply to cases in which a local subsidiary is in a position progressively to reduce its organic ties to the multinational system without great losses in economic efficiency. Such cases do exist, as history indicates. But they are found as a rule in industries in which technology and markets have become fairly static and in which scale economies are limited, as well as in industries whose products are sold entirely on the basis of a trade name. In these cases, a sloughing-off process could be encouraged, either by a deliberate policy of the government or by the initiative of the foreign enterprises. If such a policy were developed, it could achieve some of the social benefits of a divestiture policy while avoiding some of the costs.

Still, the basic problem remains. How can the seeming reserve power of the foreign-owned enterprise be made to lose some of its threatening quality, so that the tension associated with the presence of the subsidiary is reduced?

Genuine Reduction in Tension

The fundamental problem in reducing the tension that is generated by the presence of the multinational enterprise is that few countries, operating alone, are in a position to do much about it. Though there are many situations in which countries can hurt such enterprises by repressive action, such action generally entails a certain amount of injury for the country itself. Even if that were not the case, the unilateral action of any country could easily hurt others. For that reason, the policy maker who wants to reduce the tension while retaining the benefits that are associated with the activities of multinational enterprises finds his thoughts turning to the possibility of joint international action.

In some cases, relevant international action relating to the multi-

47. That fact also indicates why great gaps often separate the evaluation placed on a subsidiary by a parent firm from the evaluation by a host country. By the parent, the company is viewed as part of a larger system; by the country, as a disjointed entity.

national enterprise would have to cast its net wider than the multinational enterprise alone. That fact is illustrated by the problem of "hot money" flows. Many types of institutions besides the multinational enterprise are involved in such flows, and the appropriate remedy in the end is bound to be one that is very far-reaching in scope.

On the other hand, there are various other areas of policy in which joint international action could be considered explicitly in relation to the multinational enterprise. There have been many proposals along these lines.[48] A common weakness of these proposals is their excessive generality and simplicity. The special problems associated with the multinational enterprise cover the whole range of issues ordinarily associated with industrial policy: taxation, competition, technology transfer, labor relations, and so on. No single international institution and no simple set of principles can address so wide a range of issues. An effective set of policies will require, in the end, a very wide range of institutions and agreements.

One category of agreement which would have salutary consequences would aim at preventing governments from directly influencing the behavior of the overseas subsidiaries of their home enterprises in certain specified fields of activity, such as the fields of antitrust, of security controls, and of investment; the possibility of developing such agreements is fairly real, especially if they were confined in the first instance to the more advanced countries. Another source of tension would be reduced if governments could be brought to agree that enterprises were explicitly barred from calling on the diplomatic support of the parent firm's government to defend subsidiaries in foreign countries. It would be too much to ask the home companies—even if they were imbued with an intense desire to discharge their social responsibilities—to surrender their subsidiaries wholly to the mercies of foreign governments. But if there were international agreement on the principle that subsidiaries could not have recourse to the government of the parent company, it

48. For example, P. M. Goldberg and C. P. Kindleberger, "Toward a GATT for Investment: A Proposal for Supervision of the International Corporation," *Law and Policy in International Business,* Vol. 2 (Summer 1970), pp. 295–323. See also the testimony of Heribert Maier, for the International Confederation of Free Trade Unions, before the Joint Economic Committee of the U.S. Congress, July 28, 1970, as reproduced in "The International Free Trade Union Movement and Multinational Corporations," *ICFTU Economic and Social Bulletin,* Vol. 18 (August 1970); C. Fred Bergsten and others, *Reshaping the International Economic Order* (Brookings Institution, 1972), p. 2.

might be possible at the same time to agree on some international body to which the enterprises could have recourse, along with some standards to guide such a body.

Each of the suggestions proposed in the last few sentences would demand some form of international organization for its application, with all the inadequacies which organizations of that sort entail. But even if the arrangements were much less than wholly effective, their capacity to deal equitably with the interests of the foreign-owned enterprises could easily be an improvement over the primitive system of remedies that now exists.[49]

Another contribution to social accountability could be made by improving the system under which governments levy taxes on multinational enterprises. As matters now stand, there is both incentive and opportunity for such enterprises to slip between the various taxing jurisdictions. That well-known fact has bred dark suspicions in the minds of many countries; as a result, the enterprises are probably credited with more success in their tax-avoiding efforts than they have so far managed to achieve. Such suspicions could be allayed by international agreements aimed at two objectives: providing national tax authorities with better data, notably data on the operations of the multinational enterprise outside the taxing jurisdiction, whenever such outside operations affect the reported profit of the unit that is being taxed; and establishing rules of the game regarding the treatment of those items of income and expense in which multinational enterprises now have the greatest scope for arbitrary choice. The rules of the game would have to address such difficult issues as the fixing of transfer prices in transactions between parent and subsidiary, the use of debt and equity as the means of financing subsidiaries, the allocation of fixed charges to units of the multinational enterprise, the charging of royalties among affiliated units, and a number of other complex issues.

Even if the taxing authorities received the necessary data for their purposes, however, many larger questions of disclosure would remain. As matters stand today, many governments have exercised their power to

---

49. Some readers will be aware that one multinational approach to the problem has already been tried and proved sterile, in the form of a Convention on the Settlement of Investment Disputes between States and Nationals of Other States, administered under the aegis of the World Bank. But that approach is much more limited in subject matter and more lopsided in application than what is suggested here.

demand disclosure on the bits or pieces of the multinational enterprise that fall inside their jurisdiction. But none—not even the government in the country of the parent company—demands data that effectively describe the operations of the multinational enterprise as a whole. This is a source of the frustration and misgiving on the part of the national interests that confront such enterprises. Yet it is a problem that can be solved in principle by appropriate international agreements.

Still another kind of international agreement seems needed to deal with the problem of competitive inducements which various countries offer in their efforts to attract multinational enterprises. Those inducements commonly take the form of tax exemptions, capital grants, and subsidies. There are some circumstances in which measures of this sort would receive international acceptance; but in most cases, countries are being forced into such competition by the uninhibited acts of rivals. The effect is to generate tension and resentment, initially in the countries that feel deprived of the investment, eventually in the country that provides the inducement. This is an obvious field for joint international action. In this case, the object of such action would be to sort out and to sanction situations in which some social purpose was being served by such devices, while eliminating the cases in which countries were being forced into granting such fiscal favors by the competition of other countries.

Various other possibilities of this sort offer some promise of reducing the reserve power of the multinational enterprise and increasing its social accountability. Constraints could be placed on the powers now exercised by multinational enterprises, and some of those powers might be shifted to national governments and intergovernmental organizations. The possibility of shifting powers has a special bearing on the conduct of the mature oligopolies, where leaders often act in the role of price setters and market regulators. Proposals to shift such powers to public hands are based on the assumption that if prices and quantities must be decided so as to promote some social goal, the apparatus for that decision should be an apparatus with explicit social responsibilities. Otherwise, as in the case of the oil crisis, the actions of the enterprises will be condemned as an arrogation of power. To be sure, the probability that governments would botch the job in any individual case is quite considerable; their lack of expertise, their diversity of interests, their willingness to respond to narrow industrial and regional pressures, would no doubt get in the way of effective negotiation and effective administration. But these problems are not mitigated by delegating social tasks to private instrumentalities whose responsibilities run in quite different directions.[50]

A closely related proposal is that governments should be encouraged to set up more effective international instruments for the control of restrictive business practices. Proposals of this sort have been developed intermittently since the International Trade Organization charter of 1948. As a rule, they have been looked on by U.S. business with hostility. Some of the grounds for that hostility, such as the fear that state-owned enterprises would be allowed more freedom than private enterprises, have a basis in fact. But much of the hostility has been based simply on an unwillingness on the part of business to be accountable to yet another regulatory body, especially a regulatory body whose political and philosophical character would reflect the interests of countries other than the United States. The resistance of business to an international approach is easy enough to understand; yet unless some system of international accountability is developed, the only curb on the latent power of business to do social harm through restrictive arrangements will be the conflicting and haphazard measures of individual countries.

Though enterprises engaged in foreign operations will confront the problems of social accountability in a good many different contexts over the next decade or so, some of the most challenging problems will relate to the exploitation of the international sea bed and of outer space.[51] Given the industrial capabilities of U.S. enterprises, they are bound to be among the leaders in frontier activities of this sort. If present trends continue, for instance, they will be among the principal agents through which oil and minerals will be taken from international waters. And if the U.S. enterprises involved exhibit the instincts that govern most organizations when they are leading the race, their tolerance for measures of accountability—especially measures of an international sort— will be very limited. The vested interests in preventing international regu-

50. The Teheran agreement of 1971, which effectively determined the price of world oil, is a case in point. In this case, negotiations over the terms at which the world would buy its oil from that area were conducted between the leading oil companies and the leading oil-producing countries. But neither of these parties was charged with representing the social interests of the consuming countries. Indeed, though their debate was exceedingly complex, it was largely that of two groups of partners struggling over the division of rewards from the sale of the oil.

51. The scope and immediacy of these developments are well described in E. B. Skolnikoff, *The International Imperatives of Technology* (Berkeley: University of California Institute of International Studies, 1972).

lation will soon be formidable. Yet if a regulatory mechanism is not established, costly and perhaps even tragic consequences may follow; the political frictions and the ecological costs could be enormous.

Social responsibility on the part of multinational enterprises may oblige them to recognize that any private organization which is capable of the exercise of substantial power should be accountable to some effective public authority and that, when the private organization is multinational in scope, the public authority probably will have to be multinational, in order to be effective. So far, principles of this sort have played no role in the extensive discussions of businessmen over the issue of social responsibility. Nor can they be expected to unless and until the unilateral and uncoordinated acts of numerous national governments seem seriously to threaten the vitality of the multinational enterprises. Then, a system of multinational public control may be seen as the lesser threat.

CHAPTER TWELVE

Management and the Employee

CHARLES A. MYERS

DURING the American anthracite strike of 1902, when the mineowners' intransigence was generally considered to have caused the stoppage, a Wilkes-Barre, Pennsylvania, photographer implored George F. Baer, president of one of the railroads controlling the mines, to be more conciliatory, as a "Christian gentleman," in his dealings with the mineworkers' union. Baer's letter of reply assured the photographer that "the rights and interests of the laboring man will be protected and cared for, not by labor agitators, but by the Christian men to whom God in his infinite wisdom has given control of the property interests of the country."[1]

In the 1970s, nearly three-quarters of a century later, such views on the treatment of employees are rare. Business is expected by its employees and impelled by present social values to do more than it was expected to do even twenty-five years ago. Some of the new expectations have developed out of enlightened self-interest in the pursuit of business goals; some have been the consequence of legislation and administrative action, and some have come as the result of various social pressures. The range of choices and alternatives open to businessmen and managers in this context is a central theme of this chapter.

What Employers Are Expected to Provide

Some of the goals and values that business is expected to work toward today with respect to employees are more difficult to achieve than are others. Progressive firms, particularly the larger and more visible ones which are often the pacesetters, have made many of the goals and values

1. Quoted in Herbert Harris, *American Labor* (Yale University Press, 1938), pp. 126–27.

311

discussed below part of their published personnel policies with the strong support of top management. They have understood how a firm may maximize profits over the long run by special concern for the human component in the organization. Some of these may be oligopolistic firms, protected somewhat from competitive pressures, and some may have relatively low labor costs as a percentage of total costs. Most other firms are followers, pulled along by the example of the leaders, by the need to compete for workers, and by various external forces or pressures.

A number of goals apply to employees as productive members of the business organization.[2] Employers are expected to provide sufficient pay, job content, job security, and other job satisfactions to enable employees to achieve some of their personal goals through work. There has been increasing concern for what is considered "meaningful work" which gives employees a feeling of personal achievement and job accomplishment. This is related to opportunities for employee training and development within the organization to realize one's full potential. Increasingly, firms are providing opportunities for employees at various occupational levels to participate in some way in the process of reaching decisions which directly affect them; collective bargaining being one method and informal consultation prior to decision making another.

Employers are also expected to reduce social inequality by providing more jobs and promotions for nonwhites and for women. Working mothers look for day-care facilities for preschool children. Jobs and conditions of employment which are safe from week to week and not injurious to health in the long run are also expected by employees. Employers are becoming more involved in handling problems of employee alcoholism, emotional disturbance, and drug addiction, as illnesses to be treated rather than offenses to be punished.

Employees displaced by technological change, plant or office relocation, and plant or office closing are increasingly protected by job retraining, relocation allowances, severance pay related to prior employment, and assistance in finding new employment. Finally, employees as producers expect adequate retirement incomes after long service, and they seek earlier vesting of pension rights for those who are laid off or who quit before retirement. Protection against pension fund defaults and making earlier retirement attractive are increasingly expected.

2. Most of these goals and values are equally applicable to employees of nonprofit organizations in the private sector and of governmental organizations.

For employees as "citizens" of the industrial or business community, employers are expected to provide some established or formal procedure for hearing and acting upon complaints and grievances. The right of appeal to higher levels, without discrimination, is part of this goal. Employers are expected to recognize the right of employees to organize and bargain collectively through unions, to choose by majority vote which union (if any) shall represent them, and to carry on union activities without employer harassment.

The right to strike if agreement on a new contract cannot be reached after collective bargaining is less contested now than formerly by American businessmen, except perhaps in those cases where it can be clearly shown that the public health or safety is seriously threatened. When strikes are ruled out for reasons of public safety, alternative procedures are expected to be available for settling disputes; increasingly this is true of collective bargaining in the public sector. Organized employees expect voluntary and binding arbitration of disputes (grievances) arising under collective agreements.

Finally, certain goals or values have emerged for dealing with employees as citizens in the wider community or society. For example, employers are often expected to encourage employee participation (without loss of pay) in community affairs such as community fund drives, special school activities, interracial councils, minority employment efforts, assistance to minority businesses. Some firms are experimenting with paid leaves of absence for social service.[3] Correspondingly, employers are expected to be attentive to the social concerns which employees as citizens may have about the firm's responsibility to the wider society, in environmental improvement, in contributions to improve education, and in undertaking some socially useful activities in the local community. Some employees also expect to "blow the whistle" on what they consider to be morally questionable U.S. business activities (accepting apartheid in South Africa is a current example) without affecting their continued employee status. These kinds of goals and values arising in employer-

3. In 1972, the Xerox Corporation announced a special leave program with the statement, "If you think you can help our world a little, Xerox will help you." Twenty-one employees were chosen from two hundred applicants for leaves of absence with pay of up to one year, for a variety of specific projects outside the company. Favorable initial reports led the company to announce continuance of the program in 1973. *New York Times,* July 14, 1972. See also Grace J. Finley, *Policies on Leaves for Political and Social Action* (New York: Conference Board, 1972).

employee relations raise new questions about the traditional goals of business organizations.

To some readers, this review of goals and values in employer-employee relations for the early 1970s may seem impractical or excessively liberal. But if any businessmen consider this list unrealistic, let them ponder the fact that pressures in these directions are growing, like it or not, and those who embrace the new expectations may have a comparative advantage in employee performance and productivity over the laggard firms. And if, as the Opinion Research Corporation reported in June 1972, "Americans have been turning sour on America—on its dreams, its promises, its leaders," then business must strive to regain the allegiance of employees.[4] This involves initiative and risk-taking; the result is never guaranteed.

Changes during the Past Fifty Years

Since the 1920s, there have been dramatic changes in business conceptions of the firm's responsibilities to the employee. If there had been *no* changes over that period, business would be having many more problems with employees than it does now.

Before 1920, the scientific management approach to productivity took hold. The movement's father was Frederick W. Taylor, whose book *The Principles of Scientific Management* (1916) emphasized planning and simplification of tasks through analysis of employee motions, materials, and equipment; "the scientific selection of the workman" (p. 43); training and development of the worker; and compensation of his efforts by a straight piece-rate system. Though Taylor stressed friendly cooperation between management and workers, both unorganized and organized workers often opposed the imposition of scientific management, especially as it was practiced by some industrial engineers. The scientific management approach persists up to the present, but it has been modified by this opposition. Moreover, the work force no longer contains the high proportion of immigrants and unskilled laborers it did in Taylor's day.

Concurrent with Taylorism in the early 1920s was an alternative

4. *Business Week,* No. 2233 (June 17, 1972), p. 100. The American Management Association later reported that nearly two out of three industrial companies feel they have serious "corporate image" problems. *Business Week,* No. 2246 (September 16, 1972), p. 70.

emphasis on employee welfare and employer paternalism. Some leading employers improved plant health facilities, added lunchrooms, lockers and washrooms, and recreation programs, and provided modest group insurance and pension programs. These employers hoped their benevolence would increase the loyalty of employees and lead them to resist the blandishments of unions. Such employers became somewhat disillusioned when programs arranged for employees did not increase efficiency or win their undying loyalty.

Some large employers in the 1920s also sought to avoid outside unionism by the establishment of employee representation plans. During the 1920s union membership declined as a result of employer policies as well as lack of government protection of the right of employees to join unions. With the passage of the National Labor Relations Act (Wagner Act) in 1935, however, these company-dominated organizations were considered an "unfair labor practice," as were other employer efforts to discourage employees from forming and joining unions. The rapid rise of the strength of organized labor subsequent to 1937, when the Wagner Act was held constitutional by the Supreme Court, led in turn to the growth of the professional industrial relations function in management. Though many progressive firms had much earlier established personnel departments, drawing in part from the earlier experience with "employment management" in the period before and after 1920, the personnel function also came fully into its own after the mid-1930s.

In some firms, personnel administration and the concurrent management interest in better "human relations" in the enterprise were designed to avoid outside unionism as well as to improve employee productivity. In other firms, the principal objective of personnel administration was to provide an organizational climate in which employees could satisfy more of their needs and satisfactions through work. At the same time, development of human resources rather than simply better human relations as such was the central focus of the personnel administration effort, seen as a staff function and as a line management *responsibility*. Industrial relations in the union-management perspective became more professional as skilled negotiators gained vice-presidential status in many large firms and as staff specialists were added to advise line management in handling grievances and negotiations in others.

These developments are continuing, for business has come to accept the importance of the human factor in management and, in unionized industries, the idea of a pluralistic system of industrial relations in which management, organized labor, and government all play a role. Any generalization along these lines must be qualified by the observation that there is a vast difference between what some firms have done voluntarily (because they believe that personnel administration and industrial relations efforts improve their competitive advantage through better-motivated employees) and what other firms have done reluctantly when forced to give up unchecked managerial authority or paternalism. Even among the reluctant, however, the goals and values outlined earlier are supported by more than external pressures such as government decrees and labor shortages. Certain management concepts have developed that legitimize the new personnel policies.

The Influence of Management Concepts on Business Policies

Among the most important emerging management concepts over the past twenty-five years which have encouraged business to adopt progressive employment policies are the following.

1. Much of the writing and research in the behavioral sciences gives support to managerial styles and organizational structures that offer wider scope to employee initiative and self-motivation. Earlier, industrial psychology emphasized individual employee differences, but probably the first major study which brought out the importance of *group* behavior as a response to managerial leadership was the book by F. J. Roethlisberger and W. J. Dickson, *Management and the Worker* (1940), based on extensive research in the Western Electric Company. Even more influential in management thinking were the later books of Douglas McGregor, *The Human Side of Enterprise* (1960) and *The Professional Manager* (1967); Rensis Likert, *New Patterns of Management* (1961) and *The Human Organization* (1967); and Robert R. Blake and Jane H. S. Mouton, *The Managerial Grid: Key Orientations for Achieving Production through People* (1964). All of these stressed the value to the enterprise of a managerial approach which encouraged self-development and self-motivation of employees. For the past decade, such concepts have been used in many management training and development programs within enterprises, in management organizations, and in many university executive development programs.[5]

5. The chief executive of Westinghouse, in lectures at Carnegie-Mellon Uni-

2. Systematic wage and salary administration, utilizing job evaluation techniques and pay surveys to relate the internal compensation structure to the external labor market, is now widely used in business. Foreshadowed by wage and salary controls during World War II, these procedures have been utilized by management to reduce inequities in the compensation structure and to establish rates on new jobs as they occur through changes in machinery, processes, or products.

3. In contrast with the paternalism of the 1920s, fringe benefits, often negotiated with unions, have spread as a part of the compensation structure, usually related to length of an employee's service with the company. These benefits include protection against the high costs of medical care, unemployment compensation and retirement pay (often vested) supplementary to federal social security, group life insurance, paid holidays and vacations, and seniority protection against arbitrary layoff and recall. Nonunion firms may have gone further in providing more generous employee benefits such as profit sharing, partly to avoid unionization. Provisions for early retirement have been negotiated for blue-collar workers in the auto, steel, and other industries, and many more firms have voluntarily offered early retirement pensions. The four-day, forty-hour week is also spreading slowly among smaller companies, as is "flexible working time."

4. Experience and research on management approaches to constructive labor-management relations have had the effect of reducing animosity in this relationship over the past twenty years. Case studies written under the auspices of the National Planning Association (and published in an NPA series called "Causes of Industrial Peace under Collective Bargaining") had wide circulation among businessmen in the 1950s, as have other studies and reports from seminars run by management associations. At the same time, more managers have taken the initiative in negotiations, rather than simply reacting to union demands. Typically, the agreement that results is less the outcome of a win-lose contest and more a pact in which both parties have gained something and have laid the basis for reasonably harmonious day-to-day relationships. The concepts of joint consultation, human relations committees, and labor-management cooperation to increase productivity (the Scanlon Plan) have been limited in application but influential in affecting management thinking about the relationship.

---

versity, recently endorsed Likert's emphasis on employee-centered management. See Donald C. Burnham, *Productivity Improvement* (Carnegie Press, 1973).

5. At the same time, there has been growing acceptance of employee rights in jobs, including some form of job security and a procedure for redress of grievances. Faced with the human costs of economic change, more businesses have negotiated advance notice, severance pay, transfer and relocation to other company plants, and job retraining provisions in their agreements with unions. Sometimes assistance to displaced employees has been offered voluntarily, and sometimes heavy union pressure has been brought to bear, but in any case the concept has become familiar. The general level of employment in the economy and the level of employment in the specific industry are especially important where relocation and dislocation are at issue. Declining firms and industries, such as the railroads, face more difficult problems than do those which are more stable or expanding. In particular, industries faced with severe foreign competition need to increase productivity and reduce unit labor costs, and this requires union understanding of the employment implications of remaining competitive. On the other hand, economic factors are less pertinent in developing effective procedures for redress of grievances—a basic employee right which is now widely recognized through negotiated multistep grievance procedures in unionized firms and with fewer formalities in nonunion businesses. (Some firms, however, still believe that the "open door" of the chief executive is all that is necessary.)

The significance of the above five points is simply that there is an important role for business *voluntarism* in meeting standards of responsibility toward employees. Many of the goals listed in the opening section of this chapter—those having to do with employees as producers and as citizens of the industrial or business community—are now considered legitimate by many firms which have been influenced by the concepts just reviewed. This development is clearly strengthened by the conviction that employees are more committed to the goals of the enterprise when management holds and practices these concepts. Employee commitment is vital for the survival of jobs in highly competitive firms and industries.

Governmental Efforts and Policies

The federal government, more than most state governments, has through legislation and administrative agencies imposed obligations on business with respect to employees, although some firms have moved ahead of legislative developments in their employee relations. Apart from the legislation on unions and collective bargaining which dates back to the 1930s, most of the laws have been passed within the last decade. Not all are punitive; a considerable educational effort is involved, and voluntary compliance is generally preferred to enforcement proceedings. Here again, the range of alternatives open to business is broad: many employers make an effort to observe the spirit of the new laws and change their previous practices; some resist or drag their feet and then find themselves faced with punitive actions to bring compliance. Generally, there is more enforcement in the period immediately after new legislation than in succeeding years, when more firms realize that there are positive values in the objectives sought by the legislation. Changes within the labor force have also encouraged compliance.

Civil Rights Legislation and Enforcement

Perhaps the most dramatic legislative development affecting employer-employee relations in the past decade was the passage of the Civil Rights Act in 1964, with the establishment of the Equal Employment Opportunity Commission (EEOC) and the subsequent establishment of the Office of Federal Contract Compliance (OFCC). Some firms had already made commitments voluntarily to "Plans for Progress," but others needed the prodding of EEOC and OFCC.

A number of states also developed antidiscrimination laws and agencies, with power to issue enforcement orders. Title VII of the Civil Rights Act of 1964 dealing with employment discrimination was amended by the Equal Employment Opportunity Act of 1972 (effective March 24, 1972) to provide stronger enforcement powers for the EEOC. This agency may now seek an order in a federal district court if it is unable to secure an acceptable conciliation agreement within thirty days after the filing of a charge under the act.

Prior to 1972, the commission's enforcement authority was limited to informal methods of conference, conciliation, and persuasion, and only the aggrieved individual had the remedy of going to court. The failure of voluntary conciliation, according to a review by the Senate Labor Committee, was reflected in the EEOC workload. Up to 1972, some 81,000 charges of discrimination had been filed since the commission's inception in 1965; of these, satisfactory conciliation was achieved in less than half, with the result that the majority of aggrieved employees either had to give up their claim or find the funds and time to take it through the federal courts.[6] Under the law passed in 1972, coverage was also extended to employers of fifteen or more persons, labor unions with fifteen or more members, all educational institutions, and joint labor-management committees (such as apprenticeship committees). Furthermore, employers are now required to make reasonable accommodations for employees whose religion may include observances, practices, and beliefs which differ from the employer's standard schedules of work. Under the new law, the EEOC has brought court charges against a number of firms that are alleged to have continued discriminating practices, and increasingly such cases are brought as "class actions" rather than individual complaints.

The basic obligation of any employer covered under the Civil Rights Act of 1964 is expressed in the negative. He may not: ". . . fail or refuse to hire or to discharge any individual, or otherwise to discriminate against any individual with respect to his compensation, terms, conditions, or privileges of employment, because of such individual's race, color, religion, sex, or national origin."[7] Generally, this was first applied to blacks and other nonwhites; discrimination charges filed by women as such have not received attention until fairly recently, as in the widely publicized EEOC-FCC settlement reached with AT&T.[8] In April 1972, the EEOC enlarged its discrimination guidelines, which state that to deny a woman a job because she is pregnant is a violation of the law and that disabilities related to pregnancy, including recovery from childbirth, miscarriage, and abortion, should be treated the same as any other temporary disability in terms of leave, seniority protection, and insurance payments. Fringe benefits are to be equally applied to men and women. Unless it can be shown that sex is a bona fide occupational qualification

6. Bureau of National Affairs, *The Equal Employment Opportunity Act of 1972* (Washington: BNA, 1972), p. 1.

7. Equal Employment Opportunity Act as amended in 1972, sec. 703(a)(1).

8. In a compliance agreement, the company consented to give $15 million in back pay and $23 million a year in raises to women and minority males against whom it allegedly discriminated in job assignments, pay, and promotions. About 15,000 employees (mostly women) were estimated to share in the back pay (including 1,500 college-educated women who were hired earlier for management jobs but allegedly barred from special rapid advancement training programs). Some 36,000 were to share in the pay increases as they were advanced to higher-rated jobs. *New York Times,* January 19, 1973. For a complete review of federal action, see Ruth G. Shaeffer, *Nondiscrimination in Employment: Changing Perspectives, 1963–1972* (New York: Conference Board, 1973).

for a particular job, it is unlawful to classify jobs as "male" or "female" or to maintain separate lines of progression or seniority lists.

The OFCC under the U.S. Department of Labor has gone further in its dealings with firms and other organizations that receive federal government contracts. The Labor Department's Revised Order No. 4 (December 4, 1971) requires every government contractor to adopt an "affirmative action program." This program must "include an analysis of areas within which the contractor is deficient in the utilization of minority groups and women, and further, goals and timetables to which the contractor's good faith efforts must be directed to correct the deficiencies and, thus, to increase materially the utilization of minorities and women, at all levels and in all segments of his work force where deficiencies exist."[9] Various numerical tests are provided, including the percentages of minorities and women in each classification, relative to the proportions in the total work force in the immediate area.

The effectiveness of the OFCC lies in its power to recommend cancellation of federal contracts with any firm. However, Revised Order No. 4 spells out many suggested methods of implementing "goals and timetables," including involving the personnel staff, department and division heads, and local and unit managers in the goal-setting process and in periodic audits of performance. Personnel policies such as selection procedures, training programs, promotion policies, seniority practices, and recreational programs are subject to review. Employers are urged actively to recruit minorities and women and to encourage child-care, housing, and transportation programs designed to improve the employment opportunities for these groups.

Despite thousands of cases in which the EEOC has failed to secure satisfactory voluntary compliance, the pressure exerted by this agency (and by the Department of Health, Education, and Welfare in the case of educational institutions) has undoubtedly brought changes in employment practices in the direction of the objectives of the legislation. In the case of government contractors, the OFCC has been a potent influence in increasing the proportion of women and minority members hired, especially at the technical, professional, and managerial levels. Perhaps the numbers are not yet "right" by proportional guidelines, but there has been clear progress toward targets established. Is there any doubt that blacks and women have more and better employment opportunities and

9. *Federal Register,* Vol. 36 (December 4, 1971), p. 23153.

a better chance of being promoted than they had ten years ago? There may even have been some reverse discrimination, justified as necessary to compensate for past discrimination and because of the legislative and administrative pressures.[10]

The employment of members of minority groups hitherto at a disadvantage in the labor market (little regular employment, persistent unemployment, poor education, etc.) has also been encouraged and even subsidized through federal manpower programs which have grown out of the Manpower Development and Training Act of 1962. Private employers have been involved through the government-sponsored efforts of the National Alliance of Businessmen, headed first by Henry Ford II, and its program of Job Opportunities in the Business Sector (JOBS). This began in 1968 with a June 1971 target of 500,000 to be hired, plus 200,000 in summer jobs. The business recession of 1970–71 made this target impossible to reach, and many of those hired subsequently left or were laid off.

But the effort enlisted the support of top management in many firms, and there is little doubt that an improved number of young blacks found and are finding job opportunities at entry levels, and many have been promoted after further training and experience. Again, expectations as to the number that would be hired fell short of realization, as did the targets originally set, but many firms made lasting commitments to hiring minority members. Not the least of the problems faced is the potential conflict between the expectations of the newly hired employees and the established seniority and promotion practices of earlier employees and their unions. Prior to NAB-JOBS and prior to more pressure from EEOC, there were already a number of voluntary efforts to hire more disadvantaged minorities in such firms as Equitable Life, General Electric, IBM, Westinghouse, and Western Electric.[11] In each, there was

10. See Theodore V. Purcell, "The Case of the Borderline Black," *Harvard Business Review,* Vol. 49 (November–December 1971), pp. 128ff. For a different view, see Daniel Seligman, "How 'Equal Opportunity' Turned into Employment Quotas," *Fortune,* Vol. 87 (March 1973), pp. 160–68.

11. See Peter B. Doeringer (ed.), *Programs to Employ the Disadvantaged* (Prentice-Hall, 1969). For a review of the whole experience and NAB-JOBS, see Charles A. Myers, *The Role of the Private Sector in Manpower Development* (Johns Hopkins Press, 1971), Chap. 3. The NAB-JOBS experience of 2,300 firms has been reviewed by Allen R. Janger, *Employing the Disadvantaged: A Company Perspective* (New York: Conference Board, 1972).

an important *top management commitment* to the program—a requirement which is vital for any new program affecting employment policies.

Protection of Older Employees

Another type of discrimination—against older workers—has been
proscribed by the Age Discrimination in Employment Act of 1967. Enforcement lies with the Wage and Hour Division of the Department of
Labor, which has reported a rise in the number of complaints about firing
or refusing to hire workers over the age of 40. The 40-to-65 age group
constitutes some 43 percent of the nation's civilian labor force. Unlike
the EEOC or the OFCC, the Department of Labor has not imposed a
target or goal system for employment of older workers. But in May 1974
it secured an agreement with the Standard Oil Company of California
to pay $2 million in back wages to 160 released older employees (40
to 65) and to rehire 120 of them.[12]

Despite the rapid growth of private pension plans since 1940, from 4
million to more than 30 million "covered" employees, less than half of
all employees in the private sector are covered by any plan. Until 1974,
older employees who looked forward to private employer-funded pensions to supplement their social security benefits at retirement lost out
when firms closed, laid them off before they met eligibility requirements,
or lacked funds to meet pension obligations. In response to the lack
of full "vesting" of pension rights after a certain period (ten or fifteen
years) and other alleged abuses, both the Nixon administration and a
bipartisan Senate-House group during 1971–72 pushed for federal
regulation of private plans, beyond the modest registration requirements of an earlier 1959 act. The tougher Senate-House bills, reintroduced in 1973 with proposals for vesting and federal reinsurance of
pension rights, grew out of Senate Labor Committee disclosures of
abuses in pension fund management, inadequate funding, weak vesting,
and undeserved loss of all benefits. It was found, for example, that in a
sample of fifty-one plans established before 1950 and covering some 7
million workers, more than 5 million have left and are no longer covered.
A second study of thirty-six better-structured plans covering 2.9 million
workers showed that only 8 percent received normal anticipated retire-

12. *New York Times*, May 17, 1974.

ment benefits.[13] Although many of the larger, more progressive firms have provided better-than-average pension plans, the limited protection for employees in other firms and the absence of any protection whatever in some firms, meant that federal regulation was coming, along with more generous social security benefits in the years ahead. The recent substantial increase in the latter benefits is an illustration of the trend. Finally, on Labor Day 1974, a pension reform bill, the Employee Retirement Income Security Act, was signed by President Ford. It provides for federal reinsurance of bankrupt pension funds, vesting rights for long-term employees in pension plans, and other regulation of pension funds.

Occupational Safety and Health

The failure of most employers on a voluntary basis to provide safe working conditions, despite the outstanding safety record of well-known firms, led to a stringent piece of federal legislation: the Occupational Safety and Health Act of 1970 (OSHA), a bipartisan bill which took effect on April 28, 1971. The basis for this bill was the slackening safety and health record in private industry. To quote the assistant secretary of labor in charge of administering the act, the voluntary safety movement had "substantially reduced workplace accidents from 1919 to 1960, but . . . since then voluntary compliance has faltered."[14] In 1972, the National Safety Council reported that about 14,000 persons died from accidents at work in 1971, and 2.2 million suffered temporarily or permanently disabling injuries on the job.[15]

13. Fred J. Cook, "The Case of the Disappearing Pension," *New York Times Magazine* (March 19, 1972), p. 31. For a more recent review, see "The Push for Pension Reform," *Business Week,* No. 2271 (March 17, 1973), pp. 46ff. "In short," said *Business Week*'s writer, "the private pension system, which like Topsy has 'just growed,' is headed toward a stage of guided development in which it will be increasingly shaped by imperatives of national social policy. Realistic businessmen are already accepting the idea that reform is inevitable" (p. 47).

14. Quoted in *New York Times,* March 30, 1971.

15. Fred K. Foulkes, "Learning To Live with OSHA," *Harvard Business Review,* Vol. 51 (November–December 1973). There was a substantial number of additional deaths each year from occupational diseases. However, the accuracy of all estimates can be questioned until better data are collected. For further information, see the papers prepared for an Industrial Relations Research Association meeting and published in *Labor Law Journal,* Vol. 23 (August 1972), pp. 501–24.

The Occupational Safety and Health Act covers 57 million workers in 4.1 million private establishments. Enforcement and administration are vested in the secretary of labor and in a new, independent, quasi-judicial agency, the Occupational Safety and Health Review Commission. The Department of Labor decrees standards and enforces them regionally through a group of safety inspectors who have the right to visit firms unannounced and issue written citations of violations found. If after a reasonable time for voluntary compliance the violations persist, the commission on appeal from OSHA can assess mandatory monetary penalties up to $1,000 for each offense. From July 1971 to January 1973, OSHA inspectors visited 45,800 establishments (1 percent of those covered by the act). More than 167,300 violations were alleged. Fines were proposed in 40 percent of these cases, averaging fines of $625 for serious violations and $45 for lesser violations.[16]

Some critics like Ralph Nader and AFL-CIO representatives have felt that the inspection staff is not large enough to enforce the act effectively, since there were only about 500 inspectors in mid-1972 to cover 4.1 million firms. The labor representatives criticized OSHA's "starvation budget" within the Department of Labor and deplored the initial Senate-House amendments to exclude firms with less than fifteen employees from coverage. Taking the opposite point of view, representatives of small business charged the government with "gestapo tactics" and called OSHA "a threat to the private enterprise system."[17] Both the secretary of labor and the assistant secretary in charge of the act's administration and enforcement have emphasized the need for development of explicit standards, education, and voluntary compliance before greatly expanding the size of the inspectorate. Under this approach, private employers have a range of options, from voluntary tightening of safety and health standards and enforcement at some increase in costs to running the risk of monetary penalties with attendant publicity for continued failure to meet established standards. It is unlikely that a small enforcement staff

16. Joe Collier, "The Federal Role in Job Safety and Health: Inspection and Enforcement at the Workplace," *Monthly Labor Review*, Vol. 96 (August 1973), pp. 41–42.

17. "Labor Attacks Congress over Safety Exemptions," *New York Times*, June 29, 1972. Former Assistant Secretary of Labor George C. Guenther was on record as opposing exclusion of small employers, for, as he said, "some of these businesses are quite hazardous." *Business Week*, No. 2238 (July 22, 1972), p. 74. Subsequently an exclusion of employers of three employees or less was agreed upon by Senate-House conferees in drafting the amended bill.

or state responsibility will achieve the degree of compliance that is necessary from those employers who continue to ignore the law.

Nothing in the act diminishes the obligation of employers under state
workmen's compensation statutes. But there has been some criticism that
much of this older state legislation dating back sixty years provides compensation that is inadequate in terms of today's dollars and for today's
occupational hazards. A special commission appointed to review state
workmen's compensation legislation found that state programs were
"inadequate and inequitable" and called for substantial reforms.[18]

Legislation Affecting Collective Bargaining

The National Labor Relations Act of 1935 established in modern
form the right of employees to organize and join unions of their own
choosing and to bargain collectively with an employer through the union
chosen as exclusive bargaining representative. In most cases, the choice
of union representation is made through a secret-ballot election conducted by the National Labor Relations Board (NLRB). This represented a revolution in labor-management relations, because in the period
prior to the early 1930s employers had virtually unlimited rights to discourage employees from joining unions and in refusing to deal with
unions which lacked enough economic strength to force recognition. The
amount of voluntary employer acceptance of unionism and collective
bargaining prior to the Wagner Act and the Supreme Court's validation
of it in 1937 was small, and it took a change in the law and dramatic
union organizing tactics to bring about the degree of unionism (about
27 percent of the private nonfarm economy) that the United States has
today.

Subsequent union organizing excesses led to the Taft-Hartley Act of
1947 (an amendment to the Wagner Act), defining and prohibiting
"unfair labor practices" for unions as well as continuing the earlier ones
for employers, with some loosening of restrictions on employers' "freedom of speech" during union organizing drives and pre-election campaigns. Certain activist union tactics, such as the secondary boycott, were
proscribed. Disclosures on corruption in some unions and restrictions
on membership rights led to the passage of the Landrum-Griffin Act of
1959. In short, the legislative pendulum has swung from unilateral re-

18. *New York Times,* July 31, 1972.

striction of employer antiunion pressures to more uniform government regulation of employer and union practices. A growing group of labor relations officials in a number of firms would like to see further restrictions on what is called "union monopoly power," but legislative prospects seem poor.

The two-pronged provisions of the Taft-Hartley Act are administered by the five-member National Labor Relations Board. That more employers than unions are charged with violating provisions of the act is evident in the 1972 figures. Of the nearly 26,500 unfair labor practice cases filed that year in all, alleged violations by employers decreased to 17,361 cases, a 12 percent drop from 1971 levels. Charges against unions decreased less than 1 percent, to 9,030 cases.[19]

As bad as this sounds, it is clear that the vast majority of employers voluntarily comply with the law, in part because charges of violations are costly in executive time, legal counsel, and potential enforcement orders and back-pay awards to employees. As each president appoints new members to the NLRB, labor leaders or industry spokesmen complain that the board is now either pro-employer or pro-labor, and perhaps the balance does shift occasionally. But the basic protections against "unfair labor practices" are generally observed by employers and unions, because the evolving rulings of the NLRB are widely disseminated. And the secret-ballot procedure for selecting exclusive bargaining representatives is in the best tradition of American political democracy.

It is worth noting here that labor legislation and regulation have set some of the rules of the collective bargaining relationship between employers and unions, but for the most part it has not affected directly the *terms* of the collective bargaining agreement. These are left largely to direct bargaining, apart from periods when wage and price controls are in effect. To be sure, some of the mandatory aspects of bargaining which have been promulgated by the NLRB and sustained in court decisions (on pensions, bonuses, etc.) come close to affecting the content of bargaining, but most of the 150,000 private collective agreements in effect in the United States are reached voluntarily before strike deadlines.

---

19. *Thirty-eighth Annual Report of the National Labor Relations Board, for the Fiscal Year Ended June 30, 1973,* p. 10. This growth of NLRB activity may also be interpreted as an undesirable increase of legal remedies in employer-employee relationships. See Douglass V. Brown, "Legalism and Industrial Relations in the United States," in Industrial Relations Research Association, *Proceedings of the Twenty-third Annual Winter Meeting, 1970* (IRRA, 1971), pp. 2–10.

There have been numerous suggestions by employers and organized labor to amend the Taft-Hartley Act, but it seems unlikely that major changes will be made in the foreseeable future. There will be changes in interpretation and application of the law through the NLRB and the courts, as the composition of each changes, with some confusion for employers as earlier decisions appear to be modified or even reversed.

The possibility that some labor disputes can seriously affect the public health and safety and should be limited in their impact or prohibited is a persistent issue in labor-management relations and public policy. Between 1947 and mid-1974, the "national emergency" provisions of the Taft-Hartley Act were invoked by the White House twenty-nine times. Following the 80-day injunction period thus enforced each time, strikes resumed in eight of these episodes (strikes by longshoremen and maritime workers). At various times, other approaches have been recommended, including the Nixon administration's 1970 bill (never passed) that would have required transportation industries to adopt "last offer" arbitration as a final settlement procedure. Generally, compulsory arbitration, because it means giving power to a third party, has little support from private employers or unions, but its use is growing slowly in the public sector in some states, particularly in disputes involving police and firemen. In the steel industry, moreover, the major companies and the steelworkers' union have agreed to submit any unresolved 1974 contract issues to arbitration. Both fear the severe consequences for earnings and jobs of a strike now that their industry faces heavy foreign competition and stockpiling by steel purchasers.

To summarize this discussion of the role of governmental legislation affecting employer-employee relations, it is clear that external pressure was necessary to achieve objectives deemed desirable by the electorate's representatives in Congress and in state legislatures. Voluntary employer progress was being made in reducing discrimination against minorities and women, in hiring older employees, in providing safe and healthful working conditions, in providing private pensions for long-service employees, and in accepting the right of employees to join unions for collective bargaining. But voluntary efforts were seen as not widespread enough or moving fast enough. Once legislation was passed and administrative agencies established, many private employers "fell in line" as good citizens. Some did not, or at least were charged with not so doing, and they were involved in the litigation process as a consequence. Some were cleared; more were subject to various punitive pressures to conform. Again, the range of options open to private employers was and still is quite wide, within the limits of the laws as they are administered.

On balance, do the laws reviewed above serve the public interest as well as the interest of employees of private firms? My judgment is in the affirmative. One can always quarrel with the details of administration and enforcement in particular cases, but the general rules point in the right direction.

The Changing U.S. Labor Force

Less direct and more subtle in their influence on management are changes in the composition and aspirations of the labor force, which induce managers to consider new responsibilities toward their employees, particularly their younger ones. Quite apart from government pressures, quantitative changes in the labor force, new life styles, and sociotechnological developments give business a range of options for voluntary action.

Changes in Composition

During the current decade, the largest percentage increase in the labor force will be in the 25–34 age group. As Table 12-1 shows, this 51.5 percent increase follows a nearly 57 percent increase in the youngest age group in the labor force during the 1960s, when those in higher education began changes in life styles and aspirations reviewed later. The next largest increase will come in the succeeding youngest age group, 16–24, whereas the 45–64 group will increase by only 3.3 percent. The 35–44 age group, from which new top managerial talent is usually

Table 12-1. Percentage Change in the Labor Force by Age Group, Actual 1950–70 and Projected 1970–90

Age	1950–60	1960–70	1970–80	1980–90
16–24	2.2	56.6	19.4	−14.6
25–34	−0.3	17.1	51.5	14.0
35–44	18.8	0.1	11.5	47.5
45–64	26.2	17.3	3.3	4.6
65 and over	11.3	−4.7	2.4	6.9

Source: *Manpower Report of the President* (March 1972), p. 253, Table E-3 (for 1950–60), and (March 1973), p. 220, Table E-3 (for later decades).

drawn, hardly increased in the 1960–70 decade and will increase less than 12 percent during the 1970s. The drop in labor force growth of those 65 and over in the decade 1960–70 and the very slight increase projected for 1970–80 undoubtedly reflect the spread of compulsory retirement at 65. The 1980–90 projections, however, suggest a greater percentage increase of older people desiring jobs than in any decade since the 1950s. The impact of this for management policies lies farther in the future, when the proportion of youth in the labor force declines.

Data on educational levels in the changing labor force are not available by decades, but Table 12-2 summarizes what information we have. The labor force is clearly better educated as measured by the increase since 1952 in the proportion of workers who have completed high school and the proportion who have completed college. Between 1952 and 1980, the median figure for years of schooling is expected to rise from 10.9 to 12.5, or an increase of nearly 15 percent.

The labor force projected to 1980 (of people 16 years old and over) will include nearly 63 million men and 39 million women. The proportion of the total adult population participating in the labor force will rise through increasing participation rates for women (from 37 percent in 1960 to an estimated 45 percent in 1980), as contrasted with a steady rate for men (around 79 percent). In recent years white male labor force

Table 12-2. Percentage Distribution of Years of Schooling among the Labor Force, 1952, 1962, 1972, and 1980 (Projected)

| Schooling completed | Percent of labor force | | | |
	1952	1962	1972	1980
Elementary				
Less than 5 years	7.3	4.6	2.1	1.8
5 to 8 years	30.2	22.4	12.9	10.1
High school				
1 to 3 years	18.5	19.3	19.2	16.8
4 years (graduate)	26.6	32.1	38.7	42.4
College				
1 to 3 years	8.3	10.7	13.6	12.0
4 years or more	7.9	11.0	13.6	16.9
Median number of school years completed	10.9	12.1	12.4	12.5

Source: *Manpower Report of the President* (March 1973), p. 176, Table B-9, and p. 226, Table E-11. Minor adjustments made for comparability. 1952 data are for October; 1962 and 1972 are for March; all refer to workers 18 years old and over. 1980 data are for the year and refer to workers 25 and over.

participation rates have been slightly higher than those of nonwhite males; but nonwhite females have had higher labor force participation rates than white females. The overall increase in female participation rates will be largely among white females.[20]

Similar projections organized according to occupational group up to 1980 indicate that the largest annual rates of increase will be in professional and technical workers, service workers, and clerical workers— in that order. By industry, the service-producing industries will have a higher annual rate of growth than the goods-producing industries.[21] With the exception of service workers and craftsmen and foremen, the other leading occupational groups will rise less rapidly than they did in the 1960–70 decade. The same is true of the industry groups, but the trend toward a service economy is clear.

What are the implications for employer responsibilities? Business is now drawing upon a labor force in which the younger workers who entered the labor force in the preceding decade will continue to account for nearly half of the total labor force increase in the present decade. They are more experienced and older, but still under 35. They are better educated than in the past and may be increasingly drawn to service-producing industries. An increasing percentage of women will join the labor force. These aggregates, however, tell us little about attitudes and aspirations, which will also affect the performance of these employees.

Changes in Life Styles and Aspirations

One conclusion is inescapable: the former 16–24 age group moving into the 25–34 group during the 1970s has different life styles and different aspirations in work than did their counterparts a decade ago and especially two decades ago.[22] Management has become accustomed to

20. *Manpower Report of the President* (March 1973), pp. 220–21, Tables E-2 and E-4.

21. Ibid., p. 225, Tables E-9 and E-10. The projections assume a 3 percent unemployment rate and a service economy by 1980. The goods-producing industries include mining, contract construction, and manufacturing. Service-producing industries are transportation and public utilities; wholesale and retail trade; finance, insurance, and real estate; other services; and government—federal, state, and local.

22. This conclusion must be tempered with the observation that only a small minority of the younger age group drops out of hired work, choosing instead some form of communal living, tilling the soil, or engaging in simple handicrafts.

some of the obvious changes in hair styles and dress.[23] These styles have been widely adopted by many age groups. What is more important is the kind of expectations younger people have on the job. Here we can take note of the following important bits of evidence in recent years (in the absence of systematic longitudinal studies of an adequate sample).

1. In 1961, 1962, 1963, and 1964 questionnaires were mailed to a 35 percent sample of nearly 57,000 men who had graduated from college in 1961. The respondents ranked various occupational values in the following order of importance: opportunities to be helpful to others or useful to society; opportunities to be original and creative; opportunities to work with people rather than things; a chance to exercise leadership; living and working in the world of ideas; opportunities for moderate but steady progress rather than the chance of extreme success or failure; and making a lot of money. The sample included graduates in all fields who elected to work for a business employer.[24]

2. A 1970 survey of 5,000 holders of the master's degree in business administration from the graduating classes of 1965–68 showed that on the average only 61 percent remained with their first employer; whereas 29 percent had moved to a second employer, 8 percent to a third, and 1 percent to a fourth. In the 1965 class, with the longest experience, the comparable percentages were 47, 35, 15, and 2.5. The main reasons given for job-hopping, in order of importance, were: limited opportunity for promotion; limited job responsibility; underutilization of MBA training; inadequate salary growth; limited opportunity to develop functional skills; and supervision unresponsive to new ideas. It is perhaps significant

23. A survey of views about "the hippy dresser" held by 3,453 *Harvard Business Review* subscribers found that less than 1 percent would dismiss him outright and that there was more tolerance among the younger managers. David W. Ewing, "Who Wants Employee Rights?" *Harvard Business Review,* Vol. 49 (November–December 1971), pp. 22ff. For a review of these same subscribers' opinions on related issues, see Ewing, "Who Wants Corporate Democracy?" *Harvard Business Review,* Vol. 49 (September–October 1971), pp. 12ff.

24. "Attitudes of College Students toward Business Careers," Report No. 1 (Bethlehem, Pa.: Research Information Center, College Placement Council, Inc., 1968; processed). A slightly different ordering was reported by the Procter & Gamble Company's periodic surveys of job expectations of college graduates entering the company: (1) to feel they are *progressing;* (2) to have *responsibilities* commensurate with their abilities; (3) to get a feeling of *achievement* from their work; (4) to know their *ideas* are welcomed; (5) to believe what they do is *important.* J. M. Ewell, *The Effect of Change on Organizations* (Cincinnati: Procter & Gamble Co., no date).

that geographical location, physical working conditions, the company's lack of social concern, lack of job security, and heavy travel were the least important reasons, among this group, for leaving an employer.[25]

3. Some disenchantment is found among recent college seniors and graduates about employment in large organizations. There is apparently a feeling that an employee in a large organization sacrifices his individuality, has little opportunity to shape the environment in which he works and to shape his own career.[26] The lack of the latter opportunity was found to be one of the major reasons why young executives left AT&T, as compared with those who remained and progressed. The young manager's participation in his own career development seems to him a significant reason for staying with the firm.

4. More participation in decision making as well as in one's own career planning has assumed greater importance in what has been called "the accelerated generation." *Fortune*'s study of young executives in the early 1970s found that "they differ strikingly from their predecessors— the Organization Man of the 1950s and the Young Executive of the 1960s, both subjects of previous *Fortune* series." According to the author of the study:

Today's junior managers, by contrast, reflect the passionate concerns of youth in the 1970's—for individuality, openness, humanism, concern, and change —and they are determined to be heard. If they find no response, their deep anger at what they view as imperfections in society and business could infect their colleagues, and subordinates, resulting in a sort of industrial mutiny.[27]

These young managers want early responsibility, even more than in the 1960s; they "thirst for risk and challenge" and desire rapid promotion, "not so much for the money promotion brings, but for the chance to have authority and a real voice in company decisions." Arjay Miller, former Ford Motor Company president and now dean of the Stanford Graduate School of Business, is quoted by Gooding as follows (p. 115):

The young executive will insist on being party to the decision-making process. This is part of the new life style. It is the kind of change organiza-

25. John A. De Pasquale and Richard A. Lange, "Job-hopping and the MBA," *Harvard Business Review,* Vol. 49 (November–December 1971), pp. 4, 5, 8.

26. Eugene Gulland (Princeton University senior), "The Disenchanted Generation," *Business Today,* Vol. 3 (Spring 1969), pp. 47, 49.

27. Judson Gooding, "The Accelerated Generation Moves into Management," *Fortune,* Vol. 83 (March 1971), p. 101. For some later supporting evidence, see Dale Tarnowieski, *The Changing Success Ethic* (New York: American Management Associations, 1973).

tions of the future must make in order to operate in the new environment, in this new participatory democracy.

5. The so-called student revolution of 1969 to 1971 carried with it "changes in cultural attitudes toward authority, work, marriage, sexual morality, religion, and money," to quote Daniel Yankelovich, whose organization conducted hour-long interviews with some 1,200 graduate and undergraduate students at 53 colleges and universities in 1971.[28] More relevant to employer-employee relations are the growing challenge to authority (including a reluctance "to accept outward conformity for the sake of career advancement") and the desire for career rewards different from those sought by the previous generation. "Opportunity to make a contribution," "job challenge," "the ability to find self-expression," and "free time for outside interests" count heavily with recent graduates (though perhaps these categories are not so different from the values held by the class of 1961 reported above). There appears to be a new attitude toward work. "Some 69% of all students no longer believe 'hard work will pay off.'" Work is ranked behind love, friendship, education, self-expression, family, and privacy in their hierarchy of values.[29] Whether this value hierarchy will persist into the late 1970s for this college group is less certain, for family responsibilities and a "steady" job may become more important to them. Two recent commentators, however, have concluded:

If we are correct in our assumption that the restlessness in today's society is more far-reaching than people have realized; if it is indeed rooted in a traditional willingness to challenge authority and a heightened demand for a piece of the decision-making action; and if companies are, in fact, characterized by more restlessness than people have fully recognized—then it behooves top management to look seriously at every possible way of adjusting to the temper of the times.[30]

28. Yankelovich, "The Real Meaning of the Student Revolution," *Conference Board Record*, Vol. 9 (March 1972), p. 8. This article was drawn from Yankelovich's subsequent book, *The Changing Values on Campus: Political and Personal Attitudes of Today's College Students* (Washington Square Press, 1972).

29. Yankelovich also reported that a recent survey he did of chief executives of 300 leading American corporations, divided by those who had a son or daughter in college and those who did not, revealed that "those with college-age children had moved closer to the new campus values. They had been educated by their own offspring. This influence is one of the most important sources of social change affecting business today. It represents the very opposite of the so-called generation gap." "The Real Meaning of the Student Revolution," p. 13.

30. Dan H. Fenn, Jr., and Daniel Yankelovich, "Responding to the Employee Voice," *Harvard Business Review*, Vol. 50 (May–June 1972), p. 90. Among methods by which management can respond, the authors list special councils,

6. Are the "student revolution" views of the early 1970s shared by noncollege youth? The evidence is much less clear, for the noncollege group is much larger and more diverse. In the new voting group, 18 to 21 years old, some 26 percent were in college in 1971–72, 4 percent still in high school, and the remaining 70 percent working or looking for work. Almost half the women and one-third of the men in this latter group were married, with somewhat different responsibilities from those of college youth.[31] Since many of the noncollege young people at work or seeking work are high school graduates, the findings of a study of work attitudes of 5,000 high school students in 1970 are relevant. For the majority, the highest aspirations and concerns in work were for self-expression, personal influence, fame, and self-development.[32] These are more similar to the student views of the early 1960s reported above than to those of the recent "student revolution," which may have moderated in the meantime, with more concern for the job market.[33]

Are Employees Alienated by Work?

The failure of some noncollege youths to realize their aspirations may account for the kind of reaction typified by the widely publicized three-

junior boards of directors, nonmanagement task forces, ombudsmen, and employee committees.

31. *New York Times,* March 11, 1972.

32. George B. Graen and Rene V. Dawis, "A Measure of Work Attitudes for High-School-Age Youth," *Journal of Vocational Behavior,* Vol. 1 (October 1971), pp. 343–53.

33. In the judgment of one writer: ". . . reports from the campus, whether of continuing revolution or of counterrevolution, have been exaggerated. A distinctive youth culture has spread from a trend-setting minority to the majority, but in the process of assimilation has lost most of its ideological content. . . . Moreover, today's competitive job market, particularly for college graduates, appears to be pulling students toward the mainstream." Edmund Faltermayer, "Youth after the Revolution," *Fortune,* Vol. 87 (March 1973), p. 158.

A similar conclusion was reached by social scientists who conducted a study of 1,860 male and female members of the class of 1972 at five Pennsylvania universities and colleges. "From the information provided by the respondents, we would have to reject the position of those who maintain that the work ethic is dead or dying . . . there appears to be emerging a work ethic which places a much greater demand on work. The expectation is that work can and should be of greater significance to the individual and of greater value to society." David Gottlieb and others, *Youth and the Meaning of Work* (Center for Youth Studies and Social Policy, College of Human Development, Pennsylvania State University, 1973). This was a report prepared for the Manpower Administration, U.S. Department of Labor.

week strike in the Chevrolet Vega plant at Lordstown, Ohio, in 1972. The work force was relatively young. One 27-year-old assembly line worker said: "There's no way to beat it [boredom]. You just try not to think about it, or you can go insane. You just sort of get numb."[34] But strikes occurred at other assembly plants, with older work forces. Perhaps automated assembly line work simply intensifies the reaction to routine tasks by many workers who have the "blue-collar blues."[35] An alternative explanation of strikes in GM assembly plants is that the consolidation of two previously separate operations necessarily required manpower reductions which were opposed by workers and their union. Whatever the complex reasons, the degree of alienation felt by assembly line workers is not present among workers in contract construction, for example. In this industry there is less direct supervision, no machine pacing, and some pride in work accomplishment. The degree of work satisfaction in contract construction, as reported in a summary of the national survey drawn on by *Work in America*, was higher than any occupational group except "managerial" and "technical and professional."[36]

All of this raises the question of work dissatisfaction and alienation among present employees, particularly the younger ones. The conclusion of *Work in America: Report of a Special Task Force to the Secretary of Health, Education, and Welfare* is striking:

Albert Camus wrote that "Without work all life goes rotten. But when work is soulless, life stifles and dies." Our analysis of work in America leads to much the same conclusion: Because work is central to the lives of so many Americans, either the absence of work or employment in meaningless work is creating an increasingly intolerable situation. The human costs of this state of affairs are manifested in worker alienation, alcoholism, drug addiction, and other symptoms of poor mental health.[37]

34. "Turn the Nut, Turn the Nut, Turn the . . . ," *New York Times*, February 6, 1972. See also "The Spreading Lordstown Syndrome" and "The GM Efficiency Move That Backfired," *Business Week*, No. 2218 (March 4, 1972), pp. 69–70, and No. 2221 (March 25, 1972), pp. 46ff.

35. See Judson Gooding, "Blue-Collar Blues on the Assembly Line," *Fortune*, Vol. 82 (July 1970); Sar A. Levitan (ed.), *Blue-Collar Workers: A Symposium on Middle America* (McGraw-Hill, 1971).

36. Neal Q. Herrick, "Who's Unhappy at Work and Why," *Manpower*, Vol. 4 (January 1972), pp. 2–7. Full details are reported in University of Michigan Survey Research Center, *Survey of Working Conditions* (U.S. Department of Labor, 1971). This survey was based on a sample of 1,533 American employees at all occupational levels. It may be significant that among whites those 30 or younger with "some college" expressed the greatest work dissatisfaction.

37. The report was prepared under a contract with the W. E. Upjohn Institute

Whether this conclusion applies to a *majority* of all employees is not specified. It is also a fair question whether some of these conclusions are a projection of the scholarly background of the researchers and their own revulsion to repetitive, boring work.[38] The *variety* of work revealed by the complexity of the U.S. occupational structure suggests that work alienation may be confined to those jobs in which there is little room for employee pride in work accomplishment. As *Work in America* points out: "It is clear that classically alienating jobs (such as on the assembly line) that allow the worker no control over the conditions of work and that seriously affect his mental and physical function off the job probably comprise less than 2% of the jobs in America" (p. 13).

Despite the further contention that "a growing number of white-collar jobs" may have these characteristics, there are no quantitative data to support the view that alienation is widespread in the work force, apart from citing varying percentages of selected occupational groups responding to a question, "What type of work would you try to get into if you could start all over again?" A "cross section" of blue-collar workers showed that only 24 percent would choose their jobs again, but the size of the sample is not specified in the report. Unskilled steelworkers and unskilled autoworkers are a part of this group.

In any case, it is clear that some groups of workers are dissatisfied with the content of their jobs and that some managers have begun to consider ways of redesigning jobs and organization of work to reduce

---

for Employment Research at the request of HEW Secretary Elliot L. Richardson, who in his Foreword terms the study "doughty, controversial, and yet responsible," although he expresses disagreement with some particulars and a wish for "more adequate" data.

Work in America was published by M.I.T. Press in 1973. The passage quoted above, about meaningless work, appears on p. 186. Much of the literature on worker alienation is listed in the Bibliography of the M.I.T. edition.

Following delivery of the original report to Secretary Richardson, two members of the "task force," Harold L. Sheppard and Neal Q. Herrick, wrote a book entitled *Where Have All the Robots Gone? Worker Dissatisfaction in the '70s* (Free Press, 1972).

38. A more balanced review of this question is found in "The Job Blahs: Who Wants To Work?" *Newsweek,* Vol. 81 (March 26, 1973), pp. 79ff. See also David Jenkins, "Democracy in the Factory," *Atlantic Monthly,* Vol. 231 (April 1973), pp. 78–83; David Sirota, "Job Enrichment—Another Management Fad?" *Conference Board Record,* Vol. 10 (April 1973), pp. 40–45. Sirota points out that job enrichment is not a solution for low pay, lack of fringe benefits, employment insecurity, poor tooling or materials, and so on. There have been a number of later criticisms of the conclusions in *Work in America.*

this kind of work dissatisfaction and increase the opportunities for better performance. Possibly the nature of work itself has not changed, but *expectations* have—the expectations of younger, better-educated people with different life styles.[39]

Experience with Job Enrichment

Within the past few years the idea of job enrichment or job enlargement has dominated much of the management literature (as well as receiving attention in more popular publications).[40] What is meant by job enrichment? The following statement by a management consultant indicates the complexity of attempting a successful program:

Job enrichment means the redesigning of jobs, intelligently building into them the necessary psychological nutrients. These include such elements as: increased responsibility; opportunities for achievement and recognition for that achievement; chances for new learning; and a steady movement toward more complex tasks. The latter item does not necessarily mean promotion, although that may be an end result, particularly when a job cannot be further changed. . . . Job enrichment [the author warns farther on] is definitely not a program that one simply "plugs in" and walks away from. It is not a "packaged vehicle," similar to programs that so many training staffs are disposed to use.[41]

More specifically, job enrichment involves managers, supervisors, and workers in improving existing jobs by rearranging existing duties, bringing work into the job from earlier stages in the development of the product and putting later work stages into the job, pulling down responsi-

39. There is historical evidence that the "work ethic" developed with difficulty in the United States because "artisan work habits and diverse ethnic working-class subcultures" of immigrant groups clashed with the need for factory discipline. See Herbert G. Gutman, "Work, Culture, and Society in Industrializing America, 1815–1919," *American Historical Review,* Vol. 78 (June 1973), pp. 531–88.

40. For example, Robert N. Ford, *Motivation through the Work Itself* (American Management Association, 1969), and his article, "Job Enrichment Lessons from AT&T," *Harvard Business Review,* Vol. 51 (January–February 1973), pp. 96–106; Fred K. Foulkes, *Creating More Meaningful Work* (American Management Association, 1969); Harold M. F. Rush, *Job Design for Motivation* (Conference Board, 1971); and Richard E. Walton, "How To Counter Alienation in the Plant," *Harvard Business Review,* Vol. 50 (November–December 1972), pp. 70–81 (describing a specially designed pet-food plant).

41. Roy W. Walters, "Job Enrichment Isn't Easy," *Personnel Administration and Public Personnel Review,* Vol. 1 (September–October 1972), pp. 61–66. The quotation is from pp. 61 and 65. Mr. Walters was formerly with Bell Telephone of Pennsylvania and AT&T in New York, where some of the early job enrichment experiments began.

bilities from above and pushing some work to lower job classifications or automating it.[42]

A number of firms, among them some well-known ones such as AT&T, General Foods, Procter & Gamble, Monsanto, Texas Instruments, Corning Glass, TRW Systems, Bankers Trust, and Travellers Insurance, have undertaken limited efforts to enrich specific jobs or occupations within the totality of their employment. General Motors has begun experimenting with the "team" approach to assembly of a new mobile home, and Chrysler has encouraged other approaches to making jobs more interesting in a number of its plants. The more favorable reports from Saab and Volvo in Sweden are as yet inconclusive, as are indeed many of the other job enrichment efforts in the United States. An analysis of the thirty-four "Case Studies in the Humanization of Work" reported in the Appendix to *Work in America,* with the addition of five more cases reported subsequently in other sources, indicates the limited spread of job enrichment up to mid-1973. Probably there were not more than twenty well-documented U.S. cases, involving perhaps 7,000 employees. Those cases which are on record in some fashion but poorly documented might add another 7,000. In contrast, cases reported abroad (Norway, England, the Netherlands, and Yugoslavia) could total 20,000 for the well-documented and 14,000 for those less persuasive. In the cases on which the evidence is clear, the results included improved job satisfaction, lower labor turnover, reduced costs, and fewer errors. Top management support for the change is essential.

These results are not greatly different from the experience with an older and somewhat different approach to job enrichment, although the term was not in use when the Scanlon Plan of labor-management cooperation spread in the 1950s. Under this plan, still being adopted by a number of firms each year, "participation" is the key concept. Employee members are elected to production and screening committees, and, with management-appointed members, they review employee suggestions for improving productivity, ways of reducing waste, and other job improvements related to the employee's specific job or department. There is also provision for sharing the savings from any reduction in labor costs —this incentive taking the form of a monthly "bonus" based on such savings. The bonus calculations measure the general effectiveness of the joint committees as well.[43] Probably fifty companies now have the Scan-

---

42. Ford, "Job Enrichment Lessons from AT&T," p. 101.
43. Fred G. Lesieur and Elbridge S. Puckett, "The Scanlon Plan Has Proved

lan Plan in operation, some unionized and others nonunion. The total number of employees covered is at least as great as in the well-documented job enrichment cases summarized above.

To sum up, there is a growing recognition that new approaches are needed to motivate employees on their jobs, especially those who are "turned off" by routine or highly subdivided jobs and who resent managerial attitudes which place little value on what employees can contribute as jobs and organizations change. Higher management has been more concerned with the expressed desire of junior managers to become involved in responsible, decision-making jobs.[44] This desire may be spreading more broadly among all employees.

Hiring and Training Minority Employees

Young blacks, Chicanos, and other nonwhite minorities may have the same aspirations and attitudes toward work of young people generally, but they also have special problems associated with actual and alleged discrimination barring them from skilled jobs and especially from professional and managerial posts. Many leading business firms have made substantial progress, as they see it, in the employment and upgrading of blacks in particular. But minority recruiting firms and spokesmen for black organizations such as the National Urban League and the NAACP claim that progress has not been fast enough.[45] So pressure for more minority hiring and upgrading, particularly in managerial positions, will continue to come from the black community, in addition to growing pressure from government agencies.

Itself," *Harvard Business Review,* Vol. 47 (September–October 1969), pp. 109–18. This article covers three cases in which the plan had been in effect at a firm for fourteen years or more: Atwood Vacuum Machine Company, Parker Pen Company, and the Pfaudler Company. More documentation is available in Fred G. Lesieur (ed.), *The Scanlon Plan: A Frontier in Labor-Management Cooperation* (M.I.T. Press, 1958).

44. Recent evidence on this is reviewed in Larry E. Greiner, "What Managers Think of Participative Leadership," *Harvard Business Review,* Vol. 51 (March–April 1973), pp. 111–17. The "organization development" approach is also spreading. This approach emphasizes wider opportunities within the organization to participate in solving the problems of the organization.

45. Vernon E. Jordan, Jr., executive director of the National Urban League, has said, "Businessmen aren't scared anymore and should stop responding on an emergency basis. What is needed are consistent, ongoing programs to hire blacks." "The Black Message: Business Must Do More," *Business Week,* No. 2211 (January 22, 1972), pp. 79–80.

One problem facing business is that its accounting procedures often do not, as one writer puts it, "allow for adjustment of comparative operating costs of plants with progressive hiring practices. Accounting systems do not allocate the extra payroll and training costs incurred to the public relations department or to the company's 'central-office overhead' activities."[46] Some firms have adjusted their accounting procedures. Others, like the General Electric Company, have circulated policy statements such as "Equal Opportunity/Minority Relations: A New Emphasis," issued in 1970 by Fred J. Borch, then chairman and chief executive officer of GE. Borch made the following point:

> The successful manager of tomorrow will be the individual who can effectively manage the new work force in our changing environment. He will be the manager who can convince all employees and our community neighbors that our actions are in the long term best interests of all employees, the business, and the country.
>
> Society will measure General Electric and all industry on this basis. The Corporate Executive Office, in turn, will measure all levels of General Electric management and supervision in the same way.[47]

Still another approach is the one taken by Eastern Gas and Fuel Associates of Boston, which now includes "social accounting" in its reports to shareholders.

A major challenge will be in access to higher management positions. A December 1971 survey of 163 companies indicated that one-fourth had no minority-group members in professional and technical jobs, one-half had none in first-level supervision, 45 percent had none in middle management, and two-thirds had none in top management.[48] Although some major companies have appointed black directors, relatively few blacks are in senior line management either in the top 50 U.S. corporations or among the 500 largest companies. More young blacks are entering graduate business schools now, and some of them will reach higher management positions eventually. In the meantime, the effort to advance

46. Theodore L. Cross, *Black Capitalism: Strategy for Business in the Ghetto* (rev. ed., Atheneum, 1971), p. 79.

47. *General Electric's Commitment to Progress in Equal Opportunity and Minority Relations* (New York: General Electric, Corporate Business Environment, 1970), p. 1. GE's program grew out of reports produced by twenty-seven task forces over nine months.

48. Bureau of National Affairs, *Personnel Policies Forum: Women and Minorities in Management and in Personnel Management* (Washington: BNA, 1971), pp. 1, 2. In another study, 500 black male college graduates in managerial and professional jobs in industry were surveyed in 1971 along with some white man-

currently employed blacks will continue, as will the recruiting of black professionals and managers.

While considering the pressures business is under to advance minorities to more responsible positions, it is worth noting that the record of the federal government itself is at best marginal. When the U.S. Commission on Civil Rights evaluated federal departments and agencies in a November 1971 report, four of five groups were rated only "marginal" (better than "poor"): (1) the Civil Service Commission, EEOC, and OFCC; (2) HEW and the Internal Revenue Service; (3) federally assisted programs in regular government departments such as Labor, Interior, Commerce, etc.; and (4) the Office of Management and Budget and the White House staff. The last group had the best relative improvement compared with May 1971 minority employment.[49]

Hiring Women at All Occupational Levels

Similar pressures on management have arisen from the so-called women's liberation movement, in addition to EEOC directives to hire more women at all occupational levels. Some perceptive comments by Juanita Kreps on this question are worth quoting:

The strength women have gained from the liberation movement is difficult to assess at this early stage. If the failure to gain passage of the Equal Rights Amendment is the test, the movement's political position is a weak one. But the widespread interest in women's rights that surrounded that debate and the present sensitivity of employers to antidiscriminatory legislation surely attest to the effectiveness of women's activism on their own behalf.

. . . Analogies between Negroes' fight for equal rights and that of women have frequently been drawn, but comparison of the two cases reveals as many differences as similarities. Women, like Negroes, have had the poorer paying jobs, have been expected to assume a certain role, and have been denied access to particular areas of activity. But the class and income a woman achieves is dependent primarily on the success of her father or husband, and she has every reason to promote his cause, often even when it conflicts with her own career interests. No such commonality exists between blacks and whites.[50]

---

agers. Though nearly 90 percent of the whites and 48 percent of the blacks replied that their companies had programs for equal opportunity for blacks, their perception of whether "equal opportunity" actually existed was much lower: 48 percent for the whites, 28 percent for the blacks. Evelyn S. Freeman and Charles L. Fields, *A Study of Black Male Professionals in Industry,* U.S. Department of Labor, Manpower Administration (1973), Table MR-6, p. 250.

49. *New York Times,* November 21, 1971.

50. Kreps, *Sex in the Marketplace: American Women at Work* (Johns Hopkins

It is clear that many American women aspire to jobs and careers, especially with the restriction of family size and the availability of child-care centers for preschool children. What is not so clear is the force of their aspiration. On the one hand, advances were quite slow in the past. The proportion of women employed as professional and technical workers barely increased between 1940 and 1972—from 13.2 percent to 14.5 percent. The percentage of women in the managers-officials-proprietors group crept from 3.8 in 1940 to 4.5 in 1972. Most of the women who have gone to work in the postwar period have found jobs only in the traditional "women's" occupations—as clerical workers and service workers (except private household). On the other hand, projections to 1980 indicate that women may come to hold as many as 35 percent of all professional and technical jobs including those in fields such as systems analysis, computer programming, and medical laboratory testing. But again, the larger percentages are likely to be in such "women's" occupations as registered nurses, elementary and secondary school teachers, social workers, clerical workers, and service workers. Only 1 percent will be engineers.[51] As for management positions, the 1971 survey of firms mentioned above showed that over three-fourths had no women in top management jobs, and in four-fifths of these firms women held only 2 percent or less of the top management positions. Some women have been appointed to boards of directors in 1973 and 1974, but these are not in operating management.

Various women's groups and leaders in the movement have asked whether this addition of a woman to a board here and there is not simply "corporate tokenism," similar to the charges sometimes leveled at business when a single black is appointed to a board or to a higher management position. Admittedly, some executives consider the "woman question" more as a compliance problem under OFCC and EEOC pressures than as an opportunity to draw on a talented group of women in ways that are socially acceptable and give evidence of corporate responsibility. The same comment can be made about the effort to hire and promote talented blacks.

As a consequence, it may well be true that competent women and nonwhites, especially those coming from colleges and graduate schools

University Press, 1971), pp. 104–05. The equal rights amendment was passed by Congress in March 1972 and must be ratified by 38 states to take effect.

51. Ibid., pp. 37 (Table 2.4) and 80 (Table 5.1); *Manpower Report of the President, March 1973.*

today, initially have a better opportunity to choose between competing offers than do white males but that they find it harder to build a career. For example, male stereotypes handicap career-oriented women in management. Their attitudes "have an immediate effect on the motivation of women already at work." One study of male managers showed that they held the following attitudes: men should be courteous to women and women deferential to men; women can't supervise men; and women are less dependable employees than men.[52] Somewhat ambiguously, several writers have stressed the supportive role that males (both husbands and managers) can play in helping women advance to more responsible positions in business and the professions.

Business responsibility for establishing private child-care centers (or supporting government-funded programs) is also relevant to the employment of women. Some firms have set up their own day-care facilities as a way of attracting more women employees and reducing absenteeism and turn-over. Few child-care centers make a profit. The likelihood that company-sponsored centers will be expanded to meet the problem of the working mother is slight; externally supported centers are likely to spread. The difficulties facing the working mother may not have been lost on career-oriented young single women, who are sometimes quoted as saying they will not marry at all or, if they do, will not have children. There is even the suggestion that wives and husbands may each work part time, sharing household duties, including child care. All of this indicates that managers will need to consider more flexible work arrangements in the future if they are to utilize many talented employees.

Early Retirement

Some older employees at nearly all levels believe that business should permit retirement prior to 65 with generous pensions. For blue-collar workers in the auto industry, for example, this has been negotiated through collective bargaining, although an additional objective was to make room for young employees. Beginning with the 1964 contract, the United Auto Workers negotiated higher monthly retirement benefits for

---

52. Bernard M. Bass, Judith Krusell, and Ralph A. Alexander, "Male Managers' Attitudes toward Working Women," *American Behavioral Scientist*, Vol. 15 (November–December 1971), pp. 221–36. See also Doris H. Merritt, "Discrimination and the Woman Executive," *Business Horizons*, Vol. 12 (December 1969), pp. 15–22.

workers retiring before 65; by the 1970 contract a worker could retire with a $500 monthly pension as early as 58; by October 1972 it was 56.[53] There have been a substantial number of early retirements under these provisions; nearly 10,000 auto workers retired early during the first four months of the full-benefit plan (about one-fourth of those eligible to retire early). The 1973 union agreement with Chrysler provided a full pension after thirty years of service.

Early retirement for executives may be spreading, although there is a suspicion that some of this is the consequence of "retirement at company convenience" as belt tightening proceeds.[54] Financially generous arrangements may enable managers retiring early to develop new part-time careers, but too little attention has been paid to this possibility. The earlier the retirement, the greater the likelihood that a second career can be developed, as experience with officers retired from the armed services has indicated. Pre-retirement counseling, far enough in advance of actual retirement, is a responsibility of business toward long-service employees. The shock of abrupt transition from productive work to full retirement, especially for those who enjoyed their work, should be anticipated with retirement planning; but for those who consider work as drudgery or boring, early retirement may be a blessing requiring little advance planning. Even in these cases, however, the problem of "keeping busy" with some other activity seems to arise. There appears to be no substitute for considering various options after retirement, and business management may be expected by employees at all levels to assist them in thinking ahead.

Summary and Conclusions

In this final section, some broad conclusions will be drawn from the preceding sections, along with some implications for the profit goals of business.

A number of goals which pertain to the employee's welfare and which are generally considered to be the responsibility of business have been

---

53. *Business Week*, No. 2257 (December 2, 1972), p. 62.

54. "The Gentle Boot: To Tighten Operations, Firms Force Men in Their 50s and 60s to Retire Early," *Wall Street Journal*, March 15, 1972. These observations do not apply to those chief executives who have recently announced their voluntary retirements before they reach 65, as at IBM, General Electric, and several other large firms.

realized by an increasing number of firms. Obviously, many fall short of these goals, but there has been considerable change during the last twenty-five years. The range for voluntary action by business management toward achievement of these goals is fairly wide. Many firms have been influenced by the spread of a number of managerial concepts, growing out of behavioral science and industrial relations research and experience, which legitimate policies to achieve these goals. Strong-willed top managers with a "social responsibility outlook" have been crucial to the success of voluntary actions.

Nevertheless, it is also clear that external pressures have played a part in getting firms to assume social responsibility. The Civil Rights Act of 1964 and the activities of the Equal Employment Opportunity Commission and the Office of Federal Contract Compliance discouraged discrimination on the basis of race or sex; federal manpower programs and the National Alliance of Businessmen's Job Opportunities in the Business Sector program encouraged employment of disadvantaged minorities; the Occupational Safety and Health Act of 1970 established new standards for the well-being of the employee; the Age Discrimination in Employment Act prohibited bias against older employees; the Employee Retirement Income Security Act of 1974 affects private pension plans. Earlier, the Wagner Act and related laws had established and enforced the right of employees to join unions and bargain collectively; and the Taft-Hartley Act added obligations for unions and dealt with labor disputes of a national emergency nature.

Additional factors or pressures have influenced business responsibilities toward employees. Changes in the composition of the labor force during the 1960s brought an influx of younger workers (16 to 24 years old), now moving into the next age group in the 1970s as the younger group declines relatively. Younger workers appear to have different aspirations and life styles than did their counterparts ten to fifteen years ago. By many accounts, they are less likely to accept managerial authority uncritically, they anticipate having more responsibility earlier or at least more challenging jobs, and they want some say in the decisions that affect them. These comments may be more true of the recent college generation than of noncollege youth, although work alienation exists among some of these, leading to management efforts toward job enrichment. Black organizations are critical of the slow progress blacks have been making in business, even though this same pace appears to management as fairly rapid since the mid-1960s. The gap between black expectations and present jobs, particularly in the higher occupational positions, will continue to face business, and a similar gap will be an issue in the employment of women. Affirmative action programs, with targets or goals set for future years, will become more widespread under these pressures as well as under the legislative-administrative ones. At the same time, pressures for early retirement and for pre-retirement planning and counseling will grow.

How does business hope to achieve more fully the goals expected of the employer and at the same time realize profit goals to satisfy its stockholders and to provide internal investment funds? Will being more "responsible" in economic and social terms dilute the traditional goal of profit-making private business? One answer is that the long-run profitability of a business may be enhanced by working toward the new goals or values in employer-employee relations, even though there may be some short-run *costs* which raise prices and/or reduce short-run profits. No doubt many of today's exploratory programs are costly. To mention a few, it costs money to hire and upgrade disadvantaged minorities when qualified whites might be available; it costs money to meet tougher standards for the safety and health of employees; it costs money to reach agreements with unions; it costs money to retire employees younger than 65; and it costs money to help finance day-care centers and provide pregnancy benefits for employees. It may also be costly to respond constructively to the new aspirations and life styles of younger employees. It is important for business to quantify these costs, so that managers and society can better evaluate what tradeoffs are important.

Business is confronted with new problems but also new opportunities to develop employment policies which may be necessary to achieve corporate profit objectives over the long pull. Employees have goals in work and outside which need to be reflected in organizational goals, but these do not necessarily exclude profits, and business is used to striking a balance. As Cyert and March have observed, there are a number of participants in a business organization—managers, stockholders, suppliers, and customers, as well as employees, and the "goals of a business firm are a series of more or less independent constraints imposed on the organization through a process of bargaining among potential coalition members and elaborated over time in response to short-run pressures."[55]

---

55. Richard M. Cyert and James G. March, *A Behavioral Theory of the Firm* (Prentice-Hall, 1963), p. 43.

In accepting greater responsibility toward employees, either voluntarily or under the pressures mentioned, business firms have increasingly set themselves subgoals. Some instruct managers to hire nonwhite job applicants ahead of equally qualified whites. Others require their plant managers to report periodically the percentage of nonwhites in their locale, and to submit five-year plans for increasing minority employment. Firms have beefed up their safety and health programs by assigning responsibility higher in the management structure. More and more, employment goals are better achieved if the *top man in the business gives them his personal commitment,* communicated to all levels of management.[56]

The assumption is now common that the business firm exists as a part of an interdependent society and cannot ignore its responsibilities to deal with community and social problems. Failure to abide by this assumption exposes companies to two types of risks, both inimical to profit objectives: (1) more government intervention and (2) higher business costs and public expenditures later if wider business commitments are not made now.

The consequences of a manager's failure to respond adequately to the newer goals and values may be measured within the firm by "human resources accounting." This new accounting approach considers human resources as equivalent to other assets in the firm.[57] They require "investment" over time to make them productive: hiring, training, and development costs which are capitalized and amortized over an assumed probable productive life for the human resource, taking into account attrition and eventual deterioration. (Wage and salary costs, with fringe benefits, are considered current costs of employment.) If the employee voluntarily leaves the firm prior to this average period, there is a "loss" of a capital asset, and labor turnover has a new measurable cost. More than this, however, is the assumed impact on management. Managers

56. "For Many Corporations, Social Responsibility Is Now a Major Concern," *Wall Street Journal,* October 26, 1971.

57. This approach grew out of the work of Rensis Likert at the University of Michigan. For a summary of the approach, as applied in a Columbus, Ohio, firm, see William C. Pyle, "Monitoring Human Resources—'On Line,'" *Michigan Business Review,* Vol. 22 (July 1970), pp. 19–32. For an alternative approach, see Eli Goldston, *The Quantification of Concern: Some Aspects of Social Accounting* (Columbia University Press for Carnegie-Mellon University, 1972). The late Mr. Goldston was president of Eastern Gas and Fuel Associates, Boston.

are now measured on a new dimension: how well they develop their human resources and how well they utilize and retain them over their productive life. What were once the "social costs," or even costs borne by the individual employee himself, now become internal costs on an equal footing with others. Henceforth managerial decisions will take utilization of human resources into account as a performance factor.

Human resources accounting will probably be slow to spread because of the change it involves in existing accounting policies and practices and because of admitted difficulties in measuring the value of human resources. Pioneering in social responsibility may well be economically difficult, if not impossible, in some highly competitive industries. If a firm should move ahead of what others are required to do by governmental and employee pressures, it is likely to land in financial difficulties. But the concept of development, utilization, and conservation of human resources is still central to the goals and values which are important in employer-employee relations. In all likelihood the business that best meets these goals constructively and voluntarily, though the pressures to do so are always in the background, will *in the long run* have the competitive edge over those firms that hang back and are eventually coerced into line at higher costs. To absorb the short-run adverse cost differential facing the socially responsible firm until other pressures force competitor firms into line requires a courageous and far-sighted management.

Contributors

James W. McKie, the editor of this volume, is dean of the College of Social and Behavioral Sciences, University of Texas at Austin. A past president of the Southern Economic Association, he has served as chairman of the economics department at Vanderbilt University and chief economist of the Cabinet Task Force on Oil Import Control. He is the author of *Tin Cans and Tin Plate* and of numerous articles on regulation and industrial organization.

Martin Bronfenbrenner is Kenan Professor of Economics at Duke University, having previously taught at Roosevelt University, the University of Wisconsin, the University of Minnesota, and Carnegie-Mellon University. He is the author of *Income Distribution Theory* and editor of *Is the Business Cycle Obsolete?* His public service assignments have included work with the Treasury Department, the U.S. occupation authority in Japan after World War II, and the United Nations Economic Commission for Asia and the Far East.

Benjamin Chinitz served as Deputy Assistant Secretary of Commerce for Economic Development in the Johnson administration. He is currently professor of economics and director of the Economic Growth Institute at the State University of New York in Binghamton. He is the editor of *City and Suburb* and has worked on economic studies of the New York and Pittsburgh areas.

Marvin A. Chirelstein is professor of law at Yale University. His fields of special interest are federal taxation and corporate finance. He is co-author of *Taxation in the United States.*

John F. Kain is professor of economics at Harvard University and a member of the senior research staff of the National Bureau of Economic Research. He is the author of *The Urban Transportation Problem* (with John R. Meyer and Martin Wohl), *The Detroit Prototype of the NBER Urban Simulation Model* (with Gregory K. Ingram and J. Royce Ginn), and a number of articles dealing with urban and regional problems. His most

351

recent book, *Housing Markets and Racial Discrimination: A Microeconomic Analysis* (with John M. Quigley) is scheduled for publication in 1975 by the National Bureau of Economic Research.

Roland N. McKean, now Commonwealth Professor of Economics at the University of Virginia, formerly taught economics at Vanderbilt University and the University of California at Los Angeles. He is the author of *Public Spending* and of *Efficiency in Government through Systems Analysis*, co-author with Charles J. Hitch of *The Economics of Defense in the Nuclear Age*, and co-author with Joseph A. Kershaw of *Teacher Shortages and Salary Schedules*. Professor McKean has served as president of the Southern Economic Association.

Charles A. Myers, Sloan Fellows Professor of Management and director of the Industrial Relations Section in the Sloan School of Management, Massachusetts Institute of Technology, is the author of numerous books and articles on industrial relations, labor economics, and personnel administration. He has served as a consultant on personnel problems to a number of companies and as an arbitrator in disputes arising under collective agreements. His books include *Role of the Private Sector in Manpower Development* and *Education, Manpower, and Economic Growth* (with Frederick Harbison).

Jerome Rothenberg is professor of economics at the Massachusetts Institute of Technology. His work centers on the economics of the public sector, urban economics, and the economics of pollution and congestion. He is the author of *Economic Evaluation of Urban Renewal* and *The Measurement of Social Welfare*.

Thomas C. Schelling is professor of economics at Harvard University and a member of the faculty of the John F. Kennedy School of Government. In 1969 he helped originate the graduate program in public policy at the Kennedy School, and he has served as the program's chairman. His books include *Arms and Influence* and *Strategy of Conflict*.

Raymond Vernon, director of the Harvard University Center for International Affairs, is the Herbert F. Johnson Professor of International Business Administration at the Harvard Business School. He is the author of *Sovereignty at Bay* and *Metropolis 1985*, and he is director of Harvard's Multinational Enterprise Project.

James Q. Wilson is the Henry Lee Shattuck Professor of Government at Harvard University. His most recent book is *Political Organizations*; he is also the author of *Varieties of Police Behavior*.

Index